CHARGING
THROUGH THE AFL
Los Angeles and San Diego
Chargers' Football in the 1960s

CHARGING
THROUGH THE AFL

Los Angeles and San Diego Chargers' Football in the 1960s

Todd Tobias

Turner Publishing Company
Nashville, Tennessee • Paducah, Kentucky

PHOTO CREDITS

PUBLISHING COMPANY

412 Broadway • P.O. Box 3101
Paducah, Kentucky 42002-3101
(270) 443-0121

www.turnerpublishing.com

Copyright © 2004 Todd Tobias

Turner Publishing Company Staff:
Keith R. Steel, Publishing Consultant
Steve Abell, Project Coordinator
Shelley R. Davidson, Designer

Library of Congress Control No. 2004110555

ISBN: 1-59652-012-4

Printed in the United States of America

0 1 2 3 4 5 6 7 8 9

CONTENTS

FOREWORD

Ka-Boom ——The year was 1963, and that cannon in Balboa Stadium made quite a statement! It nearly blew me down once as I ran into the end zone with a pass from John Hadl. With the high-powered Chargers' offense of the 1960s, that cannon was constantly "smoke" in action.

In 1963 we trained in Boulevard, California... It was 90 miles east from San Diego, and on the way to nowhere. Well into the middle of the desert, it had the only green grass in 100 miles. The nights were cold, and wolves, bobcats, and coyotes roamed our practice fields. The fields were watered at night, so rodents, rabbits and rattlesnakes came out in the evening. After our nightly meetings Paul Lowe had to be escorted to his cabin by the equipment manager who carried a flashlight. No one sneaked out! There was no place to go. It was a player's nightmare. Nothing but football – study football, practice football, football meetings... but it was a COACH'S DREAM... We came out of Boulevard in great physical shape and mentally prepared to play. All that we had endured physically and mentally, we had done as a team. Boulevard gave us the chemistry. We had great players, the best coaches, and we all shared a common goal – winning football games.

Lance Alworth against the New York Jets in 1963.

We had it all. On offense were Keith Lincoln, the most underrated player of our time, and Paul Lowe. Get Lowe to the corner and watch him go! The blocking backs were Bobby Jackson and Gerry McDougall. On the line were Ron Mix, Walt "Suds" Sweeney, Don Rogers, Pat Shea, Ernie Wright, Sam DeLuca, Sam Gruneisen and Ernie Park. Tobin Rote started at quarterback, with John Hadl, everybody's All-American, waiting in the wings. Dave Kocourek and Jacque MacKinnon were at end, and our wideouts were Don Norton, Reg Carolan, Jerry Robinson and myself. Our offense was designed by Sid Gillman, and was the best the game had ever seen. All of the current passing offenses are based on Gillman's theories and are from his playbooks, which were shared with today's offensive coaching phenoms.

Our defense was coached by Chuck Noll, and set professional records that still stand today. Ernie Ladd, Earl Faison, Bob Petrich, George Gross and Hank Schmidt made up the defensive line. In the backfield were Dick Harris, Bud Whitehead, Charlie McNeil, Dick Westmoreland, Gary Glick and George Blair. Chuck Allen, Frank Buncom, Emil Karas, Bob Mitinger, Bob Lane and Paul Maguire were the linebackers.

This team was a coach's dream. We were the most exciting team in football. It's too bad that the Super Bowl had not yet been organized. The Chicago Bears, the 1963 champs from that other league, would have quickly known how good we were, and recognized that their hands would have been a bit too full.

We won the 1963 AFL Championship, but what is even more special to the players is the bond we made as teammates. It is hard to believe, but that championship season was more than 40 years ago... I can't believe it myself. The friendships that were formed among the members of that team still exist today. The most important things in my life have always been God, family and country, but my teammates on the 1963 Chargers are not far behind.

My time with the Chargers was a wonderful part of my life, and I made so many friends that I have been close with ever since. I wanted to mention something about each one of them, but knew that I would accidentally forget someone, and I did not want to do that. There is just something special about people that go through difficult situations together. We survived our Rough Acres training camp as a group. We bitched and moaned, killed snakes and spiders on the practice field, and lived on crappy food, but we did it as a team. We were as much of a family as 35 young men could ever hope to be. When we came down from the mountain we were ready for anything. It becomes much easier to win when everyone is prepared, and we were prepared. Anything that came our way, we had an answer for it.

As I read *Charging through the AFL*, so many memories come flooding back to me. I see our lives through the eyes of my friends and teammates. I remember how it hurt when the turk came calling and a close friend was cut from the team. I share a teammate's jubilation when he recalls making an interception or a game-winning tackle. I remember how we all suffered through contract negotiations with Coach Gillman, one of the toughest deal-makers pro football has ever known. I feel the indignity of seeing my black teammates refused service is public places in the South, and the camaraderie of the entire team leaving the establishment, black and white united. I live through all of the ups-and-downs all over again.

I think this is a great football book. All of the touchdowns, tackles and interceptions are in here. But more than that, it gives the reader glimpses at the inner workings of our football team. It shows how a bunch of young guys from all different backgrounds come together as a unit. Northerners and Southerners, big and small, rich and poor, fast and slow; we had it all.

I hope you take some time and enjoy the following stories as they are told by my friends and I, the Chargers of the American Football League. This was our life during the 1960s, and I am pleased that so many of us took the time to share our memories, good and bad, for Chargers' fans of all ages.

Lance Alworth

INTRODUCTION

It is funny how seemingly small decisions can sometimes be the introduction to major changes in our lives. While in graduate school, I was fortunate enough to be an intern for the San Diego Chargers. My main task was to organize their team archives. As I went along, cleaning out filing cabinets and slipping photos into protective sleeves, I read bits and pieces of the material that I was sorting. I happened to also be in search of a topic for my master's thesis at the time, and since I had access to all of this material, I figured that it would be to my advantage to research something in the Chargers' team history.

After several more sessions in the Chargers' archive, I decided to research and write about Sid Gillman, the Chargers' first coach during their days in the old American Football League. I spent the next several months contacting many of Sid's former players, and asking them questions about their coach and his offensive theories. As they spoke, many of the players would sort of drift away from the question that I had asked, and instead pass along a story that they were more interested in telling. Earl Faison and Keith Lincoln spoke about the team leaving pool halls and movie theaters that would not service the Chargers' African-American players in racially segregated areas in the South during the 1960s. Dick Westmoreland discussed the Chargers' training camp in 1963 and his roommate, former Arkansas basketball coach Nolan Richardson, who didn't make the final cut. Ernie Wright remembered that on road trips Coach Gillman would sometimes join in a poker game with his players; a bunch of teammates sitting around a hotel bed in their boxer shorts playing cards. In all I spoke with nearly 20 old Chargers, and found that I had some really interesting material. Much of it dealt with football, but really, a lot of it focused on other things that were an integral part of being on a team; friendships, conflicts, practical jokes, sorrow and joy. It was really wonderful stuff.

Visiting with Sid Gillman in his video room.

I completed my thesis in the spring of 1999, but soon found myself wishing that I was still interviewing players. It was about that time that my friend and baseball historian, Bill Swank, finished writing *Echoes from Lane Field*, a book of oral histories about the San Diego Padres minor league baseball team from 1936-1957. Bill suggested that I continue interviewing the old Chargers with the hopes of one day doing a book. I took his suggestion as a good one, and though I questioned whether I would ever be able to write a book, I continued to do the interviews.

Four years passed since I first spoke to Bill about my project, and my life became increasingly busy. My wife, Kym, and I got married in the summer of 2000. Our son, Toby, was born one year later. Through it all, I continued to interview the AFL Chargers. But then in May 2001, we were dealt a blow when a doctor told us that the coughing, fevers and night sweats that I was experiencing were due to Hodgkin's Lymphoma. I had cancer.

If anything could have postponed my interview project, I figured that cancer would be it. But strangely, I actually did many of my best interviews when I was home, feeling ill from the effects of chemotherapy that I went through every two weeks. Speaking to the players served as a kind of tonic or elixir that transported me, even if only for 30 minutes at a time, to another place where my health was not an issue.

With the help of doctors, hospital staff and my loving family and friends, I was declared free of cancer in February 2003, after eight months of chemotherapy and countless prayers. With a clean bill of health I put in a final push and finished this book.

This project has been a lot of things to me; a dream, a job, therapy, as well as an occasional pain in the ass. But after all, I am incredibly glad that I did it. I had much help along the way and there is no way that I ever would have completed this book without the support of my wife, Kym and our sons, Toby and Will. I am also thankful for my parents, Ed and Pam Tobias, and grandparents John and Dorothy Lenore, as well as my in-laws Bill and Marion Doss and Lizzie Ponce de Leon, who made sure that I was taken care of along the way. Thanks also to my brother Geoff and his wife, Sara, my sister, Tara, and youngest brother, Tim.

The San Diego Chargers' organization has been extremely helpful in allowing me to research in their archives and use their photos. I would especially like to thank Bill Johnston, Scott Yoffe, Jamaal LaFrance and Jennifer Rojas for their assistance.

I am of course indebted to all of the former players that took the time to speak with me for this book, but several of them have given additional help and become friends. Thanks to Earl Faison, Lance Alworth, Hank Schmidt, Walt Sweeney and Ron Mix.

Lastly, I would like to thank my friends and other acquaintances that helped me with this project: Tom Black, Glenn Turgeon, Don King (not the guy in Las Vegas), Bob Hood, Jerry Magee, Mark Palczewski, Pat Rogers-Thompson, John Street, Margaret Peters, Pete Lowry (with his early Chargers photos) and Mike Sheeran (a great proofreader). Ange Coniglio was also very helpful. He has an outstanding web site dedicated to the American Football League (www.remember the AFL.com). Another good website is run by Rafael Alvarez and Bolt Pride. Some of the most dedicated Chargers fans on the web can be found at www.boltpride.com. One final thanks goes to Dr. Jonathan Polikoff for leading me through the battle with cancer and keeping me alive so that I could finish this book, among many other things.

I hope that you enjoy reading the stories of the AFL Chargers. It has been more than 40 years since the first Charger team stepped out onto the grass at the Los Angeles Coliseum in 1960, and as a result, some memories may be a bit fuzzy. I tried to confirm the stories I could, but many of the recollections include behind-the-scenes stuff that was never documented. If you spot any glaring errors, or would just like to make a comment, I would enjoy hearing from you. Please feel free to contact me via email at toddtobias@cox.net, or by mail at 9276 Lemon Avenue, La Mesa, California, 91941. Thanks for reading my book. I hope you enjoy it.

HISTORY OF THE AFL CHARGERS

The story of the American Football League, and ultimately the San Diego Chargers, begins with a young man named Lamar Hunt and his bid to purchase the Chicago Cardinals of the National Football League in the late 1950s. While in college, Hunt, who was the son of Texas oil billionaire, H.L. Hunt, had been a substitute offensive end on the Southern Methodist University football team. After college graduation Hunt's interest in football shifted from the playing field to the front office. Hunt wanted to own an NFL franchise in his hometown of Dallas, Texas.

Aware that the Chicago Cardinals were experiencing financial difficulties, Lamar Hunt contacted the Cardinals' owner, Walter Wolfner. Hunt expressed interest in buying the team and moving them to Texas, and made an offer to purchase the Cardinals. There appeared to be substantial interest in the team, as Wolfner actually had several offers to purchase the Cardinals. Among those interested in taking over the struggling club were future AFL owners, Bud Adams and Bob Howsam.

Wolfner ultimately refused all offers to purchase the team outright. He did not want to lose control of the Cardinals. He instead informed the interested parties that they could purchase a minority share in the team, but that he would retain the controlling interest. Partial ownership of an NFL franchise did not interest Hunt or the other men, and all negotiations ended.

Though his attempts to purchase the Cardinals had failed, Hunt's desire to own a professional football team had not waned in the least. In fact, it was on the trip home from his final meeting with Wolfner that the idea of beginning a brand new professional football league came to him.

Wolfner had mentioned that Bud Adams had also contacted him in regards to purchasing the Cardinals. Adams was also a Texas millionaire that had an interest in owning a professional football team in the Lone Star State. Hunt called Bud Adams, and asked the fellow Texan if they might meet for lunch. Adams agreed and the two spent an afternoon discussing everything other than football. It was near the end of their meeting when Hunt finally presented his idea of a new professional football league to Adams. Hunt posed the question; if he were able to secure ownership for teams in four other cities, would Adams be interested in joining? Adams responded with unwavering affirmation. Thus began the foundation of the American Football League.

After Adams was confirmed, the other potential owners quickly fell into place. Bob Howsam, owner of the Denver Bears minor league baseball team was interested in putting a team in Denver. Harry Wismer, the famous football announcer, guaranteed a franchise in New York. Barron Hilton, son of Conrad Hilton, the founder of the Hilton Hotels chain agreed to build a team in Los Angeles, and a group led by Max Winter, H.P. Skoglund and Bill Boyer began working on a club in Minneapolis. In the coming months there would be several additions and one notable subtraction in the ownership groups. Ralph Wilson took a team in Buffalo, Billy Sullivan took one in Boston and a group led by Wayne Valley took a team in Oakland after the Minneapolis contingent dropped out of the AFL and instead formed the Minnesota Vikings of the NFL. The formation of the American Football League, and statement of the first games to be played was announced to the public. With less than one year to develop the league before the first exhibition games were to be played, the individual ownership groups went to work building their teams, securing a television contract and promoting their new league.

To build his team, Barron Hilton secured the services of one of the most highly respected men in football, former Notre Dame head coach, Frank Leahy. On October 14, 1959. A career football man, Leahy had been the head coach for the Fighting Irish from 1941-1953 (with a break in 1945 to serve in the U.S. Navy during

World War II) and had won four national championships with an .887 winning percentage during his reign.

One of Leahy's first tasks was to name and promote the team. In an effort to engage the public and at the same time secure a name for the Hilton's franchise, Leahy enlisted the help of the people of Los Angeles. Leahy advertised a "Name the Team" contest in the area newspapers. Entries came rushing in with names including the Branders, Knaves, Aces, Nuggets and Stags. One football fan went so far as to suggest that the team be called the Los Angeles Hiltons. Then on October 28th, Gerald Courtney, of Hollywood, California, submitted an entry suggesting the name, "Chargers." Hilton and Leahy liked the name and chose it for the team. For his efforts, Gerald Courtney received an all-expenses paid vacation to both Mexico City and Acapulco.

Los Angeles Chargers' Head Coach Sid Gillman.

In later years the rumor prevailed that Hilton chose the name "Chargers" as a means of promoting his credit card company, Carte Blanche. On several occasions Hilton was called upon to dispel the rumor. "I was president of Hilton Carte Blanche, all right, but that had nothing to do with it," Hilton later told *The San Diego Union* Sports Editor, Jack Murphy. "Frank Leahy chose the name and I liked it because they were yelling 'charge!' and sounding the bugle at Dodger Stadium and at USC games."

The Chargers' next step in building the Chargers came in January of 1960 when they hired Sid Gillman to coach the team. With 20 years of collegiate coaching experience and five years running an NFL club, Gillman was considered one of the best coaches in America. Gillman's most recent coaching job had been a five-year term as head coach of the Los Angeles Rams. He led the Rams to the NFL Championship Game in 1955, but after player disputes and other controversies led to a losing record in 1959, Gillman was relieved of his duties. Once free from the Rams, Gillman had nearly convinced himself to give up coaching for good and take employment as a New York stockbroker. But Hilton and the Chargers came calling and Gillman jumped aboard. He signed a three-year deal and was announced as the Chargers' new head coach.

Hilton, Leahy and Gillman "charged" forward, building the new football team from the ground up. Gillman began to assemble his coaching staff. Though they were not well-known at the time, the members of the Chargers' first coaching staff all achieved greatness in professional football; Sid Gillman, Head Coach; Joe Madro, Offensive Line Coach; Al Davis, Offensive End Coach; Chuck Noll, Defensive Line Coach; Jack Faulkner, Defensive Backfield Coach. In the years to come, Madro would be the only one to not hold a head coaching position in pro football. Davis went on to become head coach of the Oakland Raiders, Commissioner of the American Football League and ultimately, Managing General Partner of the Los Angeles and Oakland Raiders. In 1962 Faulkner took over as Head Coach of the Denver Broncos and put together a career in professional football that lasted more than 40 years. Chuck Noll was eventually hired as Head Coach of the Pittsburgh Steelers, where he won four Super Bowls during the 1970s. Gillman, Davis and Noll are now enshrined in the Pro Football Hall of Fame.

Los Angeles Chargers' coaching staff: front row, Sid Gillman; back row, Joe Madro, Chuck Noll, Al Davis and Jack Faulkner.

But while greatness was in their future, in 1960 they were just a group of coaches trying to build a team and help form a league.

The Chargers made their first attempt at gathering players in April of 1960. Answering newspaper advertisements to become professional football players, some 207 "players" showed up to an open tryout in Burbank. Gillman later recalled "every bartender in Los Angeles thought he could play football." By the end of the four-day tryout, only three players had proven themselves worthy of being invited back to training camp in July.

The team hit a minor setback in late June when Frank Leahy was forced to resign due to his failing health. The Chargers adapted and one week later Gillman assumed the dual role of head coach and general manager, a title that he would hold for the next 10 years. Gillman felt that the two positions complimented each other perfectly, and allowed the head coach to make all personnel decisions and truly take responsibility of the team. Many players thought differently, however. Some players had difficulty receiving compliments from Gillman on the field, but being criticized when it came time to negotiate contracts.

The Los Angeles Chargers opened their summer training camp on July 8th, on the campus of Chapman College, some 30 miles Southeast of Los Angeles. Players came to the camp in three waves. "It was like every Friday, literally, just a bus-load of guys would come in," remembered Don Rogers, who was the Chargers' center from 1960-64. "Then they would cut half of them the first day and they'd cut half of what was left, and by the end of the week you'd be down to three or four guys from the previous busload. Always kept enough guys around so you could practice and scrimmage and hold the dummies and what-have-you."

But by the end of training camp the Chargers had many fine athletes on the team and several players that would make lasting marks on the American Football League. It was a blend of NFL cast-offs like quarterback Jack Kemp, running back Paul Lowe and defensive tackle Volney Peters; former Canadian Football League players like Ron Nery and Sam DeLuca; and collegiate stars such as tackles Ron Mix and Ernie Wright, and running back Charlie Flowers.

On August 6th the Chargers played their first exhibition game. Their opponents were the New York Titans and the contest was held before 27,778 curious football fans in Los Angeles' Memorial Coliseum. The fans got their moneys worth when on the first play in Chargers' history, Paul Lowe received the opening kickoff five yards deep in his own end zone and returned it 105 yards for a touchdown.

August 8, 1960 Game Program, Los Angeles Chargers vs. New York Titans.

The Chargers opened the regular season against league founder, Lamar Hunt, and his Dallas Texans. The 21-20 victory was the first of 10 wins for the Los Angeles Chargers. In fact, that first season was nearly all positive, until tragedy struck the Chargers on November 26th. Ralph Anderson, a talented receiver and someone from whom the Chargers' expected great things, died suddenly of a diabetic seizure. The team was stunned at the unexpected passing of such a young and strong teammate. Regardless the Chargers were able to put their emotions aside at game-time, and the team rallied to win the final four games of the season. The Chargers' 10-4 regular season record put them in first place in the AFL's Western Division, ahead of the Dallas Texans, Oakland Raiders and Denver Broncos. Their opponents in the inaugural American Football League Championship Game would be Bud Adams' Houston Oilers, who won the AFL's Eastern Division by also posting a 10-4 record.

On January 1, 1961, the Chargers and Oilers gathered on a slightly soggy field at Houston's Jeppesen Stadium to play the AFL Championship Game. Houston featured former Chicago Bear George Blanda at quarterback. At running back was Billy Cannon, the most highly sought after rookie of the previous year's draft. The Chargers' offense starred Jack Kemp under center, and the graceful ball carrying of running back Paul Lowe.

It promised to be a showcase of offensive power as both teams had passed for more than 3,100 yards during the regular season. But perhaps as a foreshadowing of championship games to come, the Chargers' offense met its match in Houston's defense. Los Angeles managed just three field goals by kicker Ben Agajanian and one Paul Lowe touchdown. The Oilers got touchdown passes of 17, 7 and 88-yards from George Blanda. Blanda, who doubled as the Houston kicker, also booted an 18-yard field goal. When the final gun sounded it was Houston 24, Los Angeles 16.

The Chargers had provided the Los Angeles football fans with plenty to appreciate. Sid Gillman's offense was based on a strong passing game and Jack Kemp lit up the Southern California skies with long passes to receivers Royce Womble, Don Norton, Howard Clark and Dave Kocourek. The rushing game with Paul Lowe, Howie Ferguson and Charlie Flowers totaled 1,900 yards on the ground and the Chargers finished third in the AFL in scoring with 373 points.

But even a world-class offense and first-place team was not enough to draw fans to the Coliseum. Chargers' home games averaged just over 15,000 fans per game in the vast Coliseum, which seated more than 100,000 when at capacity. Barron Hilton had expected to lose money in his first few years of ownership, but the Chargers' first-year losses totaled over $900,000. Hilton quickly realized that if the Chargers were to survive, they had to get out of Los Angeles.

One newspaper columnist that had been following the Chargers and the development of the AFL was Jack Murphy, Sports Editor of *The San Diego Union*. San

Diego was a small town in 1960, known mainly for being a home to the Navy. In the area of sports, San Diego was limited to the Del Mar Race Track, the Padres of the Pacific Coast League and a PGA Golf Tournament. San Diego High vs. Hoover High provided the greatest football excitement in town, although San Diego State College and various military teams also played in San Diego.

Murphy knew that Barron Hilton was unhappy with Los Angeles and was looking for a new home for his football team. Believing that a professional football team would be greatly supported by sports-starved San Diegans, Murphy began his campaign to woo the Chargers south to San Diego. Murphy first made mention of the Chargers' potential move in his column of December 21, 1960. "The story will be denied, and I'll probably be denounced as a third-rate fiction writer," Murphy wrote, "but it comes on excellent authority that the Los Angeles Charger franchise is San Diego's for the asking." Murphy went on to explain that even the Chargers' first-rate ownership, coaching and winning record could not entice the Los Angelenos into the Coliseum for Chargers' games. "That's why the Chargers are odds-on to play football in another city next season, and San Diego heads the list of eligibles," Murphy

Los Angeles Chargers vs. Houston Oilers, November 11, 1960. Note the empty stands at the Coliseum for this regular season game.

wrote. "The other possibilities are Seattle and Atlanta, but they won't have a chance if San Diego seizes its opportunity."

Murphy urged the San Diego City Council, Chamber of Commerce and other notable officials to move on this opportunity. He outlined a plan for the Chargers to play in Balboa Stadium, on the campus of San Diego High School. At that time the stadium held 24,500 at capacity, but would later be expanded to hold an additional 11,000. Murphy even went so far as to propose a rental plan for the stadium and to suggest that Chargers' games would be televised, which would give additional advertising to the San Diego Convention and Tourist Bureau.

With that one article, Jack Murphy and San Diego's campaign to bring the Chargers to San Diego began. From that point on, *The San Diego Union* (and other newspapers, radio and television stations) ran daily stories about the possibilities of the Chargers coming to town. The idea immediately had potential. The headline of the December 24th sports section read, "Chargers' Owner Plans S.D. Visit; Will Investigate Possible Grid Move To City." On January 6th San Diego's civic leaders formed the Greater San Diego Sports Association to attract major sports and events to San Diego.

Negotiations between the Chargers and the City progressed quickly. Hilton showed nearly as much interest in San Diego as San Diego had in the Chargers. On January 12th the AFL owners gave their approval for the Chargers' move to San Diego. A plan to expand Balboa Stadium was proposed and approved by the City Council. The city was a whirlwind of excitement over the possibility of the Chargers' coming to town. Then on January 25th, just over a month after the idea had first gone into print, *The San Diego Union* Sports headline cried out, "It's San Diego Chargers!

Chargers' Owner Barron Hilton.

Council Okay Seals Deal." The deal was done and the Chargers' would now call San Diego and Balboa Stadium home.

While much of San Diego was wrapped up in wooing Barron Hilton and his team South, Sid Gillman and the Chargers coaching staff continued to bolster their already impressive team by adding an exciting group of draftees. The 1961 AFL draft was held, and amongst the Chargers' group of 30 draftees were five names that would make major contributions to the team for years to come; Earl Faison, a defensive end from Indiana; Keith Lincoln, a halfback from Washington State; Ernie Ladd, a defensive tackle from Grambling; Bud Whitehead, a defensive back from Florida State and Chuck Allen, a guard-turned-linebacker from Washington. From those five players the Chargers would receive more than 34 years of service and multiple all-league selections.

Adding the second deck to San Diego's Balboa Stadium.

The Chargers' move to San Diego was quick and painless. They set up their business and ticket offices in the Lafayette Hotel on El Cajon Boulevard, less than five miles from Balboa Stadium. Ticket sales went well. In fact, some 12,000 season ticket pledges had been made by January 27th. On May 1st workers began the process of adding an 11,000-seat upper deck to the stadium.

The months went by and the Chargers became more familiar with their new home. In July the team opened training camp at the University of San Diego, a small Catholic school overlooking Mission Bay to the West and downtown to the South. The Chargers trained at USD in 1961 and 1962, and typically had numerous spectators at their training camp practices.

The Chargers opened the regular season on September 10th, with a 26-10 win at Dallas, and came home the following week to beat the Oakland Raiders 44-0 in their first home game in San Diego. The move to San Diego appeared to invigorate an already dominant team. The Chargers took immediate control of first place in the AFL's Western Division and did not relinquish their lead the entire season. They won the first 11 games of the season before dropping a 33-13 game at Houston. The team was led again on offense by quarterback Jack Kemp and running back Paul Lowe, but other offensive stars began to emerge as well. Dave Kocourek led the team in receiving for the second year, and increased his 1960 totals by nearly 400 yards. He became the first Chargers' player to have more than 1,000 receiving yards in a single season. On the line, tackle Ron Mix continued his high level of play. Mix had a rare combination of size, speed and unmatched intellect that many believe made him the most technically perfect tackle to ever play pro football.

The Chargers dominated defensively as well. Up front they featured the largest line in all of pro football. The original Fearsome Foursome was made up of Earl

San Diegans line up to purchase Chargers tickets at the team office in the Lafayette Hotel.

The San Diego Chargers held their first two training camps at the University of San Diego.

The Fearsome Foursome: Bill Hudson, Ron Nery, Ernie Ladd and Earl Faison.

The Seven Bandits: front row, Paul Maguire, Chuck Allen, Maury Schleicher; back row, Dick Harris, Charlie McNeil, George Blair, Claude Gibson.

Faison, Ernie Ladd, Bill Hudson and Ron Nery. Nery was the lightweight at 6'6" and 245 pounds. Faison stood 6'5" and weighed 256, Hudson was 6'4" and 277, while Ernie Ladd towered over them all at 6'9" and 325 lbs. The Chargers' pass rush was unrelenting, and allowed the linebackers and defensive backs to achieve new levels of success. Given the nickname, The Seven Bandits, the Chargers' defensive backfield set a pro football record with 49 interceptions in 1961. Led by players like Charlie McNeil and Dick Harris, the Chargers also scored nine touchdowns on interception returns.

The Chargers finished out their season with one more win and one loss, ending with a 12-2 record, and winning the AFL West. Their opponents in the championship game were again the Houston Oilers who had finished atop the AFL East with a 10-3-1 record.

The two teams met on a crisp Christmas Eve Day to play the second AFL Championship Game before 29,556 fans in Balboa Stadium. The Chargers' defense played well, holding George Blanda and the Oilers' offense to just 10 points. But the offense proved even more anemic than the year before. Their only bit of scoring was one fourth-quarter field goal by kicker George Blair. Twice the Chargers had played the Oilers in the championship, neither time producing a victory.

Unfortunately for San Diegans, the painful playoff loss was just the beginning of a year full of heartbreak. Death again struck the Chargers, this time taking reserve quarterback and linebacker, Bob Laraba. Laraba was involved in an auto accident that claimed his life on February 16, 1962, in the Pacific Beach area of San Diego.

The lone bright spot for the Chargers in 1962 came in the draft. Like the year before, San Diego added talent to the team that would last for years to come. They worked a draft and trade situation with the Oakland Raiders to obtain the rights to Lance Alworth. Alworth had been a running back at Arkansas, but the Chargers' coaches projected him as a receiver in pro ball. They also drafted quarterback John Hadl of Kansas, defensive end Bob Mitinger of Penn State, linebacker Frank Buncom of USC, center Sam Gruneisen of Villanova and defensive tackle George Gross of Auburn as a future.

Alworth became the AFL's first true superstar. A naturally gifted athlete, Alworth had speed and could leap. He also had an amazing ability to pull the ball out of the air. He would later become the first member of the AFL to be inducted into the Pro Football Hall of Fame. A two-time All-American at Kansas, John Hadl would play quarterback for the San Diego Chargers through the 1972 season, and Gruneisen would play center and guard for 10 years. Buncom, Gross and Mitinger would all make significant defensive contributions for at least three years each.

But few of the Chargers' future successes were apparent when the team took the field in 1962. Paul Lowe had broken his arm in the second exhibition game of the season and would not carry the ball all year. Earl Faison, Charlie McNeil, Lance Alworth, Bert Coan, Wayne Frazier and Chuck Allen each missed more than half of the games that season due to injury. In all, twenty-three Chargers missed two or more games because of injury. Another major setback to the Chargers was the controversial loss of their quarterback, Jack Kemp.

Linebacker Bob Laraba died tragically in an auto accident in 1962.

The San Diego Chargers' 1962 rookie class.

15

The Chargers lost quarterback Jack Kemp when the Buffalo Bills claimed him off waivers.

Kemp severely dislocated the middle finger of his throwing hand when it landed on the helmet of a Titans' defender during the September 16th game against New York. Within minutes of Kemp going down, rookie backup John Hadl suffered a separation of his rib cartilage. Gillman faced the problem of which quarterback had suffered a greater injury, and which would be more likely to return to play the quickest. He made his decision and placed Kemp on waivers. At this time, when a player was placed on waivers, he could be recalled if claimed by another team. However, waivers sought on a weekend preceding a game could not be recalled.

It came to the attention of the Buffalo Bills, a team sorely needing a quarterback, that Kemp was available. Bills' owner, Ralph Wilson, claimed Kemp for the $100 waiver fee. Gillman attempted to reclaim Kemp, but was informed by the league that he could not. The true reason that Kemp was placed on waivers was never fully explained by Gillman. Had Gillman not understood the waiver rules? Had he given up on Kemp after two losses in championship games? Had he feared that Kemp might not completely return from his hand injury? Gillman never truly explained his reasoning, but regardless, the Chargers lost their starting quarterback and their backup was injured as well. They were forced to finish the season with veterans Dick Wood and Val Keckin, and the healing Hadl.

The steady number of injured players took its toll on the Chargers' season record. They finished the year at 4-10, seven games behind the Dallas Texans in the AFL West. It was to be the first and only time that the Chargers' had finished the season with a losing record during the American Football League years.

Determined not to repeat their miserable season of 1962, several significant changes took place during the off-season. Before the 1962 season began, Jack Faulkner, the Chargers' defensive backfield coach, had left the team to take over as head coach of the Denver Broncos. One year later in January 1963, Al Davis departed from San Diego to become the head coach and general manager of the struggling Oakland Raiders. While Gillman could fill the coaching vacancy left by Davis, he could not adequately replace Davis' ability to bring new talent to the Chargers. Al Davis had been influential in convincing many top draft choices to sign with the Chargers instead of going into the NFL. Ron Mix, Lance Alworth and Walt Sweeney were just three of the players scouted and signed by Davis. His work ethic and desire to build a winning team was matched perhaps only by Gillman. Similar to when Faulkner left in 1962, Davis going to Oakland brought about a new reason for the Chargers to want to beat the Raiders, and vice-versa. In fact, Davis' taking over the Raiders was the first step in what has become a 40-year rivalry between the Chargers and Raiders.

In the area of player personnel, the Chargers made a significant addition to their roster when they signed quarterback Tobin Rote of the Canadian Football League. During the off-season a trade was made with the Buffalo Bills for the rights to Rote, who had won championships both in the NFL and CFL. In Rote, the Chargers not only got a starting quarterback, but also a mentor to young John Hadl and a leader to guide their still-young team.

A small change took place in the area of team ownership also. Barron and Conrad Hilton sold one-third of their interest in the Chargers to San Diego businessmen John Mabee, George Pernicano, Kenneth Swanson, James Copley and M.L. Bengston. These gentlemen had only a minority ownership, but in the case of

Former NFL and CFL quarterback Tobin Rote led the Chargers in 1963.

Always ready for a good time, George Pernicano cuts loose.

Pernicano, he did not let that keep him from getting a majority-share of fun out of the deal. Pernicano, who settled in San Diego from Detroit, owned a chain of popular pizza restaurants in San Diego, including the Casa di Baffi in Hillcrest. Pernicano earned the nickname of "Road Warrior" by making sure he attended every Chargers game, home and away (a promise that was still being kept 40 years later). He helped make the trips more palatable by having his restaurants cater all of the Chargers' flights to away games. Prior to the plane taking off, George would come aboard with pizzas, Italian sausage and cheese, sandwiches and whatever else his kitchens may have produced for the trip, ensuring that the players would not have to bother with the airplane food. Pernicano's Casa di Baffi soon became a regular point of destination, not only to the Chargers, but also to players and coaches of opposing teams, and most every celebrity that visited San Diego and was in search of fine Italian cuisine.

More than losing Al Davis and gaining George Pernicano and Tobin Rote, the biggest change among the Chargers of 1963 was the location and structure of their training camp. The University of San Diego, where the Chargers had trained the previous two years, sits atop a hill overlooking San Diego Bay. A breeze often flows through the campus, keeping things cool and comfortable, even on hot days. It is just a 10-minute drive to either downtown or the beach communities and for a player determined to completely forget football for the evening, Tijuana is less than 20 miles away. All of these factors, and the exorbitant number of injuries suffered by Chargers' players in 1962 led Gillman to believe that the previous training camp had been too easy for the players.

In an effort to toughen his players during camp and ensure that football was their sole focus, Gillman secured a training site in Boulevard, California, some 60 miles East of San Diego. Amidst the rocks and tumbleweed that was Boulevard, sat a dilapidated facility called the Rough Acres Ranch. For the next several weeks the players called Rough Acres many things, but unfortunately for them, one of them was "home."

The players that went through the Rough Acres training camp laugh about it now. The "field" was just a barren patch of dirt. Grass would not grow there, so the ball boys spread sawdust over the dirt each morning hoping to resemble the softness of grass. Living amongst the Chargers was a host of snakes, spiders and other things that crawl, and in the evening the players fell asleep to the sound of bats screeching in the rafters. The only way for the players to maintain their sanity was to jump in a car after team meetings ended and make a run each evening to a local watering hole. Once there, the players would have roughly one hour in which to wet their whistles before having to be back at camp for the 10:30 curfew.

The players didn't necessarily like their spartan accomodations at the Rough Acres Training Camp, as demonstrated by draftee Rufus Guthrie on the far right.

Indeed the training camp at Rough Acres was not a pleasant one. The Chargers could not help but concentrate on football. Aside from a couple of warped billiards and ping-pong tables there was nothing else to do. Whether because of Rough Acres or in spite of it, when the Chargers came down from the mountain to open the season on September 8th, they were one cohesive unit, trained to win football games.

The Chargers opened the season with three wins in a row. They lost to Jack Faulkner and his Denver Broncos on October 6th, and then won twice more. It was a testament to Al Davis that the Chargers' only other two losses that season came at the hands of Davis and his Raiders. Oakland had gone just 1-13 the year before, but under Davis the Raiders came roaring into the spotlight. The Chargers provided but two of Oakland's 10 wins in 1963. Al Davis was named AFL Coach of the Year.

Unfortunately for Oakland, the Chargers had more wins than the Raiders at the end of the season. On December 22nd eight different Chargers scored in a 58-20 victory over the Denver Broncos. The win gave the Chargers their third Western Division title in four years, and again placed them in the AFL Championship Game. Their opponent was to be the Boston Patriots, whose key to success came in the form of a smothering defense that confused its opponents with numerous and rapid blitzes.

But Gillman had a trick up his sleeve. He designed a game plan that he called "Feast or Famine," and featured things that the Chargers had not previously done all

Keith Lincoln had one of the greatest individual post season performances in the 1963 AFL Championship.

Lance Alworth celebrates the Chargers only AFL championship victory.

Center Don Rogers chats with Al LoCasale at the Chargers 1964 training camp in Escondido.

year. Gillman countered the Boston blitzes by sending running back Paul Lowe into motion, which was to keep Boston off balance all day by disorganizing their usually precise defense. Another "Feast or Famine" innovation was the East formation. In a typical offensive formation, end Dave Kocourek would be positioned on the strong side of the line with Lance Alworth lined up outside of him. Receiver Don Norton would be alone on the weak side. In the East formation Kocourek played a weak side tight end, while both Norton and Alworth split out together on the strong side. This was done to draw Boston's linebackers up to the line. They were good cover men, but were too light to play defensive end, thus giving the Chargers an advantage at the line of scrimmage.

Gillman's plan worked to perfection and the result was the Chargers' total domination of the Patriots. Fullback Keith Lincoln ran wild with 206 yards rushing, 123 yards receiving and making one 20-yard pass completion. The Chargers scored 51 points to Boston's 10, and when the final whistle blew, San Diego had its first professional league championship of any kind.

The champagne flowed freely in the Chargers' locker room while the team celebrated, as they never had before. Shouts of "Bring on the Bears" could be heard throughout the locker room. Sid Gillman would later propose a "world championship" game to George Halas, whose Chicago Bears had won the NFL Championship. Halas declined the offer.

Although the Chargers had won the AFL Championship after training at Rough Acres, the team did not return to Boulevard. Complications with the Rough Acres ownership forced a change of training camp location. For the 1964 season the Chargers trained in Escondido, roughly 30 miles North of San Diego. The TraveLodge of Escondido served as the official site of training camp.

The Chargers opened the 1964 season with a 27-21 victory over the Houston Oilers at Balboa Stadium. The 1964 season appeared to be something of a turning point in the overall quality of the AFL. In January, league officials secured a new television contract with the National Broadcasting Company. The deal was for $36 million to be split amongst the eight teams over a five-year period. This influx of cash helped to stabilize some of the teams that had previously been on shaky financial ground. It also allowed teams more money to pay for talent, and helped bring some bit of parity to the league. Teams such as Buffalo and Kansas City (formerly the Dallas Texans), improved greatly, which made things more challenging for the Chargers.

San Diego won the Western Division again in 1964, but did so with only a one-game margin over the Kansas City Chiefs. Their 8-5-1 record was the teams second lowest only to the miserable 1962 season when they went 4-10. Still, the Chargers were favored in the championship over the Buffalo Bills, winners of the Eastern Division title.

The Chargers traveled to Buffalo's War Memorial Stadium to play the '64 championship game. The temperature at kick off was a cool 47 degrees, but it did not seem to bother the Chargers who needed just four plays to score their first touchdown. Buffalo got the ball on the ensuing kick off, but quickly turned it over. The Chargers appeared ready to drive for another score, when on second down and 10, quarterback Tobin Rote threw a swing pass to Keith Lincoln in the flat. Buffalo linebacker Mike Stratton read the play perfectly and arrived at Lincoln at the same time as the ball, crushing Lincoln who had been outstretched in his effort to catch the ball. A hush fell over

Keith Lincoln was knocked out of the game by Bills' linebacker Mike Stratton. The play became known, at least in Buffalo, as "The tackle heard 'round the world."

San Diegans voted to build a new stadium for the Chargers in 1965.

the Chargers' sideline as Lincoln lay writhing in pain. After several minutes Lincoln was helped off the field, but would not return to the game. The tackle had broken several of his ribs.

Lance Alworth was already sitting out of this game, unable to play because of a leg injury, and now Lincoln was out with broken ribs. Stratton's tackle had shifted the momentum in favor of Buffalo. It never returned to the Chargers. The Bills scored 20 unanswered points and brought the AFL Championship to upstate New York. Once again the Chargers had to settle for being the second-best team in the league.

With the league growing stronger and becoming an increasing threat to the NFL, there was little worry of the "rebel" league folding. The Chargers had grown increasingly popular in San Diego, and as the team continued to entrench itself into the San Diego community, the need for new facilities became increasingly apparent. Though Balboa Stadium had been a good home for the Chargers, realists understood that the stadium had serious drawbacks. Balboa Stadium was built in 1915 in conjunction with the Panama-California Exposition. There were no seats; spectators sat on long, concrete rows. If someone spilled a Coke in the upper rows, it ran down the stands, soaking the backsides of people the whole way down. The locker rooms were far from satisfactory and the toilets often overflowed. It was with the backing of the Mayor of San Diego that on April 27, 1965, the San Diego City Council endorsed construction of a multipurpose stadium in the Mission Valley area of San Diego. One month later the city approved spending $750,000 for architectural and engineering drawings for a 50,000-seat stadium. On November 2, the citizens of San Diego approved the construction of a $27 million stadium with a 73% vote. On December 24th the groundbreaking ceremonies were held and San Diego Stadium was underway.

Meanwhile, the Chargers again held their training camp at Escondido and opened the season with a narrow 34-31 win over Denver. Like the year previous, 1965 proved to be a more challenging year for the Chargers. Teams throughout the league were signing players to higher contracts and the quality of play continued to get better. In New York a brash, young quarterback from the University of Alabama signed a $400,000 contract with the Jets. His name was Joe Namath and there would soon be great things in store for New York fans.

Back in San Diego the Chargers could not mount a winning streak. Win, win, tie, win, win, tie, win, loss, win, loss, tie, win, win, and win, so went the Chargers' season. They finished with a 9-2-3 record, despite dominating the league in offensive statistics. The Chargers led the AFL in rushing yardage, receiving yardage, total offensive yardage, and in scoring. Once again the Chargers won the AFL West, and they were heavily favored to beat the Buffalo Bills in the championship game. But as had happened in years before, the Chargers broke down in the post season. Playing in what would be San Diego's final AFL Championship Game, the Chargers took a 23-0 beating at the hands of the Bills. For two consecutive years the Chargers' castoff quarterback, Jack Kemp, had beaten his former team.

As is often the case with winning teams, individual players enjoyed great success in 1965. John Hadl had taken over the reigns as starting quarterback and threw for nearly 2,800 yards. Lance Alworth led the league in receiving yardage with 1,602

Barron Hilton and Al Hartunian at the San Diego Stadium groundbreaking ceremony.

Buffalo Bills' quarterback Jack Kemp defeated his old team twice in AFL championship games.

19

yards. Paul Lowe led the league in rushing with 1,119 yards. Lowe and Alworth finished 1-2 in balloting for AFL Player of the Year. But to the truly competitive athlete, individual success means little if the team is not successful.

The season of 1966 brought about great change in the future of the American Football League. After six years of struggle against the mighty NFL, the two leagues came together and announced a plan to merge. The merger was to be finalized in 1970, though some changes would be implemented immediately, such as the top teams in each league playing each other in the AFL-NFL World Championship Game, soon to be called the Super Bowl. The fledgling AFL had finally earned the respect of the NFL.

The next two years brought many changes to the Chargers as well. This was the beginning of the breakup of the great nucleus of San Diego players. Ernie Ladd was the first to go. Unhappy with team management, Ladd had played out his option in 1965 and signed with the Houston Oilers for the 1966 season. Popular tight end Dave Kocourek, guard Ernie Park, and cornerbacks Dick Westmoreland and Jimmy Warren were lost to the Miami Dolphins in the expansion draft. In years to come, many familiar names would leave the Chargers. Hadl, Alworth, Buncom, Mix, Ladd, Faison, Sweeney, Kocourek and Lowe; none of these players would end their careers in a Chargers' uniform.

The most significant change to the Chargers came in August of 1966 when Barron Hilton announced that he had sold controlling interest in the team to a group of 21 businessmen, headed by Eugene V. Klein. Hilton had assumed the position of president and chief executive officer of the Hilton Hotel Corporation in February of 1966. The new position demanded his full attention, and forced him to divest the majority of his holdings in the Chargers. The sale was announced on August 25th, and the purchase price was $10 million, a then-record transaction in professional football. Hilton maintained a 10% ownership after the sale.

Barron Hilton, Sam Schulman, Sid Gillman and Gene Klein.

Gene Klein was a self-made millionaire who had begun his career in automobile sales. A born salesman, Klein first gained notoriety when he advertised that he was selling his cars "cheaper by the pound than hamburger. Instead of putting a final price on his cars, potential customers might see cars on Klein's lot priced at 33-, 44- or 66-cents per pound, all cheaper than hamburger. Klein built his business empire over the years, and when he purchased the Chargers in 1966, he was president of National General Corporation, a Southern California –based organization that had major holdings in movie theaters and movie and television production. Sam Schulman, Klein's partner and recently named Chairman of the Board of the Chargers, was a senior vice president of National General Corporation.

There was change for the Chargers on the field as well. The 1966 season was the Chargers' final season in Balboa Stadium, their home since arriving in San Diego in 1961. They would open the following season in San Diego Stadium in Mission Valley. The Chargers began the season with a four-game winning streak, but stumbled at mid-season, and lost three in a row in November. Two more wins and a loss was not enough to put them in the playoffs. They finished the 1966 season with a 7-6-1 record. Their record put them in third place in the West, behind Kansas City and Oakland.

The Chargers opened their 1967 training camp on July 10th in Escondido. Although their draft list did not produce any big name stars, there was still reason for optimism. The offense featured a strong line that included Ron Mix, Ernie Wright, Sam Gruneisen and Walt Sweeney, with Jacque MacKinnon at end. John Hadl remained at quarterback and had developed into one of the top passers in the league. Lance Alworth and second-year man, Gary Garrison were one of the best receiver duos the league had ever seen. Paul Lowe, Jim Allison, Gene Foster and rookie Dick Post were at running back.

But while the Chargers' offense remained strong, the defense had lost considerable strength over the years. Gone were all four

Quarterback John Hadl and the Chargers' offensive front.

Above: Lance Alworth and Dickie Post led the Chargers in receiving and rushing in 1967.

Left: The Chargers lost to the Detroit Lions in their first meeting with an NFL team.

members of the Fearsome Foursome. Second-year man Steve DeLong was developing into a fine defensive end, but he was still young and had little support. Chuck Allen and Frank Buncom still headed the linebackers, and their supporting cast was talented, but very young. In the secondary were Bud Whitehead and Kenny Graham, supported by up-and-comers Joe Beauchamp, Leslie "Speedy" Duncan and Jim Tolbert. In total, the Charger defense had potential, but lacked the dominating figures that led the team in the early days of the AFL.

The Chargers played their first game in San Diego Stadium on August 20th. A crowd of 45,988 turned out to see the Chargers play an exhibition game against the Detroit Lions. This game was also notable as it was the Chargers first contest against an NFL team. But fortune was not in the Chargers' favor and Detroit handed San Diego a 38-17 defeat.

There were many individual highlights in 1967. Alworth had over 1,000 yards receiving and John Hadl passed for 3,365 yards and 24 touchdowns. Running backs Dick Post and Brad Hubbert emerged as fine runners, leading the team with 663 and 643 yards, respectively. Defensively a cornerback named Speedy Duncan had become a reason for excitement among fans. He was a thrilling special teams player and often entertained fans and teammates with long returns. Such was the case on October 15th, when Duncan had 203 yards in returns for the day. He ran 35 yards for a touchdown on a fumble recovery, and had 68 yards on four kick-off returns. He also intercepted a pass that he ran back 100 yards for a touchdown and a new AFL record as the Chargers defeated the Kansas City Chiefs 45-31.

But the few highlights were not enough to carry the team through a 14-game season. San Diego finished the 1967 season with an 8-5-1 record, again good for third in the AFL West behind Oakland at 13-1 and Kansas City at 9-5. They had come charging out of the gates early, posting an 8-1-1 record through 10 games, but dropped their final four and finished well out of the playoff race. The offense was third in the league in total yards and fourth in scoring.

Just as finishing first in their division had once been an annual occurrence, finishing in third place had now become a regular event for the Chargers. Similar to the 1967 season, the Chargers offense had a great year in 1968, while their defense struggled along. Both Alworth and Garrison had over 1,000 yards receiving. Alworth led the league with 1,312. In his second year in the league, the small but exciting Dick Post led the Chargers with 758 rushing yards. The Chargers led the AFL in passing yards with 3,813 and ranked third in total scoring with 382 points. In true form, Speedy Duncan set another AFL record, this time with a 95-yard punt return for a touchdown against the New York Jets. But once again the Chargers finished in third place in the AFL West, this time with a 9-5 record.

With the beginning of the 1969 season came the end of an era. The 1970 season would see the merger between the AFL and NFL complete, and the two

Special teams star Leslie "Speedy" Duncan.

leagues would then represent American and National conferences within the National Football League.

The Chargers began 1969 with a change the location of their training camp. After spending the previous five years holding training camp in Escondido, the team moved 85 miles North and did their 1969 pre-season training on the University of California - Irvine campus. Alworth, Hadl, Post, and Mix again led the offense, while DeLong, Rick Redman and Speedy Duncan emerged as defensive leaders.

The regular season opened two months later with a loss to Kansas City at home. A second loss to Cincinnati was followed by four wins and then a four-game losing streak.

But the losing streak was somewhat forgotten on November 14th, when the man that had molded the Chargers throughout their existence, Sid Gillman, stepped down as head coach. A stomach ulcer and chest hernia were cited as Gillman's reasons for leaving. His son-in-law and physician, Dr. Jay Malkoff had urged Gillman to resign his post. Gillman swore that his ailments needed only rest to heal and that his resigning as head coach was strictly a health-based decision.

Gillman and Kansas City's Hank Stram were the only head coaches left in the AFL that had been in place since the league's inception in 1960. Gillman had built an impressive 78-42-6 record during his term. Gillman retained his position as general manager to keep close to the team, and handed over the on-field reins to Charlie Waller, previously the offensive backfield coach. Waller finished out the 1969 season in fine form. His first game, just two days after taking over for Gillman, was a 21-16 loss to Oakland, but then the Chargers won their final four games of the season.

As mentioned previously, the AFL-NFL merger would be completed in 1970, and December 14th against the Buffalo Bills pitted two of the league's original teams in their last game in the AFL. It was also Ron Mix Day. The great offensive tackle from USC and one of the first stars to sign with the AFL in 1960, had decided to end

Poor health forced Sid Gillman to give up his post as Chargers' head coach in 1969.

Ron Mix retired from the Chargers in 1969.

22

his playing career (though he would be coaxed out of retirement to play with the Oakland Raiders in 1971). His number 74 was to be ceremoniously retired at half-time. Finally, Lance Alworth had made history the week prior when he tied the record of the great Green Bay Packer, Don Hutson, by making a reception in 95-straight games. A catch against Buffalo and Lance would have the record to himself.

The weather couldn't have been nicer for the Chargers on their last day in the AFL. It was sunny, with a temperature of 66 degrees. A slight breeze was coming out of the West when the Chargers' Dennis Partee kicked off to begin the game. The Buffalo offense began the game with the ball on their own 24-yard line. The first offensive play was a handoff to their brilliant young running back, O.J. Simpson who took the ball but was stopped at the line of scrimmage. Three plays later and the Bills were forced to punt.

The Chargers got the ball on the Buffalo 41, after a 38-yard punt return by Speedy Duncan. John Hadl dropped back to pass on the Chargers' first play and fired a 33-yard pass to Gary Garrison who hauled it in and trotted the final eight yards for the touchdown. A Dennis Partee kick made the score Chargers 7, Bills 0.

The Bills again got the ball and began a 14-play drive that after penalties totaled just 16 yards.

On the first play of the Chargers' second possession, Hadl threw a pass to Alworth, who hauled it in for a gain of nine and a new professional football record. Don Hutson had come to the game in anticipation, and came out on the field to congratulate the new record holder. Play resumed a short time later and the Chargers picked up where they left off. When halftime rolled around, San Diego had a commanding 24-0 lead. Alworth had three more receptions in the half.

San Diego came out after the half and continued to play like the Chargers of old. Dick Post had touchdown runs of 34 and two yards, and young quarterback Marty Domres scored on a nine-yard run. The Chargers were in the lead 45-0 in the fourth quarter before Buffalo scored on a 19-yard pass play. The final score was 45-6 after the Chargers blocked the Bills' extra point attempt.

When the final gun sounded, the game, the season and the league came to a close. For the fourth year in a row, the Chargers had finished in third place in their division, this time with an 8-6 record. Alworth had again led the league with 64 catches for 1,003 yards. Dick Post was the league leader with 873 yards rushing.

With the end of the league came the end of an era. Sid Gillman and his Chargers had been the class of the American Football League. Their exciting aerial offensive attack had been the most potent in professional football during the 1960s. The Chargers gained 49,652 total offensive yards during the decade. The Baltimore Colts of the NFL finished second with 49,213. The Chargers led the AFL in total passing yards and finished second in rushing yardage over the 10-year span. They also finished second to the Chiefs in total scoring, having totaled 3,528 points during the decade, an average of 25.2 points-per-game.

But while scoring points wins football games, perhaps more importantly, Sid Gillman and the Chargers helped lend cred-

Lance Alworth and Hall of Fame receiver Don Hutson.

ibility and professionalism to the AFL, something that it desperately needed, particularly in the early years. "I went to San Diego for one reason," Bones Taylor, a Chargers assistant in 1963 recalled in *The $400,000 Quarterback.* "Sid Gillman is the master of organization – the best in the business."

Gillman had been a rare commodity coming into the AFL. He was a man who had head coaching experience in the NFL. He knew how to run a football team and it showed in the Chargers. Not only did his team excel on the field, but also Gillman and the Chargers were consistently on the cutting edge in all aspects of the game. In

Keith Lincoln and Chargers' strength coach Alvin Roy.

1963 the Chargers became the first team in professional football to hire a strength coach and make weight training a mandatory part of their workout routine. Sid Gillman was also one of the first coaches to use game film and later practice film as a coaching tool.

The Chargers set precedents for race relations among pro football teams. The Chargers had always been a team that rejected racial discrimination of any kind. As a team they walked out of movie theaters and hotels when they were told that the black players would have to use alternative facilities. Gillman and several Chargers' players had been intimately involved in having the 1965 AFL All-Star Game moved from New Orleans to Houston on a day's notice after cab drivers and nightclub owners refused service to black players.

In 1968, when racial conflicts persisted in certain areas of the country, Sid Gillman dictated his players' roommate arrangements in training camp and on the road. Instead of grouping players together based on friendships or otherwise, he roomed them together by position, and thus forced black and white players to room together, again a first for professional football players. When questioned on the subject, Gillman answered matter-of-factly and was quoted in the *Los Angeles Times.* "We've really been thinking about it a long time. We just decided to Americanize our football team. That's all there is to it. We don't segregate Jews and we don't segregate Catholics and we don't segregate people because of their political beliefs. So why should we segregate them because of their race? ...I don't think it's a particularly great thing. It's a thing everybody's got to do or we're not going to make any progress or improvement. If we are designing our future with the idea that we're going to get this (racial) situation straightened out, then let's get with it."

On the field the Chargers had little success for their first several years in the NFL. Sid Gillman returned as head coach for the 1971 season, but feuds with Gene Klein led to Gillman resigning after 10 games. Lance Alworth was traded to the Dallas Cowboys in 1971. John Hadl went to the Los Angeles Rams after the 1972 season. One-by-one the Chargers of the AFL were traded, released or retired. In 1982, the Chargers released Russ Washington, a 1968 draft choice and longtime offensive tackle. In releasing Washington, the Chargers cut their last on field ties with the AFL.

The Chargers' days in the AFL are only occasionally mentioned. The old baby-blue jerseys have made a few appearances in recent years. They're called "throw-back jerseys" now, and few fans can recall the times when they were the Chargers' regular uniforms. Balboa Stadium is long gone; it was torn down after failing tests for stability in an earthquake. Sid Gillman is gone, too. He passed away peacefully in his den at age 91, surrounded by mementoes of his days coaching the Chargers. In fact, all that is left of San Diego's days in the old league are some photos, old stories and fuzzy memories. But thank God for those memories... They are damn good.

Sid Gillman.

27

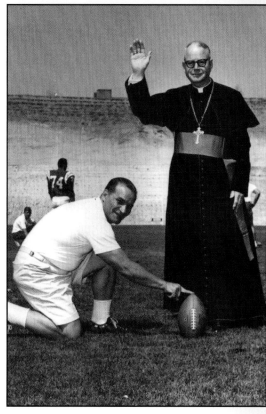

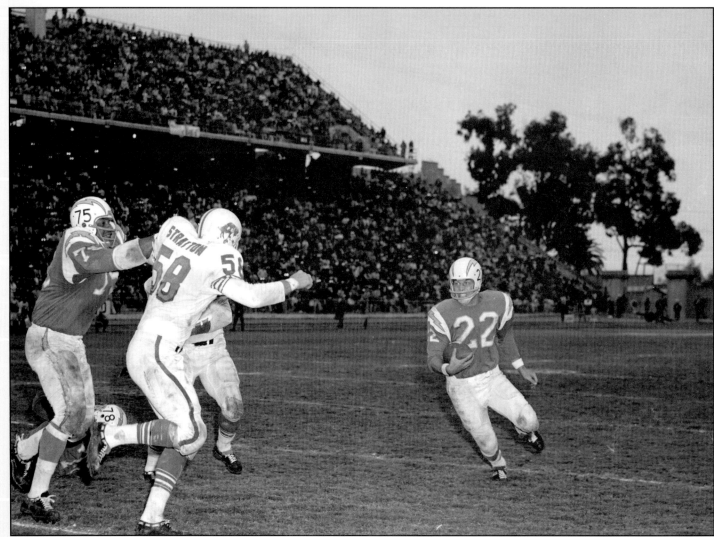

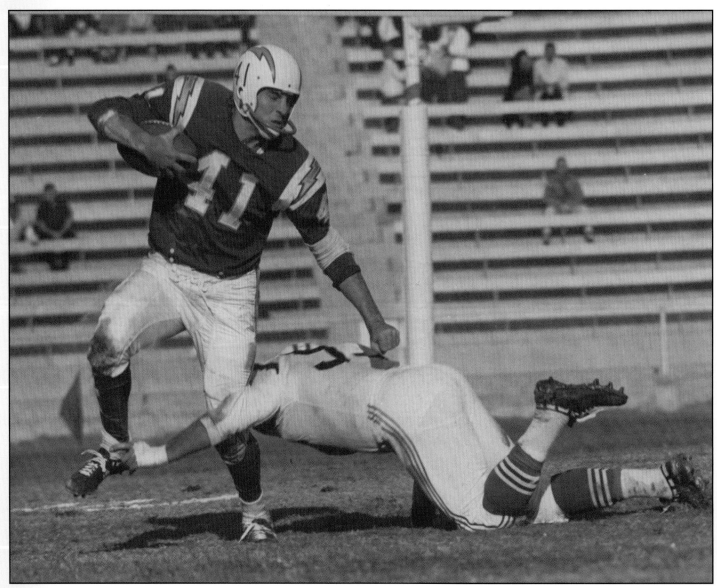

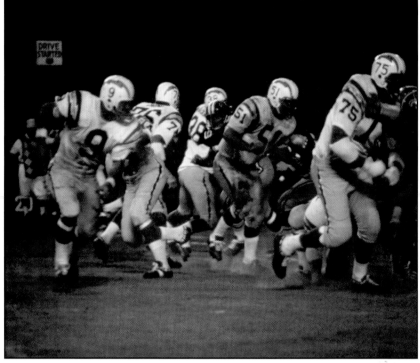

37

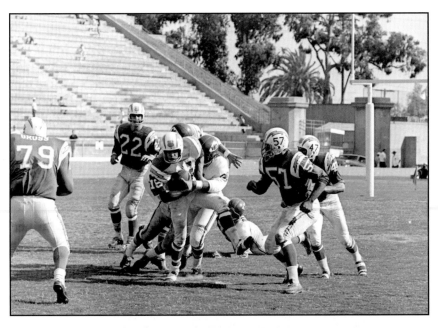

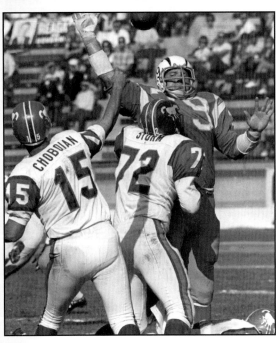

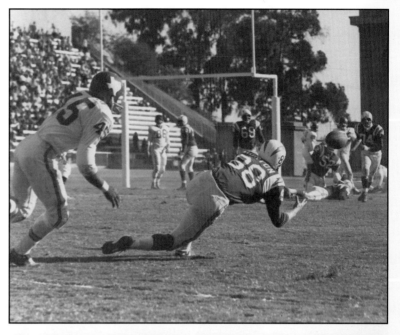

BEN AGAJANIAN, KICKER

College: Compton CC, New Mexico
Years with the Chargers: 1960, 1964

Ben Agajanian was already 41 years old when he became the Los Angeles Chargers' kicker in 1960. His professional football career began in 1942 with the Hollywood Bears of the Pacific Coast Football League. He also played for the San Diego Bombers, Hollywood Rangers, Philadelphia Eagles, Pittsburgh Steelers, Los Angeles Dons, New York Giants (twice), Los Angeles Rams, Washington Redskins, Los Angeles Chargers, Dallas Texans, Green Bay Packers, Oakland Raiders and finally the San Diego Chargers. After retiring as a player, Agajanian spent more than 20 years as kicking coach for the Dallas Cowboys.

Well, I was retired. 1957 was my last year with the New York Giants, because I wanted to fly back and forth. I held out for the Giants in '56, and the Giants told me to get someone else. I coached Gifford and Chandler, so they could kick. But Gifford couldn't kick and play, so they brought me back and we won the world championship in '56 in New York. I decided in '57 that I was going to quit, but I flew back and forth. In '58 they brought Pat Summerall in, and he did the kicking, so I retired. They asked me if I was going to retire and I said, "No, just give me a release."

So in '58 and '59 I didn't do anything, but in 1960 the Chargers were working out at camp, training camp, here in Chapman College. So I went over and sat in the bleachers to watch them. And funny thing, Sid Gillman looked at me and he yelled, "Hey, old man. Can you still kick?" And I said, "Yeah." He says, "Practice up and come over in a couple days. Let me see you." And I said, "I don't need any practice." So I went over there the next day and I kicked and we looked over, and their kicker picked up his helmet and shoulder pads and walked off the field and went home…

Then Sid Gillman says, "You're not eligible to play for us." I said, "Why?" He said, "You belong to the Titans." I said, "How come?" He said, "Well, the draft." The New York Titans selected me as one of the players from the Giants. I was on their roster so to speak. I didn't know it, but they had selected me. So what did I do? I told Sid that I would take care of it.

So I called the Titans and they said that they were in South Carolina or something where their training camp was. I said that I wanted to talk to Sammy Baugh. They gave me the number and I called Sammy Baugh. I said, "Hey Sammy Baugh, I'm coming back to kick for you." He says, "What? Who is this?" I said, "Ben Agajanian. I'm on your roster and I have decided to come out of retirement and kick for you." He said, "Oh Jeez, we already have a kicker." So I said, "Why don't we do this? Why don't we make a trade?" I said, "The kicker for the Chargers also is a player. He's a darned good player. Why don't we trade him for me?" So he said, "OK." So I made my own trade and I came back and told Sid. "Everything's fine. I made a trade and I'm on the team." He said, "OK, great." So I kicked and I had a pretty good year.

But then they decided to move to San Diego, and I said, "I can't move to San Diego. I've got my business up here. I'm in the oil well business and I have the Long Beach Athletic Club." And I had sporting goods stores and discount houses. So I didn't need the money, but at the same time, when someone says, "We want you, we need you," I go running. So he said, "Can you come down and coach one of the kids," (Keith) Lincoln, I think it was. And I said, "Sure." So I went down to San Diego for the preseason and I did some coaching. I kicked in their inter-squad game.

Then I came home and I told Sid to just give me a release. So he did. But in '61 the Dallas Texans called. They said, "We need a kicker, our kicker is hurt. Can you kick for us?" I said, "Sure." So I flew back there and met with Lamar Hunt and his man. I kicked the first game and then the second game we went to New England and I got hit in the back after a kickoff. A guy came around from behind, and I couldn't raise my leg. I kicked the ball very poorly. I tried a field goal and the ball rolled down the field. Somebody said I kicked like his grandmother and I was just as old.

Anyway, I came back and Hank Stram says, "Lombardi wants you at Green Bay." I said, "Oh Jeez, if you don't want me, then OK." I was so excited to go to Green Bay, because Lombardi and I were together in New York for five years. I said, "Well, if you don't want me, then I'll go to Green Bay." So I flew home and I flew up to Green Bay. I kicked with Bart Starr holding and Paul Hornung was still there. They made a trade. Val Keckin, a quarterback, was supposed to go to the Dallas Texans. And this was a secret trade between two leagues that were not talking to each other. But Hank [Stram] idolized Lombardi, so Hank would do anything to help Lombardi, and I would too.

Well, I kicked up there with Bart and everything, and then I got a phone call from Lamar Hunt saying that he understands that Paul Hornung's not going in the service until the following week and they need a kicker for one more week. Could I come down? I said, "Oh Jeez." I'm in Green Bay and it's Saturday, and the game is Sunday. I said, "Well, I'll come down." Lamar says, "You can be free to go to Green Bay if you'll just help us this one week." And I said, "OK." My wife was with me and it was her birthday. And I said, "What do you want for your birthday?" She said a record field goal. And I said, "You're crazy. I'm 42 years old. I can't kick."

We flew back. You won't believe this… A little DC-3, Green Bay to Oshkosh to Milwaukee to Chicago. Stop, jump, stop, jump, up, down… Then we go to O'Hare and then we have to take a helicopter to Midway. My wife hates to fly and here we are in a helicopter with an open door. Jeez! And I said, "I'm taking my shoes in my hands." Because my kicking shoe with the square toe, if I don't have it, I don't kick. So I wouldn't pack it. I carried it. I knew. Well, my clothes never showed up. I got there Saturday night. Sunday morning we got a cab and went to the Cotton Bowl. I got dressed up and went out there and I kicked one field goal, and I kicked another field goal. Then they called a 51-yard field goal. I went out there and made it, and it was a record. It was a team record and a Cotton

Bowl record. When I came jogging off the field, I looked up and my wife blew a kiss to me. I blew a kiss back everybody in the stands thought I was kissing them, so they all threw a kiss at me.

So immediately after the game, I got dressed and was leaving and this kid comes up to me limping. He says, "I'm the kicker here. I was the kicker and you came in and broke the record. I just want to shake your hand." I shook hands with him. I don't know who the guy was. I left and I flew up to San Jose to open another store. Sporting goods and discount stores was my deal then. And I opened another store and I got a phone call from Lombardi saying... He says, "The deal is off. You can't come to Green Bay." I said, "Why?" He said, "Well, they won't release you." And I said, "They already have." He said, "No way." I said, "Well, Lamar Hunt said if I went one more week, they'd let me go." When I called, I got a hold of Hank Stram and I said, "Hank, you didn't want me when I missed one, and then when I make three in a row, you want me."

He said, "Well, how could I explain to the fans? They all love you. The press... How could I explain? Jeez." I said, "Hank, you already released me. I'm not gonna come back there. I promised Vince I would go to Green Bay and help him. Paul's in the service now and they don't have a kicker." He said, "Well, if I can't talk you out of it, good luck in Green Bay." So I called Green Bay back and Lombardi got on the phone. He started chuckling, and I said, "I made my own trade again. I'll be there Friday." He said, "OK." And I flew back and forth every week, and we won the championship at Green Bay in '61.

Then in '62 I go back for the All-Star game, but I go back there and I coach. I taught Jerry Kramer how to kick, and Green Bay went that year, in '62, and won the championship also, with Kramer kicking three field goals in the championship game. Meanwhile, in '62, I get a call from the Raiders. Not Al Davis, but the Raiders called and said, "Would you kick for us?" It was in the middle of the season in '62. They said, "What did you get in Green Bay?" And I told them, "It was $1,000 a game." "Oh gee, we can't pay you that much." So I said, "That's OK, I'll kick for nothing." So for $0 salary, I flew up there and they had a contract all made out with $0 salary.

Well, I "X'ed" out the option clause and signed it, and I flew back and forth to Oakland. They didn't win a game until the last game. At one time there was nine men out on the field. I kept yelling on the kickoff. And they'd wave at me, "Nah, I'm not on that team." No one wanted to play. Hell, I'm now 43 years old, and I'm kicking. One time I kicked a field goal and they blocked it, and everybody went off the field except me. I'm chasing this guy who's going for a touchdown. I'm limping and chasing, and I can't catch him. Then we punted to them once, and the guy's going for a touchdown, and no one knew this. As he went by the bench, I went out and tackled him and went right back to the bench. Nobody knew this until Jim Otto and them were looking at films and I'm home. Jim Otto calls me here in Long Beach and he says, "Goddammit, you were the guy that made the tackle, saved the touchdown." I said, "Yeah, I sneaked off the bench and did that." He just got a big kick out of it.

But finally, the last game I told the coach, "Why don't we try an onside kick?" It was raining and muddy, and I couldn't kick it to the goal line then. Oh I could, maybe. But he said, "What for? They'll get the ball on the 40." And I said, "Well, they run them back to the 40 anyway, so what the Hell's the difference." He said, "OK, go ahead." I kicked a perfect onside kick, we got the ball, we made one or two first downs, and I kicked a field goal. 3-0 the score is until the end of the game and we scored a touchdown and won the first game in 17 games.

That was in '62. Then '63 I didn't play. In '64 Sid Gillman calls me and I go down to San Diego to watch practice. He says, "I want you to kick for us." I said, "No way. I'm retired. I'm 45." And he tells my wife, "I want Ben." And my wife tells me, so I say, "Well, if I can fly back and forth, I'm still busy with my businesses." Someone said, "Why did you kick for nothing for the Raiders?" I said, "Well, I was making more money than they were, so why should I charge them?"

I had all these oil wells and everything going. So, at 45 I went and signed with the Chargers, and the funny thing, a couple days before the first game, Sid tells me that I'm ineligible. I said, "What?" "Yeah, you're ineligible. You can't kick for us." "Why?" "You belong to the Raiders. Al Davis says you belong to the Raiders." I said, "That's a lot of baloney." I think it was the day before the game. He said, "Why?" I said, "I 'X'ed' out the option clause. I'm not that stupid. I know what the Hell's going on. I know how pro football works." So I said, "I 'X'ed' out the option clause and I don't belong to the Raiders." He said, "Well, let me call Joe Foss." In fact, Joe Foss, the commissioner, thanked me for coming into the league to help with publicity and stuff like that, an old, old kicker.

Anyway, they said, "Sure, Ben's eligible." Well, Sid didn't say anything to me until the day of the game. I think Hadl threw a pass to Alworth for a touchdown. I'm standing there, Sid looks at me and I said, "Do you want me to kick? Am I eligible?" He says, "Yeah, yeah, yeah, yeah, go kick." So I ran in and kicked. Well, after another two or three games, I think we went to Denver and I kicked a 47-yard field goal. But one of my friends was the referee and he said, "Ben kicked a 47-yard field goal that went 47 yards, 47 rows in the stands, and he's 47 years old." Well, he was exaggerating, but anyway.

Lombardi called. He said, "Paul Hornung's having trouble. Would you come coach him?" I said, "Sure." So I flew to Green Bay, and I said, "Paul, how are you doing?" And he said, "I can't kick." So anyway, I gave him a lesson and kicked there. And then I met the team in Kansas City. That's when it all ended. I flew from Green Bay to Kansas City and the wind was blowing and it was Saturday. I told Sid all this, that I was going to Green Bay to help and I would be back. And Sid had me kick off on Saturday morning, a cold, windy day. And I pulled a hamstring. Tore a muscle. I just couldn't lift my leg. They took me in the locker room and gave me about four or five shots. And it bled from my groin down to my knee; it was all black and blue. They gave me quite a few shots. I dressed up and went out Sunday, and I still couldn't lift my leg. I tried in the pre-game warm up to kick and I just couldn't kick. So they got someone else to kick and that was it. They went on and I think they won the championship or the playoff in Buffalo or something that year, in '64. And that was my last kick, and I retired.

42

Joe Amstutz, Center

College: Indiana
Years with the Chargers: 1960 Training Camp

Joe Amstutz was drafted out of the University of Indiana in the sixth round of the 1957 draft. He played one year for Paul Brown and the Cleveland Browns before a knee injury ended his time in the NFL. He attempted a comeback with the Los Angeles Chargers in 1960, but the reoccurrence of his knee injury kept him from making the team, so at age 25 he retired from pro football and began a 30-year career in the parks and recreation department of the City of Los Angeles.

Right: *In 1960 the Fleer Company decided to print bubble gum cards of AFL players. The set of cards was released prior to the end of training camp and as a result, several cards were made of players that did not actually make the team. This card of Joe Amstutz is one such example.*

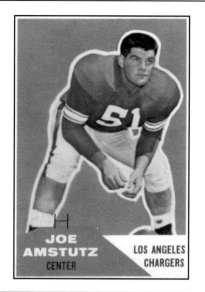

I had played with the Cleveland Browns when I graduated from college. I hurt my knee against the Giants in the last game of the season. And they didn't take me back in those days, when you got a bad knee, at my size anyway. So I taught and coached for one year and then when they started the new league, I was called by a couple of pro teams. The Oilers called me, the Chargers called me. After coming out here to play San Francisco and the Rams, I liked California. So I chose California…

At that point, I knew of Al Davis before. He didn't strike me as much of a coach, to tell you the truth. I don't know. I wasn't knowledgeable at the time. As a matter of fact, the guy that played center for them (Don Rogers), I coached myself. He was a guard originally, and I was teaching him how to snap the ball and how to block, things like that. Because, I don't know, I wasn't concerned about making the team, I guess. After some scrimmages they viewed the films and they asked me how my knee was. I said, "Fine, I guess." He said, "You favor it a lot. You look like Hopalong Cassidy out there." And I said, "Well, if my man didn't make a tackle in the whole scrimmage." And he said, "Yeah, but we can't start a season wondering if you are going to finish the season." So that was the concern, I guess, my knee. But I have no regrets. I came out here and enjoyed it. I got a job and retired from L.A. City and moved up here in the mountains where I can relax and do nothing.

Paul Brown… Knowledgeable, he knew his football frontward and backwards. A little Caesar; you didn't cross him. You didn't make remarks to him. He controlled practice. A taskmaster. I respected him. A lot of the players didn't like him, but they respected him. He was very sarcastic at times. Don Paul was running back a punt and he tripped on, I don't know. We feel that he got tripped up by somebody. But Paul Brown ridiculed him at a meeting by saying, "You know, you gotta watch those chalk marks. They're higher than normal."

Pro football is a lot different than college ball. You didn't scrimmage as much after the season started. I feel I enjoyed my football career. I was a center and I snapped the ball to probably six of the greatest quarterbacks in the history of football. Let's see if I can remember them anymore; Paul Hornung, John Brodie, Len Dawson, Otto Graham, Milt Plum, Bobby somebody, …Jack Kemp. So, I enjoyed it. Today I wish that I wouldn't have had my knee messed up because it's bothering me. My wife is a scrapbooker. She makes these books. She took one of my old scrapbooks and put one together. She finished it and I was looking through it, and I had to laugh because in the article it said I was probably one of the largest men in pro football at that time. Except for Biggie Munn and a few people like that. But I played at 265, and I had to laugh because they busted my butt to get me down there from 310 pounds. And nowadays, I'd be a lightweight.

Generally in football, what I cannot stand, and you ought to ask this of the other guys that played back in the 1950s, about the dancing. The most you would do if you made a good tackle, a guy would come and pat you on the butt and say, "Nice going." Now you make a tackle, and I would be embarrassed to dance like these people. I was watching a playoff game three or four years ago and the statistician was talking about the guy sacked the quarterback. He looked at the stats and said, "Oh, his first of the year." Well, yeah, he went through the whole season, didn't sack anyone. Now he sacks somebody and he dances around like he's a hero. I would be ashamed to do that. I've talked to some other guys who used to play years ago. I spoke at a men's club meeting once, a couple years ago, and said I couldn't play today. They asked why not and I said, "Cause I don't dance that well." I just think it's ridiculous. Paul Brown once said, a rookie caught a pass and scored a touchdown. He did his dance, walked back to the sidelines and Paul Brown called him over. He thought he was going to congratulate him, and Paul said, "Son, act like you have been there before." You are expected to be making tackles and sacking the quarterback and interceptions passes and scoring touchdowns. I guess they do it for the fans, I don't know. But when they start doing it, I turn the game off.

HOWARD CLARK, TIGHT END

College: Tennessee - Chattanooga
Years with the Chargers: 1960-1961

Howard Clark played during the first two years of the Chargers. An injury cut his career short after he had averaged 16.25 yards on 38 receptions in 1960 and 1961. After football Clark returned to Sierra Vista, Arizona, where he had been stationed in the Army, and taught school and coached P.E.

When I got out of college I went up to Montreal. Then I signed a contract with the Alouettes. Then I was drafted into the army. That was about the time of the draft and I was just out of college. So I got on the list. I was deferred until college was over. But anyway, I was drafted. That was in '58. Then just about the time I was getting out, the new league was being formed. I contacted the Chargers. I received a letter back from them and they sent me a contract. I think it was Joe Madro that remembered me from when he came to visit someone else. That's kind of what I remember of it. I think that's the way it was…

Gosh, that [1960 training camp] was at Chapman Junior College, up there by Disneyland as I recall. I think it was right there in Anaheim. But anyway, we were in the dorm there at the junior college. It was just a typical training camp. People were coming and going everyday. We would all kind of get together and talk. A little bit later in the training camp, when players would be cut loose from the NFL, we would all begin to wonder if they were coming here. And a lot of them did. We had several come in there that were cut by the NFL teams. I think we picked up two or three that stayed. Otherwise they just passed on through. In my opinion, speaking for myself, you never knew. You had a pretty good idea, but the way people came and went there was no certainty. Let's put it that way.

Well, Sid Gillman was, at the time you probably didn't realize what you're dealing with, but as I look back, he was a very good offensive-minded coach. Al and Chuck were just regular guys to me. Obviously they had a whole lot of talent also.

Sid had some funny jokes that he would tell. His mannerisms were pretty comical sometimes. I think he tried to make everybody feel pretty good and at ease. He let the other guys do the chewing. I can remember one time, just as an example of something; I think we had gone on an Eastern trip. We left Houston, I think. About the time a major hurricane, I think the biggest one, was coming in. We played… I think Buffalo was first and then New York and Boston. We had a three-week swing and we stayed over there the whole time. But anyway the Buffalo game… Anyway, to make a long story short, I can remember an incident. We were at a meeting reviewing the films. I had made a good play and Sid, he would compliment you in front of everybody. He mentioned it and I quipped back at him to hold on and let me get a tape recorder, because I might need that at contract time. He got a big kick out of that. But Sid was a good coach.

Other than probably the Chargers were one of the two or three or four teams that had good, solid financial backing. Some of the other teams struggled there for a while because of the ownership. But the Chargers, with Hilton, the checks were always there. I can remember one team in particular, the Titans, were having financial problems. I think two or three of the other teams did. But the Chargers never did have any that I know of…

We had a lot of good people and good players. And both. Some of them were good people and some were good players and some were both. I always enjoyed Ron Mix. We kidded each other a lot. He played tackle and I played tight end. I got a kick out of Ron. We kind of kidded each other back and forth a lot. But all the guys were actually pretty good. I didn't have any qualms about any one of them. They were all good people… I want to mention another one, Royce Womble. Have you interviewed him? But you saw him on the roster. He and I became real good friends. He was from Dallas. I think he played with Baltimore for a couple years before he came in. I can't remember if he came directly to the Chargers or if he was released and came in later. But Royce and I were pretty good buddies. He was a wide receiver…

I disliked the flying. About midseason or so of the first year, for some reason I began to develop not liking to fly. Do you remember the San Luis Obispo football team plane crash? Was that '60 or '61? I don't remember when it was, but that was about the time. It could have been my second year. But I think it may have been the first. But we were on a trip and we got up and read about it in the paper. I was then starting to get pretty nervous about flying. I don't fly at all now, unless it's an emergency or something. I haven't flown in years.

The camaraderie we had with the players and coaches. Our end group, we had a good time with Al. Al Davis, he was pretty funny, too. He wasn't all seriousness. He would joke around and we had a lot of fun teasing Al and he teasing us during our practices and things like that.

Fred Cole, Guard

College: Maryland
Years with the Chargers: 1960

Fred Cole was an All-American at Maryland and captain of the Terrapins football team. He spent the 1959 season with Winnipeg of the Canadian Football League, and then returned to the states to play for the Chargers in 1960. Cole retired from football after the 1960 season to begin his career as a mechanical engineer.

Well, when I was a senior, Bud Grant, who was the coach of Winnipeg, came to the University of Maryland. He came to my dorm room and offered me a signing bonus right on the spot. As far as George Halas, he had called me, and he was primarily concerned with how I stood in the draft. He said, "How do you stand in the draft?" I said," Well, I've got a college deferment." But other than that, that was it. They never really talked seriously to me. The Chicago Bears didn't. And at that time I had never made any money. My big signing bonus was $1,000. So I signed and went to Winnipeg. I went to Winnipeg that Fall.

Their season is more advanced than they are in the states. I had really racked my knee pretty good. And I was doing nothing and it was doubtful that I'd be back before the end of the season. It was like late September and their season is almost wrapped up by October. Then they have the Grey Cup. So I asked for a release so I could go back to school. I hadn't graduated yet. I still needed some more credits. So I asked for a release so I could go back to school. I registered late and then I finished my education in consecutive years. Otherwise it would have taken me two years because I would have had to go back in the spring. Then I would have to go back the following spring. So this way kind of worked out nice.

At that time there was no AFL. When I was in high school, Al Davis was coaching at the Citadel. Al Davis came to my high school and wanted me to go to the Citadel. I was from Newark, New Jersey. And then subsequently I did not go. But he tracked me down. In fact, I was with my roommate in Pennsylvania and he tracked me down there. I met with him in Pittsburgh and he assured me that I would get a good shot with the Chargers, and I signed. I went out there.

Well, when the Chargers started out that year they had open tryouts starting in April of the year. They had signed me. Al Davis signed me in the spring. I don't remember the month. But I was scheduled to come in with the last wave at the end of June. I think it was the end of June when they brought in people who either had a little experience or maybe... I don't know how they decided who came in when, but they had been running practices from April, May and in through June. Maybe it was as early as July, I forget. I remember when I first got there they had 32 guards that they were trying out. I would get at the end of the line and you'd wait in line. Then you would run one play and then go back to the end of the line again. So practices were really easy when you first got there. You hardly did anything...

We had a few veterans on the team, which were ex-NFL. And I said, "They have top-notch coaches, they have great facilities, and they are getting players from the same place that

the NFL gets them." As long as they could keep it financially going. In the beginning, I don't know what the gates were, but they weren't packing the house. But I think they had TV money. That's when TV started to play a big part in pro sports. And I think, I guess they all kind of lost money that first year, maybe. But they went about it first class. All of those owners, they didn't skimp. We had good facilities, we had good practice facilities, and we traveled well. We used to stay at the Hilton Hotels because Barron owned the team. Every place we went, we stayed at a Hilton Hotel if there was one available. But we stayed at top-notch places. The equipment was good. I wasn't concerned that they would fold...

Sid was excellent with the players. He would explain what he wanted and if he saw you made a mistake, he would put you to task or holler at you. We had a double reverse, I remember. The two guards were supposed to pull to the left and take two steps and then turn around and go to the right. Orlando (Ferrante), who was the other starting guard, on the left side, somehow we got confused and we both pulled at each other. We had a head-on collision, and Sid Gillman went nuts. He said, "My God, what's the matter with you? You're going to kill each other." Because we went head-to-head. Bang! There was no place to avoid it. If you did your best and the other guy got the better of you that was one thing. But if you made a mistake, and you blocked the wrong guy, he didn't like that. He wanted everybody to mentally do the right thing. Or at least do the thing you were supposed to do.

Bud Grant was a whole different style. Gillman would kid around a little bit. Bud Grant was so dead serious. He hardly ever even cracked a smile. Very, very methodical and quiet. He was more distant from the players. I think Sid Gillman kibitzed around with some of the players a little more than Bud Grant ever did...

Ron Mix and Ernie Wright. When we used to run wind sprints, those guys were as fast or faster than the guards were. And they were the tackles. So we had a lot of speed on that line. I think (Don) Rogers was the slowest of the group. And certainly Sam DeLuca brought up the rear. But Ron Mix and Ernie Wright were very, very quick for as big as those guys were. I forget how big they were, maybe 275 or something like that. But Ron Mix fired out; he had a spring-type stance that he was in. He would fire out of there and he was terrific. Very quick.

As we got into the season we'd start calling the blocking and we worked together real well. It might be a pass play and I'd say, "You got this guy, I got that guy." Nobody really knew what was going on. And we used to call our blocking. The system that Gillman had was that when you went up to the line of scrimmage, you called the blocking. It was like an A, B, C, or something like that. They had some code as to who was going to block who...

We started off the season great. We won our first game, and then we lost three games in a row and I guess our fifth game, we were like 1-3. I think our fifth game was in Denver and Sid Gillman called the team together and before the game said, "You guys have been playing lousy. I don't want you taking any more of these pep pills." In those days some of the guys would take Benzedrine. They thought they would get a lift from it or whatever. He said, "I don't want anybody taking anything and if you guys don't go out there and play the way I know you can, you're gonna think this place is Grand Central Station. I'm gonna bring in so many guys, your heads will be swimming." And that was the game that we kind of jelled. I think we only lost one more game the whole season. I think we lost four games that whole season and we lost three right away. Near the end of the season we were rolling 40 or 50 points a game. We had a real machine going there.

AL DAVIS, OFFENSIVE END COACH

College: Syracuse University
Years with the Chargers: 1960-1962

Al Davis is a legendary figure in modern day sports. The often despised, but equally admired and respected owner of the Oakland Raiders began his professional coaching career in 1960 with the Los Angeles Chargers. Davis left the Chargers for Oakland prior to the 1963 season. From that point he built the Raiders into one of the most dominant and successful sports franchises in history. The popular slogans, "Pride and Poise," "Commitment to Excellence," and "Just Win, Baby," are all attributed to Davis and his Raiders.

I was coaching at the University of Southern California. One night I came home. It was about 11:30 at night. My wife, Carol, said, "Sid called." And Sid and I used to talk all the time. And he liked you to call him no matter what time you got in. So I called him about one in the morning. I told him that I hoped I wasn't disturbing him. He said, "No, no, no, I was waiting for the call." He says, "I'm going to go over and take over this Charger team in this new league, the American Football League, and I'd like you to come along." And I said, "Well, what are you thinking? What would I coach?" He said, "I'm not sure exactly who I'm gonna hire yet, but I'll let you say where you want to coach." And I said, "Well I coached the defense, I was the defensive coordinator at Southern Cal, but I really want to go back on offense, the passing game." He said, "OK you've got it if you'll come." I said, "Gimme a week." And I took a week and I said I would come...

I was only with them in 1960, 1961 and 1962. But I had to compete against them the rest of my life. And they were special, there's no question about that. It was probably one of the greatest (coaching) staffs of all time. For a small staff of only five people, for three of them to be in the hall of fame (Sid Gillman, Chuck Noll and Al Davis), and I think between Chuck and myself we have nine super bowls. That's a lot of super bowls. But Sid was really the catalyst.

No, I knew Sid's offensive theory a long while. That was not the factor. The factor was working with him. We were gonna build a young team in a new league. I had opportunities in the National Football League and opportunities in college. But I liked the idea of it. I liked the idea because I also could recruit a lot of the players. Of those great teams in the early years, I'd say we got most of them. From Paul Lowe to Keith Lincoln to Ron Mix...

I signed Paul Lowe in the middle of the night. Yeah, he was a great talent. In those years there were many castoffs, which was proven by having the new league. He just had great ability. And what really got him going was the weight programs that we had. That really developed his body. He was a very explosive player. God, he and Lincoln were explosive players.

Lincoln came in '61. He was a number two choice. Earl Faison was number one. The thing is that I missed Lincoln. I missed Keith when I came to the University of Southern California. Keith had already signed at Washington State. I couldn't get him. But he was really good. I think he was from Monrovia...

We had drafted Lance (Alworth) in a prior draft that was ruled not legal. So that draft was thrown out. And in the second draft that year, the Oakland Raiders had drafted him, number two, I think, in their draft. Because they were much lower than us in the draft, they had the rights to him. But we traded Bo Roberson and several players for Lance because I thought Lance would be a brilliant athlete and a brilliant performer. It was unique that it was in November. I think it was November; we had a bye week. The Chargers did. We were in San Diego. We had moved from Los Angeles, and I was gonna go down to see Lance on that bye week. I was going down to Arkansas to see him. I got a call in the middle of the night, and I thought it was the planes calling to say that the weather had changed and they couldn't go out. But it was a call that was probably the worst call I have ever had in my life; that my father had died. So I went to the funeral back East, and then late in the week I went down to see Lance and met him for the first time. I started to sell him on the Chargers, a young team, a young city, a young league, grow with it, and then of course the point that I would be coaching him. I had the ability to sell the great Sid Gillman, and of course the owner of the team, Barron Hilton…

No, we were not an unstable team. On the contrary, we were very stable. We had signed some brilliant young players like Charlie Flowers from Mississippi, Earl Faison from Indiana, Keith Lincoln, a lot of great young players. And the class that we were bringing in when Lance's class came in… I like to call it a class… Had John Hadl and had some great young players in addition. So we had Ernie Ladd… Ron Mix, we had Ron Mix, we had Ernie Wright. We had all the earmarks of a truly great football team. As I said, it would be a young team, we would be going to a new city with a new league, and the idea was to grow with it. Of course we had great coaches and we had me…

I had seen him [Alworth] play as a junior. I had seen him play as a sophomore. And obviously had him positioned for a wide receiver early on in his college career. He had great speed, he had great leaping ability, and while some people questioned

his hands, they became great as well. But also I think one thing that he had was tremendous confidence. A very interesting story that might interest you. I think it was in 1962; Lance had just come in from the all-star game. We were going to play a pre-season game at night. I think it was a Saturday night and they played the all-star game on Friday night. Sid said we were going to start Alworth. I said that we would just give him some basic stuff, but I really didn't want to do it because the guy that had been playing the position had really worked hard the whole training camp. But Sid started him anyhow because we wanted to attract attendance. And the guy that had worked real hard the whole training camp was a guy named Jerry Richardson. He owns the Carolina Panthers…

But I have so many great memories with those players and all, and from time to time I have responded to them when they have needed things. The door was always open because that's how we built the league. The Chargers were the flagship of the American Football League.

SAM DeLUCA, GUARD
College: South Carolina
Years with the Chargers: 1960-1961, 1963

Sam DeLuca spent time as a durable offensive lineman with the Chargers and New York Jets after playing several years in the Canadian Football League. After his playing career ended, DeLuca was a radio announcer for the New York Jets, wrote books about football and became a successful businessman with McDonalds franchises and in self-storage.

Well, Al Davis, I guess was at the Citadel when… He was coaching at the Citadel when I was a player at the University of South Carolina. I was a second round pick of the Giants way back in 1957. That's when there were 12 teams. I played in the college all-star game. Anyway, I went with the Giants. I didn't make it. I wound up in Canada for a couple of years and Al had contacted me. We had a conversation, I can't remember if it was the old Sheraton or one of those old New York hotels, and I signed with them…

I'll tell you what things were like at that time. I was the second choice of the Giants in '57, which meant I was the 22nd or 23rd player chosen in the draft. Twelve teams. I got a $7,000 salary and a $500 bonus. I played in the college all-star game, joined the Giants late. The guy I was supposed to replace, Bill Austin, had returned. The year before, the Giants had gone and won the championship. So they decided to stay with a pat hand and I got there late because we played against the Giants. So I never got a chance to show what I could do during the preseason.

They sent me up to Canada. I go back the second year, and when I leave I asked Wellington Mara to pay my expenses. I was already married and was all set up in New York. I had an apartment. I said, "You want me to go up to Canada, I'm presuming you're going to pay my expenses. I have an apartment

here, I'm going to need an apartment there." He reluctantly gave me $1,000. So I made $8,000 with a $500 bonus. I came back and worked out with the Giants for six weeks after the season ended. Because the season ends early up in Canada and they didn't get into the playoffs, at least Toronto didn't that year. I go in to talk salary with Mara, because I understood that I would come back the next year and get a good shot. And he writes down on a little piece of paper, "This is what I am prepared to pay you." And on it was $6,500. I said, "You gave me $7,000 last year. Why $6,500?" He said, "Because I though by asking me for the $1,000 to go up to Canada, that you were acting immorally." That's what dollars were at that point.

So I told him that I could get $9,500 up in Canada. Since I was drafted by Toronto, and a lot of guys would go up to Canada, and that's what the original offer was. When I went back up to Toronto I got $8,500. When I signed with the Chargers, my first salary was $9,700 a year, and I think Sid gave me $10,000 or $10,500 the second year. So we're not talking about big dollars. And that was the reason that I didn't go back in '62. It was strictly a matter of money. I had a couple of kids, so taking them out there and again having the apartment in New York and the apartment out there and transportation expenses and everything else, there wasn't a helluva lot of money. You had to love it. And I did love it, but not that much. It wasn't financially that rewarding and it didn't seem to make a heck of a lot of sense. And then I guess I realized I loved it more than I thought, so I went back in '63...

The Chargers were more run-oriented. His running game was predicated on outside stuff. And again I am relating this to myself. There was a lot of pulling. The guards would pull a great deal and have to get out in front of the running backs. And I wasn't fast, so I had difficulty in doing that. And the handwriting was again on the wall. Walt Sweeney was the first pick that year, in '63. He was a tight end at Syracuse, and they moved him to guard and it was just a matter of time before he was going to be playing. So that's one of the reasons I wanted to get back to New York. I wanted to get away from Sweeney and the competition out there.

Sid's passing game was maybe a little more wide open than Weeb's. But Weeb (Ewbank) adjusted that and adapted when he got Namath. He threw long as much as anyone. Of course he had Don Maynard, so that was a natural. The object is to utilize whatever talent you have, so if it behooves you to throw long, you're gonna throw long if you have the players who can do it. I had to pull out a lot less. In other words, there was a lot less trapping and a lot less sweeping, where I would have to get out in front of the running backs. Because that was not a great strength of mine I'd get out and we'd throw the body around. But I remember Paul Lowe constantly having one hand on my shoulder saying, "Come on, come on, come on, Sam. Run!" I was running, but just not fast enough for him...

I don't know if it's a favorite memory, but we used to make a trip. When the Chargers went east, they played the Jets, the Patriots and the Bills on successive weekends. Not necessarily, obviously, in that order. In order to save transportation costs. So you'd go in on a Friday or a Saturday, whenever you were going to play that first game, and then we would spend the next week, either at Bear Mountain or at Niagara Falls. So one year at Niagara Falls, Sid didn't have a mandatory dinner. It was voluntary. If you wanted to come to dinner the night after the game... You didn't have to come to dinner, you had the day off. He gave us the day after the game off. So probably only four or five of us showed up at dinner, and the rest didn't show up. And they had lobster. I must have eaten 10 lobsters. I had a big appetite. I think it was the only time in my life, I have never had upset stomachs or had a problem with anything. And all of a sudden I'm sick. And I realized that it wasn't the lobster, or the volume of food, it was the butter that I was putting on. And it stuck in my mind because of how silly it was. I think Don Rogers was with me. He and I. We just ate everything in sight...

I guess the uncertainty, probably, to be honest with you. What I disliked was not having a helluva lot of ability, and it became a struggle. With each passing year, the lack of ability became more and more of an issue. In other words, I was able to compensate because of wisdom, experience. I was sound fundamentally, but I was somewhat undersized to begin with

and slow as I already indicated. As years passed, it became even worse. I may have lost a little bit of speed, but the difference in size became more obvious. In other words, players were getting bigger. When I started in 1957, I was a good-sized offensive guard. In fact, in 1960 or '61, they moved me from tackle. I was originally a tackle. I was 6'2", 245, and I was playing offensive tackle...

Anyway, I moved into guard and on the first play [Jack Kemp] leaned over and hit me on the rump and he said, "Nice to have you so close, big guy." Because I was a big offensive guard. The other guards were 230. Orlando Ferrante, I think was 230. The other guy, named Freddie Cole, in '60, he was 225. So I was 245 and I was a little bit taller. They were 6'0", 6'1". So I was a big guard. I've told that story a thousand times. As years went on, by the end, they had Budde and Tyrer in Kansas City, who were 6'5", 6'6" and 270-290 pounds. The whole thing had changed during that 10-year period. It was 11 years from the time I got out of college in '57 and my last year was '67. And during that time, guys just exploded.

I read an article in *Time Magazine* maybe six or seven years ago. It was tracing the size of NFL linemen going back to the '20s. There was a guy named Hunk Anderson who went to Notre Dame and was the all-decade lineman in the 1920s. And I knew the guy. He used to come down to South Carolina and help coach during the spring training. And he was all of 5'8" or 5'9" and 180 pounds. And then the following decade they'd put on 10 or 15 pounds and an inch or two. Up until today's players who are tremendous. Again this was six years ago, so it was in the '90s. But they said if that kind of growth continued, by mid century, the average NFL player would be 6'9" and 430 pounds. As silly as it sounded six years ago, and it still sounds beyond comprehension. I don't think people will grow that tall, at least not an average player. But if you had told people back in the '20s when the average height was 5'8" or 5'9", and I guess football players were maybe close to six feet, that that would happen, that you would have players that were 6'6" and 300 pounds, and that would be a common occurrence, they wouldn't have believed it either...

It was just a struggle. I had to develop a lot of techniques in order to survive. In other words, I couldn't stand up and go head to head with a guy like Ernie Ladd or Buck Buchanan. That's where I played, the left guard. So I would have to face a guy like that each week. Tom Sestak from Buffalo, a guy named Houston Antwine. And I was giving away at least 40 pounds and several inches in most instances. So it became more and more difficult. I guess that was probably the toughest part of it. I was good size in college and by the end I was not a watch charm guard, but a little guy compared to everyone else. I guess that was probably the worst part of it. And yet I take pride in that. I take pride in being able to survive based on thinking a little bit and having sound fundamentals and good technique and being able to keep a guy off-balance. So it was a struggle and yet looking back, I take pride in that I was able to survive.

BEN DONNELL, DEFENSIVE END

College: Vanderbilt
Years with the Chargers: 1960

Ben Donnell was a collegiate center and linebacker at Vanderbilt, but was switched to end when he came into the Chargers' camp in 1960. Donnell's career with the Chargers lasted for three regular season games. Although it was a short period in his life, professional football was a memorable experience for Ben Donnell. Ben suffered a stroke a number of years ago, which affected his speech, but he was still very willing to reminisce about his days in the American Football League.

Q: *Tell me about how you first came to the Chargers.*

Donnell: I was the draft choice of the Detroit Lions. Al Davis.

Q: *When you were making your decision between the Lions and Chargers, were you concerned that the American Football League might not succeed?*

Donnell: Lions '59, Chargers '60. Got homesick for the Lions and I came home.

Q: *Did you worry at all in 1960 about the Chargers not succeeding?*

Donnell: The Chargers signed me for $11,000. I didn't know whether they would make it or not.

Q: *In 1960 the Chargers had three future Hall of Famers on their coaching staff. Did the staff seem overly impressive at the time?*

Donnell: Any other coaching staff. Chuck Noll, defensive end coach, I liked him.

Q: *What was Sid Gillman like?*

Donnell: Sid Gillman, offensive-minded guy. He was head coach. I followed him the rest of the time. Sid Gillman was an OK guy.

Q: *You played only three games in 1960. Were you with the team the whole time, or did you leave early?*

Donnell: I had a heat stroke. Houston. And got cut in Buffalo.

Q: *Was there anything that you did not like about being a pro football player?*

Donnell: Away from my family. We got to Dallas Texans, Houston Oilers and Buffalo in one trip. I got a baby seven weeks old.

Q: *Was your time with the team limited to just that Eastern trip?*

Donnell: No. We played four exhibition games. The baby was born July 5th and I reported to them July 6th.

Q: *Was that training camp in 1960 pretty tough. There must have been a ton of guys out there.*

Donnell: Yeah. I was late. The baby was born. I was a linebacker. We had 17 or 18 linebackers. Sid Gillman got me to play defensive end. Defensive end suited me better.

Q: *Are there any other comments you would like to make?*

Donnell: I wouldn't take anything for it, for the experience.

CHARLIE FLOWERS, RUNNING BACK

College: Mississippi
Years with the Chargers: 1960, 1961

Charlie Flowers was an All-American running back at Mississippi, and was drafted by the Chargers in the AFL and the New York Giants of the NFL. The Chargers eventually won the rights to Flowers in a court battle with the Giants. The 6'2", 220-Flowers played for the Chargers in 1960 and 1961 before he was traded to the New York Titans in 1962. A dislocated ankle and the fact that the Titans' owner, Harry Wismer, consistently bounced the players' paychecks aided in Flowers' decision to retire in 1962.

They (the Chargers) hadn't played a game when I got there. So I don't know that we had what you would call scouts. I don't know how they drafted. But they had some people who worked for the Chargers, a man named Tom Eddy and the old coach from Notre Dame, Frank Leahy. I really don't know the process by which they drafted, because they didn't even have coaches yet. It was before Sid Gillman signed on. So I assume that they just drafted off the NFL or I'm not really sure. I don't know how. But I am positive that they didn't scout football games, because I don't think they had a staff yet…

I couldn't get used to the fact that it was 100% business. I had come from Ole' Miss and we played for the national championship every year and we felt like we represented the state, or at least half of it. We felt like if we lost, then the state would go into mourning. And we felt like we represented something, people. Whereas when I got into the pros, it was strictly business. The football was the same, but the feeling of it was not. It is hard to describe, but it was like going from Ole' Miss to all of a sudden joining General Motors. You were playing football for General Motors. And I couldn't get used to that because we always played for something and somebody. Well, you know the difference between college and pros. It's more meaningful, I think. At least to me it was…

He (Sid Gillman) was tough. He was brilliant, and very, very dedicated and single-minded. He was obviously going to produce a winner, one way or another. He was very demanding, very tough, and very unemotional. In other words, you may think that you were something special to him and he may make you think that, and then the next day you would be gone. But he was a typical… I think most great coaches are that way. They don't get that involved. It's very practical and unemotional to them. But I have never in my life seen anyone who knew as much football as he did, and come to think of it, still haven't. He was just an absolute genius, especially on our side of the ball. Believe it or not, he really coached both sides of it. You can't know that much offense and not know that much defense, because they are both the same.

Sid basically coached my group. We had come from college where we played both ways; therefore we got coached by everybody. But in the pro's you didn't really get involved with Chuck or Al Davis or Faulkner or those guys because they had their own spear of influence, whereas Sid coached the offense and the offensive backs. So I saw more of him. So we were more friends with the other coaches because they didn't come that much in contact with us. So it wouldn't be fair to say that I recognized their genius at the time, because I didn't deal with them that much. But I did like them. They were good guys.

I guess Jack Kemp was my best friend. We were roommates. Don Norton, and Keith Lincoln was a great friend of mine. Dave Kocourek was a good guy, Bob Zeman. They were just really nice, fun guys to be around. I had never been around people not from the South before, and I don't think they'd been around Southerners before, so it was kind of interesting. They'd call the coach by his first name, and they would call their college coach by their first name, and that's something we'd never in a million years do. I couldn't get used to calling Sid, Sid. It was Coach Gillman to me. But that was just a difference in the way we were raised, I guess. But there were a lot of good guys on the team…

I'd say the low point was when Sid called me in and told me that he'd traded me to New York. That was about as low as it got. I woke up one day on the beach and went to bed that night in the Bronx. Like I told him, why couldn't it have been Denver or some place like that. Why did it have to be New York? Oh Lord! But anyway, that let me know that it was just a business…

[It was] the difference between day and night. How about the difference between getting paid and not getting paid… I got my ankle dislocated and it was one of the highlights of my career. I didn't like New York; I didn't like being there. My wife was seven months pregnant. We weren't getting paid, guys would strike. They'd show up at practice if they wanted to. I had come from Ole' Miss and Sid Gillman. I had never seen anything like that. Right after I got hurt, the league took them over.

SID GILLMAN, HEAD COACH AND GENERAL MANAGER

College: Ohio State
Years with the Chargers: 1960-1969, 1971

When Sid Gillman became the head coach of the Los Angeles Chargers in 1960, he had already established himself as a top-flight coach. He had more than 20 years of college coaching experience as well as five years at the helm of the Los Angeles Rams. But it was during his time with the Chargers that Gillman permanently embedded his name in the annals of professional football with his countless contributions to the Chargers and to the game as a whole.

Well, of course I played as a youngster. I played in high school and was always, as far back as I can remember, oriented as far as athletics are concerned. I was very much interested in them. I played in high school and I played in college, played in professional football and it just carried on through life.

It is kind of an interesting story in that my coach, a fellow that I worked with, briefly, to start with, his name was Francis Schmidt. And he was probably one of the greatest minds of anybody that I've ever known. I was playing in the all-star game in Chicago. We don't have an all-star game anymore because insurance rates are so high that if any of those kids got killed, especially if somebody hurt his arm and he's got an insurance policy of $15 million, you couldn't afford to stay up with the insurance deal. So they cut it out. But I was playing in this all-star game when my coach wired me and wanted me to come back and help out in spring football practice, which I did do, although I was destined for law school. I thought that maybe I might become a lawyer. But I thought, "Well, we'll give football a try." And I went back. This was at Ohio State. I went back and I haven't seen a law school yet. Because I was taken back by football and teaching football and coaching football, I wasn't interested in anything else after that experience...

Well, the main thing in pro ball was throwing the ball and scoring quick. This was the idea. Against college football it was more run-oriented. People didn't think too much about throwing the ball in the old days when I was breaking in. They were thinking about running the football until some of us got to thinking that it was kind of a waste of time. We began to throw it. Instead of running the ball, we knew we could start the cash register going a helluva lot faster when we're throwing than when we're running. So we just decided that we're going to throw the ball and not run much.

Well, what we did was widen our outside ends. So often you see these outside ends, wide receivers are awful tight. Now that confines the area behind them. What we did is move them out. That gave us a lot of passing room, a lot of receiving room in there. That gave us the width of the field and we threw long because we had Lance Alworth and stretched the field straight away. So we just stretched the field horizontally and vertically. There are some clubs that do that now. No major deal there.

As a matter of fact I was freelancing about the time I met Barron (Hilton). I just happened to decide that instead of selling stocks and bonds, I'd prefer to stay with football. I knew that Barron was getting into another league, so he contacted me and by mutual consent we got together. Frank Leahy got sick and the general manager's job was available. I felt as though I should have it because I felt that there was a strong possibility that I would want to coach and be general manager and run the show at the same time. It worked out very well. It was much easier than any other way, because I could make all the decisions. That's exactly what I did. I just ran the whole office.

Watching film dates back to my cradle. It was college as a matter of fact; we filmed our practice sessions and carried it over into pros. When I went with the Rams we began to take film of our practices. So it dates way back, almost to day one. Of course it was very simple for me, because my parents were in the movie business. And in those days they used to have Fox Movie Tone News and Paramount and they all had newsreels and I used to clip the football out of those reels. It was against the law, but I did it anyhow. So that's what started me out. People now get television, but years ago you had the Movie Tone. Fox, Paramount, they all had shots of major games and I used to cut those major games out and study them. So that's what started me out in the movies. And then the fact that I just took the movie camera out on the practice field.

Gee, I'll never forget. I was coaching in college at the time and we were in a training camp and I had a cameraman work with us. He was shooting one day and we noticed that there was going to be a storm. The clouds were so goddamn black, you could hardly see. The guy reminded me of Gene Leff, same mode. I said, "Jimmy, come on down. It looks like were going to have a storm." Well, before he was able to get down, that storm came up and it was about a 25-foot scaffold and the son of a bitch just flopped on over and the camera and everything just smashed to smithereens. It was just a helluva thing. Nothing happened to him, thank goodness. He survived, but all our film equipment broke up. I see that in my mind every once in a while. He had just enough room to move in a direction. He was like a rat trying to find the hole and he couldn't find the hole and he decided to ride down with it. He rode down with the storm. Oh jeez, I'll never forget that...

The big change in today's game is size. Football players, unless they weigh 350, 375, they just can't play. They're big, strong, can run. That's one change. Money-wise, they're making millions of dollars, not a few bucks. But they're making millions of dollars. Free agency is what's killing it. You sign some guy up because he doesn't belong to anybody. It's terrible. Of course, that's the way it is in baseball, that's the way it is in basketball. I hate it. You get up in the morning and you don't know who in the Hell is going to play for you. It poses a major deal for a coach because you can't sustain a squad. It moves around too much. You get up in the morning and you don't know who's on your football team. It's terrible.

DICK HARRIS, CORNERBACK
College: McNeese State
Years with the Chargers: 1960-1965

Dick Harris was an undrafted cornerback that came to the Chargers' original tryouts in 1960. He quickly became a starter and led the team in interceptions in 1960 and 1963. He retired from the football in 1965, with 29 career interceptions, which still ranks second all-time for the Chargers. Harris coached high school football for many years after his professional career ended.

What happened was that I sort of jumped around a lot from college to college. I was actually supposed to go to SC and play tailback in the single wing after Jon Arnett. I screwed around and ended up going to a bunch of different places. When they formed the league, coach Phil Cantwell, who was at the time when I was growing up, had watched me play in high school. He remembers me playing against the pros when I was in high school in a touch league. I believe I made most valuable at the time. But then I went on and screwed around and wasn't very successful in college. He just recommended me and that's how it got started. The three teams that contacted me were Green Bay, Baltimore Colts and the L.A. Chargers at the time.

Well, I'm from the area. So that was the reason [I signed with the Chargers]. Just to be close to home. I'm a San Pedro kid and it was just the thing to do. I was just excited as Hell. That was a dream come true, just to get a chance to try out…

The training camp in 1960 was just brutal because they brought us in in flights. Of course, being a free agent, I came in with the first group. I think we came in around late June. We went two-a-days for a couple of weeks and out of maybe 60 guys they kept maybe five or six. The next group came in and they were the guys that were probably going to make it. In other words, that first group was just sort of a dream camp, a wish camp. And then they brought that group in and they weeded out. They kept probably two of us after that, from that first group. Then they brought in all the guys that had previous pro experience or were college All-Americans and all that. From there I was very fortunate that I hung in there and ended up starting at corner for the Chargers. Corners were hard to find then so it worked out pretty well for me.

I always respected Coach Gillman because I remember when Rich Roberts was the sports editor of the San Pedro newspaper and he took us to a Rams game. I rode down with him when I was just out of high school, maybe playing for Harbor Junior College. We went down there and watched the Rams practice at Redlands. As a kid growing up you know who Sid Gillman is and you know Ollie Matson was in that camp and all those guys. You are really impressed as a kid. I had a million idols in those days. It is a little harder to have them now because there is too much money. It is show business. When I was playing I knew all the guys had jobs in the off-season, except maybe a very few who made enough money to make it through the off-season. There wasn't the camps like they have now. You just had another job and when you reported to camp, you reported to camp. It was a different era. Everybody just loved the game. I think now the money is so big that you would probably get a lot of people that really don't love the game, but they are there

because the money is so unbelievable that they'll play anyway. Even though I don't think they love it.

Sid was a good guy. He was really a nice man. He had a wonderful family, Esther and his children. They were always very pleasant to be around. Sid and I, we all had out battles. I remember I made all pro and I came in and he offered me a $200 raise. That's how it was in those days. If you were a free agent and you were lucky enough to make it, you weren't going to make any money. So that's it. That was just the way it was in those days. You're not going to get a lot of money. There wasn't the opportunities that there are now that if you make it you get a big raise.

[Our defensive line] was the original "Fearsome Foursome." *Sports Illustrated* came down to do a story on that team because we were undefeated and we got beat, so they decided not to do the story and all of a sudden the Ram line got tagged with the fearsome foursome. But we still hold the record even though we didn't play as many games as they do now. We still hold the NFL record for interceptions in a season. Those guys… It is really great when you have a pass rush. Believe me. Even if they don't sack the quarterback, if they get near him, you can play a little more aggressively. You can take more chances, you can go for the interceptions a lot more because that guy is not going to get the ball right where he wants it. It makes it a helluva lot better. I'll tell you what. You take an average cornerback with a great defensive line and you have got a really good cornerback.

And as far as the coaches, Chuck Noll, Davis and Gillman, they were all really good coaches. Chuck didn't communicate much as the others. He was more quiet and didn't say much. But there was also Jack Faulkner who lives in this area now that was also with the Rams and the head coach with Denver. He was my first defensive backfield coach. Then he left and went to Denver and then Chuck took over as the defensive backfield coach. Jack was sort of like my… He was really a good guy. He sort of made it easier for me to play because I sort of had that devil-may-care attitude. In those days a lot of coaches didn't like that kind of attitude. It was a lot stricter then about how you behaved and everything. They didn't put up with too much.

Charlie McNeil, who played at Centennial High School, was my buddy and partner. He was a free safety and I was the corner. We worked pretty well together. He always impressed me as being… Well, he was one of my really good friends. We had Paul Maguire, who was our outside linebacker, who now is trying to make it as a broadcaster. I don't know if he is going to make it or not. Bob Zeman, he was a strong safety. Then of course we had Ernie Ladd and Earl Faison. Those were the two guys that were really the pass rushers. We had Chuck Allen at middle linebacker, who when Noll went to Pittsburgh, he took Chuck with him and put in the defensive system that he developed with the Chargers. We had Kemp. Jack, he was the quarterback for us. Sid gave him up because he injured his finger. You could only put a player in those days on waivers once. You put him on the second time and you couldn't pull him off. So Buffalo claimed him for $100. Then Tobin Rote came in. He was the old pro. Of course Lance Alworth. Paul Lowe, Keith Lincoln. We had some really good players, Don Norton, an All-American from Iowa. That was a great group of guys. Charlie Flowers. I guess he and Billy Cannon battled it out that one year for the Heisman Trophy. Flowers came here and Billy Cannon went to Houston. It was good times then, fun…

We stayed in some weird places. We stayed at Bear Mountain and we stayed at West Point. In those days when we went back East, we went back for three games in a row. We played Boston, we played Buffalo and we played the Jets. So we just stayed there. Obviously when you're there that long, the road trips can be very interesting. I know why people go to Niagara Falls for their honeymoon, too. Because there is nothing to do there, believe me. You talk about boring, God. There wasn't much to tell you about Niagara Falls, I can tell you that right now. But we had fun on a lot of the trips. We went down to Greenwich Village in New York and we went to different places and had fun.

[The Rough Acres Ranch] was unreal. They took us up there and some doctor bought this property. He had some little tiny cabins on it, if you want to call them cabins. I guess he was going to make it into a dude ranch or something. It was about 4-or 5,000 feet high and the average temperature during that time was at least 100 degrees. They watered the ground so we would get something like grass on the field. It was nowhere. They had a gas station that was also considered the post office. They sold beer there, too. I remember that. We'd sneak down and drink beer at the gas station after the second practice. That's all I remember about it. But that was the time that we really came together as a team. We were there for about six weeks. There was nothing to do. I remember they got a bus and took us down to El Centro to watch the Floyd Patterson-Sonny Liston fight. That was a great ride. We got in the bus, got out of the bus, got back in the bus. I think we were in that place to watch the fight for about 30 seconds and then back home. I'll tell you what, that definitely was a place… I don't know if guys nowadays would put up with it. They'd probably sue the team for something, but it brought us together and that's the year we won everything…

I loved playing. I always go back and say if I could have it before the injuries started piling up, it was the greatest feeling. There was nothing better. It was a game with a bunch of guys that you liked. I can't think of anything better. Really. I have no complaints. I have a complaint that they didn't pay as much, but as far as something in my life, it was probably the biggest thing that ever happened other than of course marriage and children. I think most of the guys would agree that they really had a good time.

BILL KIMBER, END
College: Florida State
Years with the Chargers: 1960 Training Camp

The New York Giants drafted Bill Kimber in 1959, but Kimber played in only one game that season. He came to the Chargers' tryout at Chapman College in 1960, but did not make the final squad. Though he was cut by the Chargers late in training camp, Kimber was able to catch on again with the Giants and later the expansion Vikings of the NFL.

Right: *Bill Kimber was another of the players featured on a bubble gum card, that did not make the team.*

BILL KIMBER
OFFENSIVE END

LOS ANGELES CHARGERS

In 1959, after I graduated in January of '59, I had to go into the service because I was in the ROTC program. So I joined the Giants back in October, was activated that year, and didn't play, but was activated. Then in 1960, somehow the word got out that I was available, as far as the New York Giants were concerned, so Al Davis called me up, had me fly to Atlanta, where he met me at a hotel there. He went through his sales pitch and the deciding factor was that instead of being paid $7,000 for the 1960 season by the New York Giants, I would be receiving $10,000 from the Los Angeles Chargers. So with the enticement of the extra money, I said, "What the heck." So that's how I ended up out at Los Angeles in the 1960 season…

At the time I was playing with the Giants, I was playing behind Kyle Rote, so I didn't see that much action. I always felt that if I had gone over to the Los Angeles Chargers I would be able to start and play football, which was my utmost desire. The money was really the big factor, but more in lines of the idea that I would be able to play full time and make my own statement. And that's, I think, the overriding factor of why I left the Giants and went out to Los Angeles.

Well, the Charger camp, when I got out there, I thought I was in good shape for the 1960 season. I had practiced in New Orleans, over there in the humidity, and had worked out with Tommy Mason, who was going to the Minnesota Vikings that year. So I thought I was in tuned to really step in to the role of being in shape and ready to compete for the position I was there for. And when I got out there to Los Angeles where we practiced, I guess there were like 18 or 19 ends, and I was taken back by that. But what was more important though, was that when I was working out, I was losing 10 pounds a session.

In the morning and the afternoon, we were in shirts then, but we went into pads later. But I was losing so much weight, and I wasn't replacing it with anything, that I started getting symptoms of rigor mortis, to sort of exaggerate the point. But I could not move or really give it my best, so I guess after about two weeks the handwriting was on the wall that I was not in the shape I thought I was. Therefore I had lost a lot of ground as far as being competitive, as far as the rest of the group. But they called me in and said, "Well, Bill, we're going to let you go." The Turk came visiting and said, "Bring your book." And that was the end of the experience that I had out there in Los Angeles.

When I came back, I immediately got on the phone and called Wellington Mara of the New York Giants, the owner at that time, still is. And I told Wellington that I'd made a mistake. Could I come over and join the Giants in Fairfield, Connecticut, at that time. And he said, "Bill, we can't promise you anything. We can't guarantee you anything, but you're welcome to come on out and give it a try." I said, "That's good enough for me." So I reported to Fairfield and needless to say, I made the active squad when the season began and spent the 1960 season with them. And then in 1961, because of the Minnesota Vikings coming into their beginning, I was one of the three that the Minnesota Vikings chose as far as the nucleus of 36 veterans that they could draw upon, as well as the draft and anyone else they could bring in there. And that's how I ended up going from New York to Minnesota for the third season. And then I got injured, pulled a hamstring, and couldn't really function as

far the function to keep my job. I was running first string when I got hurt, but Van Brocklin, I will always remember, came up to me. He was the coach at that time. He said, "Bill, we're going to shoot that leg so you can get out there and practice." I said, "Coach, I can't do that. There's too much of a possibility of a sustained injury that would probably end my career. It's not worth it to me."

So after I got rehabilitated, where I could play, I went out and had a hell of a ball game in the last exhibition game. I had a good outing, and was cut the following day. It meant that they had to see that I was back in shape to play, but I was cut before I even got out there, in their mind. So I came back, stayed for about two or three weeks, and then the Boston Patriots called me up. That's where I finished out the season. At that time, when I went to the Boston Patriots, I guess I was so out of shape that I don't think I really capitalized on the opportunity that I had. But as I was gradually getting back into shape, to play, in the style that I was accustomed to, Lou Saban was fired. But not before he released me on Thursday. He was fired on Friday and Mike Holovak, the coach that came in as head coach then, tried to reinstate me, but I had already been deactivated on Monday or Tuesday of that week, even though I was told later. So it meant sitting out for a period of time and the season was virtually over. I said, "Gentlemen, that's it. I'm taking off, and I'll see you later." So that was my third year and also my sudden burst of realization that it was time to get serious and go get a job and raise a family like I had, and chalk it up and be thankful that I had the experience and go on about life.

DAVE KOCOUREK, END

College: Wisconsin
Years with the Chargers: 1960-1965

Dave Kocourek came to the Chargers from the Canadian League in 1960, and became a perennial all-star. He was a large target for quarterbacks Jack Kemp, Tobin Rote and John Hadl. His top season was 1961 when he caught 55 passes for 1,055 yards and four touchdowns, and helped lead the Chargers to their second consecutive AFL Championship Game.

I played football in Winnipeg in 1959 and they have an import rule. So many Americans allowed maximum, and I kind of got caught in the shuffle. I was out of football for a brief time there after the '59 season in Winnipeg. I had to go back to school, the University of Wisconsin, for nine hours to get my degree, and that was very important to me. So I got back to Wisconsin and… Or I was going to go back. I registered and everything and I was in the Chicago suburbs, figuring that my football career was over. A friend of mine, Bob Zeman, who had played with Wisconsin and played in the Rose Bowl that year, they got beat by Washington by a big score. But anyway, he said he had signed with the Los Angeles Chargers and thought it was going to be a fun league.

So I wrote a bunch of letters. I wrote to the Chargers, and I pretty much wrote to what I thought were the good-weather

areas and places I'd want to be, Houston and Dallas and Denver and Los Angeles. I wrote to an old coach that had coached me at Wisconsin, Perry Moss. He was coaching in Canada. And I didn't hear from anybody for about a month. All of a sudden I got a call from Sid Gillman and he said, "Dave, this is Sid Gillman. I don't know if you remember me, but I got your letter and I'm the new head coach-general manager of the Chargers and we'd like very much to sign you to a contract."

They offered me $10,000 and a $1,000 bonus, if I made the team. That was more money than my father was making at that time and I thought it was a pretty good deal. So I signed the contract, not knowing what was going to happen or anything about the AFL. I started to learn about it. I got my schedule as far as training camp goes, and they were bringing them in. We were at Chapman College in Orange. That's where the first training camp was. They were bringing them in in boat-loads. Sid had camps all over the Los Angeles area looking for athletes and former athletes. There were truck drivers and other guys that might have played high school football and thought they could play. There were very few guys that ever made it out of those original camps, but I got fairly early into Chapman College.

I was a back-up tight end and also I started playing a little bit of wide receiver. I think that kind of helped my pass-catching skills and maneuverability skills. I started the year behind a guy named Royce Womble as wide receiver on the right, and Howard Clark was the tight end at the time. Somehow or other I worked into the starting lineup. I think my first entrance was as a wide receiver. I think it was Buffalo in Buffalo, and I had a pretty good game. I was wide receiver and Howard was the tight end. I don't know if he got hurt, I guess he got hurt in the second year and then I became the tight end and pretty much gave up the wide receiver stuff. But it was kind of fun, and I think being a wide receiver kind of helped my maneuverability and things like that. I went on from there and had some fun years, winning football teams. Al Davis was our original end coach and I learned an awful lot from Al. He was very diligent about the way the feet would go and you making an in-move or an out-move or whatever. I was just trying to soak up as much of that stuff as I could. He had coached at Baltimore a little bit and helped Raymond Berry and some other people. So I felt very comfort-able and went on to play a total of 10 years and I had a lot of fond memories.

Well, Sid was just a great, great offensive mind. He was a good coordinator of what was going on. He'd had experience and we had some real horses. You know, you look at the lineup and who we had in the early years, and Jack Kemp. I was one of Jack's favorite receivers because I was a pretty big target. But we had some wonderful skill people and a lot of camarade-rie. We had some great speed, which was important. We had some tremendous size. You know the Ernie Ladd's and some of those kinds of people. Earl Faison and the defensive line, Paul Lowe in the backfield.

I remember Paul Lowe as a 175-pound running back out of Oregon State. Opening kickoff, opening game in the Los Angeles Coliseum, he went 105 yards against the New York Titans. He could really fly. Boy, it was a real pleasure watching Paul run. We also had Bo Roberson on our team, who was an Olympic sprinter and broad jumper. They one time had a little race, which I don't think the coaches should have allowed be-cause somebody could have pulled a muscle or something. But Paul had him for most of the start and Bo kind of dropped it low, low and showed the pure sprinter's speed.

But we had some skill players and we had a lot of defense, which was wonderful. They set the all-time, and I don't think it is ever going to be broken, record, as far as intercepted passes goes. Charlie McNeil and some of those guys, Zeman and Dick Harris. We had a nice mix of people.

Paul Lowe used to call me "Iron." I said, "What do you call me 'Iron' all the time for?" He said, "You're an iron man. When-ever you're hurt, you're playing. You're always there." And prob-ably more than anything else, those words meant more to me than anything else, or any praise. I had some good years. I had some all-league years. I'm proud of the accomplishments on the field, but the fact that I was always around and always avail-able, and acknowledged that I was around. I feel very comfort-able with that. I'm very proud of that.

PAUL LOWE, RUNNING BACK
College: Oregon State
Years with the Chargers: 1960-1968

Paul Lowe came to the American Football League as a discard of the San Francisco 49ers. But when given the opportunity by the Chargers, Lowe became one of the AFL's most prolific running backs. When he retired from pro football in 1969, Paul Lowe was the League's second all-time leading rusher with 4,995 yards. He was the AFL Player of the Year in 1965 and was chosen as a member of the AFL's All-Time Team.

Well, I'll tell you how I got to the Chargers and into profes-sional football. I was with Oregon State and every year we played Cal (University of California). I would have a good season, a good year. I would make some long runs against Pappy Waldorf. He was the coach at Cal. But he was a scout for the 49ers also. He liked the way I played and he approached me and said, "What are you going to do after you finish your col-lege?" Well, I didn't get to finish college. So he said, "When you do, you get in touch with me. I'd like to see you play for the 49ers."

So I gave him a call after I left school and he gave me a contract with the 49ers. That was in 1959. I was real happy about it. So I had a successful preseason with the 49ers, very successful. For some reason I got hurt when we went to Utah to play the Giants. We had a preseason game there, and I got injured and I got released. Then I went home. My home was in L.A. So I went back home and I needed a job because I had a family at the time. I had four kids. So I went and got a job. The job so happened to be at the Carte Blanche Credit Card Cor-poration, and that was owned by the Hiltons.

Frank Leahy was the general manager. Mr. Frank Leahy was the general manager at that time and they were forming a football league. So they found out that I was in the mailroom at the time. That is where my job was. And they got in touch with me and asked me if I wanted to play professional football. They were starting a team in L.A. I told them, "Sure." So that's how I really got started with the L.A. Chargers. And then shortly after that Frank Leahy resigned, and then Sid took over the organization. Sid remembered me from when I played for the 49ers because I made a couple kick off returns and punt returns against the Rams, which had impressed him. So they asked if I wanted to play and I said, "Yeah." I was invited to camp and all that, and that's how I got started with the Chargers.

We were down in Texas (in 1960), playing the Dallas Texans at that time. Ron Waller, he had played for Sid when Sid was coaching for the Rams. Sid brought him over. I called home and talked with my wife and she said, "It's in the newspaper that they have got to make a cut and most likely it's going to be you." And I said, "What!" It was on my mind and all of that. So we were playing Dallas. Ron was on the kick off return and I was on the kick off return. Ron came up to me and he said, "Hey, you get the ball wherever the ball goes." I said, "If I'm out here I'll get it, but you get it in your area." He said, "No, you get it." I said, "OK, I'll get it." So the ball came to Ron, so I went over in his area and I got the ball and returned it. Made a pretty good return out of it. We lost to Dallas, so I guess that just made Sid pissed at anybody and everybody. So I called home again and my wife said, "Yeah, they say you're going to be released. You're going to get cut." So Sid came to my room and asked me how come I went out of my zone to receive the kick off. I said, "Ron, he didn't want to return the ball. He asked me wherever it goes, to get it." So he said, "Who told you that?" I said, "Ron did. He didn't want it." So he said, "You wait here and I'll come back. I'm going to go have a talk." He went and had a talk with Ron. So, I guess Ron saved my job. He convinced Sid that yeah, he did. So he cut Ron Waller and he kept me…

Lance. Lance. I've never seen a white boy run like a black man and do the things he did catching that ball. Lance Alworth for end. Yeah, he could get it. Lance and I, we would run after most every practice. People used to stay out after practice to see us run wind sprints. We'd run at least 5-10 before we'd go in. I was pretty fast, but Lance beat me one day by a step or something like that. I would always beat him when we ran races because I was the fastest, but he had speed. He had everything that an athlete could have. Many of the other guys look at Lance today, you can find guys bigger and all of that, but there's no one as smooth and just everything. Lance was the best. Lance Alworth as an end, was the best. He's my man.

…That's where I would send my worst enemy, would be Rough Acres, to go through what we went through. It was bad and then again it wasn't bad because after we came back from Rough Acres we succeeded in doing what we went up there for. We didn't have any nightlife, like here in the city. You couldn't see the kids or the wives or the girlfriends or whoever. Our objective was to go up there and practice and get in shape. That's what Sid got us to do. That's what great coaches do. No distractions, nothing. We went up there and we trained hard.

We lifted and we did everything we were supposed to do and we succeeded. But then again, the place was like… I just can't explain. You were eating dirt. Sometimes you ate dirt. There was dirt on your plate. There were flies you had to slap off when you eat. You would go in there and sometimes the cook didn't have the food ready. You had to sit and wait for it to finish cooking. The flies were eating you up and you would go in the big room and pretty soon there was a snake over in the corner. The guys would be over there killing a snake or killing a tarantula. All that happened. You'd go back to your room and there's a big 'ol bat hanging up in the ceiling, or a tarantula. Plenty of snakes.

We had a scrimmage one Saturday and Sid opened up the camp for the people of San Diego to come up and watch. So we had to be back in camp the next day; he only gave us one day off. We went back up there and went to warm up. I took my helmet and laid it over here. Signing autographs and all of that, I thought some lady had maybe dropped a bracelet. So I laid my helmet down there and I decided to warm up and jog down there and jog back a couple of times. Then I would pick up this bracelet. So on my way back, I'm going over to pick up my helmet and some guys are over there stomping and kicking. I said, "Goddamn. Where's that bracelet that was around here?" It was a baby diamondback rattlesnake. I would have gotten bitten because I had thought about picking it up and putting it in my helmet so I could take it home to my wife. I'll never forget. I was just lucky. I've been lucky quite a bit, I guess.

I disliked that it just didn't last long enough, the season. I liked to play everyday, it didn't matter. I was one of those guys that just wanted to play. I liked the limelight of it. I liked the enjoyment, the people, the crowds. I liked it all. If I kept playing I would have made more money. See, things were so bad. Especially for a lot of us retired black guys. As soon as the season was over, we had to go run and jump in the unemployment line. We didn't get any good jobs. So as soon as the season was over, you'd go to unemployment and then come back and get ready to play some more football the next year. It was a lot different then…

Like I say, I had some wonderful teammates and we were a family. We weren't separated like you see a lot of these things happening today in sports. We socialized a lot together. That's what made us good. Paul Maguire, Zeman, Kocourek and Jack Kemp at one time. He wasn't out like us. We were rowdy. We respected him for what he was then, Jack. We knew what he was, he was a leader. Let's see, it was Zeman, Kocourek, Maguire, and one other… And Norton. We all hung together and had some good, good times.

They tried to teach me how to water-ski and I almost drowned. I wouldn't let the ropes loose and the water kept pulling me and filling up my mouth. They said, "Let it go." I finally let it go. We were out there on the beach. We used to have a lot of fun. Paul Maguire and them, they had "The Surfer," the club, on the beach out there. We used to go out there after games and we'd be together then.

We were always together. Ernie Ladd and his wife loved to cook gumbo; they're from Louisiana. We'd go over there and play dominos and twist and eat gumbo. We were just together. We'd talk about this and that. How you're going to do this guy this week, things of that nature. We were like family. There was no color barrier or anything like that. We just had a good relationship with each and every person. My daughter used to baby-sit Jack Kemp's son so we could all go out together, out there in Point Loma.

So it was that kind of family, and that's what makes winners, too. Socialize together and be together so you can talk about this play or individual. You can talk about this or that. It just comes up. "You let this guy beat you this week. You let him do this and you're gonna be a punk." We would talk about it and express it, and you didn't want to be a punk. You wanted to be one of the best, the best that you could be. So that's what being close and having relations with your teammates [is about].

Paul Maguire, Linebacker, Punter

College: The Citadel
Years with the Chargers: 1960-1963

Prior to being known as a television commentator, Paul Maguire played for the Chargers and the Bills of the American Football League. He is one of the few players to have three AFL championship rings, from the Chargers in 1963 and the Bills in 1964 and 1965.

I played for Al Davis in college at the Citadel in 1956. I was drafted by the Chargers in the 17th round in 1959 and that's basically how I got here. Al Davis knew who I was and Jack Faulkner, who was the defensive coach, was from my hometown. So I ended up with the Chargers. I was drafted 17th by both the L.A. Chargers and the Washington Redskins. They signed me; I got an $8,000 contract with a $1,000 bonus. They were the first ones that came to me and I signed it and went to play...

I just thought that the whole AFL in those days, it was really a pleasure to play because there were only eight teams and we played each other twice and we knew everybody. So we went to a town and we'd sit down with these guys the night before, we had a few cocktails, and then there was an 11:00 curfew for everybody. But it was just the fact that all of these guys, we all knew each other. We were in a league by ourselves and it was kind of unique that the guys stayed together and it worked out very well for everybody.

I don't know if I want to be remembered as a football player. I want to be remembered as someone that contributed and not only on the field, but in the press box. It's been [more than] 41 years and I've enjoyed every moment of it. I can't ever think of anything that I would do different. The one thing I do about this game is respect the game. I respect the players and I respect what these guys are trying to do and I think it's very difficult. When people bad-mouth guys, put them down, do all these different things, and there's no reason to do that because every one of these guys are trying to win. But when I go out, I don't care. As long as I'm respected as a good person, the rest of it takes care of itself...

I love San Diego. In fact, my wife and I are trying to come back here. I just think it's a great town, the great people I've met by being here. And the friends that I've made here outside of football were more important to me than the people I've met inside of football.

Ron Mix, Tackle

College: Southern California
Years with the Chargers: 1960-1969

To this day many football experts consider Ron Mix to be the most technically perfect tackle to ever play professional football. In a career that lasted 12 years, Ron Mix was penalized for holding only twice. Mix anchored the Chargers' left tackle position through the AFL years. During the NFL's 75th Anniversary season in 1994, Ron Mix was named to the All-Decade team for the 1960s. In 1979 he followed teammate Lance Alworth when he became the second player from the American Football League to be inducted into the Pro Football Hall of Fame.

The first day of practice Sid wanted to find out how good his offensive line was, and how tough they were. So he had his assistant coaches spread out all over the field at Chapman College. That's where we trained. They were all doing individual drills with their respective players. He had the offensive linemen and the defensive linemen. He brought them up

and he ran the drill even though he wasn't the offensive line coach or the defensive line coach. He just wanted to see what he had. So he had the offensive linemen going one-on-one with the defensive linemen. Now let me tell you something about that. He would just have us line up and say, "On two." Well, any offensive lineman or defensive lineman knows that under the best of circumstances, on a one-on-one drill it is tough to block a defensive lineman. It helps in a game because you know the count and there is a little uncertainty. Is it going to be a pass? Is it going to be a run? Is it going to be a toss? So you have a little split-second advantage. When the defensive lineman knows that it is going to be a run, that is all he has to think about. All he has to do is concentrate on the body in front of him and stay low.

So we're doing the drills. Sid calls up me and [Bob] Reifsnyder. Now Bob was a very good player. He was a two-year All-American at Navy, a terrific player. And Bob weighed about 260, 270. That was my first year in pro ball and I weighed 250. I later went up to 270. So Sid says, "on two." Well, anybody that has done any athletics, amateur, recreational, knows that at some time everyone of you are going to do something as good as anybody's ever done it. Sometime everything is going to fall into place and you are going to do something. A grandmother is going to make a hole-in-one. I've read about that. This is stuff that just happens. Unfortunately for Bob Reifsnyder, everything went perfect for me. I uncurled my ankles. I unwound my back, unwound my chest, unwound my arms, my neck, all perfectly. He, on the other hand, rose up a little too high. I hit him just perfectly. The sound, I'm telling you, it was like a bomb went off. It was like an explosion. Now Bob won't like to read this, but the truth is the truth. I actually knocked Bob up into the air and back flat on his back. Up in the air and flat on his back! Sid Gillman blew the whistle and started yelling to all his assistant coaches. "Everybody come up here. Come up here. I want you to see something. Come up here. Mix just kicked the Hell out of Reifsnyder. He knocked Reifsnyder on his back and Reifsnyder was lying there like a big, fat frog. Come up here everybody. I want you to watch Mix do it again." "What?! Do it again?!" I'm thinking, "It was a fluke. Do it again?" Well, Sid is saying all this stuff and I glance over at Bob. He looked like the cartoon Yosemite Sam. His face was red. It looked like steam was coming out of his ears. He was digging some holes into the grass with both feet. He got down so low that his chin was about three inches off the ground. There was no way I was going to dig him out. There was no way he would let anybody… Three guys couldn't have beaten Bob, he was so mad. But now everybody's there. This is the first day. Sid has about 100 guys there. Sid says, "on two." So again, I don't get any benefit. He says, "on two." Well, on two we both smash into each other and not much happens. Then Sid is mad at me. Now I have embarrassed him. Now he says, "Goddammit Mix. If you're going to be a professional, you've got to be consistent." Then he says to the whole team, "you guys should have seen it the first time…"

All I wanted to do was play two years of professional football, make enough money to buy a house and a car, and be a schoolteacher. So whether it lasted or not didn't make any difference to me. The Chargers offered a lot more money than the Baltimore Colts, so I decided to sign with the Chargers. I was the number one pick of the Colts, but they offered me $7,500 for one year, plus a $1,000 bonus. The Chargers offered $12,000, two-year, no-cut contract, plus a $5,000 bonus. But I really would have preferred to play for the Colts because I liked that team. Gino Marchetti was one of my favorite players. I wanted to play on the same team as him. So I told Carroll Rosenbloom, the owner, that I would rather play for his team. I told him exactly what the Chargers offered. And I said, "I would rather play for you. If you would just give me a one-year contract at $10,000, it doesn't have to be guaranteed, and give me a $2,000 bonus, I will play for you." He said, "Ron, that would really skew our salary structure. You're asking to be paid as much as John Unitas, our quarterback. What we're going to do is this; this league is going to fold anyway. It's not going to make it. So you will be with us next year anyway, with some experience under your belt. So we will just wait for you." So that's how I signed with the Chargers…

It was a great pleasure to play for Sid because it is not for nothing that he is called the father of offensive football. He had great work habits. His work ethic was contagious, and we just felt we had an advantage with him as our coach. We were really explosive offensively, tremendously explosive. He was a very good judge of talent. But let's go back to the explosive offense. I'd like to see the statistics of what our offense produced by way of yards during the '60s compared to other football teams and compared to the NFL. I'll bet we're near the very top. As I say, he had a good eye for talent. He had a good eye for talent in his coaching department and in his personnel department and they just brought in some great players.

One thing that is something I have never seen written about Sid, and it is kind of fascinating actually, is that in 1960 the NFL seemed to have a quota system regarding black players. It seemed like five might be just about the right number. Sid immediately used as his only gauge of whether or not to sign a player, was his answer to three words: Can he play? If he can play, Sid was colorblind. So at the time the NFL had this unwritten quota system for black players, Sid brought in some of the greatest black players in San Diego Chargers' history. Ernie Ladd, Earl Faison, Frank Buncom, Joe Beauchamp, Speedy Duncan, Paul Lowe. You can just go on and on. At a time when the Washington Redskins did not have one black player. That seems shocking because right now there is probably 70% of the players in the NFL are black. At the time the Washington Redskins didn't have a single black player, Sid was assigning roommates in training camp on the basis of their position; offensive linemen roomed together, defensive linemen roomed together. The pretext was that they would be helping each other learn the plays and the nuances of the game, being able to discuss things. But Sid told me that the real reason was to have a natural integration of the team. That's very important. It's a very important thing to be done because athletics are supposed to be about sportsmanship and about judging people on the basis of their performance and character alone. And Sid was an embodiment of that. It was a great contribution to professional football.

Lance Alworth was just a great, great athlete. Now we're both in the Pro Football Hall of Fame, so theoretically we're peers. But I can tell you that, and the Chargers had some great, great players. You know who they are, both offense and defense. But Lance, we held him in special regard. The best story I can tell that illustrates that is that we were coming home from New York. We were flying home and we hit this tremendous pocket of bad weather. The plane was literally dropping 500 feet and shaking and what have you. I really thought that we were going to crash. I'm not that thrilled with flying anyway, and I was frightened. Then I remembered that Lance was on the plane and I said to myself, "I'm alright. God wouldn't kill Lance." And I felt better and relaxed. That's what high regard we had of Lance. He was a super athlete.

Ernie Ladd was just a great guy. 6'9", 340-pounds, his eyes weighed about 5-lbs each. He was probably our best all-around athlete. He was the best at everything. The best chess player, the best checkers player, the best ping-pong player, the best basketball player, although Earl Faison would probably dispute that. The best tennis player, the best card player, and just a super guy. And for about four years before his knee injuries took their toll, he played defensive tackle as well as anybody has ever played the game. If he could have had a career that lasted uninjured, if he could have had a career that lasted seven or eight year, he'd be in the Pro Football Hall of Fame. Same with Earl Faison; for about four years he was about as good as anybody that has ever played the game. And then he had a really devastating back injury and that killed him from being a great player. If he could have put together seven or eight years like he had those four years, he'd be in the Pro Football Hall of Fame. And the other players like I mentioned, they could break up a game anytime. Paul Lowe, Keith Lincoln. We had other terrific players. Dave Kocourek was an excellent tight end. Jacque MacKinnon was an excellent tight end. John Hadl was a terrific quarterback. He was a great leader and just a really super guy. That team was a joy to be around.

From public recognition in those days, I think the assistant coaches labored in anonymity primarily, and they just did a terrific job. My line coach, Joe Madro, was a great line coach. Not only from a technical standpoint, but he was a very funny guy and a humorous guy and a worldly, intellectual guy. He kept things interesting. That's hard to do. He kept us interested. He never got the kind of public attention and recognition that he deserved, but he was a good foot soldier and I bet it never even bothered him. That was his job and he just did it...

Barron Hilton, I don't know if he has got the type of recognition he should have received for having been one of the founders of the American Football League, but doing it the right way. Going about it in the highest professional manner possible and going first class from the very beginning. There were a few teams in the early teams that did not. The Oakland Raiders, for instance. We had guys who were cut from our team who signed with Oakland and we would talk to them. Their training camp, I remember on fellow was named Riley "Rattlesnake" Morris. When we played Oakland I was speaking to Riley after the game and he said, "Oh, I miss the Chargers." I said, "Why is that?" He said, "You should see our training camp. It's unbelievable. For lunch we get two baloney sandwiches and grape Kool-Aid. I had Oakland Raiders tell me that when they came down to play San Diego they would fly in the day of the game. They'd go to a hotel and the players were instructed not to turn back the covers on the beds or they would be fined an extra five bucks. It would cost the team five bucks. In the early days, the first few years, members of the Denver Broncos and New York Titans, they told me when the paychecks came that they would rush to cash them because sometimes they bounced. We never had a problem with Barron Hilton. Everything was first class. We traveled first class, hotels were first class, training camp. The salaries, people would laugh at them now, but the truth is it was good money then. He was fair, so I think he is somebody that deserves a very high place in Chargers' history.

RON NERY, DEFENSIVE END

College: Kansas State
Years with the Chargers: 1960-1962

Ron Nery was drafted by the New York Giants of the National Football League, but an injury in training camp kept him from making the final roster. He played in Canada and then became a member of the Chargers' original "Fearsome Foursome," when he joined Bill Hudson, Ernie Ladd and Earl Faison on the defensive line. Unlike the other three, Nery always had trouble keeping weight on, and as a result was the lightest of these defensive linemen.

Ron Nery was unable to conduct a telephone interview, so he instead answered several questions in written form. A few months after sending his reply, Ron Nery unexpectedly passed away from problems stemming from an enlarged heart.

In 1959 I returned to the states after I requested and received an outright release from the British Columbia Lions of Vancouver in the Western Interprovincial Football League of Canada. The Rams were still playing their preseason schedule. I spoke briefly with Coach Gillman who said it was too late to get on that season, but would I contact him for the 1960 season. In the spring of 1960 I was living in Bakersfield as I had just married a girl from there who I had previously known in college at Kansas State College as the school was known at that time.

I tracked the progress of the AFL to organize through the local newspapers. When it looked like a done deal I called the Chargers front office and was invited to drive to Los Angeles and sign a contract, which I did for $5,000. It was then that I met Sid Gillman, Chuck Noll, Joe Madro and I believe Al Davis. Training camp started a few weeks later.

It seems like there were three groups of 33 players each reporting about a week apart. This included a few of the players who reported for open tryouts in the spring of 1960. During training camp I must have had 6 different roommates, only two of which I met or learned their names.

It seems there were over a dozen defensive ends, all of whom outweighed me and three or four were taller than me.

Training camp seemed to go on forever seven days a week and mostly two practices a day. We were finally given 1 _ days off after a Saturday scrimmage and off to Laguna Beach we went. I was driving a 1948 Packard that cost me about $90.00. I made it back in good shape but a lot of guys (a bunch of defensive ends included) didn't get back to Chapman College in time and were released.

That first training camp and preseason schedule in which we won all 6 games followed by player cuts left us with 33 players to begin the first season. After the 3rd league game it seems like about 1/3 of the players were replaced by late preseason NFL cuts and we finally had our team – the 1960 LA Chargers.

Before the 1960 season I had worked almost two months in the potato fields around Bakersfield. I came into camp weighing about 205 pounds and gained eight or ten pounds during camp.

The answer to question one, no one scouted me. I came to the Chargers the hard way – lean & hungry.

I never really worried about the Chargers making it. Except for a position or two or maybe a back up or two I was looking at some of the best athletic talent I had ever seen. I saw the team improve in training camp and all through the first season. I felt if the Chargers were representative of the whole AFL it would make it fine. The frustration of the many injuries I had endured before I came to the Chargers did little to get the "Gotta Play Football" monkey off my back. If I could stay healthy, I hoped to play five years and be perfectly satisfied. I knew nothing at all about the business end of the team, much less about the league itself. There just wasn't time to concern myself with worrying about the AFL when I was hanging on to my job by fingernails only...

I made a home for my family in Granite Hills, part of El Cajon, and we were very happy there. It was the sort of place I would have been happy to spend the rest of my days at in bliss. Everything was fine till the 1964 season was about to begin. I did not get a contract offer but I did get a divorce. Oh well, it would have been nice had everything worked out. While I lived there I coached little league baseball and was somewhat active in that very worthwhile program...

Each year we did an Eastern swing, which I always enjoyed. We played Buffalo staying a week at Niagara Falls then played Boston staying a week at Bear Mountain Inn then played the NY Titans and returned to San Diego. This trip was when fall was in full swing and the leaves were beautiful is certainly memorable.

One year, in Buffalo, Hank Schmidt, who I was rooming with then, and I visited a local coin shop. Hank was an avid coin collector and I was a curious beginner. Hank purchased a few coins and I learned a lot. That night the shop was broken into and looted. The next morning the team bus was loaded and ready to leave for the airport and our flight to Boston. The local police showed, called Hank and me off the bus and questioned us in front of the whole team. I guess we were saved by the famous team bed check. We were released and went on our way.

Another road trip I remember well was an early in the season trip to Houston. The weather was typical Houston, 100 degrees and 100% humidity. The game was filmed a quarter at a time while the remaining film was stored on ice. Still the humidity nearly ruined the film while it was in the camera. I played the whole game and drank plenty of water and soft drinks. At the end of that game I weighed 198 pounds. The Chargers very imaginative publicity people always listed my program weight at 244 pounds...

The only thing I disliked about being a pro player was these things that made it so difficult for me to play. I always had trouble gaining and keeping weight. That is till I turned 50 years old, now it's easy to gain weight. I don't remember stepping on a football field with my weight over 215 pounds. My eyeballs are flat – so much so that I've never been able to wear contact lenses. I gave it my best effort and played as long as I was able, probably longer than I should have, more importantly the "Gotta Play Football" monkey is off my back. I can look back on those years with few regrets and a smile on my face.

VOLNEY PETERS, DEFENSIVE TACKLE
College: Southern California
Years with the Chargers: 1960

By the time Volney Peters came to the Chargers, he had already concluded a seven-year NFL career with the Cardinals, Redskins and Eagles. He came out of retirement to play with the Chargers. After one year with the Chargers, Peters played one year in Oakland and then retired. Volney Peters is a man of few words, so his lovely wife, Margaret contributed a few stories as well.

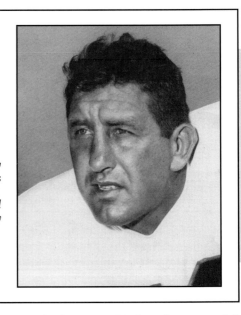

We were having a get together with some players. I had quit, in '59 I didn't play with the NFL. I didn't know they were making another league, and these friends of mine came down to San Diego and we had a party. They said that they were starting the American League and L.A. was making a team, and Houston and several others. So I contacted L.A. and they took me. And that's the way I got there. But I was drafted by Houston. Somehow Gillman got me off. They made a trade or something. And so I went to the Chargers...

Well, nobody had experience. They were all young kids. I was probably the oldest. There were a couple of others. But I was the oldest, I guess. They had some real great players. Just rookies, most of them, but they were good because they were drafted by the National Football League, a lot of them. But they went to the American instead, and they were good, very good...

Oh, we went back to New York and we stayed there for a couple weeks, and my wife bought a house when I was gone. Then she called me and surprised me. I said, "Are you kidding?" She said, "No..."

The Raiders were so disorganized. It was something. The Chargers were really... Because Sid had been with the Rams and so he was very... Well, he knew what he was doing and everything was organized. Up here, with the Raiders, it was something. You know they didn't have a stadium. They didn't have anywhere to practice.

(Raiders' coach Eddie) Erdelatz? He was much looser than Gillman. Everybody really enjoyed him but he couldn't win, so they got (Marty) Feldman. His assistant took over. But it still didn't help. They didn't have the players or the know-how until Davis got there and straightened it out.

Margaret Peters

They kid me all the time because they always say I was Pete's mouth, because he's very, very humble and very modest. But when the Chargers came to San Diego, we already owned a home down there. In fact, Esther Gillman about had a heart attack because I walked over to her at the tunnel in the Coliseum in L.A. and I said, "Are we going to be moving to San Diego?" And her mouth fell open, and she looked at me and she said, "How do you know that?" And I said, "I have my own sources."

Well, Sid brought all these players that would come in ahead of time, and there was a recession and they couldn't get jobs. So they lived at our house. They would get there around six in the morning and it was party every night. I was feeding, doing all the washing and ironing, and taking care of these ball players. One of them was Paul Maguire. And he invented "party." It was a wild time, but it was a wonderful time.

And Esther, the wives are never supposed to become friends with the coach, but she and I became friendly. And she was a wonderful person. The Charger office called our house the Chargers Annex. And they would call and leave messages for the players and did I know where Ron Nery was, or could I get a message to Ron Mix, and all this stuff.

One time they called and they wanted to know if they could do anything. They appreciated all I was doing. I said, "Well, if you want to send me some big pans, I'd appreciate that." And I was cooking 15 pounds of spaghetti. And I got it cooked and I didn't know how to drain it. Here I had all these ball players,

and I was looking out the kitchen window. So I ran outside, took the screen off, poured boiling water on the screen, laid it across the sink, and dumped the spaghetti...

It was really like a family. The Gillman's were just... She is a wonderful person, and so was he. And when Pete came up here, to the Raiders, he was the first big trade that was made, and he was very upset and didn't want to come. And when he got here a sportswriter interviewed him and asked him what he thought of the Raiders. "Well coming from the Chargers to the Raiders," he said, "you guys look like rinky-dinks." Al Davis is what he is today because of Sid Gillman, and he says that. He sat at his feet and learned everything there was to learn. It was a very, very happy time.

Well, I did get to know Barron Hilton when he owned the Chargers... And Barron Hilton was just the most delightful man. He threw a party for us the first Christmas, when it was the Los Angeles Chargers, and to date I haven't been to a nicer party. And he went to thank the players for what they had done for him and what he thought of them, and he started crying. He said it was the first time in his life that he'd ever been a regular guy. The guys would bum cigarettes off of him, and borrow money and they teased him and did terrible things to him, and he was just another man to them. And he had never been treated that way. I think it was a different time. There was still a lot of respect. I used to say, "I hope a coach never told Pete to go home and shoot me," because he'd had bought a gun and done it. The coach became their father. A lot of those guys, it was the only father figure they had.

BOB REIFSNYDER, DEFENSIVE END

College: Navy
Years with the Chargers: 1960 Training Camp

Bob Reifsnyder was a highly touted football player as a junior at the Naval Academy. He ruptured his Achilles tendon in his senior year, and the injury threatened his much-anticipated professional career. He went to camp with the Chargers in 1960, but was traded to the New York Titans prior to the opening of the regular season. Reifsnyder played two years for the Titans, but never fully recovered from his Achilles injury. Bob Reifsnyder was inducted into the College Football Hall of Fame in 1997.

Right: *Bob Reifsnyder was traded to the New York Titans during training camp, but his bubble gum card featured him with the Chargers.*

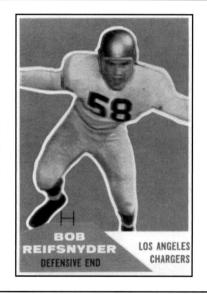

BOB REIFSNYDER
DEFENSIVE END
LOS ANGELES
CHARGERS

I graduated from the Naval Academy. I had ripped my Achilles' tendon in my senior year and as a result, got a medical discharge when I graduated. So instead of going into the service, I was drafted by the L.A. Rams. Also that year, 1959, I played in the Chicago All-Star Game, which was kind of a joke because in those days they didn't really have any of the rehabilitation and therapy that they have now. So in February, of course they didn't really know what was wrong with me. In February they cut my leg open and stitched me back up and all that stuff, and that was it.

So I was drafted by the L.A. Rams, and at that time Sid Gillman was their coach. I played in the Chicago All-Star Game against the Baltimore Colts. I was being worked out as a defensive end out there, and then when I went to the Ram camp,

they tried to make me a linebacker, which I had never really played before. But I just couldn't run the way I used to. One of my attributes at Navy, I was an All-America in my junior year, won the Maxwell Trophy when I was a junior, and a couple of years ago was elected to the College Hall of Fame. So I did have a solid college career up until my senior year, which was a disaster. I just didn't play.

So anyway, what happened was that they were dissatisfied with my progress. I was going through camp out there and they put me on special teams. I had a real good game on special teams, on kick off and punt returns. I felt like I was coming back, but they decided they were not going to keep me. What they tried to do was send me, Sid Gillman and Pete Rozelle, who was the general manager, tried to talk me into going up to

Canada and play. They had some kind of deal worked out with a Canadian team, which I forget which one it was. But I had just been married and said that I didn't want any part of doing that. The next thing I know, they wind up trading me to the Giants. So the Giants put me on injured reserve. I think they traded me for Ben Agajanian, the kicker. So anyway, I spent the whole year with the Giants and did not get activated. So by the end of the season, the contracts rules in effect in those days, since I technically had never been on an official contract, I was a free agent.

Frank Leahy became the general manager of the first Chargers team, and Sid Gillman, who got fired by the Rams, became head coach. So they contacted me and offered me a fairly decent bonus and a bigger contract than I had with the Giants, so I jumped. So anyway, I was out there and they were playing me

at defensive end and I was a place kicker, and I was still having problems with my legs. I guess things just didn't work out in their eyes. I started a couple of preseason games and the next thing I know I was traded to the Titans. I played that year with the Titans and half of a second year with the Titans. That was it. The second year I was with the Titans I broke my hand and they put me on injured reserve and then released me. I kind of think, in their case, it was a question of money. And again, in all honesty, I was not the ballplayer I was three years previously. I was kind of gimping around on a half a leg. That has always been kind of a black cloud in my life. I always wondered how successful I could have been in pro ball if I was 100%. But if I was 100%, I probably would have been in the Navy shooting guns instead of playing pro ball. So, you can't have it both ways.

DON ROGERS, CENTER
College: South Carolina
Years with the Chargers: 1960-1964

Playing football after college was not in Don Rogers' plans before Al Davis first contacted him about joining the Chargers in 1960. After several meetings with the silver-tongued Davis, Rogers signed with the team and became the starting center for the next five years. After his football days, Rogers built a successful financial planning and tax business in the San Diego area.

Well my first year out of college I was drafted by San Francisco. I didn't make it. Paul Lowe and I were, I think, the last two cuts. I think the irony was my biggest mistake there was that I probably got in too good of condition. I lost a lot of weight. I showed up at training camp at 235 and they wanted me up around 250. When I first started working out I was 265 and I just lost too much weight. That's probably the biggest single reason why I didn't make it. Anyway, when I got cut I didn't know what to do, so I called South Carolina. I guess like everybody else, when you don't know what to do, you go back to school. I called South Carolina and said I'd really like to get my fifth year. Because everybody that I'd started off with as a freshman, they red-shirted a year. So I said, "I think I'd like to get a fifth year." And they said, "Fine, we'll continue your scholarship."

So I used that fifth year to go to graduate school and I think it was spring break when I was home in New Jersey. I had absolutely no intentions of playing football and I got a call from Al Davis. He was at Newark Airport. I had never heard of the American Football League, I had never heard of Al Davis. He was on the road signing up everybody he could. He reached me at home and I said, "I'm really not interested. I gave it a shot and I have lost interest. I don't want to play football."

So he hounded me and said, "At least come down to the airport." So I went down and I talked to him and simply told him I didn't want to play. He hung around and called me the next day and I said, "I haven't changed my mind." Somehow or

other he got me to go down there again. I don't know if I felt sorry for him or what. I left him with the same message, "I'm just not interested."

While he was there he had signed a couple of guys. One of them was from South Carolina, Sam DeLuca, who was a couple years ahead of me. So finally he started pulling all kinds of crap. He's always going to the phone booth and making calls and coming back saying, "We can do this, we can do that." So he finally came back and said, "Look. I'll give you $500 if you sign the damn contract." I said, "Well, I'll sign the contract, I'll take the $500, but I'm not going to camp. This is the last you're going to see of me and the last you're going to see of the $500." He said, "Here's the $500, sign the contract." So I did. I really had no intentions of playing football. I was in graduate school and I was studying and I was locking myself in the library everyday and I was enjoying it.

By the end of the school year I was a little fed up with that, and they sent a couple hundred bucks for an airline ticket. I thought maybe I'll go out and see California anyway. I had interviewed with a couple of companies that were California-based and said, "maybe I'll just use the money and go out there." I never worked out a day. The training camp was in Orange County and I had this old junky car. I gave myself about three weeks to drive out because I really didn't think the car would make it. I got in the car and I just couldn't stop driving. I drove straight through. I got to training camp about two weeks before I was scheduled to be there.

They really had it well organized. They just had busloads of guys coming in that first year. I pulled into the parking lot of the training camp where the dormitories were and it must have been about six o'clock in the morning. I had been driving all night long. The first guy I ran into was Gillman. I didn't know him, he didn't know me. I told him who I was and that I'd been driving all night and would really like to get some sleep. He said, "Sure, no problem. C'mon over and have breakfast first."

I get out of breakfast and the equipment manager comes over and says, "Mr. Gillman wants you on the field at 9 o'clock." I must have weighed 265-270, hadn't worked out a day, and I was on the field in uniform at 9 o'clock just like everybody else. All we did all morning was one-on-one drills and I was kicking ass. I was running over these guys. So basically I made the team that first morning. In the afternoon, the first thing out, he's timing everybody. I was just as tight as could be. I ran 40 yards, got half way down there and pulled a hamstring and I was out for maybe a month. Just walking around the track, I had already made the team...

I really had no intentions of playing any more football, didn't care, and I just drove out to L.A. on a lark. And I figured I'd see what's going on, spend some time, see what's going on in California, maybe look for a job or something. I really didn't expect to make it, didn't particularly care, and I made it. So once I made it I got a little bit serious about it. Maybe by the end of the season I was in shape. It was an interesting first year. It was a great experience...

It was pretty obvious that we weren't making any headway in Los Angeles. Another guy on the team and I, Don Norton, I don't know if you've been in the Coliseum, but to get from the dressing rooms to the field you go through these really long tunnels. Every time we'd come out on the field we'd always be next to each other and we'd say, "They've stayed away by the thousands." Nobody was there. A couple thousand people in the stadium and then they'd start putting them all together. You've got this 100,000-seat stadium and you've got 2,000 people there. We never did draw very well.

So it didn't surprise me, but it was like, "What do I care?" San Diego is California, just like L.A. is. I didn't particularly like L.A. It was big, dirty, freeways, traffic, and smog. The first time I came to San Diego I said, "Hey, this is a great little town." Highway 8 down in Mission Valley was still a two-lane blacktop road. It looked like a farm community. I thought, "Shit, this is O.K." The weather was good, air was clean. Everything was a little more spread out. So once I saw San Diego I really liked it. With the beginning of training camp and all, San Diego was really behind the team. I think it was a really smart choice. But it really didn't make any difference to me where we played. I was kind of like, "I'm not sure what I'm doing out here anyway, so what the Hell is the difference whether I play in San Diego or Los Angeles?" But I didn't particularly like L.A. and we obviously weren't getting the crowds we needed. And San Diego got behind the team 100% right away. It worked out well.

I think [Balboa Stadium] was a real good stadium for viewing football because the fans were close. The game wasn't as much of a theatrical production as it is today. So it was a real down-to-earth, basic stadium. It held 30-35,000. It was an existing facility, so it kind of made sense. It was pretty much as big as any other stadium in the league, or even in the NFL. I think the best thing about it is the stands were full. Playing in the Coliseum in L.A. was absurd. You couldn't even see the people in the stands. You couldn't hear them. There was no interaction. There was no 12th Man effect at all, whereas in San Diego the fans were very much a part of the game. I think that's an important aspect of winning and losing, getting the fans involved. And in San Diego they were definitely involved. So I think from that aspect it was a good stadium.

ERNIE WRIGHT, TACKLE
College: Ohio State
Years with the Chargers: 1960-1967, 1972

Ernie Wright was an outstanding offensive tackle for the great Chargers' teams of the AFL. In 1960 Wright was the youngest player in the league, but that did not stop him from earning a starting position and keeping it for eight years. Wright went to the Cincinnati Bengals in the 1968 expansion draft, and helped Coach Paul Brown build the fledgling franchise.

Well, I came to the Chargers when I was a junior at Ohio State and out of school at the time. The old Ohio State coach was a friend of Sid Gillman. He said, "Ernie, would you be interested in playing pro football?" I said yeah. In those days you had to wait until the NFL draft. He said, "We'll have somebody call you." So then I got a call from Sid Gillman saying, "We're starting this new league and Ernie Gottfried says you're a helluva player, and he knows football. So I would like to talk to you about being a Charger." So I subsequently flew out from Columbus to Los Angeles without an agent. I sat down in a room with Sid Gillman, Jack Faulkner, Al Davis and started talking about the new league and before I went home in about four days I signed a contract to become a player in the American Football League for the Los Angeles Chargers. I was married at the time, had one child and was expecting another one. It was, I don't remember, a $500 or $1,000 signing bonus and a $10,000 contract. Of course they made it guaranteed for three years, $10,000, $11,000, $12,000. In those days, I know Jim Parker had been a great All-American at Ohio State. He was with the Baltimore Colts and he was only making $6,500 or $7,500 a year. I thought this was too good a deal to pass up. So that's how I became a Charger…

I didn't compare the Chargers to any other AFL team. I compared them more to the NFL. I think when I signed with the Chargers they had eight teams in the league. There were only 14 teams in the National Football League. There were certain things going on in the National Football League that we talked about because we weren't thinking about the American Football League, but it would have been more of a concern if I had been drafted in the National Football League. For instance, we knew that as African-American players even then, that African-Americans didn't sit on the bench. You had to be a starter. There was a quota system. They didn't want to have over 10 African-American players. Usually 6 or 8 because it would have been difficult on the road because you had to have a roommate. There was bullshit like that going on and we knew all about it. We knew all about it…

Sid Gillman, the little bow-tied man. He signed me. He was my coach and general manager. There were times, especially in contract negotiations that I couldn't stand him, although I played for him. I couldn't stand him, and I couldn't hate him. I don't know if you know what I am talking about. He was one of the first individuals that had me look at life as life. Life is not fair. You don't live your life expecting other people to give you things. You have got to do it; you have got to take it. Eventually, after I got out of football and got into the agent business…Well after I got out of football I went one year into the World Football League. The team was supposed to be in Los Angeles then Mexico City, but they ended up back in Philadelphia. I was working with Ron Waller. I was the offensive line coach. We had to run some camps out here because you're trying to find anybody that can breathe to play. I hired Sid to help organize my camp. So I went from being a player that he recruited and coached to hiring him and telling him what we were going to do.

But I have seen him take a guy with limited talent and he's such a great teacher, he was such a great teacher. He could show you how to run a pass route and become open just by this and that. He was a very technical person. He knew all aspects of the game. I had quite a time with Sid. Sid used to be a member of La Costa. I am a member of La Costa. Before he got to the point where he couldn't move around, before he had his surgeries, he'd be down in the men's locker room and he would always say what a great football player I was and so on and so forth. I said, "If I was so great, why would you screw me out of $1,000 back in 1962?" And he said, "Uh, that was my job and that was your job."

I have never thought of him as having a racist bone in him. You could room with anyone you wanted to room with. During the 60s, that's when you had all the sit-ins and demonstrations. Some Southern cities were hopeful of getting pro football franchises. So a lot of things happened. Our first year we went to play the Houston Oilers in Houston. We stayed at the Rice Institute and we stayed in the dormitories. Everywhere else we were going we stayed in Hilton Hotels because the owner was Barron Hilton. And so we're saying, "Why are we staying in these funky-ass dormitories?" Well, because the Shamrock Hilton is segregated. If you're black, you have got to work there. That's the only way you could get in there. "We ain't coming here anymore. You can tell the commissioner that." So Sid Gillman got on the phone and lobbied, and we never stayed anywhere but a Hilton after that. When we walked into the Shamrock Hilton a year later, the employees stood up an applauded because we were the first African-Americans to be guests at the hotel. Now I don't think Sid did that because he believes in legal rights for everybody. He did that because he had some great African-American talent on his team and he wanted to put the team out there and he wanted to win. He did not try to bluff us or say, "We're gonna cut you and so on and so forth. You better play or else." He made things happen.

We had two other incidents. We had to play an exhibition game against the Jets in Atlanta. It's hard to believe in this day and age. This was back in the early '60s. We stayed at the Hilton by the airport. We went to the mall next door to shoot pool. It was Ernie Ladd, myself, Earl Faison, Lance Alworth, it was about 12 or 15 guys, mixed half black, half white. Of course we were noisy wherever we would go. So we noticed that the kid running the pool rack would only give the balls and the cues to the white guys. We saw him get on the phone and after a while he came over and said, "I'm sorry." It was kind of difficult for this kid, this young man who was working at the pool hall. But he had called his employer who said they didn't allow any black guys. So we all left. We called Sid and said, "We're not playing any exhibition game tomorrow in this racist damn place. This was at like 8:00 on a Friday, because we played the exhibition game at 8:00 on a Saturday. By 11:00 the Mayor of Atlanta and the Governor of the State of Georgia were in meetings with us at the hotel, apologizing and saying, "Please play and we will straighten this all out." So you know the history of Atlanta and the Falcons and so forth.

We had a year where we flew from San Diego to New Orleans to play in the all-star game, the AFL All-Star Game. The All-Star Game was supposed to be in New Orleans. We get in there at 11:00 at night and on the plane were guys from the Chargers and the Raiders. So we go to get a cab and the cab driver says, "No, you have to go over there to those cabs with the black cab drivers." So here we go again. "We're not playing in this place." Now this is league-wide. So they move the game from New Orleans to Houston, the headquarters of the Shamrock Hilton. See how this stuff goes? So we play the game in Houston on five-day notice and New Orleans is out of the picture. The next goddang year the all-star game was going to be in Houston. The airport is so fogged-in that we have to go to New Orleans and head back the next morning. We land at the airport and go over to the New Orleans Hilton by the airport. So we want to go down to the French Quarter. So we get in a cab. It is Dave Grayson, myself and Earl Faison. The guy says he'll take us down to Acme's or wherever we wanted to go. We wanted to go get oysters and all of that. And this was a black cab driver. So we started talking to him and he said, "Aw, I thought I recognized you guys. You're football players, right?" "Yeah, yeah." "You don't know what you guys did last year. Now we have public accommodations on bussing and cabs. They can't refuse people." And so on and so forth. This city wants an NFL team so bad that they have changed years and years of segregated policies because they see something that they want. All of this had taken place during Sid Gillman's time. Again, I don't think he was motivated to do all of this because he was a clone of Martin Luther King, but he certainly didn't disagree with it. And if it meant having a football team, he'd rather do it that way…

Well, my roommate for years and years was Paul Lowe. My first wife and Paul's wife, Sophie became great friends. When we moved here from L.A. in 1961, we lived in houses that were right next to each other. Two of our kids were born within 18 hours of each other. So Paul Lowe and I ran around a lot. Earl Faison, Ernie Ladd. I played a lot of golf with Sam Gruneisen, John Hadl, Lance Alworth. I say that would probably be the bunch back then. We did a lot of things together as families. My first wife has picture albums with all these people growing up together and now they're having kids.

We had some guys that hung together. It was kind of interesting too because being from Ohio, that was the first time I had dealt with Southern blacks or Southern whites. Take like a George Blair from Mississippi, Charlie Flowers from Mississippi. It was interesting getting to know these people and them getting to know us. Some of the stereotypical monikers that were attached to people disappear when you're out there hot and sweating and showering naked and seeing who is doing what. You find out who you can trust and who you can rely on and who you can't rely on, because in the course of a game, there is going to be a chance to win and a chance to lose. There are some guys that will find a way to lose and some guys that will find a chance to win. If a guy is going to help you win, I don't care what color he is, how his breath smells or what his thoughts are. If our whole society was more oriented that way as opposed to "I don't like you because you are white. And you're lazy because you're Mexican, blah, blah, blah." It gave me a chance to take a good look at the difference in people and races from all over the country.

There are some African-Americans that were on our team that I did not associate with because I didn't like them. I didn't like they way they thought about things and I didn't like the way they did things. There were some white guys that I felt very close to. And then golf has always had me out with the white population anyway. I was playing golf when I was 13 years old. I started caddying and playing golf. So I got used to being around the Caucasian population. It's kind of funny. Even today, if you're somebody, you're not just black anymore; you're a football player. It is just our society. My thing is that my friends are based on who they are, not what color they are. My friends today come from all walks of life and we may joke about racist times and so on and so forth, but it's who you are, not what color your skin is…

Remember I said I had a no-cut contract? In the first year of the Chargers, guys were coming and going like crazy. They would be here today and three people would be here tomorrow with the same helmet and same jersey. You wouldn't know who in the Hell they were. We started out on the road. Our first game that year was down in Texas somewhere. I think the Dallas Texans. Then we were going to go to Buffalo. We took the bus from the game to the airport. There was another bus there. About 15 guys got off this bus and got on our bus. They called the names of 15 guys on our bus. They took 15 guys off our bus and they went back to San Diego when we went to Buffalo. So we were going to Buffalo and start practicing and there are 15 guys that I have never seen in my life before. It was a treadmill. You were always looking for players. The Ron Mix's and Ernie Wright's and Paul Lowe's, the Charlie McNeil's and some of those certain guys are going to be there forever. But the other supporting cast, they came and they went.

We used to always have the Eastern swing. We would be gone for 17 days. Depending on who we were playing, we used to play a lot on Saturday nights. We would leave here on a Thursday and we would play the Titans, New York Titans, Boston and Buffalo. So instead of coming back, we would just go to the next place. We stayed in Lynn, Massachusetts, we stayed in Bear Mountain. I used to really enjoy going to Bear Mountain, New York. We would go down to West Point. It was quite a place. Of all places, we used to stay quite often at Niagara Falls, outside of Buffalo. We used to say, "Who in the Hell would have a football team stay in the Hotel Niagara for a week with nothing but newlyweds around here?" We're practicing and horsing around, gambling and drinking. But that 17-day road trip was a lot of fun. We would get per diem for food. Some guys would spend more than they got, and some guys would come home making a profit. We had a guy named Henry Schmidt who used to bring a hot plate and canned beans to save money. We would have a big poker game going on the whole time where we kept score by paper and then the big argument was who was going to pay off the most money. We spent a lot of time together. Teams don't spend a lot of time together anymore. You have so many specialists. We would have a team meeting and do a lot of things with everybody and then the special team meeting was everybody on the team because you participated on special teams. Then defense would go in this room and offense would go in that room. Now you have not only that, but you have a run cluster, a pass cluster, a pass-rush cluster. Today I don't see them having the camaraderie that we had in those days… The guys that I remember the most are the guys that I played with before you had so many teams in the merger. Stories are rampant. Guys getting into trouble. Some of those stories you couldn't print.

BOB ZEMAN, SAFETY

College: Wisconsin
Years with the Chargers: 1960-1961, 1965-1966

Bob Zeman played for the Denver Broncos in between stints with the Chargers. He was a popular guy with his teammates, and at one period, owned a bar near the beach called The Surfer, with teammates Dave Kocourek and Paul Maguire. After retiring as a player, Zeman coached professionally for 22 years. Most recently he joined the 1999 Seattle Seahawk staff to help Head Coach Mike Holmgren during his first year with the team.

That first year of the Chargers, that was one of the great years that I have ever spent in football. I remember we were all playing in the Rose Bowl. I was at Wisconsin. After the Rose Bowl they took us to a party over at, I think it was Barron Hilton's house, or somebody's house. Anyway, Barron Hilton and his wife, Marilyn, were there, and all the executives from the Chargers. I was one of the first selection rounds. So we went over there after the bowl game and they told me that I was one of their guys that were chosen. Me and Ron Mix and I forget who else. But that was my first visit with them and then I went back to school in Wisconsin. Then I got a call from Sid Gillman. He was down in Chicago, so I went down there and talked to him, and I signed a contract with him. I also was drafted by the Cleveland Browns, but I just felt like signing with the Chargers, so I did.

Well, [training camp] started at the end of June and I was still in the service. I went in the service right after I graduated in January. At officers' school in Virginia, and then I asked for a transfer out to the West Coast. They brought in a bunch of guys and a couple of hundred guys early in June. And then the drafted guys didn't have to be down there until July. My case commander let me go down there and sign out so I could go down there and practice and then I wouldn't have to go back and sign off duty. Anyhow, we went two-a-days for three or four weeks. It was in Orange, California, at Chapman College. I remember the little town there had a barbecue there for us on a Saturday afternoon. We couldn't wait for that barbecue because we knew we had a half a day off. Then we had a scrimmage with the Orange County Rhinos, which was a semi-pro team. They called it off in the third quarter because there were so many fights going on. We had so many guys coming in and out of camp, but that was the longest camp I had ever been at. Plus six preseason games. It was rough, but we got a lot done and got a lot of camaraderie. All the guys that made it through and stuck together, we're still close to this day...

I'll tell you what; Ernie (Ladd) was 6'9". Earl (Faison) was 6'6". Bill Hudson was 6'4" or 6'5". We were big. We would have been big at this time. And then Ron Nery was our right defensive end. He was our speed rusher, which everybody is using now. Guys like Charles Haley and Kabeer Gbaja-Biamila with the Packers. They are speed rushers and that's what Ron Nery was. But everybody contributed intercepting passes. Defensive linemen would knock them up in the air and catch them. Linebackers, everybody was grabbing passes that year. Of course we had the good pressure and good height up front. But they got their share too...

Keith Lincoln was one of the great athletes we had, and Lance Alworth. Talk about two guys that could run and do ev-

erything. Keith could kick, pass and run. Lance was just so athletic. He could jump a mile high and run and had great hands. Just being around those guys, they were in a different category themselves. Good guys, too. So probably those two players stood out in my mind as being... Well, Lance is in the Hall of Fame, so that speaks for itself. But Ron Mix was another guy. I don't think he ever had a holding call on him in his career. He was so consistent and dominated his position. Those three guys were really impressive to me.

You know Don Norton was a wide receiver at the time. He was my roommate on the road. In fact, one of my sons is named after him. He passed away a couple of years ago. But we were on a road trip and we were staying in Boston and playing the Patriots. We were allowed to come to our hotel rooms, but they told us not to use the beds because we were just going to come there and rest up for a while before we went to the game that night. We had been staying up in New York the previous week. Anyhow, Don and I and Dave (Kocourek) were in the room. Don had the window open and he was looking out. Dave and I were horsing around. There was a ledge out the window. Don was kind of being wise to us, so we pushed him out on the ledge. He was hollering and screaming at us, and we pulled his pants down and shut the window. Of course he was hollering and cussing and swearing at us, and it was raining outside. We were always thinking of something like that to do. That was one of the funniest things. He dared us to do it and we did it. He couldn't believe it. But he didn't fall, so that was one good thing.

Volney Peters, I'm trying to think if it was after a game or... It was some night. He was going home and he ran out of gas. It was dark out, so he was cutting across this farmer's field. Anyhow, he fell into an old outhouse hole. He had to dig little ledges in the side to get himself out. Then he walked across the field and he found a gas station and called a cab. Then he got some gas for his car and went home. Of course when he knocked the door was locked. His wife came to the door and there he was, standing there full from falling in the outhouse. That was an awesome story.

Well, that was quite a trip [to Hawaii to play in the Oilers in a 1961 exhibition game]. We were supposed to go there longer, but the plane broke down, so we got delayed a day or two. But we went over there for about three days, I think. We went surfing and stuff. But on the way home we were in the plane and one of the players went in the back and found the champagne that they had on the plane. Guys were drinking mai-tais and we stayed a day after the game. But Don Norton got on the plane and he had a lei around his neck and shorts on. In those days you dressed up when you flew. Anyhow, the players and coaches sat together, so his seat was next to Chuck Noll. Anyhow, Chuck Noll looked at him and just gave him a dirty look. In those days, after practice we used to go watch the Three Stooges. You know how they poked each other in the eye with the two fingers? Well, Chuck had been looking at Norton, and finally Norton took his hand out and gave Chuck three jabs in the eyes with his two fingers. Just like the Three Stooges would do. We were all sitting around watching that. Of course Chuck was pretty straight and he didn't appreciate that. But we went surfing over there. It was the first time I had been surfing. Jack Kemp, he was a West Coast guy and we went out on surfboards. It was most of our first trip over to Hawaii. I was over there and met this Hawaiian hula dancer. She came back over. I invited her over that year and we got engaged. Barron Hilton really liked her and was going to buy the ring for us if we got married. But it didn't work out. Good thing for her. So that was that trip.

Chuck Allen, Linebacker
College: Washington
Years with the Chargers: 1961-1969

Chuck Allen came to the Chargers in the 1961 draft that brought Earl Faison, Keith Lincoln, Ernie Ladd, Bud Whitehead and Luther Hayes. He had played guard at Washington, but was moved to linebacker with the Chargers. Allen played for the Chargers through the end of the AFL in 1969, then played two years in Pittsburgh and ended his career with one season in Philadelphia.

Well, I think Jack Faulkner and Chuck Noll and Al Davis, Joe Madro, all the coaches were there at the time. I was fortunate enough to play in a couple Rose Bowls with the Huskies, so they saw me there. They came up after the second Rose Bowl in 1961. That was in January, and mentioned that they were with the Chargers. Would I be interested in playing? From that point on, everything just fell into place. I had a couple other opportunities, but it was pretty intimidating to go to the Rams when they had Myron Pottios, Les Richter and, who was the other great All-Pro? Anyway, Saskatchewan didn't appeal to me, but San Diego sure looked great. It was an easy choice.

You have got the master coach there [in Sid Gillman]. He pulled everything together. He knew organization; his assistants were all knowledgeable. Jack Faulkner was the defensive coordinator. And of course I'm looking at it from the defensive standpoint, but he had Al Davis, wide receiver coach, Chuck Noll was their defensive linebacker coach, secondary coach. We just had a great staff and their reputation was there. And it looked like if the league caught on at that time, we knew we were going to be doing real well. And we did.

Well I dealt with him (Sid Gillman) on contracts. That was the worst part. Don't have to say too much more about that. He's legendary in that area too. But you know what? This guy had a tremendous heart and we were counting the years that some of us were together with our wives. We were married, most of us in San Diego. We got together, it was Ernie Ladd, Earl Faison, Paul Lowe; we had almost 200 years of married life. My wife and I have been married 40 years and most of my friends, Mitinger has been married for almost 40 and Bud Whitehead, he's at 38 or 37. But we all hung together and we had a great group of guys. Everybody got along pretty darn well with one another. Now that's part of the chemistry that created some outstanding Charger teams there…

You know, one of the things Sid used to do was have a group of underprivileged children, a lot of times mentally handicapped or physically handicapped kids, come to training camp. He'd call us all together in a huddle before and he said, "You know, you people are the luckiest people on earth to play this game." And that's one of the things that he instilled in us. This is the greatest game on earth, and it really is. But he said, "You have this great talent and you should get down on your knees and thank God every day because you are able to exhibit this and you are able to do this." And he says, "These poor kids, they idolize you and I want all of you to go over there and shake their hands, give them a hug as you leave practice." And we did. And I'll tell you it's a humbling experience. I think that put a lot of character in some of the players, because we realized how lucky we really are to do this.

GEORGE BLAIR, DEFENSIVE BACK, KICKER

College: Mississippi
Years with the Chargers: 1961-1964

George Blair was drafted out of Mississippi as a defensive back, but also developed into a fine place kicker. He led the Chargers in scoring in 1961, '62 and '63, and pulled down five interceptions during his career as a cornerback.

We had some great coaches and some great teammates. We didn't get paid very much, but friendships, we've come through playing together like we did with the early Chargers, that's invaluable. Again, we didn't make a lot of money, but the friendships and playing with the great group that we had, was priceless...

I enjoyed playing in Balboa because of the fans. We had some great fans. We had a full house every game and, like you said, they were close. Of course, we would have played anywhere, but I enjoyed playing in Balboa. It's been a long time since I played there. It was a small stadium with crowd noise. We had great backing then and they did make a lot of racket and noise, but I enjoyed it...

We just had a great relationship, everybody. I think that came not only from Sid, but from the players. We'd joke with each other and call each other names and laugh. We just got along, more so than... Sid, they say Sid had a lot to do about that, but I just think it was the guys that came through there. They were all just good guys. They played a lot with each other and got mad at each other and the next day we forgot it. I think it was just a great group of guys.

Bud Whitehead and I were talking today about it. Sid, you know he was strictly offense and we'd go peel and deal on offense and defense and he'd be over with the passing game and we'd be over trying to cover these receivers, which were great. I think that's what made our defense so good, is trying to cover them. Every once in a while Sid would see one of us

defensive backs and he called us peekers. He'd come over and cuss us and get onto us about peeking. So we'd go up to Oakland and play Al Davis up there and I don't know, but the week before we may have gotten beat a couple times [in practice]. But anyway we were in the dressing room and the defensive people always got in the way back and the offense always got near the door. So we were back in the back with Chuck Noll having a little meeting before the ball game and I look up and see here comes Sid walking towards us and I said, "Oh Hell, he don't ever come back here unless something's wrong." But he came back there and said, "You damn defensive backs. If one guy gets behind you guys, you all will be gone by Monday." We went and played the game and went into our team meetings and Chuck Noll starts zapping the film and starts looking and says, "Hell, where's our defensive backs?" We were so far back that we weren't even in the film. But that was one of the funniest road trips that we've had. He laid the law on us and scared us to death. We were rookies and, man, we were so far back we weren't even in the film...

I've been very fortunate in that I've played on some good college programs at Ole Miss and had some great coaches and came out here and played under a great staff and great bunch of teammates. To me it's priceless. Like I said a while ago, we didn't get paid much, but the memories and experience we had is priceless. We had a great football team in '63. We get together and talk and we feel like we could have played with anybody. I'm just very fortunate that I was a part of it. Real happy.

Earl Faison, Defensive End

College: Indiana
Years with the Chargers: 1961-1966

By signing Earl Faison the Chargers got arguably the most dominant pass rusher the AFL had ever seen. He was an all-league selection in four of his six years in San Diego, and was selected to play in the all-star games from 1961-1967. As a member of the original "Fearsome Foursome," Faison also pulled down six interceptions in his six-year career that was cut short by back injuries.

I was drafted by the Chargers number one and I was drafted by the Detroit Lions number three. In the process there was the fact that the Canadian team wanted me. But I wanted to play in the AFL because they were then the Los Angeles Chargers. So my last game, which was against Purdue, I was flown the next day to Los Angeles and got to meet with a lot of the people from the Chargers – the Hiltons, Al Davis, Klosterman, a bunch of the executives. We cut a deal…

As far as my going to the Los Angeles team, Los Angeles Chargers, it was my thinking that that's where we would play. When I came back and as the year progresses, I read in the newspaper that the team was moving to San Diego. My first reaction was "San Diego? Where the Hell is San Diego?" Somebody said, "Close to Mexico." And I had never seen it, never heard of the place, or anything. So I wondered about it, but when I came out here it was love at first sight…

I remember one game in particular, my first year. I was sitting on the bench and I looked across the track behind me into the stands and I see Charlie McNeil sitting in the stands. So I knew I had seen Charlie McNeil in the locker room prior to the game. We dressed close to each other. And I ran over to Ernie Ladd and I told him, "Ladd, the goddamn Sid has cut Charlie, he cut Charlie. He cut him before the game." And he said, "No, no, Charlie's down there." And I said, "Look behind me, look over there." And he looked in the stands and there was Charlie McNeil, or so we thought was Charlie McNeil. Then we ran over to the defensive coach. "Coach. Charlie is in the stands. Charlie is in the stands." The coach looked at us and said, "No. Charlie's standing right over there." Charlie had a twin brother and we didn't know. Looked just like him, the spitting image. But we were that close to the fans and we thought something drastic had happened to Charlie and we raised Hell there.

But the fans were absolutely tremendous in the acceptance of the team at that time. The city just opened for us. It was a good marriage, right from the very start. And we did things for the city, as players, that the players now expect to be paid for, like public appearances and things like that. We thought it was an honor that somebody asked you to come speak at a school assembly. We didn't anticipate any type of payment; we looked forward to it. But to answer your question, it was just great. It was a tremendous thing to play at Balboa Stadium. Even though the airplanes would come over…

I was a rookie and came to San Diego to play and Paul Maguire was the first guy that really made me feel accepted on the team. I wasn't a drinker or anything and I went to this nightclub with some of the guys. Now I guess they had already come in, but they were seated at one end of the bar, some of the players and Paul Maguire. I was a rookie and I was seated on the other end of the bar. He came over and got me and said, "Hey come over here with us. You're part of our team." That made me feel real good…

And Ernie Ladd, he was just his own man. God, the man had a tremendous… Little Sampson, we never called him that. But he had a wonderful working relationship with Sid Gillman. I think Sid feared him. We were up in Denver playing at one game and this was a negotiation year for Ladd and myself and we hadn't signed a contract. So we changed up for the game, went out for pregame warm up. And we came back. The defensive team got together, offensive team got together. Everybody looked around, "Where's Ernie Ladd?" He was gone. Come to find out, we played the first half without him. He had gone across the street to a bar and watched the game on the TV screen and came back at half time. "You need me now don't you? You know you need me. You need the big fellow all the time. You tell me that you don't need me, I saw what you were doing." And he was over there drinking in his football pads and helmet, everything. Across the street at the local bar. He'd do that all the time.

He and I were roommates. He used to tell me, "Hey roomie. Watch me piss Sid off. I'm gonna piss Sid off." He'd get on the phone, "Hey Sid, I'm thinking I'm not gonna play in the game tomorrow." "What's wrong? What's wrong?" "I don't want to, I think I need some shrimp down here. I'm hungry." Any kind of reason. Everything would be forthcoming. He'd send it right on down to him…

I remember when Speedy Duncan came into the league. As a rookie he used to think he was tough. He used to run back kickoffs with his head up. "I gotta see, I gotta see." You know how Speedy used to talk real fast. "I gotta see where I'm going, I gotta see where I'm going." We'd tell him, Ernie and I pulled him aside one game. "Hey, keep your head tucked in when you're going through a pile. Otherwise somebody's gonna stick their arm out and cold-cock you." "No, no. They can't catch me." Sure enough, he was running a kick off back one game and he's got his head on a pivot. Somebody stuck an arm out and caught him. He came back, his jaw was broken, his face bones were broken. He told us, "I should have listened." Through his wire that they had put in his mouth after the ball game. Ended up drinking out of a straw for two weeks. Milkshakes.

You remember when Lance Alworth, we were up in Rough Acres. No, we were in Escondido at the training camp there. The season had gotten started, about two weeks into the season and we had been working out pretty good. You know how hot it gets up there. So Sid gives us one Wednesday off, he cuts out practice. And we go out to one of the little bars and sit around and drink some beer and everyone's feeling pretty good with a 10:00 curfew. We come back to the dorms and were walking around outside the dorms, waiting to go in the hotel where we were staying. Lance comes out, he's a little toasty and Don Norton comes out of another car. So Lance has found a rattlesnake somewhere on the highway. So he gets out of the car and Don gets out of the other car and Lance just hurls the rattlesnake and it wraps around Don's neck. Don looks back, "OOOOOOOH!!!" Nothing happened, but I swear to God it was comical to see a guy sober up instantly with a six-foot rattlesnake wrapped around his neck...

Bob Petrich, he's another crazy guy... As football players, with the Chargers, he and I were on our way to Houston and we sat next to each other on the airplane. We hit such bad air turbulence; we were bouncing, bouncing for what seemed like over an hour. I don't think it was really that long, but it seemed like it. But then all of a sudden we're bouncing, bouncing and bouncing and the plane just dropped off to the right. It just kept going down. It didn't seem like it would ever come up. The stewardess and everybody that were walking along in the aisles, they were thrown up to the roof and landing all over everything. But when it finally straightened out, fortunately it did straighten out, Bob and I found ourselves wrapped up in each other's arms. Digging into each other. And when it leveled off, we didn't realize that we were like this, and we turned and looked into each other's faces and said, "Oh man, get away from me." But I'm sure that everybody else was doing the same thing...

Jimmy Warren, Illinois. Jimmy and I, his rookie year and I think I was a year ahead of him. We were in New York, and this is true. We were in New York, we had just gotten in and we were into our hotel, the Hilton Hotel. I look out my window and I'm looking up at this gigantic building and there are clouds around the top of it. I exclaimed, "My God. That's the tallest building I've ever seen in my life." And Jim come over looks out and matter-of-factly says, "Hey man that's the entire state building." I said, "What did you say?" "That's the entire state building." "You mean the empire state building." "Yeah, well whatever..."

Alvin Roy, "Earl you are the strongest man in football. You're going to be the strongest man in the world. You're stronger than the Russians." And that's what he used to think. He's the one that got us on steroids. We were the original team to use steroids until we found out that they weren't good for us. Mix, somehow Mix found out from a doctor that steroids would hurt your chances of producing children. When we heard that, we just stopped it. Wouldn't take it...

Boston Patriots. This game here was a masterful game plan by Coach Gillman. I mean we had just beaten this team 7-6 in the season and then to come back and beat them 51-10 in a tremendous achievement. They had a very good team, but Sid put together a beautiful offensive plan. Deception, a lot of veers and swings to take advantage of their pursuit patterns and there was holes all over the field for the runners...

Dick Wood. I remember when the Chargers traded him to the New York Jets. He came back to play a game against us in Balboa Stadium. He dropped back to pass and I started after him. He let the ball go, I jumped up, caught it, started down the field and somehow he got between me and the goal line. He was going to tackle me. I said now, "Do I want a touchdown or do I want to run over a quarterback?" So I started right for him. I headed right for him. He turned and ran. He turned away from me. Smarter than I thought he was. But he played a long time, so he was very smart.

Jack Kemp, our congressman. He and I used to argue on the planes, talking politics. He was a Goldwater man, back in those days. John Birch. One day I received a package at home, a bunch of stuff advocating John Birch Society. I thought that it had to come from Kemp. So whenever we practiced, or whenever we played against each other, I delighted in trying to hit him. I mean we would argue, he, myself and Dave Kocourek. We'd get off the plane at some stop, go to the restroom and be standing next to each other and we were still arguing politics. As fate would have it, back in '63, I replaced Kemp at *The Evening Tribune*. He was doing the PR work prior to my doing it, and I replaced him there. Those are good memories.

One of the things that I am most proud of the Chargers is that we were at the forefront of Civil Rights, the Chargers were. And I think it stemmed from the fact that Barron Hilton owned hotels. The Chargers used to stay at those Hilton Hotels and we were the first blacks to ever stay in many of them in the South.

I remember there were Civil Rights pickets in front of our game in Houston at old Jeppesen Stadium. Lloyd Wells used to be a photographer for the Kansas City Chiefs and then turned photographer for Muhammad Ali. Well, somehow he was a newspaper reporter with a black newspaper in Houston. He would come around to us and ask us not to play the games because the blacks weren't allowed in the middle of the stadium; they had to sit in the end zones. So we protested some of those games and didn't play a couple of them. Well we played, but we let it be known that we didn't like it. So eventually they started giving open admittance to blacks.

Little Rock, Arkansas, Dallas, Texas, we went into certain movies that we would go to Saturday night before a ball game. In Dallas there was one theater there that we went into. We had the whole mezzanine to ourselves; we were seated up in the mezzanine. And during the course of the movie, we kept hearing laughter behind us. We didn't know what was going on. And the lights came on and there were black people seated up in the very top of the theater behind chicken wire. Naturally we had to leave. They wouldn't allow us to go down to the lobby to get popcorn and drinks, so we walked out of the theater.

But the Chargers, at that time, integrated a lot of places, and helped the South along. Because a lot of the other teams, Boston Patriots, and all of those other teams that were coming down there, if they went to Houston, Texas, to play the Oilers, whites lived in a hotel and the black guys lived someplace else, separately. Except for the Chargers. All those places, we'd open them up. Players and management, they would support us. We would go to them and let them know that we didn't like what was going on and they supported our cause. If you were thinking about boycotting the game, I mean there were games in Atlanta, Georgia where we decided that we were not going to play and the mayors and everybody else came in to try to talk us into playing the game. Convince us to play the game. We let it be known that it took more than that. That never made the newspaper, those types of things. Never made the newspaper for some reason.

LUTHER HAYES, SPLIT END

College: Southern California
Years with the Chargers: 1961

Luther Hayes only played one year for the Chargers, but it happened to be the Chargers' first year in Luther's hometown of San Diego. Hayes was a football and track star who had gone to USC after graduating from Lincoln High School in San Diego. Hayes was productive during his year with the Chargers, averaging 20 yards per reception and scoring three touchdowns.

Al Davis was the backs position coach at USC. He went with the Chargers in 1960. I came out of college in '61; my last season was '60. In '61 I played with the Chargers. Al was the man and I had the most contact with. Naturally I got introduced to Sid. He had quite a coaching staff at the time. That's who I dealt with, mostly...

Playing professional football, I don't know about now, it was so much different from playing college football. And it was so much better than playing college football. Regardless of what people say, trying to go to school... I'm going to give you a typical day at USC, for me. And then I will give you a typical day at the Chargers. You can make the comparisons.

During the season I would get up, I had to go to 8:00 class. You couldn't take class later because you had to practice. So, 8:00, 9, 10, 11, you had class. You go to lunch and at 1:00 you had to go to the whirlpool in the athletic facilities to make sure if you had injuries or whatever. And then we had a chalk talk from 2:00 to 3:00, supposedly. We would leave at about 2:15, 2:30, and go out on the field and have unsupervised practice because of rules that you couldn't practice at the time, more than two hours with a coach. So our coach would have a chalk talk, send us through our warm up exercise. This was all before we were supposed to be on the field. Now by the time the rest of the squad comes out, or other parts of the squad come out, everybody would have been out there two hours, which would have violated the rules at the time. But, that's the way they did it. Not just at USC, but UCLA, everybody was doing the same thing. They were all playing the game. But then after you got through with that, it is 5:00 or 5:30. You get through your shower at 6:00, 6:30; you gotta go to the training table to eat. So that's from 6:00 to 7:00. You may get out of there at about 7:30 or 8:00. So at 7:30 you're there and you have to go back and start studying, whereas your classmates have had all afternoon off to study. We left class at 12:00, and they had from 12:00 to 8:00 before you get in. They had eight hours more to study than you did. And then at the time, the reflection was, "Well, you're not very bright. Look at those athletes getting those bad grades." A lot of times we practiced so hard, that you were sore. You were getting beat up in practice worse than you would get beat up in games. By the time you got through the stiffness and the pain, and then on Friday nights we played, home or away, we spent the night together at hotels, which was very nice. It was very nice. It gave me exposure. Being a poor kind, it gave me exposure to first class living. So it had both it's good and it's bad.

And the good part was that we all wore blue blazers with the SC emblem on it. We stayed at the best hotels. This is '61.

This is before the civil rights movement really takes off. So it was unusual. SC had to make arrangements with people so that there was no embarrassment or bad feelings. We had integrated rooms. That sounds so stupid to say integrated rooms, but before that it wasn't integrated. So you're teammate may be a white young man or maybe a black. It didn't matter, because they were integrated so you may wind up with whatever. That was different...

When I went to the Chargers, we'd get up and we'd be on the practice field at 10:00, maybe. A chalk talk. That's when you'd go over the plays and what you want to do. The defense is all set, depending on what unit you are with. Now that you're there, you have practice for an hour and 45 minutes. They didn't try to kill you, because they needed you for Sunday. They didn't try to beat you to death, or establish and re-establish if you were the starter. They weren't going to get you injured in practice. And we played better football with the Chargers than with SC, just from the players perspective, because we weren't hurt and in pain. Not that you never got hurt in the game, sure enough. But you didn't pick up injuries in practice, and that was the difference. And then they paid you. We got paid every week. I was getting $500 a week, like I just told you, the teachers were getting $500 a month. So I'm getting $500 a week, I'm getting paid, I'm working out, we'll stretch it and say 10:00 to 2:00, and then I'm through. That's a four-hour day, a four-hour day. And coming from almost a 12-hour day at college, I'm going, "Wow."

And the respect and adulation that you get from the fans and storekeepers, it is just unmatched. They had a Charger discount. They just created a Charger discount. They were glad. That was the first year the Chargers were in San Diego. The year before they had been in L.A., and they were glad to have them. So the merchants were very accommodating, very nice. As a poor kid, when I needed a discount, that's when I didn't have any money. Now I had money, I didn't need a discount. Life just happens to be that way. It was very nice. That was an experience that will always be in my mind. I wish that I would have been able to write and express what I saw and the experiences that I was going through at the time that I was going through them. People have written about them since, and so there is not the need for it now. That was the comparison.

My fondest memories are that we played the Houston Oilers for the championship, and at the time the Chargers had a winning streak on the '61 team that exceeded anyone else's in the history of pro football. It was broken by Miami, but before that we had won about 11 or 12 games straight. When we came out of the blocks, we were off to a flying start. But we lost the AFL championship to Houston. It was played in Balboa Stadium. Balboa Stadium, I had played there when I went to San Diego High School. So that was familiar. And it was nice to be around. One nice thing, my mother would get on the bus... My mother would get on the bus to go and come to work, and she was so proud because they would be talking about myself and other players. She would almost just burst out and say, "That's my son! That's my son!" She felt so proud about it...

It was a nice experience. I thank God for it. I am happy I am able to walk and everything. In one hand it was too short, but on the other side of it I am retired and I am able to get around on my own power. And I think I appreciate that more than anything.

BILL HUDSON, DEFENSIVE TACKLE

College: Clemson
Years with the Chargers: 1961, 1962

Bill Hudson was one of five brothers to receive football scholarships to Clemson. After college he was drafted by the Chicago Cardinals of the NFL in 1957, but signed instead with the Montreal Alouettes of the Canadian Football League. He came to the Chargers in 1961 and was named defensive captain for his two years with the team. In 1961 Hudson got the opportunity to play against his brother, Bob, who was a defensive back with the Denver Broncos.

I was drafted by the Chicago Cardinals in the second round. That's how old I am, back when the Cardinals were in Chicago. Their final offer was $7,000 and my college coach's best friend was coaching in Canada, P. Ed Walker, so I went to Canada for twice the money. Then they started the American League in 1960. Al Davis called and after my fourth year I found out that I had made the All-Pro team on offense and defense in the same year, and he called and found out that I was unhappy with the new coach we'd had the last year. So it just worked out. They were in L.A. and I went to camp and signed with them and it looked good at the time. I wasn't crazy about L.A.

When they moved to San Diego, that was great. I moved to San Diego immediately and went to work with Coca-Cola in the off-season. I just started playing. We had a pretty good football team. I think we broke the pass interception record in the pros. It stood for over 30 years. We had the biggest line in the history of professional football at that time, with Ernie Ladd and myself and Faison and Nery. So it was a good experience. I enjoyed it and got to be good friends with them, and thought the world of Sid Gillman and of course, Al Davis. I ended up being a part-time scout. I went with him when he was appointed commissioner of the league. I was one of six that went in the league office with him. Then they merged the leagues, as you know, about six months later. So we all got fired. I ended up as an area scout, a part-time weekend scout for Al for 17 years. Living in the South, here. And then started a business.

I had no problem with him (Sid Gillman). I felt that probably the only thing I could say is I had a problem negotiating with him on contracts. In those days we didn't have lawyers or agents negotiating for us. So I was negotiating and then go out and play for him. It made you have a little different attitude because he was a pretty good negotiator in contracts. But when Al went to Oakland I wanted to go up with Al Davis to Oakland and in those days, it was pretty well known that if you told Sid

that you weren't going to sign a contract, you were going to play out your option, he would trade you. He would trade you or cut you. I was hoping that he would cut me because I already had a deal worked out with Al Davis, and he surprised me. He traded me to the New England Patriots with the stipulation that they couldn't trade me to Oakland. So I ended up going out there one year and then frankly, I'd gotten tired. In the Canadian League I was playing both ways, 60 minutes a game, 25 games a year. I was getting pretty well tired of training camps and wear and tear on the body was pretty much when you were playing that much football. So I decided to give it up. And that's when I started scouting for Al Davis...

People think... In fact, Chuck Noll did an interview with *Sports Illustrated* a couple of years ago and he was asked if that line he had at Pittsburgh was the best defensive line he'd ever had. He said, "No. The best line I ever had was the original Fearsome Foursome in San Diego." He did an article in *Sports Illustrated* and mentioned that. We had a good line...

Well, of course Ladd's potential was as good as I had ever seen at that point. 6'9", 360, those days we understated our weight. Nowadays they put it higher. But Ladd was a tight guy, strong as a bull. If a fight broke out, you made sure you got out of the way because he was swinging and he'd hit anything in sight. But he was a good player, good speed. We used to get out and have a little fun on Saturday before games. We'd have a foot race between Ladd and our fullback, Charlie Flowers. Ladd could beat him most of the time in a foot race. As big as he was... Of course Earl Faison was probably one of the best 10-yard people that you have ever seen. That meant get up the field. We had an unusually good pass-rushing team. That's why, I guess, we were successful. We had very little blitzing of the linebackers. That's why we broke the pass interception record. It stood for so long because we put so much pressure on the passers and we had enough people in the backfield to catch them, I guess. Anyway, Nery was just a good, basic, sound player. I had just heard that he had died. We had a good group of guys. We used to work out a little bit.

You know Lance Alworth. John Hadl and Lance was there in my second year there. Jack Kemp and I were team captains in '61 and '62. Charlie Flowers and I were out working out before the camp started at the college, and Charlie and I were watching Hadl throw the ball to Lance. The kid could leap. I don't know if you have had the opportunity to see films on him, but his leaping ability was unbelievable and he'd catch the football. It looked like a deer running. And I made a comment to Charlie, I said, "He looks like a deer running, doesn't he?" And Charlie said, "Yeah, let's call him Bambi." And that's kind of why he got started with the Bambi nickname. But he was quite a player and Hadl and I got to be good friends. John was a good man. We had a good team right there. We should have won the whole thing a couple times, but a few things happened that didn't let us do it.

ERNIE LADD, DEFENSIVE TACKLE
College: Grambling
Years with the Chargers: 1961-1965

One of the biggest names (and men) in the American Football League was Ernie "Giant Cat" Ladd. A dominant defensive tackle, Ladd teamed with Earl Faison, Ron Nery and Bill Hudson to form the original "Fearsome Foursome." During the off-season, Ernie Ladd toured on the professional wrestling circuit, which he continued with long after his football career ended. As a wrestler, Ladd was particularly known for his longtime "feud" with fellow wrestler, Andre the Giant.

I came up from Grambling to see the championship game and the next thing I know I am confronted with coaches that I have never seen before, that I know nothing about. And a trip to go out to California. Really, in a sense, it was almost like a kidnapping. They got me on the plane, and the plane took off before I had even agreed to go. The next thing I know they had Brad Brockenberry. Two black guys, who were drawn in, tricked into the Chargers. A very good friend of mine, he passed away. Brockenberry and Brad Pye, who later became a very good friend, very close, and is still close to this day. These were the brothers. Because everything was still segregated in the South and they really had to have someone to smooth everything over for them. Pye and Brockenberry were two strong black men.

I wasn't really concerned about the league being new because one of them had suggested a no-cut contract. You have to remember, in 1960, Johnny Unitas was the highest paid football player in the world at $15,000. And a schoolteacher was making like $3,400-$3,700 a year in the state of Louisiana. If you signed a contract for $10,000 or more, you tripled what a schoolteacher was making during that time...

My relationship with Sid Gillman was good and bad. He was a bad negotiator. I didn't like a lot of years that he was a bad negotiator. He should have been our coach and not general manager. He had the best team in football and broke it up. I considered this a lot of years, because I didn't understand it in early years. You don't break up a team of Earl Faison and Ernie Ladd. We were the first Fearsome Foursome in football. We were the best pass rushers in all of football, Earl Faison and Ernie Ladd. The best pass rushers in all of football, NFL. Earl Faison was the number one player picked in the draft in 1961. You let guys like that season, get about 8-10 years out of them. And Sid, with his foolishness, and I said foolishness, not knowing how to handle men...

I look back at the Rams and other places. He had a brilliant mind for coaching offense, but he had no understanding and no concept of people staying together. I look back and all of what happened is a reflection of young, great owners like Barron Hilton and Lamar Hunt. People like that, who gave coaches an opportunity to do what they wanted to do. Sid was a brilliant coach, but he knew zero about men and kinds of personalities. You couldn't deal with me in any kind of way because I would rebel. You had to shoot straight at me. I didn't care about getting put out of football. I admired a girl, my wife. She told me that if you get put out of football, you become a schoolteacher and we can both work and make a living. That was one of the worst things my wife could have ever done. That made me stand up to everything I didn't like. I stood up to it or I walked out on it...

Well, there's not really much to tell about Chuck (Noll), except that Chuck is the greatest line coach I have ever seen or ever known. You can't add a lot to that. Chuck Noll was the best line coach, but Chuck Noll had some psychology too. I was kind of a simple guy from a small school. I worked hard. I would work hard in practice and I would work hard before the season would start. Chuck wanted to stop me from using my forearm, and I thought the forearm was the best weapon in football. But I was wrong. Chuck Noll told me the club was the best move in football, and a hop-around. Chuck had to trick me to get me to change my style. Chuck said, "If you deal with it for two weeks, just don't use your forearm at all, let me teach you one move. Use it for two weeks. If you don't like it, then go back to the forearm." Well, I wasn't too eager to go to something that Chuck wanted me to go to, but I respected him enough to do what he told me. So I worked at it for two weeks, and the first week I didn't like it at all. But I kept working at it. It came in the middle of the second week, and it was the best move that ever happened to me. Best move that ever happened to me. Chuck had a way of reaching out and touching his players. If you brought something to the table, Chuck would develop it for you.

My actual height was 6' 9", when I was measured as a young man. I was a bonafide 300-pounder that looked like he weighed about 250. I played one year at 330. I trained to get down to 280 one time and Sid Gillman called me and told me, "Man, you're too light. They're gonna blow you off the line, big fella. It just ain't gonna work." I stepped on the scale and weighed 281, he said, "Goddamn, get out of here." I stepped on the scale and weighed 281, I was like 35, 36 in the waist.

I got something really special that you got to put in this piece. He (Sid Gillman) put Earl Faison on the weight table. I could eat anything I want. Earl Faison was a fat man. They had to put Earl Faison on the fat man's table. And he loved apple pie. And I would get him an apple pie every time they had apple pie. I'd sneak it to him under the table when he was not supposed to eat it. Boy, he'd have pie going everywhere. Then I would squeal on him. I'd set him up with the apple pie. Earl and I were roommates the whole time we played together. We're still close friends.

Earl was the greatest defensive lineman that I ever saw as a rookie. Because I never saw myself, either. He had more moves and skills that anybody I ever saw as a lineman. The only problem was, I don't think they developed his skills to the max that he could have played at, or to his potential. Even as brilliant a coach as Chuck Noll was. I guess Earl and I probably... You gotta remember this was during segregated years. And I came from the Deep South and I might have brought a little bit of attitude with me too. And Chuck had to work with that. I thought it made Chuck a very brilliant man. He took all the licks that Sid and other coaches didn't take, from his two devastating black forces. He had to be a psychologist as well as a great coach.

And when I look back on the years and I reflected, he was both. He was brilliant.

Rough Acres Ranch was a great, great training place. It was hot and you were isolated. It had a lot of rattlesnakes out there. That was the only problem that you had. We'd practice twice a day at Rough Acres. Get up in the morning... I rode up with Earl. Charlie McNeil, Ernie Ladd and Earl Faison in his (Charlie's) Volkswagen to Rough Acres. I thought it was a great training facility. Sid was very unique in certain things and certain things I think he was terrible at. That was one of the unique things about him, taking us to a great area. Sid said, "We'll feed you good, keep you in good facilities. We give you first class food, first class facilities and we expect a first class performance on Sunday." And we gave it to him. He kept us in great facilities and we gave him a great, first class performance on Sunday...

Ron Mix was a very close friend of mine. Bob Petrich, Earl (Faison), Paul (Lowe), Ernie (Wright), Dick Westmoreland. The Chargers were a very unique team. Everybody had relations on the Chargers. It wasn't a black and white issue with the Chargers. You were a football player and you had relations because we broke that foolishness up before it got off the ground. If somebody said something wrong, one of the black guys would come tell me and I would (put an end to it). There wasn't going to be no foolishness. We had a team that we thought was a good team, and we respected one another. The great thing the Chargers did as teammates, we had parties together, with the wives. We all came together, and we did everything together. You'd have your isolated parties, black and white, periodically, but it was no thing. And we had a guy that understood relations real good, named Bob Burdick. Bob Burdick understood relations among blacks and whites in the '60s and he was a great guy for that.

KEITH LINCOLN, RUNNING BACK
College: Washington State
Years with the Chargers: 1961-1966, 1968

Keith Lincoln came to the Chargers from Washington State University. An incredibly gifted athlete, the Chargers tried him out at several positions before settling him in at fullback. Lincoln was a star for many years in the AFL, but his best day came in the 1963 AFL Championship game against the Boston Patriots when he rushed for 206 yards and one touchdown, had seven receptions for 123 yards and one touchdown and threw a 20-yard pass. In all he accounted for 349 yards of total offense and two touchdowns.

Well, back then I got drafted by both leagues. I was drafted by the Bears and by San Diego and by a Canadian team. Then it was just a matter of negotiating where you wanted to go. An interesting thing, a sidelight was that I got a telegram from Vince Lombardi telling me that they would take me number one if I agreed to play defensive back. Of course when I played here (at Washington) I think my junior year, I averaged something like 58.5 or 59 minutes a game. I just never left the field. But Vince wanted me to be a defensive back. So I went through that. And, Jeez, what's the scout's name? He became

a GM (Don Klosterman). Anyway, he was the lead scout that had contacts with me for San Diego.

I certainly knew that the AFL was only two years old at that time. There were a couple of things that were key, and at the end of it you get down to money. Then, of course, the AFL was signing guys for double what all-pro guys were making in the NFL. So it was attractive financially. I think Sid Gillman was a big key for me. You're knowing that he was a well-respected coach. And we didn't know it at that time, but he had an awfully good staff with him also. But I think the key for me was that I wasn't anxious to go play in the cold, being a West Coast guy… and the financial part of it. My feeling was that you have got to have confidence in yourself. If I sign and do the thing with the Chargers and they disband the league, then I will go play in the other league…

I probably could have held out, but I didn't do that. There were five or six of us that went back to the college all-star game on that team. Were you aware of that? And then I got a little bit more money out of them because when I signed with them they were in Los Angeles and changed the franchise to San Diego. When I was drafted, it was the L.A. Chargers and then after I signed and Faison, all of us had signed, they moved the franchise to San Diego. So then I went back to them and said I need more money if I am going to play in San Diego. Just another avenue. Goddamn 20-year old kid, don't know what in the Hell I am doing, but I thought I might get a couple more bucks and I did…

[Rough Acres] was quite an experience. It was out in the middle of nowhere. The timing on it was probably good for Sid to take us out there. As far as not having distractions and doing this type thing, it was sure as heck a location for being geographically isolated out there. And with the weather and stuff you could really get the social fat off people, if that's what you had to do. You could get people in shape. I think you basically had full attention of all the players that were there as it was very Spartan. And the field was a mess, to be honest with you. They were mixing in sawdust and whatever, trying to make a practice field out of the thing. It was a thing, I think, where once again I talk about family and team unity and that. And I think it really strengthened that once again. And of course, you've got the full attention. There's no distractions. From those standpoints, we had everything there that we needed. Like I said, the field wasn't the best field, or this type thing, but God, it worked. In retrospect it was pretty positive…

Tobin Rote was like a coach on the field. It was like having Sid Gillman out there. He really had that… He was a wily old veteran. He had the experience, he could read defenses, he had all those things going. He had good leadership skills. But was he past his prime? Yes. Because at one point in his career, Tobin was an awfully good runner. He maybe ran for as much

yardage, or more yardage than any quarterback for a couple years in the NFL. But that skill was beyond him and his arm wasn't as strong. But what he did with that, mentally, he could read a defense and he'd put a little more air under the ball. He'd let Alworth or someone run underneath it, or he'd get rid of it a little bit quicker. But I think it was Tobin's command and sense of the game plan and what we're trying to do. What Sid wanted to implement, going against tendencies, anticipating what might be there, he had a huge advantage in that. But no, other than that, you might go out there and run a pattern and the ball might not be there as quickly as you wanted, but most times Tobin would adjust and he'd throw it earlier than most quarterbacks or something like that. Put a little more air under it. But no, we didn't make any major adjustments for him…

Well, my roommate Lance Alworth was a heck of an athlete. He just had that given talent, the eye-hand coordination, the leaping ability, the whole thing. The speed, acceleration, he was gifted. Earl Faison was, when healthy, a heck of an athlete. The guy that might at some point have been a little bit under appreciated, and I thought was a football player that any team would be lucky to have on their roster, was Gary Garrison. I think he got over shadowed sometimes, but was there. Ron Mix, in our era, a self-made football player. A guy that really hit the weights and did the things he had to do to reach and maintain a body weight to be competitive, was very impressive…

If you step back and look, it is almost mind-boggling if you look at the collection of assistant coaches that went through there. That says something. It was light years ahead. Hell, they talk about the West Coast Offense. Hell, Sid started the West Coast Offense. There's no question in my mind about that. Look at what they're doing today and what they're trying to do. Sid was a trailblazer on that. Not Bill Walsh or somebody like that, it was Sid. Coryell came along and followed it and of course Coryell was out at our practices all the time taking notes and watching. That's how he grew with his philosophy. I think it was that. It was a well-run, well-managed team. Better than anyplace. …. I respect that. I think that whatever you do in life, if you're going to be successful, you better have some discipline and organization to what you want to do.

JERRY MAGEE

Jerry Magee never played football for the Chargers. But as the San Diego Union *beat reporter covering the team, he breathed, ate and lived San Diego Chargers' football. He covered the Chargers for 25 years, from 1961 through the 1986 season*

To me, the community was languishing in a sports sense, in the doldrums that had set in after World War II. It was just looking for a catalyst, something to lift up the people, something the people could rally around. The Chargers became the catalyst. I got here in 1956 and I think the big sports event in town was the Hoover-San Diego High football game. We had the Padres in the Coast League. We had some military sports that didn't really amount to all that much. Marine Corps Recruit Depot had a good football team, but they were just playing the Orange County Rhinos and other semi-pro teams. Well, we had the Del Mar Racetrack, we had the Caliente Racetrack, we had a golf event. There was a golf event in Tijuana then, too, a PGA event. There was very little, certainly no major sports here then in 1956. It was just a sleep, little, old... It was viewed anyhow as kind of a sleepy old navy town. And I think the Chargers changed that. They gave the citizenry something to rally around...

I tried to be objective. I don't know that I ever tried, in effect, to promote the team. I'm sure though, that consciously or subconsciously I tried to promote the league. You know, when you're around an event, even on the periphery as a newspaper guy... What the AFL was doing almost seemed like a crusade. They were tilting against the mighty giant that was the NFL. I guess that I have always been a guy that supported the underdog. But at least I hope I didn't try to promote the team to fiercely. I'm sure there were some who felt I wasn't promoting it at all. I remember in the early '60s if they didn't play well, at least I tried to be critical. All these professionals in this day and era of television, I kind of think that what the newspaper should do is provide sort of a review of what has happened. Otherwise you can't say whether they were good or bad. That was just my idea of journalism. It still is, as a matter of fact. I don't remember, anyhow, trying to promote them. I wanted them to do well.

I was very close to many of those people, to Sid and all those people. But I hope it didn't show too much in my copy. Sid used to get really mad at me. Oh, Hell yeah. I had a very difficult association with him. Times we were up in training camp. I'd write something he didn't like; he'd take all the newspapers and throw them away before the players could read them. We had kind of an antagonistic relationship many, many times. But when it was over, the good thing about it was that he realized what I was trying to do and I certainly realized what he was trying to do. We were probably closer after he was through than we were when he was working. I appreciated how good he was at what he did, and the effort he put into it...

I can't help but think of that 1963 Chargers championship team and the team that won the NFL championship that year, the Bears. This was pre-Gale Sayers remember. They didn't have Gale Sayers. They had Billy Wade as their quarterback. Their best running back was Ronnie Bull, who in my thinking in no way compared to either Keith Lincoln or Paul Lowe. They'd run rings around Ronnie Bull. He was a pretty average back. The Bears did have some good defensive players, some good defenses. But so did the Chargers. I think to this day that if the Chargers played them, that the Chargers' would beat them. They didn't have anybody like Lance Alworth. Who did? So I think that was one point that you might pick. I'm not saying that the AFL from top to bottom was equal to the NFL, but for one game between those two teams, I think the Chargers would have done real well. I think they would have beat them pretty easy. Maybe not easy, but they had good talent. The best teams in the AFL had damn good talent.

The teams that did go out and fight for the players, the Chiefs, and the Houston Oilers and the Chargers and the Bills. There were teams in the early part of the AFL that didn't have all that great of talent. The Raiders being the leading example. And the Patriots. Hell, the Patriots got along with a lot of guys from Bates. They were playing Maine and Boston College. They still did pretty well. Then the New York Titans were a joke until Sonny Werblin bought them and went out and signed Namath. That was a really big event in the history of the league, Namath signing with the Jets. Because it gave the league a greater core in New York, where every league has to have a strong center.

[The Chargers' coaching staff] seemed impressive, but I don't think you can judge a matter like that until there's a passing of the years. Until these people have had time to establish what they could do. And look at what they could do. Noll won four Super Bowls with the Pittsburgh Steelers. He's gotta be considered one of the leading NFL coaches of all time. He didn't lose any. Davis has had a profound influence on pro football, as profound probably as any man you could name. He became commissioner of the league. He had a great bearing on the AFL-NFL merger. And Sid's in the Hall of Fame. He's one of the leading maestro's of the passing game that football is now. But when they first came here, I don't think we could have known that, that they were gonna be that good. A lot of people said that Noll had left football too early; that he could still be playing. And Al Davis was not a big figure then. He had been a coach at USC. He was still a very young guy. He didn't have any great image then. Joe Madro was a good coach, the guy that followed Sid all through his life. Great little guy, he was. When he was up in Oakland in his declining years he used to come down and spend the day with me. I think he was just lonely. He was a real good coach. He and Sid got along together fine. You know we didn't have the big coaching staffs then that they have now. And Jack Faulkner is a damn good coach. He later became the head coach of the Broncos. He's still working for the Rams as a scout. He's the only guy left in the Rams organization that still lives in Southern California. He is an extremely well known guy in the football community. That was their whole staff. Now they have 12 or 15 guys on the staff. We had what, five? But they did have a strong staff. But there was no way to know then, I think, how good it really was.

Emil (Karas) was a very nice guy. He had played in the NFL. I think he played with the Redskins. He was a nice guy. He was a good-looking guy. He was aware that he was good looking, which is nothing to slight him. The thing I remember about Emil is he would be doing arm curls to improve his biceps and things like that. Emil was a good player. He was not a great one, but as a person he was a fine fellow… Emil was a real nice guy and should have lived longer than he did.

You know we had a lot of guys in the early years of the Chargers get killed. Bob Laraba got killed in an auto accident. Jacque MacKinnon. He got killed running from the police. He had been incarcerated for some previous incident and he was a free spirit and just couldn't stand the thought of going back to jail. One night they stopped him and he was running to escape the police. There was a wall there. He leaped over the wall to get away from the cops and he wasn't aware that there was quite a plunge on the other side. He suffered an injury that took his life.

I think Sid was a personality that interested me. And we know all about him. The guy that really attracted me a lot was Paul Lowe. I thought he had immense talent. A very rhythmic athlete. I used to go to the stadium early so I could watch him warm up. He had this thing that he would first walk 100 yards down the sidelines. Then he would stride 100 yards, then he would sprint 100 yards before a game. He had been a hurdler and he had just a beautiful gait. And he had an interesting story too. I think he worked in the mailroom for Barron Hilton while they were stowing him away. I still think he was a great player. He's a cook now out at the federal penitentiary. I talk to him

once in a while. But I always thought he was an interesting guy, simply from the standpoint of the skills that he had.

Kemp was an interesting guy. Amazing that being put on waivers put him in congress. They got him for $100 and Sid never would admit that he made a mistake in putting him on waivers when he did, but he did. I still see him once in a while. He's doing something now for the league. He's employed by the league. I think it's in attracting more people to play football. Hell, he could have been president. He had a shot. He always did seem to have a political lean. Good-looking guy, real good-looking guy, when he was young.

Ernie Ladd was a guy that I thought was immensely interesting. I knew Ernie pretty well. He loved to play games and he was good at them. He was a good pool player. He could play ping-pong pretty good. Not as good as he thought, maybe, but he could play. And he loved to play poker. He loved games. And he liked projecting this image of being this big, strong guy. A huge person. And he was a very good chess player. I have a twin brother who was a state chess champion in Nebraska for a number of years and played in the U.S. Open. So I was around chess quite a bit. I knew how to play, but Ernie always beat me. Years later when he would come back to town to wrestle, he would bring his chess board and sometimes he would call me up and invite me down to the Coliseum to play chess with him. He was an interesting guy. Just the size of him. He was a big son of a bitch. 6'9", 325. And you remember he had that tether that he had on his arms. There aren't too many defensive tackles that could just pick up a center and throw him into the fullback. He could play. He couldn't run all that fast, but he was an interesting guy.

There were a lot of interesting guys in those years. Mix is an interesting guy. He could write. He did some articles for *Sports Illustrated* and they were good. You wouldn't think he would be a very good athlete. I don't think he could hit a curveball in a week. But he could block and he could run. He could run. That's what separated him from others. Plus he would apply himself. But I never thought he was a great athlete. A lot of those guys are interesting guys.

HANK SCHMIDT, DEFENSIVE TACKLE

College: Southern California
Years with the Chargers: 1961-1964

Hank Schmidt was a tough defensive tackle who played football on the Marine Corps Recruit Depot teams of the late 1950s, with the San Francisco 49ers in 1959 and 1960, the Chargers from 1961-1964, the Buffalo Bills in 1965 and the New York Jets in 1966. Schmidt was such a force on special teams that Sports Illustrated's Dr. Z. selected him as the wedge-buster on his All-Century football team.

Well, I was up with the 49ers and the new head coach, Red Hickey, in 1961. The last training camp game he cut me and said that they would put me on their taxi squad. I was [contacted] by the British Columbia Lions. Then Jack Kemp was down here with the San Diego Chargers. Because Kemp went through the 49ers' camp, we had gotten to know each other. He asked me to come down and I came down to San Diego. The training camp was at MCRD and I had been in the Marine Corps and played at MCRD.

So Sid Gillman signed me to a contract. They suited me up and boarded me on an airplane and we went to Dallas to play the Dallas Texans. When we arrived there at the airport, there was this other ball player that was in the Marine Corps with me back in the '50s, Mike Connolly. He was the center of the Dallas Cowboys. Well, unbeknownst to me, I was picked up by the Dallas Cowboys and he was there to pick me up and take me over to Tom Landry. I told Sid Gillman about this and Sid said that he would work it out. So he worked it out somehow where I stayed with the Chargers. I had basically jumped leagues. So that's how that basically occurred. Then we played the Dallas Texans and I really don't remember if we won or lost...

There were only 12 teams in the United States back then, in the NFL. There was a lot of good talent coming out (of college) and there were not that many ball players kept on a team, only 30-someodd players. And there were a lot of players that were let go that could play excellent ball. There were good ball players coming out of college and out of service ball. They just wanted to play pro ball. Not semi-pro, they wanted to play pro ball. So I never had any doubts that [the AFL] would continue at all...

I was very impressed with Chuck Noll. He was very technique-oriented. He also was a very brilliant defensive strategist. Sid Gillman was offense. He was so far ahead of the game... And then Al Davis, what can you say about Al Davis? The guy was just a great coach, great management-type of coach. He knew talent, Al Davis did. So definitely, there was a big difference from what I came from with the 49ers. I saw a tremendous difference in technique and their knowledge of the game. And their knowledge of ball players too. They knew their talent...

I think the comradeship was excellent... Chuck Noll was very impressive to me, and Al Davis. Those two, and some of the ball players. With other teams you still had the comradeship a lot. In fact, I go back to the 49ers reunion every now and then. It's still there. They have a different feel than the Chargers. But the Chargers, that '63 year we put it together. But other than that, I think there was a better feel for football up at the 49ers than at the Chargers, to be honest with you. Even with the Jets. I was very, very intrigued with the Jets and the

New York crowd. It was completely different than San Diego. In fact, if I had it to do over again, I would never come to San Diego. I would have went to New York and played. It's a different atmosphere and I would have gone there if I could...

Tobin Rote was very impressive. Tobin Rote. He was a leader. He could get the guys together. The defensive line players, we were always communicating, always good together. The defensive line had a good relationship with each other. All the ballplayers, there was no hard feelings towards each other or anything like that. There was no jealousy. Everybody just played their style and Chuck and Walt Hackett, the defensive line coach, knew how to use that talent. We just all meshed together. It was all meshed, it seemed together. Just like gears. With some coaches the gears just don't hit. But it just seemed that we all hit together. And like I say, the one ballplayer that really struck me as should be a hall of famer was Tobin Rote. His leadership quality was there. He said something and you did it, you believed in it.

Back then, looking back now, at least I wasn't paid properly. I had to have a job during the off-season. Al Davis was good at getting us a job. He'd get me a job in construction. I worked for Trepte Construction. In fact, building a bank building downtown. Arnholdt Smith's bank building. I was on that project. I worked at Andy Kitzman Plumbing, driving a truck and delivering plumbing supplies to work areas. Bathtubs and such, it kept me in shape. But we just had to have, at least I did, we had to have a job and it was hard to find anything except in construction or labor. You didn't have a career. That's the only dislike I had. The only career you had was football, at least myself, that I was concentrating on. The other jobs I just had as a job, to make money during the off-season to survive. I had a family to support. That was the only dislike. There was never enough money there. I don't think I ever made over $10,000 in any of the years I played.

Fondest memories. Besides Jerry Magee being thrown in a swimming pool out in Boulevard? I don't remember that much, but I remember we were out at Boulevard and Sid took all of us in a bus to El Centro to a television station to watch a boxing match. I believe it was Muhammad Ali. It ended in one or two rounds, a typical Muhammad Ali boxing match. Afterwards we left. We stopped at a motel to eat and somehow Jerry Magee ended up in the swimming pool, the reporter. But he was a good guy. I like Jerry...

I remember when we were playing Buffalo in Balboa Stadium. Billy Shaw, he was a guard for them. He was giving me a real rough time. What you always tried to do is you try to weaken an opponent up, but not cheap shots in the legs. But you try to weaken him up by hitting him. I'll never forget in this game, a play was over. I looked to my left, looked to my right and straight-ahead; there was no officials by. Billy Shaw walked right by me and I nailed him right in the back with a forearm. I knocked him down. Then I heard a whistle and a flag went up. The official was right behind me. We got a 15-yard [penalty]. Then Sid Gillman came off the bench and went bananas and got a technical foul. That's what I remember on that one. They had to restrain Sid on that one. But I used to try to weaken them up.

Like I say, I didn't try to hurt anybody intentionally on the knees. That's a no-no. I didn't do any cheap shots...

I don't think I ever wore a cage on my face. I only wore the two bars. I never wore a facemask until I went with the 49ers and I only had a one-bar. I came with the Chargers and they had the two plastic bars. I didn't want anyone grabbing the facemask and using it on my neck. I never had a cage on my face, ever.

Bud Whitehead, Safety
College: Florida State
Years with the Chargers: 1961-1968

Bud Whitehead came to the Chargers as the 128th player selected in the 1961 AFL draft. He had led the nation in interceptions with nine as a junior at Florida State in 1959. Whitehead became a fixture in the Chargers' secondary and also spent time as a kick returner. He retired after the 1968 season and went into coaching.

I would say, probably, the one that found out about my playing abilities at Florida State University was Al LoCasale. He was involved in personnel with the San Diego Chargers at that time and has now been with the Oakland Raiders a number of years. He was the one that kind of contacted me and let me know more or less that I would probably be drafted by the Chargers; and I was drafted by the Green Bay Packers because you had the two leagues against each other. So I was a draft choice by the Packers and the San Diego Chargers. I just felt like the opportunity for me to play would be in a new league that was actually looking for ball players. At that time Lombardi had a real powerhouse. They didn't really need a lot of bodies and I thought I might just get a cup of coffee and be sent home. I wanted to go play where it looked like there was a real opportunity that I'd get a real chance and I was given that and a very enjoyable time...

You would think, seeing the financial backing and not having the support right off the get-go, which is normal, there might have been some inklings of "Man, we may not make it." But I don't think I ever thought about that. I don't think I ever worried that, "You know, this thing might go under." I felt like this organization was very solid. We had a strong owner in Barron Hilton, as you know. He had financial success with the hotels and came from a family that had a lot of money, and he could probably back us a long way before he might give up, if no money was coming in through TV and ticket sales.

But I don't think as a player, in my mind, I thought that we would ever go under. I don't think that really crossed my mind. Maybe I was being naive about that, not knowing what the financial picture was, but I thought we looked like a marketable product because I've heard so many people say that, "Man, you guys kind of brought pro football out of the twilight zone because it wasn't three yards and a cloud of dust. You opened up the passing game, you put people in motion, different for-

mations, you made football exciting." And that's not to knock the NFL, I don't mean that derogatory in any way, but it was appealing. They liked to see scores. To a fan, 7-3 or 10-10 is nothing. They don't get pumped up. They want to see that ball move down the football field because most fans are not defensive people.

That's what the AFL was. It was highly explosive. Most teams were very good offensively. We had some good defenses with the Chargers; I'm not saying we didn't. We had some excellent defensive ball players. But I think it is a little more wide open, a little more appealing to the fans. And as I said, I don't think in my own mind I thought we would fail. I thought if the league went under, I thought we had maybe one of the stronger teams and we might keep moving along and maybe incorporate some other teams somewhere else if we had to. Maybe go to other cities with teams that might be failing, maybe move out of that city and go to another one...

Sid, I'll never forget Sid's opening comments at training camp. I almost had it memorized for a little bit. Sid would always tell us in training camp, and one statement always stood out in my mind. He said, "Guys, I'll tell you what. I'm not interested if you like me. I'm not here on a popularity contest. But you will respect me." And he had the respect, I guarantee you. But I don't think Sid ever did anything in a vicious way. I think when he did chew on you, and get on your rear end, it was to improve you and make you a better human being and a better athlete. Because one of the things I learned real quick, if a coach isn't on you, he's probably given up on you. So when you're screwing up, and you're not getting your little behind reamed out, they've probably said, "Hey, he's never going to make it, why waste your breath." So you felt like, "Hey, if I'm getting my butt chewed out, they see something in me and they're trying to make me better some way, somehow." So I appreciate that in Coach Gillman. And he was just a great coach, just a super guy to play under. Yeah we had a great time.

Oh my goodness. I think of the story that I tell about Earl Faison, I guess when we were back in Buffalo. I think Earl was out signing Jimmy Jones on chits for lunches and meals and drinks for all his pals, and sending them to the hotel in care of the Chargers. Sid says, "If I ever find out who that damn Jimmy Jones is, he's gone." Everybody was looking around, "Who's Jimmy Jones?" "Who the Hell is Jimmy Jones?" And ole' big Earl, he's been sending those chits. Sid's getting all these receipts, "Who the Hell has been spending all this money and writing down the Chargers organization?" We laughed about that; that cracked us up. That was so funny. And ole', big Earl, he was having a good time just treating anybody who wanted a drink; he'd buy them a drink and sign the Chargers. Really good times. Those years went too fast. Time moves on, doesn't it?

I'll tell you the hardest thing… It was my last year, the camaraderie. I miss these guys. And they were family. They become family, these guys that you spend a lot of years with. A lot of these guys I spent more than a college career where you are there four years, some of these guys you spend eight years with, because I was here eight and they were here the whole time with you. Some maybe four, five, six years, and they became like family.

LANCE ALWORTH, FLANKER

College: Arkansas
Years with the Chargers: 1962-1970

Lance Alworth was the American Football League's first true superstar. He combined his natural ability with a fiercely competitive nature to become the greatest receiver the game had ever seen. His acrobatic catches and touchdown runs are among the most vivid memories of the people who watched the early Chargers. Perhaps the Houston Oilers' former receiver Charlie Hennigan said it best. "A player comes along once in a lifetime who alone is worth the price of admission. That player is Lance Alworth."

Al (Davis) was the receiver coach for the Chargers. He was the one that recruited me for the AFL versus the NFL, so to speak. At that point in time I didn't know that much about the leagues because I wasn't paying that much attention to it. I was a running back and I didn't feel like at that time, the NFL was any place for me to be, or the AFL. Then when it got down close to draft time, I was being recruited by them to play outside receiver. It was a position that I thought I would really enjoy because I loved to catch the ball. Always liked doing that. But Al was the one that recruited me…

Sid had a system to throw the ball that was unparalleled. Football was just beginning to come into the phases that we have now, which is throwing the ball a lot. We went from running the ball 90% of the time to where we threw maybe 30% of the time. Or 25% of the time. And that was the big change, in the fact that Sid was so smart in what he did. He is the original guy for the origination of the West Coast Offense.

Really, Sid was just so far ahead of his time. We controlled everybody on the field, offensively by what our offensive backs did, how we released from the line of scrimmage. We had passing zones, roaming zones, things that simplified the game, but at the same time made it complicated from the standpoint of learning everything you had to learn. Then when he started doing all that, then the defense turns around and starts doing other things too, to compensate for that.

But as far as Sid was concerned, the only reason, and I've told him this, the only reason that I feel like I'm in the Hall of Fame is because we had such a great passing attack. We didn't throw the ball that much, because we also had a great running attack. It was just a well-rounded game and there was not any circumstance that we could get ourselves into that the quarter-back could not get us out of with some kind of audible. It was just that simple. We had probably, and I'm sure they probably do today, we had 100 audibles. But they're all simple. So it wasn't complicated. Then the linemen had certain blocking combinations…

But Sid was just so far ahead of his time that I think he had the talent to work with us. We did have a lot of talent on our team, but at the same time we got great coaching. If we went out on that field, there was not any way that I felt that anybody could score more points than we could. If the defense could just stop them, we could score enough to win. So that was sort of our whole attitude. As far as Sid was concerned, he was where it all started. I mean that's where Al Davis came from. That's where Chuck Noll came from. There are so many guys that are winners today, Bum Phillips. I mean you name them, and those guys have benefited from being around Sid and the way he conducted his offense. His defense I don't know about because I was on the other side. But I know this; offensively he is the guy that started it all. In both leagues.

He was the originator of the West Coast Offense. That's where Coryell learned everything. Coryell spent time on our field. He came down and stayed with us for two or three years during training camp. That's where his whole offense came from, his whole philosophy, everything came from Sid Gillman. There is not anyone at this point in time, in the game, or that has been in the game, that I think provided as much and gave as much to the game as Sid has. You look at all the people that are playing, including the coaches that played with him, players that played with him, the systems that have come about because of him, and they're all based on him. They're all based on the premise that Sid had, and that's he didn't mind putting the ball in the air when we needed to. We didn't put it in as much as we would have if we were playing today, because we had such a great running offense. We had some great running backs. We had a great offensive line. They just nailed them…

Well, I got hurt my first year wearing number 24. The first year I came in, I wore 30. I had asked for 23, just to keep the numbers right. Paul Lowe had 23 and he said, "I'll sell it to you for $10,000." Well, that was 50% of what I was making, so there wasn't anyway I could do that. So, after I got hurt, I decided I wanted 19. 19 was the number of a guy in high school who, when I was like eight or nine, I guess, his name was Harold Lofton. He was number 19 in high school. One of the things I remember is I went to Lofton's Department Store. I had watched him play on a Friday night, and then Saturday morning he took the time and lifted me up on some bolts of cloth, because that's the kind of store…Small, little town. And he talked to me. And I'll never forget that. And that was why I decided to use 19…

Sweeney, I'll tell you what's really funny. We threw the ball fairly often. We didn't have many long passes called back. The reason why we didn't is because we would get in the huddle and say, "OK guys, I think we can get them, but no holding." And everybody would look over at Sweeney and say, "NO HOLDING, WALT! OK, SUDS? Don't you hold, you sumbitch." Walt was really one of the players that… He was a great guard. He never got the recognition he deserved, but he should have been a middle linebacker. Oh yeah, he would have been a terror. He would have been the equal of Butkus. He would have been equal to him, or even better. He could run, he was quick, he was fast. He weighed 250 pounds. Mean. They put him at guard because we needed him for the running game. He could pull and be around the corner real quick. It worked. He didn't like it. And I do feel like he was miscast. The game would have remembered him a long time, if he would have played middle linebacker. Yeah, he was that good. He was that talented. Unfortunately he never got to play that position…

Ernie Ladd was a great big hulk of a guy and one of the smartest guys I have ever been around. And one of the greatest ping pong players. Now you'd never believe that, but he could beat everybody at ping-pong. He was great. Of course Ron Mix. Ron Mix was a totally different player in the position that he played and played so well. The Intellectual Assassin. He was extremely smart and didn't look like he could play a lick and he'd kill you. Gary Garrison, and of course John Hadl, everybody's All-American. And we just won. That's it. Which was fun. We knew we could score points. What happened is that we lost our defensive guys and our defensive team. And when we lost certain people, that was sort of the beginning of the end. We could score points; we just couldn't keep people from scoring, and a lot of them…

Tobin Rote's the reason why we won [in 1963]. Tobin was a guy who came with lots of experience. He was a man that called his own plays. They weren't sent in, as did John, too, for a number of years. But Tobin was a guy that when he first came in I said, "Well why is he doing that?" And then after about six games I was like, "Whatever you call is OK because it always works." The thing I remember about Tobin too is sitting on the barstool. He'd just sit up there and have a few beers and bring everybody around. It was fun to be around him. He was just a great football player…

[We had] one of the greatest years as a result of [Rough Acres]. I still don't understand why more teams don't do that and why we didn't do it more often after that. We were out in a place where you couldn't do anything else. You couldn't sneak out at night because, where in the Hell are you going to go? Coyotes gonna get you. It's the only place within 40 miles where there was green grass and water, and because of that everything came there at night. Paul Lowe wouldn't go out after dark. We would have meetings at night and they would have to have somebody escort him back to his room. This was a guy who every night he was out anywhere else, and sneaking out after curfew. He wouldn't leave the cabin. He was scared of snakes and there were rattlesnakes all over. I mean they were really all over the place.

We knocked a ping-pong ball over in the bushes and wrapped around in the bottom of the bushes was a big rattlesnake. Somebody almost got bit. Then Sid heard so much about it that it pissed him off. So he said, "OK, the next person that mentions rattlesnakes or does anything of that nature, I'm gonna fine him $5,000." I forget exactly what it was. But that was the first year that Tobin Rote was there. Tobin and a couple of guys would go down before dinner and they'd have a couple suds in one little bar down there and then they'd come back. One day they were driving back and they saw this huge rattlesnake. Six, seven feet long, it was big around as your leg. Anyway, they chased it down and killed it. And they bring it down there, right in front of where we ate. It was this lodge. Right in front of the lodge they parked the car with this great big old snake across the hood. Everybody's eyes going by it were just getting huge. Then Sid walked up. Sid says, "Goddammit. Who did this? I told you guys if you ever brought any of these damn things up here again I was gonna…Who did this? Who's the sumbitch that did this?" Somebody said, "Coach. Tobin." And he said, "Oh. Goddamn that's a big ol' rattlesnake, isn't it?" I mean he just forgot it. I'll never forget that.

But I felt like that was something that brought the team together. The camaraderie that came out of there we still have today. I think it was a great move and I think they should do it again. I think the Chargers should do it now. It is really sad that that went by the wayside. That was the greatest training camp in the world.

SAM GRUNEISEN, CENTER
College: Villanova
Years with the Chargers: 1962-1972

Sam Gruneisen came to the Chargers in the same AFL draft that brought Lance Alworth, John Hadl, George Gross, Bob Mitinger and Bobby Jackson, among others. Gruneisen played both center and guard and became a pillar on the Chargers' offensive line through the 1972 season.

Al Davis was our receiver coach at the time and he was the one who scouted me. Al Davis and Al LoCasale ended up scouting me and signing me...

Well, I didn't have any experience, but I could tell that Sid was always a tremendous coach. And of course, my coach (Joe Madro), the o-line coach, they were just so knowledgeable. Over and above anything I had in college, as far as knowledge. Chuck Noll, you could tell was a good coach, but I didn't play defense. I just played guard and center. All of them obviously were good and they had great personalities. Probably Joe Madro never got the respect that he deserved. He was just tremendous. He took us as a group of no-names and made us play pretty well...

Well, I had good longevity. I didn't get injured frequently and I had a high pain threshold. And I played, played fairly decent, and I kept our group of linemen together. On the field you share the passion, but you also share what you don't know. You are not afraid to ask each other and help each other to know exactly what to do in a given situation. So all of that communication, it's always present. Or it needs to be present so that you can depend on your buddies.

As I look back now, Sid was our father image, our grandfather image. We all had, I guess, the personal side with him as general manager and you didn't want to face that. I hope he treated us as fairly as he could, from a monetary point of view. But as a coach he was still a father figure and loved us and that's how he treated us. We knew that we were cared for and about, and that's why we busted our butts for him. He very much was a father image to almost all of the guys, and our families too. He and Esther, they were really a family image for us. Because we were all young, all just married, most of us just married and starting to have our own families. They helped us through a lot of things. They were the ones we called.

Rough Acres is where we started [in 1963]. They had our training camp out there and Sid made the deal with us that if we won the preseason games, that he allowed us to stay home an extra day. If my mind is right, we won all our preseason games and I think we won our first 12 games in a row, until we lost. But the Rough Acres was a coming together. I really believe this. We got to know each other better.

Tobin Rote was very, very key in all of that. Sid trusted him explicitly and he was the type of personality that he surrounded us, as opposed to us surrounding him. He was a character, but a very honest person and he made demands on us because of his experience. I think Tobin at that time was about 37 years old and had been through the wars. I mean he made demands on Keith (Lincoln) and Paul Lowe and Lance (Alworth) and our receivers that they had to do what they were supposed to do.

And I think we grew up a lot that year. I think the Rough Acres experience itself had a lot to do with that because we were forced to be together, whether we liked it or not, and he was the inspiration to keep us together and keep it fun. Even though it was probably miserable. I don't remember it being so miserable, it's a long time ago. But at the time it was just a unique situation and Tobin was the key to the chemistry. Hell, we just banded together and did what we were supposed to do. I think that was a huge key or a huge factor...

I think I was always impressed with Paul Lowe's ability to run with the football and Keith Lincoln's ability to run between the tackles with the football. Obviously Lance was just a terrific athlete, one of the first truly great ones who was always was one of the first one's on the field and the last ones to leave. Always trying to improve. But our defensive guys were equally important. I think that Emil Karas and Chuck Allen were great influences on everybody as far as working as hard as you can and getting the most out of their bodies. Probably a kid that is never mentioned, Kenny Graham. I think Kenny Graham went to Washington State and played safety. What a competitor.

There was just a number of players who were just the leaders. It wasn't so much their athletic ability. Lance stands out with that. It was that the guys would work that hard in practice and make it happen in a game. John, John, what a competitor John Hadl was. A good athlete, not the greatest quarterback per say, but his knowledge of the game and his ability to lead. His character, that's what a team's all about. We had a team of good characters who played hard for and with each other.

I think that's what made us very successful. And I know I'm leaving a lot of guys out. Steve DeLong, Dick Harris. Dick Harris may still own the AFL record for number of interceptions in a season, I don't know. But I know Dick played a helluva football game. Walt Sweeney and Ron Mix, Ernie Wright. You can go on and on and name them all. After a couple of years they were special people because you lined up with them and guarded each other's backs. You trusted them. And I think that's the most remembered thing in my mind. You played the same guys all the time. I know a lot of the Raiders; I know a lot of the Chiefs and all that kind of thing. And you look forward to playing because you know you can count on each other. It wasn't maybe so much winning the game, although at the time it was. But its just guys that you learned to trust and love and you went out and played. So it was an exciting, exciting time. It was an exciting time in my life. I know I still awake some nights thinking about certain things that happened. But we had some good athletes and great competitors.

I don't know that there's anything to dislike about [pro football]. In my own mind I never thought about it like that. I thought it was exciting to go on the road and play. We used to go on and play Buffalo, Boston and the Jets or Titans all in the same series, where you were gone for two weeks or a little bit more. I always thought that was exciting. That's how you did it; that was part of it. After I got older and had my own children, I guess going away to training camp was hard to do, but that was expected too. I don't know if I ever thought of anything as a true dislike. Hated to see friends get cut, guys you'd played with. I don't know if there is anything to dislike. I hated when people got hurt. As we've gotten older, a few guys have died off. It seems unnecessary. But I'm sure that we put our bodies through so many wrecks that... You can see a broken arm; you just don't know what you did to your internal organs and stuff like that. It's hard now and seeing young people, at my age I still think we're young. People who died because we beat our bodies up so bad, that's probably the worst part. But I'd do it again tomorrow and so would they. I don't think that there's anybody that wouldn't do it...

I would just think the family atmosphere; it's something that I've always cherished. The camaraderie and the camaraderie of the families. We were a young, new league, so everybody was basically the same age and all having families at the same time. There's a life-long of football memories and a lifetime of family members. We shared each other's births and as I look back on it, that was just a tremendous time in our lives. I'm not sure if you're in the military or whatever at that same age group that you'd be doing the same thing, but a lot of it has to do with the age group and that we were just out of college and starting our own lives and own families. There was so much compliment to each other. There was very little negative. I just see that as one of the real positive influences in my life and in my children's lives, that they got to experience that at their young age. We talk about it constantly. My boys are 39 and 38 and my daughter is 33, and that's what they talk about. That was their life. The Chargers were their life, their memories. I just think from a family point of view it was crucial and vital...

You talk about Earl Faison. Earl Faison was... He was one of the special people. He was such a great football player. Obviously we were lucky to have him at the Chargers in those days when the NFL and AFL tried to get him and sign him. What a great, great football player and a great person. He's outstanding. You ask about memories. The guys were good guys. They were good characters. There were always a few characters, but they were good, moral people that did a good job. You could count on them. That's just what I remember. You just could count on each other.

JOHN HADL, QUARTERBACK
College: Kansas
Years with the Chargers: 1962-1972

When the Chargers drafted John Hadl in the third round of the 1961 AFL draft, they secured their starting quarterback through the 1972 season. Hadl and Lance Alworth quickly became one of the most celebrated quarterback-receiver duos in the history of the American Football League.

Well, I'll tell you, Don Klosterman was the chief scout for the Chargers when I was in my senior year in college. And he's the one that thought that I could be a quarterback and that's basically it. He was out at spring practice one day and saw me throwing and that's how it happened. Because we didn't throw very much in college. I played more of a running game, with options and all that kind of stuff. One day we were doing drop backs and he saw something he liked and that was it. If he hadn't been there that day, I don't know what would have happened. We only threw four or five times a game in those days. But anyway, that's how I got started.

I think the opportunity to play quicker [was with the Chargers]. It was a new league with new opportunities for people like myself. Coming out of a major college in a major college conference, I thought that I would have a pretty good opportunity to get started earlier than if I went somewhere like Detroit or in the old league NFL somewhere...

Well, it began when Sid signed me to the first contract and we had our first year together. It was a whole new learning process for me as far as learning the pro offense and understanding the total picture, what the linemen were doing and what everybody else was doing on every play. You had to know all that. That helped an awful lot to know all that. He worked us very, very hard, which was good. I think the first four years we, the quarterbacks, didn't have a day off. I know I didn't. He had me in there every Monday after the games and we were looking at films the whole way through Thursday. It was heavy duty during the season. But that's where I really learned everything. He taught me how to get up and get to work. That's for sure...

Whatever Sid saw [in me], he liked. I guess it was good enough to keep me. We had plenty of fights, though. Don't kid yourself. We had some hoop-de-groups and he won most of them, of course, because he was the coach. But there were times that I wanted out and he said he was going to get me out, but it never happened. So we always settled the issue, whatever it was. Thankfully the last 10 years I made sure I got to see him every time I came out here. We were real close in later life, with Sid.

Well, you know Jack (Kemp) when I first came in my rookie year, he was my roommate. In training camp, the first night I walked in and he was reading a book on Goldwater. I said, "What are you reading." And he was telling me that he worked for Goldwater in the off-season. He was into politics and that kind of thing. We had a lot of political discussions and I just didn't know that he wanted to be president. He was a sharp guy. But you know, he got traded about halfway through the season. So I have stayed in touch with Jack through the years. But he was really a nice guy. Tobin (Rote) is the one that really taught me on and off the field how to be a quarterback. The things you had to do and he was a real pro. He helped me a lot and brought me along pretty fast...

The biggest problem was Sid and (Chargers' owner, Gene) Klein were getting into fights all the time, I think. I don't know what happened because I wasn't in those meetings, but you could tell that Sid would be upset coming out of meetings with him. Sid, at times, basically felt like he owned the team, because he made it go from the get-go. Anyway, Barron Hilton was the great owner and he let Sid run things. I think Klein came in and tried to take over and do what he did. Then he brought in some other people in a management setup and got in between Sid and him. They would give Klein other ideas, other ways to do things and that kind of stuff. Klein didn't know anything about football anyway, so you didn't know what to believe. I remember one day I was coming in a quarterback

meeting and Sid was charging out. This was like 7:00 in the morning. I said, "Where are you going? We got a meeting." He said, "I'm going to L.A. and I'm going to tell Klein..." I said, "Don't do that coach, he'll fire you. You'll be fired by noon." They had a 1:30 press conference and he was fired. That's how quick that was. That's true...

Well, if Earl Faison hadn't have got hurt, he probably would have been the greatest. He would have been Deacon Jones, easily, without question. He was the same kind of speed and strength and quickness. He just got his knees tore up too early. He would have been a really, really great one. Of course, Lance. Lance was an all-around, as-good-as-you-can-be receiver in any league. But I'll tell you, Gary Garrison. He was the opposite, kind of. He was a great receiver, but he ran great routes. He was an intellectual-type receiver. He understood coverages really well and had great moves. You could hit him really easily, throwing the ball. So I had two great receivers all the way...

Walt Sweeney. He got a lot of credit early, but he was the best guard that ever played football, in my opinion. He was a fantastic player. If we get the films out I can prove it. Sam Gruneisen was a real heady football player. He was an overachiever, but he started and played guard and center. During the course of the game if someone made a bad line call, he'd correct it right there on the spot. Things like that. But he was more of a coach on the field. He didn't get enough credit in my opinion.

BOB JACKSON, FULLBACK
College: New Mexico
Years with the Chargers: 1962, 1963

Bob Jackson came to the Chargers after playing in the All-America Bowls at Tucson and Buffalo as a college senior. He played just two years for the Chargers, but contributed by scoring nine touchdowns in 106 rushes, and scoring twice more on 19 receptions. He went from San Diego to Houston, then Oakland and finished his career in 1965 back in Houston.

I'm not sure who scouted me, but I came to the Chargers, I think I was drafted in the seventh round by the AFL San Diego Chargers, and in the second round by the St. Louis Cardinals. And then I was also drafted by the Canadian League. And that time there was a war between all the leagues. So I chose to go to San Diego because of the weather and it was close to home.

To me, Sid was one of the best coaches I ever played for. He was a team coach. He kept the team together. And I played for several other teams and by far San Diego, with Sid Gillman, was the best as far as team unity, playing together as a family. Just, it was totally different. He was very much into team effort. Everything was team. There was no individual type thing or players. And back then they did it that was because when you came out, you could single one person out or whatever, but he was a team coach.

...Rough Acres, yeah. It was rough. It was way out in the boonies. But I think it was there for a reason. I don't think anybody complained that much about it, we just had to work out a little time off to run into Oakland. That was pretty rough... And then everybody just kind of pulled together and everybody was pretty healthy [in '63]. We had especially good defensive personnel with Faison, Ladd, Hank Schmidt, Ron Nery. They were good defensive players, which helped a lot...

Well, I think that I can say to be in pro football is something like the service. You are drafted and they will send you anywhere they want to send you. That I didn't like because you had no place to say, "This is my home." You play, and if they want to trade you... I know that when I first got sent to Oakland, I had no say so whatsoever. They never talked to you about it. It was just between the managers and the coaches or whatever. They did all the negotiating. We had no say so whatsoever, back then. We had no agents or nothing to represent us. We had to represent ourselves. That was the toughest part about when I was playing...

My fondest memories of being a Charger are just being a part of that organization. Of all the teams I played for, I played for Denver, Oakland, San Diego, Houston... Just being part of the San Diego unity. It was just a family-type organization, where the other teams weren't too much of a family. Everybody went their separate ways after practice or after games. But Sid made it possible. If after a game he had something going on, everybody was invited. And then in Houston and Oakland, everybody just kind of went their separate ways. They weren't together too much. That was a big difference that I noticed.

GERRY McDOUGALL, RUNNING BACK

College: UCLA
Years with the Chargers: 1962-1964, 1968

Gerry McDougall came to the Chargers for the last four games of the 1962 season, greatly aiding a team that had been ravaged by injury. McDougall, a veteran of the Canadian Football League, also assisted in the process that brought quarterback Tobin Rote to the Chargers in 1963.

I actually started in 1957, up in Canada, before the AFL started. I believe they started in 1960. I had played my option out in Canada because I was thinking about coming and playing for the New York Giants. I was on vacation prior to the 1962 season out there in Los Angeles. I was contacted by the Rams because somehow they had found out that I was playing my option out, and I said to myself, "Well, maybe I should give Sid Gillman a call down in San Diego," because that was more appealing to me than the Rams at that time.

So I talked to Sid Gillman and he said, "Well, until you do play your option out, there is no sense in talking right now. If and when you don't make a deal, then contact me." This was in October, and our season actually ended before the playoffs. We didn't make the playoffs. I was with the Toronto Argonauts at the time and our season ended, I believe in the latter part of October. So I contacted Sid Gillman and he said, "Yes, come on out, we are very interested and we would like to talk to you." So I said, "Well, there is also a quarterback who is playing his option out in Toronto, by the name of Tobin Rote." And he said, "Well, let me get a hold of Tobin and we will have both of you come out here and talk." So I got a hold of Tobin and told him what happened, because he was going to retire at the time. And the two of us, at their expense, flew to San Diego and talked to them. Meanwhile I am in contact with the Giants and they made a pretty lucrative offer, but being born and raised in Long Beach, California, I figured that really I would like to return to the southland. And the Chargers came really close to what the Giants had offered, so I decided to sign with them...

Lance Alworth, myself and John Hadl would always play gin on the airplane traveling back and forth. Ernie Ladd was the same way. There is a story about Ernie Ladd. He had an old Mustang. This was in like '62. He had taken the front seat out and had done some type of conversion with the back seat so that he could actually get in and drive the car. Not only that, I remember in 1962 I had my football shoe on. So I took my football shoe and put it inside his football shoe. And I wear a size 11.

Alvin Roy. Now he was the guy that actually introduced the pills, the steroids to the Chargers. Nobody liked him. He was a real asshole... Emil Karas was a health nut. Again, unbeknownst to the team, they had these bowls at the training camp. When we would go in for lunch they would have bowls of two different types of pills. And they said, these pills would add twenty pounds of muscle. If you took these pills it would add twenty pounds of muscle on you. And I said to Tobin, "Tobin, we don't need to be taking that. I am already 28 years old and I am all right with my body. I don't need to add 20 pounds of muscle." And he said, "Yeah, you're right. I don't need anything either." As you took these pills, a couple of coaches would stand there and make sure that you took the pills and swallowed them and took you water and stuff. Well, Tobin and I would put the pills under our tongues and then go spit them out in the bush after we left the dining room. Now I understand that the linebacker (Emil Karas) was eating that stuff like candy, and he died in 1974 from stomach cancer. I attribute that to his downfall. He didn't drink, he didn't smoke, ate nothing but the best of foods, and here he dies of stomach cancer. Anyway, he was eating that stuff left and right. It was ridiculous. It is kind of the dark side of football...

I was a punter, John Hadl was a punter and Paul Maguire was a punter. This was in 1963 at the training camp up in Rough Acres. And it was between the three of us to see who was going to be the punter for the season. And Paul was really a character, and we needed characters on that team. I said to John, "Paul told me that he will give you $10 if you shank a couple of balls." So I shanked a couple, John shanked a couple, and Paul became the punter. Because Sid Gillman and Paul did not get along. It was like Mutt and Jeff or whatever, they just didn't see eye to eye. So anyway, Sid had to keep Paul because he was the best out of the three. So that night, after dinner, John says, "Where is my $10?" I said, "Oh come on, John. I just said that to keep Paul on the team." And that's what happened.

Pat Shea, Guard
College: Southern California
Years with the Chargers: 1962-1965

Pat Shea attended Mission Bay High School in San Diego where he was a champion wrestler and star football player. He played college ball at USC and then returned to San Diego to play for the Chargers. Shea was a hard-working offensive lineman who made himself better through diligent weight training and an aggressive playing style.

Well, I was going to SC and I didn't get drafted or anything. But Coach Madro was watching a practice and saw that I was fairly aggressive and he liked my style. I didn't graduate from SC, but I had to quit because I was married and I had a child. So I called and asked the Chargers for a tryout, because I believe it was Joe Madro that told Sid, "Yeah, let's take a look at this guy. He's kind of like an animal guy; let's get him down here. He seems nutty enough to do it." So I talked to Sid and he said come on down. Actually, I didn't even have money for a bus or anything else. I hitchhiked down. He said, "Oh yeah, we'll take you on. $8,000 per year." "Oh you're gonna pay me for this?" That's the truth, though, $8,000 for the first year. So I came on down and started in 1962. In '62 I just started a couple games in that season. I didn't really become a starter fulltime until '63…

Winning the championship in 1963 was probably the high-light. It was one of those games where you couldn't do any-thing wrong. Everyone was just so perfect. It was unbelievable. To be out there and not be worried and have a good time at the same time, it was an amazing game. That's the highlight of my whole career, the championship of '63. Just nailing Nick Buoniconti one time. That was about it. He was such a fast guy, hard to catch. I tagged him a couple times. I though that was quite an accomplishment…

Walt Sweeney, he was my roommate and we ran together, we drank together, played together. We would always before a game sit together. It was kind of weird; we'd smoke a cigarette together. We'd smoke a cigarette at halftime. Try to calm down, sit by ourselves. Not say much, but just be sitting there with each other. We were buddies, close.

Oh Rough Acres, I couldn't believe how hot it was there. It was unbearable. Between practices I would go sit in one of the hot tubs. I would fill it full of cold water and just sit there all the time between the practices, just to cool off. I couldn't take the heat. I can't stand it. But bugs and mosquitoes, snakes, it was insane. It was a true test.

Tobin Rote, he was older. 36 years old at that time, and we thought that was an old guy. He was like our dad. He kind of led us down to the bar after practices, into the evening. We'd go down and drink and play drinking games. He'd be buying rounds for everybody. He didn't care how drunk anybody got. But he was our leader. We respected him. Great leader. He'd won the championship in the Canadian League and the NFL also. It was kind of amazing he came here and won that one in '63 in the American Football League.

Oh Ladd. I went against Ladd a lot. It's impossible, you couldn't hold him back because his arms were so long, he could just swat you. That's one of his techniques, to swat you in the helmet. He was 6'9" and 335 pounds, solid, no fat at all. Not like some of these guys you see today. And he could move, very agile. Yeah I had to go against him in pass protection and it's just ridiculous. You end up grinning because you know what is going to happen, he'd just swat you.

Earl, the Tree. Just like hitting a damn tree, solid as a rock. They had a drill one time where the coaches wanted me to go after him and I said, "Are you serious?" Because he was ready for me, he knew I was coming at him. I said, "C'mon." But I did it and he rang my bell pretty good. What a guy…

Keith Lincoln with the way he could run, his quickness. We all respected him. He was the guy that after every game he'd come in and individually thank all the linemen. Buy us cocktails. But he'd make a point of it every game, he'd come up into our rooms when we were traveling or wherever, and thank us. Quite a guy.

GEORGE GROSS,
DEFENSIVE TACKLE
College: Auburn
Years with the Chargers: 1963-1967

George Gross was born in Rumania and came to the United States as a young boy. He went to Auburn on a football scholarship. On a Chargers team full of physically strong athletes, Gross was perhaps the strongest. Nicknamed "Mr. Muscles," Gross had a 50-inch chest, the result of a large natural frame and dedicated work in the weight room.

Well you had to like the guy (Sid Gillman). I'll tell you a little story about him. I guess it was the first or second year that I went in. See, back then we didn't have any agents. And Sid wouldn't talk to anybody that had an agent anyway. But he says, "Georgie." He sat there at his table smoking his pipe. He says, "Georgie, I love you like a son." It was true. But you had to negotiate with him. "But you didn't have too good a season." So he cut you down. That's when the guys didn't like him. Because he also negotiated your contract and he was your coach.

Sid had Chuck Noll, but we didn't have as many coaches as these guys do. We did have some damn good coaches who taught you some new things. It's completely different coming out of college. You're playing guys all your size or bigger, but I'll tell you a little story. They put me on the kickoff return team. They called them the "Four Bulls," the big guys. My first game down at Balboa stadium they kickoff to us and we're coming up the field and I block somebody. And you know those great big cages we wore? I mean this helmet, the cage was crushed and my helmet was turned around, and I said, "Shit. These guys hit a lot harder than they do in college." Cause they're all your size. That was my introduction my first game…

Back then we had five defensive linemen. I mean it was a pleasure to play with these guys. Ladd would always get double-teamed, so that would leave the other guys open, right? Well, he was big enough to handle two guys. That was a good defensive line, and the linebackers, and the whole backfield. He just picked the right players. They all came together. I guess he thought by taking us out to Rough Acres that it would pull us all together. It just made us mad, out in the middle of nowhere…

I guess it was supposed to be like a motel. They had these little units, two guys to a cabin. There was no air conditioning. The only fans that we had were the bathroom fans. My first year I'm roommates with Sam DeLuca, from New York. Sam and I'd be laying there at night and the place is full of bats and he says, "George. You hear'em, you hear'em?" They're scratching. I guess they were in the attic or something. He was afraid of any kind of bugs or anything like that. You know he later played for the Jets. But some of the guys, we had rooms, right. At night the bats are flying around and they're swatting at them. That's one story. And then the field was terrible. Bobby Hood and the other boys would have to go check for snakes before we could practice, for rattlesnakes. To practice in 104 degrees, it was like a Spartan camp, but you couldn't get that much done. The guys were always trying to get water or something. It was an experience, but I wouldn't want to do it again.

KEITH KINDERMAN, RUNNING BACK

College: Florida State
Years with the Chargers: 1963-1964

Keith Kinderman played his rookie season with the Chargers at safety, but was moved into the offensive backfield during his second season. Injuries robbed Kinderman of much playing time with the Chargers. After playing 11 games with the Chargers over a two-year span, Kinderman played four games with Houston in 1965, and then retired from pro football.

Well, Sid Gillman and my coach, Bill Peterson, were pretty good friends. San Diego was interested in me initially as a strong safety. They scouted me. Al LoCasale came down and Al Davis, he came down when he was with the Chargers. He was with the Chargers before he went to Oakland. They liked me as a defensive back, although I was primarily a running back...

But the reason they put me at running back is that they did move some guys out. They had some older guys playing in the offensive backfield. Sid wasn't real happy with everybody. One of the guys couldn't catch. We called him ping-pong-paddle hands. But he told me after the season was over, he said, "I want you to put on 20 pounds and next year you are going to be a running back." So I worked on the weights during the off-season and came back as a running back. Unfortunately I partially tore my ACL in my left knee. I worked myself up to a starting position twice in my second year in San Diego. The first time I partially tore the ACL in my left knee, it was an exhibition game in Atlanta, of all places, against the Jets. I rehabilitated and came back, although I probably had lost a half a step. Because back then they didn't know how to repair torn ACL's, the orthopedic guy. So I just let it heal, and I went with tape. But I worked my way up to start again, playing Denver in Denver. They had a back named Odell Barry that ran about a 9.2-100. I guess he ran about a 4.3-40 or something like that. I was the starting running back because they had some real strong dogging linebackers. They had me as a safety on the kick off team, just to get my feet wet before we started running the ball. So this Odell Barry gets the ball. He comes into his wedge, then moves out to the sideline and he's running free except for me and the sideline. I worked the sideline as another player. I used it for leverage. I pushed him out of bounds and landed funny on my hand. Something I did a hundred times a day, and dislocated my elbow. So that put me out for about four or five weeks. That was basically my career with the Chargers. I just did special teams after that. Then the next year I played for Houston. Then I decided that I was going to leave Houston, or leave the pros, and go to law school, which I did...

I guess the biggest thing I disliked about being a pro football player was that I felt like a part of a racecar engine. Let's say I was a carburetor and I went bad. They'd just throw you away and put a new one in there. Which basically happened after I dislocated my elbow. The human element is missing, but what in the Hell can you expect, though?

I'm sure that you know from writing your book that Sid Gillman is the engineer behind the wide open passing offense, which a lot of other people have taken credit for as, "This is our West Coast Offense." That is a bunch of crap. Sid Gillman was the guy that opened the game up. Sid Gillman was a brilliant, brilliant offensive mind. The best I have ever seen. And he trained a lot of guys. Dan Henning is now the offensive coordinator for the Panthers. He and I were rookies together, out there at San Diego. Dan never played. He was a marginal player, but he was a very bright guy too. Sid had him and another quarterback from McNeese State named Don Breaux. He was the offensive coordinator for Joe Gibbs at Washington. He had them making up the game plan with him. In their rookie year, or maybe it was their second year. But they learned a helluva lot from Sid Gillman...

The sophistication of the game, compared to what I was used to... That's an interesting point. Seeing the sophistication of our game, the schemes, the plays, formations, everything like that, on a 1-10, say we were a 10. On the college level it was about a two or three. Interestingly, I talked with Henning and a few of the guys I played with who are coaching in modern-day pros now. I asked them the same question, because I have noticed watching on TV that they don't do the stuff that we did. I asked Henning point-blank, I said, "On a scale of 1-10, if the sophistication of our game was a 10 when you and I played at San Diego, what is it today now that you are coaching?" He said, "We have had to dumb it down. It is about a five today. Five or six..."

But the truth of the matter is, I think the NFL had 12 teams at that time. We had eight teams. And there weren't enough... I've heard Gillman say this and I've heard Davis say this. There weren't enough quality players in the country to put 22 men on 20 rosters to play the level of football that was expected of them. See what I'm saying. I see that today. Now they have 32 teams. I see millionaires dropping passes, fumbling the ball. They changed the fumble rule. If you hit the ground and the ball pops out, it is not a fumble. Well, it was a fumble for us. But we rarely fumbled. The whole league was like that. You rarely saw a fumble. You rarely saw a dropped pass. Now it is a bit diluted. The talent pool is diluted today, in my opinion. They say the players are so much bigger and so much faster. I think Alworth ran a 9.6-100. I ran a 9.7 or 9.8, which equates to about a 4.4-40. Alworth ran a 4.3-40. They say about the size. I can point you to some of these 400-pound linemen today that have 125-pounds of fat on them. We had Ernie Ladd, 6'9", 325-pounds. And if you took two separate photographs of him and me from the back, and had each of us in a different photograph, he was built just like I was as a running back. He had no fat on him. Earl Faison was 300-pounds, 6'7". He didn't have an ounce of fat on him. There are a lot of bellies hanging over the belts today.

I really respected Ron Mix for his intellect and his ability. He and I kind of tee-hawed pretty good because we both had pretty good minds. Both ended up as lawyers. I think Keith Lincoln is the most underrated player that ever played professional football. He ought to be in the Hall of Fame. Are you aware of that game he played against Boston in 1963? 320 yards. I happened to see that on NFL Classics. Ten of the best games played by any player...

Pat Shea and Walt Sweeney. I love those two guys. We'd run what they called the Green Bay Sweep. You'd have the fullback as a lead blocker, the offside back carrying the ball. We'd have a double-team with the tight end and the tackle mixing down. These two guards pulled. You could see their heads going right and left. They looked like the blue ball on a police car, looking for somebody to knock down. They impressed me...

Bernie (Don) Rogers and I fished every Monday when we had off. He had a boat. We were trying to catch marlin then when none of us knew what we were doing. We got into a damn school of marlin one time. They're coming right up along-side the boat. I said, "Bernie, what the Hell are these right here?" He said, "Goddammit, those are marlin!" We took Lincoln and Alworth and me and Bernie went out one Monday. I'm a pretty good fisher guy and I don't get sick. But Alworth got sick. He was throwing up. He offered Bernie Rogers his next game check if he'd please take him into shore.

Comparing the players then and now, I'd say we loved the game a little bit more than they do. We did it for the game. The love of the game sounds corny, but we weren't making any money. Now they take themselves out of the game if they have a sprained finger or something. We used to dislocate finger and then just put it back in place. Dave Kocourek. Have you talked to him? He had his four front teeth kicked out by Smokey Stover, playing the Chiefs. And he came right back to the huddle. We were in the huddle and I'm looking at the guy bleeding down his jersey. We had to take him out of the game. He wouldn't get out. Just things like that. We loved it more, I guess. I'm sorry it's over, but everything's gotta end. But I'd do it again if I could. It was exciting. It's something that everybody can't do.

BOB MITINGER, LINEBACKER
College: Penn State
Years with the Chargers: 1963-1966, 1968

Bob Mitinger was a consensus All-American in 1961 while playing linebacker for the Penn State Nittany Lions. Mitinger attended the University of San Diego Law School while playing for the Chargers. After retiring from pro football, the hard-hitting linebacker became an attorney and practiced law in his native Pennsylvania.

To the best of my recollection, I had been a known property by Al Davis. Al Davis, at the time, was working on Sid's staff. He had recruited me in high school, to go to the University of Southern California, which I didn't do. I went to Penn State. But periodically, probably my junior year at Penn State, when I was named as an All-American for whatever reason, Al Davis had gone through to see what Penn State was doing and we exchanged pleasantries again at that time. And then when I graduated I was contacted, again by Al Davis. Would I be interested in coming to San Diego? Certainly I would be. And we talked that they were going to try to draft me. And then there was an original draft, and I was drafted by the Washington Redskins and by the Buffalo Bills. The American League, the first draft for whatever reason was negated and the second time around I was drafted by San Diego. I guess that's how they made that determination. I know that when we played in Boston, that senior year, that I had met Sid Gillman and Al Davis for the first time. They made known that they were going to be in the stands and watch the game...

Sid was a unique individual. If you don't think he's unique, let me ask you if you've ever seen another coach to this day, who appears in bow tie and sports jacket on the sideline. He had great vision... He early on recognized that you have to have speed and quickness and courage. And even today, when they say that the current teams are better than the other teams, 4.5 or 4.6 in the 40 is still the same, quickness is still the same and courage is still the same. That doesn't change.

That was just really an experience [the Rough Acres training camp in 1963]. It was just hotter than the Hades of Hell. The facilities were something unusual. We'd kill rattlesnakes and leave them in people's rooms and the tarantulas were crawling around. Various tricks we would play on people. Sam DeLuca, for instance, was terribly afraid of spiders and snakes and we were forever playing tricks on Sam DeLuca, until he eventually just went to Sid and said, "Either you trade me or I quit. I'm not staying here another day." Jesse Murdoch and Ernie Ladd were playing ping-pong one night and Ernie Ladd hit the ball to him, he turned around to pick it up and the ball was laying on top of a coiled rattlesnake. That was a unique experience, but when we came down out of the mountains there, we were really in shape. There wasn't any place that you could get into trouble. It was hot, we worked hard, and the Rough Acres Ranch was the beginning of the '63 season.

ERNIE PARK, GUARD

College: McMurray, Texas
Years with the Chargers: 1963-1965

Ernie Park was an Honorable Mention Little All-American coming out of McMurray College. He played three years with the Chargers before going to the Miami Dolphins in the 1966 Expansion Draft with Dave Kocourek, Dick Westmoreland and Jimmy Warren. He stayed one year in Miami and played for the Denver Broncos in 1967 before retiring from the Cincinnati Bengals in 1969

Well, I think it was Al LoCasale that was doing the scouting then. They gave me a call. I was at McMurray College in Abilene, Texas. I thought I was going to get to play a fifth year. I though I'd had a successful redshirt year. Come to find out, some of us who had thought that we had redshirted, they suited us up for a homecoming game and we got in the game. I believe I might have got a little injury, turned an ankle or something. One guy made a tackle and three of us were ruled ineligible. Our names got in the paper. The guy covering the story was an ex from the cross-town rival and made sure our names got in the paper whenever they got a chance. It came up right before our fifth year. Our names came up and he said, "Well, these guys played that year that they were supposed to have laid out." So I got a call in July from Sid Gillman. I had a call waiting from him. When I got home my mother said, "Sid Gillman called. From the Chargers." Then a few minutes later I got a call from the Dallas Cowboys. I knew they had been looking at me as a future, but they thought I had another year of eligibility. But they called and Sid said, "Hey, we got you a plane ticket. Why don't you come on out?" After I heard all of this, then my college coach, he had been trying to get a hold of me. He explained what had happened and that our school wasn't going to contest this guy's statement. Anyway, they were already in camp out in San Diego, and they had put me on a plane and flew me out there. I weighed about 220 pounds. My weight was down during the summer. When I had played college ball I played at about 225, somewhere like that. So they put me on a weight program and I stuck around for three years...

Well, they started me out with the offensive line and I was sort of a project. I suppose I had pretty good potential, but coming in at no more than 220 pounds, I certainly was a project. In fact, I think I weighed in at 215. I believe that's what the scales out there said. I looked more like a receiver or something. Of course, your linemen, 250 or 260 was kind of average for an offensive lineman. I had the frame. I was almost 6'4" and had the framework to carry more weight and it didn't take me too long before I got in the 240-range, which was very respectable. They fed me. We had everything you wanted to eat out there. But Sid told me, "I want you to stick around. We're going to put you on a one-year contract, no cut. Then we'll see what you can make of yourself." So that's what I signed, really. Then I was activated. It might have been October, September or October. Then they activated me...

Well, I thought Sid was extremely intense, no question about it. He knew football, no question about it. But one thing about him that almost shocked me was that there were no holds barred. He would chew anybody out. I don't know what his dog thought.

But Chuck Noll, it just didn't matter. "Now Chuck, we have got to get this." He didn't spare anybody. But at the same time, he was very kind and gracious. It was all business to him. No question about it. He knew football. He ate and slept football. That was his life, I'll tell you. No question about it. Of course I didn't realize his genius being right there with him. I didn't know how much to appreciate him until later while listening to other people and their respect for his innovations and whatnot. I think it kind of opened my eyes to what it was all about.

I think the Chargers lost some depth with the expansion draft (in 1966). Kocourek went and maybe Sid went with someone else and they weren't quite ready. I know a guy that they counted on, Earl Faison, came up with a bunch of injuries, and Ernie Ladd was plagued by knee and back and other injuries. Several things happened, I know that year, that took place over there that affected their performance. There is no question it affected their performance. But not being over there, I think another thing that was coming around, and it is kind of a long story, there was some dissention I think. Sid Gillman ran everything from top to bottom. I mean he was the guy in charge of the club, and he was the guy that you sat down with and negotiated your contract. It was hard sometimes. Some of the guys, I think... It is hard to separate the two. Dealing for your salary and then playing for a guy. I think most teams got away from that way of doing things. Everything was run pretty simple. I don't know how many people were in the front office, but not nearly as many as today. They just don't have the baggage, they didn't have it like they have today. Sid was doing all of the contract negotiation and I think that hurt. No question about it, the contracts were getting larger and Sid was trying to save money and make things work and bargain for holding guys salaries down. I think that hurt. That was about the time that people began to divulge what they were making. I had no idea what the guys were making. A lot of the guy around the league, they were shocked when they found out what other people were making. Guys that had played and played well, I have heard of several stories that they had no idea that they were playing for half of what some other guy was playing for. I think some of that affected San Diego a lot...

I think it's interesting to see the different styles of the coaches. I played for George Wilson down at Miami and he had a pretty loose operation. He left a lot of it up to his assistants. He wasn't as intense as Sid Gillman. Paul Brown hired excellent assistants and just sat back and let them coach. He was more of the manager type. Of course he had his input in the coaches meetings every Monday. Sid ran everything. I kind of got the idea that he ran everything from the top down. If Chuck Noll wanted to put in a new defensive coverage, he sure had to clear it with Sid Gillman. I guess Sid essentially was the offensive coordinator. He ran it. There is nothing wrong with that. All the guys were successful. It was just amazing to see the different styles of coaching and the way they structured their staffs and workouts and everything.

The game has changed quite a bit I think. I think we played with San Diego and were right on the edge of the change. Weight training equipment just seemed like it got better right during that period. This West Coast Offense had its beginnings in those times. The teams had 33 active players instead of all the players they have now. It's just a different game and it is kind of exciting to be a part of the old school and yet to be on the edge of modern football. I thought it was kind of a unique period there where it began to change. Observing the two leagues battle and the American Football League battling for credibility I thought was an interesting thing to live through. And the salary escalation; When I went to Miami there were guys that had no chance of playing that got $30-$40,000 bonuses. Some of them got their bonus just because they were friends of another guy that they wanted. Here I was. In my biggest year I made $20,000. I was a starter and I made $20,000. And here were some guys that before the merger had made $25-$30,000 just as a signing bonus. To live through that time was kind of unique.

BOB PETRICH, DEFENSIVE END
College: West Texas State
Years with the Chargers: 1963-1966

Bob Petrich was drafted by the Chargers in the 11th round of the 1963 draft. He earned a starting job on the Chargers' defensive line as a rookie, and his hard work kept him in the starting lineup for his four years with the Chargers. In his retirement from football Petrich has among other things, enjoyed a bit of acting in the television series, Walker, Texas Ranger.

I was used to Spartan facilities, coming from West Texas. So the only place I saw was Boulevard, the dude ranch out there. So that was my first impression of professional football, wood shavings on a football field.

My impression when I came in, the morning after I got there, I looked out and I saw this guy walking down the middle of these ponderosa little duplex rooms that we were staying in. There was a row of them. And then there was a big opening in the middle, and then there was another row on the other side. I woke up and there was this Black Angus coming through. I looked out the window, and here are these cattle coming right through the middle of this thing. A little while later, here comes Earl Faison. He had shorts on and thongs, I mean on his feet. I looked out there, and my roommate was a guy that I went to West Texas with. His name is Jim Cunningham. His bed was on the other side. He goes, "Golldang, look at that!" I turned around, and I saw these cattle, but he was talking about, it wasn't the cattle, it was Earl walking down. Man, there's muscles all over the place, the guy's walking down with the meanest look on his face you've ever seen. Jim just said, "Dude." I was very thankful that Earl was a defensive player. At the time, I didn't know if I was competing against him or not, which I figured I was. Of course, I was a little, got a little fired up, so to speak. But he was very impressive. And then the next guy I saw was Ernie Ladd, a day later. And all the rest of the guys.

It was a different circumstance; probably nobody else ever experienced that kind of a camp, because it was just so unique to professional football. We had our own weight trainer. We had a weight set-up. Outdoor showers, everything was makeshift. They didn't even have freezers. The food was brought up every day from San Diego. Probably the most impressive thing that I can remember was getting help from Hank Schmidt, who stayed up to practice with me because I really wanted to learn...

I guess my favorite team to play against was the Raiders. I developed a truly instinctive hate for them. There was an instance my rookie year, we were playing up there. We played at a stadium called Frank Youell Field... You could never take your helmet off. I remember in Oakland, Coach said, "Leave your helmets on." All the rookies grumbled. This one guy, Ernie Barnes, took his helmet off for one second; somebody hit him in the head with a full beer can. He couldn't play...

Anyway, this particular night we were playing Denver, and I said, "I'll see you in the back field, Earl." He said all right... Anyway, I made a move on my guy on the outside. My understanding was that Earl did the same. We didn't even get held up. It was so quick, I was flying. I had a full head of steam, and I had a high on that quarterback, I was up the field and even with him. I turned and I started towards him. And I left my feet, and he ducked, and on the other side was Earl. And we hit face to face, going as hard as we could go, and we were just splattered all over the place... I said, "Jesus Christ!" I looked up and it was Earl. He goes, "Bob, what did you do?" Quarterback just went down, though. We didn't even hit him, but he went down and saved us...

We were playing Kansas City one time in San Diego, Kenny (Graham) was our safety. He was like Rodney Harrison, you know, that type of guy. Fearless, antagonistic. We were just controlling these guys; they wouldn't run on our side. We stopped them everywhere. They stopped running. Kenny would get up to the line and start yelling, "Why don't you run over here, you chicken shit!" "Come on, just shut up, Kenny. We got it made, man. Leave well enough alone."

Frank Buncom was the most gentlest person you would ever met. And I was with him in Cincinnati when he died. Frank was just like, the little kids loved him. He was just the happiest, nicest man, and he hit like a mule on the field. That was a guy that I'd lay down my life for, in a heartbeat. I really would. He was just, there wasn't anybody like him. He was almost to the point of, if you didn't know him real well, and you knew he went to SC, that you'd think he was too nice. Frank was an angel. He's up in heaven somewhere.

(Pat) Shea, such a bull. He used to practice when we were training in the off-season, he was from the beach. His brother's a lifeguard and he was a lifeguard, too. He would get a two-man sled, and stick the harness to it, and take his wife and two, I think he had two boys at the time, two little boys. He'd put on a pair of Army combat boots, and he'd get in the soft sand at the beach and run the beach, pulling them.

...So there was a guy named Chief Patterson. Patterson was an Indian guy who used to play on the college circuit. He even went to West Texas State the year before I was there. He played about 10 years of college football. Different names, you know. Through the Southwest, the South. Then he tried out with the Chargers, and he was a crazy guy. They roomed him with Pat Shea. Ernie Ladd was telling me this story. Up at USD,

every night... They didn't like each other. Shea was just raw animal. So every night, what they would do is they would move the beds against the wall, move the chairs out, and they'd fight. They would go at it. Bang each other up. Then, after they were done, they'd move all the stuff back and go to bed. They'd do this every day. You could hear them hitting the walls, the doors, but they'd move the furniture so they'd have room to fight.

Remember Billy Cannon? Well we were playing Houston. Charlie McNeil was, pound for pound, probably the hardest-hitting football player ever. We were down in Houston. Billy Cannon had just gotten all the biggest bonuses and everything and just really got a lot of money. We were in the game. Every time Cannon came out to catch a pass, Charlie would hit him. He would pot it or drop it or he would just hit him. Just hurt him. Just killing him. And Cannon was starting to feel it, and you could see it. What happened was, when I was rushing in and missed the quarterback, you'd turn around and go to follow the play, see who's got the ball or whatever. It was like a boxer. Every time he hit him, he made a sound. Charlie would literally go, "Augh." And he'd hit him. Cannon got to hearing that, and I think he'd just about had enough. Near the end of the game, he went up for a pass, and Charlie went, "Urgh!" Cannon came down, let the ball go, and Charlie didn't hit him. Talk about people booing really bad. They just ragged on him pretty good.

WALT SWEENEY, GUARD

College: Syracuse
Years with the Chargers: 1963-1973

Walt Sweeney came to the Chargers as an end, but developed into one of the greatest guards the game has ever known. He was an extremely tough and physical player, but also had speed, which proved very valuable on sweeps and pitch-outs. In recent years Sweeney has chronicled his life story in his autobiography, Off Guard, *which he plans to publish.*

Al Davis did all the scouting on me at Syracuse. Al's a former Syracuse guy himself. It's funny. Green Bay told me... Back then the draft was a couple of weeks apart, the AFL and the NFL. Green Bay told me I was going to be their number-one draft choice. When I got drafted so high by the Chargers, they thought I had a pre-arranged deal with them. A lot of that stuff was going on; they were hiding guys in hotels and stuff like that back then. But I didn't. So I got drafted in the sixth round by the Browns. But Sid and Al came out and saw me in Los Angeles. We were staying in the Biltmore. Syracuse had one last game against UCLA. That was my first time in California and me and a couple of my buddies went out and had a few beers on Sunset Boulevard. When we got back there was a message that Gillman and Davis were waiting to see me in the Coconut Grove. That was the restaurant in the hotel at the Ambassador. I panicked. I threw on aftershave and started chewing gum. I must have smelled like a French whore by the time I got down to see those

guys. I was half-looped and I signed my first contract the night before the game. I was so happy that they didn't realize that I was drinking. I had all of this paranoia going on... I would have signed anything. The next day I had a great game against UCLA and they had another contract for me to sign in the end zone after the game. The guy from Cleveland was tugging on my arm saying, "We will give you anything you want." But I already signed with San Diego.

I was at the College All-Star Game where we beat the Packers. So I missed most of the training camp at Rough Acres. Sid had sent me a bunch of brochures about this million-dollar dude ranch, back when a million was a million. That place was just an old dump. The snakes, the spiders, the sand everywhere. The practice field had sand on it. I wasn't too impressed. Then he threw me in with Alvin Roy to start lifting weights. The first thing that got me down was that I was an end at college, and then they made a guard out of me. I was supposed to play defense, but Chuck Noll didn't want me on defense because I had a rowdy reputation. So they made a guard out of me and I was really disappointed in that. I hated it. In high school I was a back who scored 120 points my senior year. In college I was a good defensive end and a tight end that could catch the pass. Then all of a sudden I was at the lowest spot on the team as far as I was concerned at the time. It was tough. I had a lot to learn. Joe Madro did a great job with me.

It was real hard [to practice against Ernie Ladd and Earl Faison], but it was good for me because those guys were really good players. I had so much to learn. The first couple of games I played, the guys I played against weren't that good. So I kind of thought I was better than I was. Then I came up against Tom Sestak. He played for Buffalo and this guy, as one reporter in Buffalo said, he handled me like I was on roller skates. It was a real introduction to someone who was really talented. That was a big lesson for me, I learned a lot from that guy. Hadl was screaming at me in the huddle. It's hard for a guy to throw a pass when he's on his back. But it was a good experience for me. I was humiliated and then it never happened to me again. I decided then and there that I would do anything to keep the quarterback from getting tackled or leg-whipped, or his facemask pulled down. And I did...

I always liked the eastern swing. We would go to Buffalo, Boston and New York. We would stay in Niagara Falls. It was always nice to get out of the house, get away from the kids, drink some good Canadian beer.

I can tell you my worst road trip. My worst road trip was my second year. We played Boston in Boston and we were flying to New York to stay at Bear Mountain for a week to get ready for the Jets. Sid gave us the night off in New York and we didn't have to be back in Bear Mountain, which is about 60 miles north, until 5:00 the next day for dinner. I remember it

was Pat Shea and Bob Zeman. We went to this bar called Sullivan's on East 71st Street. We started bullshitting with an off-duty cop and an off-duty fireman. We were getting pretty tanked. Zeman was really tanked. These guys wanted to go with us. We wanted to get rid of them. There was a scuffle in the bar and then we left. They came running after us down the street. To make a long story short, someone called the cops. The cops came, put Zeman and I against the wall. This fireman was about 5'6". He lunges out and Zeman and I. We both put our hands up. So hits them, goes back, hits his head on the cement and goes into a coma for 24 hours. They arrest us for felonious assault. We really didn't do anything. They moved us to 11 different cells in 13 hours. But I had to call my wife in San Diego. It was headlines in the San Diego paper, "Two San Diego Chargers Arrested for Felonious Assault." Headlines in the East Coast papers, I had to call my mother and my in-laws to say it was all a mistake. At any rate, we had to give $500 bucks to a guy that used to be in the D.A.'s office, $100 each to the arresting officers so they would tell the truth and not change the story. We gave $750 each to a lawyer. We went to court the Friday before the game. I was just so pissed off. My wife was pissed off at me. I had my best game against the Jets that night. I took all my frustrations out on those guys. But that was my worst road trip. I got arrested...

Alworth. He was fantastic. Tremendous upper-body coordination. He could leap. We had some good defensive players like Ladd and Faison and Chuck Allen. Hadl. Hadl, I thought, was great. He was very underrated. But Alworth was the most impressive for his raw talent...

I think Gillman is overlooked. I keep hearing that they always give Bill Walsh all this credit. He never gives any to Gillman and he got all that shit from Sid. I just think Sid doesn't get enough credit for what he did as far as the passing offense goes.

DICK WESTMORELAND, CORNERBACK
College: North Carolina A&T
Years with the Chargers: 1963-1965

Dick Westmoreland signed with the Chargers as a free agent in 1963, and went on to be the runner-up to Denver's Billy Joe as the AFL's Rookie of the Year. He was an outstanding cover-corner for three years with the Chargers, and hauled down 7 interceptions in 32 games. He also averaged 20.1 yards on kickoff returns.

What we had then is just amazing. We didn't have racial problems. We were like a big family, from the trainer right on up to everyone else. It was just like good times all the way around. We played hard. We had good times at practice. Do you know what that is, to have a good time at practice?

My career started with San Diego when I got a call from Al LoCasale. He called to my school, North Carolina A&T, which is in Greensboro, North Carolina. I am from Charlotte, North Carolina. Football season was over. I think we were getting

ready to go home for either Christmas or Thanksgiving. The season was just over. Anyway, I get a call one night in the dorm and it's Al LoCasale, who is Chargers' personnel. He called me and asked me if I would be interested in playing with the Chargers. I was elated because I was told by the Detroit Lions and by the Buffalo Bills that they were going to draft me, but I was injured my senior year in college. So I didn't get drafted and I was sort of downhearted. So when I got that call from the Chargers I was elated. He talked about that he wanted to sign me to a free agent contract. So I was like, "Yeah, I'd be glad to do that." So it really happened fast.

It blew my mind because he's in California. What he did in fact was call a coach from North Carolina Central, which was called North Carolina College at that time. It is in Durham, North Carolina, maybe an hour away from Greensboro. So he called one of their scouts there, which is one of their coaches, and asked him to come over and sign me up. So I had about an hour before they signed me after that phone call. I can remember being kind of excited, but we were getting ready to go home and me and some of the boys were having a few drinks to celebrate the end of the year. I can remember thinking he was going to come sign me and smell alcohol on my breath. So I was up there trying to brush my teeth and all this other kind of stuff. When the Dean of the dorm came down, he was a pretty strict guy. He came down and he said to me, "Westmoreland, you've got a phone call," because the phones were down at the end of the hall. I said, "Thank you Dean Boone." Then he said, "Seems like I smell alcohol in here too." "Uh, no..."

But anyway, that was my experience with signing with the Chargers and so I was real happy about that. I trained and got ready to go out in July. That was my first plane ride. So I went out to Chicago and from Chicago to San Diego. Then from San Diego right out to Rough Acres, which is Boulevard, California... That was the first spot I came to in California. The camp was excellent for training because there was nothing there but us and rattlesnakes and things like that. All we had to look forward to was practice and things like that.

I can remember Nolan Richardson was my roommate. He [was later] the basketball coach at the University of Arkansas. I can remember thinking that guys who had done better than me were getting cut. I thought, "Gee, I'm stumbling all around." But Chuck Noll, who later coached the Pittsburgh Steelers to the Super Bowl champs, he was my defensive coordinator. He coached the defensive backs. He really inspired me. He was always training me to be optimistic. I'm an optimistic person. If you kind of yell at me and curse me out I might not do as well as if you let me know that you're depending on me, and "don't let me down." That kind of thing. I would do my all for you. So he always kept me going. He always told me, "No, you don't look bad at all." He always told me that I was looking and

doing this sort of thing. I said, "Am I? I feel like I'm skipping around and falling." But like it came on and I got the hang of it. I started being good at it...

Balboa Stadium was a sight. Because playing downtown, that atmosphere downtown, with planes coming over about five feet off the ground. People inside the city, it was just great. We had a double-decker. Balboa Stadium was a double-decker stadium. So basically we played to capacity, I think it held 35 or 39,000. We had the stadium basically filled. We were a great team to watch and Mickey Finn's cannon, we used to run that guy out of ammo. Touchdowns and field goals. But it was just so exciting playing there. I remember being superstitious and I'd walk out the same way. They had some walls, some gothic things, Roman-style things out in front where we came through the stadium. I would walk a certain way all the time. You can really get superstitious, do the same thing the same way. But it was just elating because the crowds were loud and close to us...

But we had a lot of love, a lot of camaraderie that everybody had. It went from Barron Hilton down to Bobby Hood, who was our ball boy. Jimmy Van Deusen was our trainer. We just had a great time with the coaching staff. The fans loved us. I don't know what was happening before that, but the fans loved us. We were a big deal here in San Diego. But the players were different in that we were... I wouldn't want to say more dedicated than anybody else, but we were really dedicated about our jobs. It was kind of like if you're not doing your job, I'm waiting right outside, waiting to take it because I'll come right in and do this job...

Hey, this is football, something you played when you didn't get paid for it. It's like the game of life, football is. It's like a war that you get a chance to live again after. Some genuine relationships come out of that. So you can't have problems like, "Well, I don't want to play today." What! It's time to play. "I don't feel like practicing." What! It's time to practice. We had good characters on there. Good leadership with Lance, Ladd, Earl, Paul Lowe. Charlie McNeil really took me under his wing as a defensive player and helped me out a lot. Helped make me tough, too. We were always wrestling upstairs. We were trying to out-do each other. But Balboa Stadium, there was some magic down there.

RON CARPENTER, LINEBACKER

College: Texas A&M
Years with the Chargers: 1964-1965

Ron Carpenter came into the league in 1964 and played for two years. After retiring from football, Sid Gillman recommended him as a potential employee to the Spalding Sporting Goods Company. Carpenter got a job with Spalding and remained in the sporting goods industry for more than 30 years.

I can remember coming to San Diego and it's kind of like being in the army. You probably haven't been in the army, but, I arrived in Los Angeles from Texas and changed planes there to come down to San Diego and kind of sat there in the airport looking around, trying to decide who else is going to San Diego. You meet guys; there were several of us that came in at the same time. It's like instant friendship that you make. Coming from a small town in Texas, and not knowing anything about pro football, I look back on it sometimes and it was kind of like a dream come true. Because when I went to college, I wanted to play baseball. I was a baseball player, but they didn't give that many baseball scholarships. And my dad said, "You're going to college." But I went on a football scholarship where they were gonna let me play baseball and then of course when I got there, I really fell in love more with football than I did baseball. My junior year, when I was going through spring training, a friend of mine who was graduated who was drafted by the, well he ended up in the Packers but he was drafted by the Eagles. Came up to me one day in spring training and said, "You know, you're gonna be drafted." And I don't want to go in the army. That to me was being drafted. So he said, "Oh, no. There was a lot of scouts in here looking at you and you're gonna be drafted next year." And that was the first time I'd even heard of it. I was drafted by San Diego and Minnesota, and signed with the Chargers because I thought I'd have a better chance of playing, being it was a new league. I just felt my chances were better there...

I thought, "Geez, I'm gonna play pro football." But they forget to tell you one thing: that you gotta make the team. There's only a few guys that come in with those guaranteed contracts. I came out, and I'll never forget, the first day, we went out and we ran wind sprints, and kind of went through a few drills. Basically, I remember we were running for time. They were timing us in the 20, 40, 50, whatever. We went back to our room, and I'm sitting in a room with a guy, in fact it was a guy that I met in Los Angeles on the exchange of planes to come down here. I'm sure some of the guys might have talked about it, who was the angel of death that brought you the bad news, a guy by the name of Bobby Hood who worked for the Chargers for many years. I don't think Bobby's with them anymore.

Bobby was a super guy back then. He was going to school and working his way through college or whatever. But at that time, we didn't know what Bobby was. He knocked on the door and this guy and I are sitting in his room and talking. He kind of looked in at us, and he said to this other guy, and I don't even remember his name now, he said, "Coach Gillman wants to see you, bring your play book." And actually, at the time, I

thought, "Jiminy. We go up and do it this morning and nothing real big, and now this guy's got a private meeting with Coach Gillman. What's going on here? This is great for him. He came back and the guy was crying. I'm like, "What's going on?" He goes, "I was just cut." That's when I knew that it was a lot tougher business than I had imagined it was gonna be.

In my rookie year, we used to sit in the rooms. You always had a roster of every player that was still on the team and you would go through and check off the guys you knew were gonna make it. The Alworth's and the Hadl's and the Mix's. God, all the other guys you knew that were gonna be on that team. Back then, we only carried 35 or 37 guys on the team, so no matter how you figured it out, you were not gonna be in that mix. It just wasn't gonna happen. You're sitting there, trying to figure it out. We're in camp for about a week, and the veterans come in and then we're there another week. Things start stepping up a little bit. Then we have our first scrimmage in Escondido. I'm sure people told you that's where the training camp was. We have a scrimmage on a Saturday night. It's for the Charger Boosters, so there's a pretty good crowd there. Of course, all of us rookies get to play, because they're coming and looking who's gonna do what.

The next morning, the only people left in camp, because we had Sunday off, the only people left in camp, basically, were the rookies. Because none of us had cars, or if we had our cars here, we didn't know where to go. There was no place for us to go. So we stayed. We went over to breakfast, and I'm sitting there with all the other guys eating breakfast, and Coach Gillman comes in and sits down with us. We're all just sitting there eating breakfast, and all of a sudden, Coach Gillman goes, "who was number 89 last night on defense?" My heart stops, because I figured, "Oh, that's it. I'm out of here." I couldn't even probably lift my fork up when he said that. So I'm sitting there and I finally said, "That was me." And he said, "You did a heck of a job last night." I went back to my room, and I laid down on my bed, and I went over every play I was in the night before, trying to figure out what I had done that caught there eye. And I laid there all weekend trying to figure out what the heck did I do? What did I do?

My first year was 1964 and even by 1964, -65, there was talk that eventually a merger was gonna come about. My first year, San Diego was already talking about building a new stadium. We'd played in Balboa, as you well know. Either '64, '65 there was a stadium vote on the new stadium. I remember at that time, we were told that if the stadium was voted down, that we were gonna move to Anaheim. And we would've played in Anaheim Stadium. But the people of San Diego approved the stadium, so of course the Chargers were here to stay...

I always thought we had a very outstanding defensive ball team. When you look back in that era, who the Chargers had, with people like Earl Faison and Chuck Allen at middle linebacker and Ernie Ladd and Frank Buncom was a linebacker who later died with a blood clot going to his heart and it killed him. He went to, I think, Cincinnati - expansion drafter, could've been Miami, I don't remember which. George Gross, we had a lot of outstanding defensive football players. Speedy Duncan was a defensive back. Kenny Graham, I don't know where Kenny Graham is today, but Kenny Graham was the early free safety. He just came off and nailed you. The guy could just hit like a ton of bricks. We had some really outstanding defensive football players, and we always felt we had a very good defensive football team. We always felt we could've played with any team in the NFL.

I think my biggest disappointment was that my rookie year and the next year, we played Kansas City, oh we played Buffalo both years in the championship game. The following year, the third year was the first Super Bowl. We had always beaten Kansas City, kind of like we owned them. And then they won it that year and of course, San Diego didn't get to go to the championship game. That was always the big disappointment, that I couldn't stay around long enough, that we could've gone to an early Super Bowl. That would've been fantastic, but things always work out differently, sometimes for better. At the time, I look back, and I would have like to play for a lot of years. But I look back on it now, and getting out as early as I did, I think, was great, because I got on with my life, I got on with the career that I was gonna do. I think a lot of guys have a hard time, that play pro sports, because they don't know how to adapt to the real world when they come out. I think its even more true today than it was back then because there wasn't as much show business as it is now. Guys have a hard time all of a sudden going from being catered to, to having to face the real world and getting up every morning and going to work and putting in a full day and the whole thing. It's a different way of life. So I got that out of my system and got on with what I wanted to do and made the most of it. It was good from that standpoint.

SPEEDY DUNCAN, CORNERBACK
College: Jackson State
Years with the Chargers: 1964-1970

Undrafted out of college, Leslie "Speedy" Duncan became one of the most feared kick returners in pro football history. On October 15, 1967, he set a league record with 203 return yards in a single game. He had 21 interceptions as a Chargers' defensive back, and was inducted into the Chargers' Hall of Fame in 1995.

I was scouted by Al LoCasale, who later became vice president of the Oakland Raiders. He was a scout for the San Diego Chargers at the time. That was back in 1963 or the end of the '63 year in college. Actually it was kind of a bond session. I was sitting around on the steps of the band building at Jackson State College. Willie Richardson had been drafted by the Baltimore Colts in the NFL and then he was drafted by the New York Jets in the AFL. He chose to go with the Baltimore Colts, which he ended up having a super career, but he didn't go into the AFL. So Willie was standing around. I was hurt most of my senior year. I had what they call calcium deposits settle along my right leg after the third ballgame. Teams didn't give me any more of a look my senior year. Al LoCasale was in the area and he came by. Willie was just returning from the Colts and his rookie year. So we were standing there. We were all talking when Willie turned to LoCasale and told him, "If you want a ballplayer, this is a guy you need to sign." Al kind of laughed and then the next day Al LoCasale came back and signed me to a contract. And that's how it all got started. I was signed as a free agent during that time. As a free agent you just come into camp. They bring you to camp and you're really not listed on the depth chart. At that particular time the Chargers weren't carrying but six defensive backs. They had the starting four backs from the year before. I think that was Dick Harris, Charlie McNeil, George Blair and Bud Whitehead. I wasn't even listed. We had four teams that were listed on the depth chart, and then there was a fifth team. Two players were on the fifth team and I was one of the two players on that fifth team. That's how it basically all got started. It got started in training camp...

During that particular time I think one of the main reasons that I was still around and had the opportunity to stay around was that... Most people will know this young man. He's not a young man anymore, but he was the defensive backfield coach for the Chargers, and that was Chuck Noll. Chuck Noll recognized some things in my ability and immediately inserted me into the depth chart and started moving me up the ladder. People got cut and people got hurt and I continued to move. The key at that particular time was being able to get the opportunity to show what you could do. In college they never had me return punts. I returned kickoffs, but I never returned punts. As you know, that was one of my greatest abilities. They ended up putting me in preseason, back on punt returns. I think the first punt I touched I put it down about 60 yards up the field. That immediately caught the eye of a lot of the coaches and stuff. I had a real good ability. I was what they call shifty. I could change directions real fast, and stop on a dime and go. That was also another asset that they were looking for. And basically, during that time, most all of the black colleges in the South were like the training grounds for most of the old AFL players. The NFL basically looked over most of them. The AFL got the chance to get those guys and if you look back at all of them in the AFL, they all came out of the South. Buck Buchanan, Verlon Biggs, Frank Molden, Jim Hayes, Harold Cooley, Archie Cooley, Willie Richardson, Gloster Richardson. We were all on the same ball club. We basically played each other. We played Grambling, Texas Southern, Southern and Prairie View. Those areas. Otis Taylor was a wide receiver, one of the best ever, and he came out of Prairie View. There was a lot of talent in those colleges that the NFL, at that time, didn't even touch. They didn't even go that way. It was an opportunity for those guys to get a chance to perform on the main stage. And when they got that opportunity, it was a different brand of football. It was a wide-open style of football. I think that's one of the assets of the AFL. By being in the AFL, you saw a different brand of football. It was a run-and-gun type of football. The NFL was a three downs and a cloud of dust. Throw it on third down. Most people liked it, but they enjoyed the way the American Football League put the ball in the air. They came out and you had to be ready to defend. They were going airborne on you. At the particular time that I was with the Chargers, we had a coach by the name of Sid Gillman. His whole thing was the run and gun. Put it in the air. He was a mastermind at what they now call the West Coast Offense. The Chargers were doing that then. Basically it really came down. The AFL, like I said, was a training ground and it got all the ballplayers that the NFL really didn't want or for some reason overlooked. It's kind of funny. I wasn't even drafted. I was a free agent, a guy begging for a chance to come in and get the opportunity to play. Then seven years later I got traded to the Washington Redskins for three or four of the top five draft choices. I think that was saying a lot.

I didn't have a lot of contact with [Sid Gillman]. The only time I had contact with him is when I had to go in and try to beg for some more money. That was challenging. Sid was a kind of funny man. I think I led the NFL in punt returns and kickoff returns in the same year. I think I made $12,000 that year. He indoctrinated a rule on me because I got hurt during my rookie year preseason. I got my jaw broke. And when I got my jaw broke they put me on the taxi squad. I stayed down there on the taxi squad until my mouth healed. I came back around the ninth week. He brought me up and put me back on the team. Then he had me returning punts and kickoffs. I wasn't playing much cornerback. I was getting in sparingly. But basically I was returning punts and kickoffs. I think in the last five games I had a 30.2 kickoff average and I was averaging 15-point-something on punt returns. What Sid did… I love him and God bless him. He's dead and gone on now. Sid called me into his office before he brought me up and he said, "The league doesn't have a contract. I don't know what happened to it, but they don't have a contract for you. So I need you to sign this right here. I have to send them a copy." So I signed a blank contract and then the next year when it came time to negotiate, he told me, "You're already signed." So he had gotten me to sign a blank contract and then he put in the numbers. I think he gave me a $3,000 raise, so I was already signed. Well, I was up a creek. There was nothing I could do about it. There was no such thing as challenging stuff like that back then. You couldn't do that. Nobody negotiated your contract; you had to do it yourself. So me not knowing anything, I got stuck. I was really, really bitter about that. It took a long time for me to get over that. The next time

my contract came up for negotiations, I made him double it. He had to double the whole thing. He was pretty bitter about it. But from a management standpoint I thought he was in kind of an awkward position because he had to be coach and general manager. You don't see a lot of that anymore. It is hard for you to tell me that I am the best to ever do something one day when you are trying to get the best out of me, then you tell me I'm the worst there is when it is time to give me some money. It was kind of a complicated situation, but overall I think I really kind of enjoyed playing for Sid because he was kind of a no-nonsense guy. He was kind of funny, but Sid only was concerned about your performance on that Sunday evening or whenever you were playing.

I think one of the greatest road trips was when we went to… We would make what we call the Eastern Swing. We would play New York, Boston and Buffalo in a three-week period. And the league scheduled things then so you would just make that swing one time and you would stay gone. We trained at Niagara Falls, Canada. That is across the line from Niagara Falls, New York. We had a practice and it was really snowing and going on. This was in the early years. I didn't know anything about all this. I was just on the team. So we were waiting to get ready to start and we didn't have any coaches. None of the coaches were around. Ron Mix tells this all the time. So we were throwing the ball around and we said, "Let's do something, it's cold out here." So they all decided that we were going to play a football game. So Ernie Ladd, one of the craziest guys on the team, he says, "Man, let's play the blacks against the whites." And I think that was one of the funniest things I have ever had happen to me. We'd go on those road trips and we would always do something stupid. That was one of the most memorable ones because we showed how far we really had come. We were just a together team. Just to see the blacks on one side and the whites on the other side, running up and down the field, clowning and acting silly and falling in the snow. That was really one of my greatest experiences.

I never really disliked anything [about being a professional football player]. I think it was great. But I think it is a false kind of recognition and false world that you can get caught in. See, we live in a real world. Ballplayers, for some reason, you get to a point in your life where you live in a fantasy world. You basically think that you can do that forever. See, that's not the real life. The real life is after football. If you are lucky and you can be around 10 or 12 years, that is beautiful. The ones that don't have an adjustment period. You have got to go back to the real world and now you have to go back and be able to cope and deal with life as it really is. I thought that was one of the biggest adjustments that I had to make. I had to come to grips with the fact that during the time I played, then the job opportunities and all just weren't there. You have to come back to the real world and then get your head screwed on right and get out there and really go to make a living. Now when football is over with, you have to get back into the real world. I think that's the biggest adjustment that I had to make. Being able to come from one world to another world and get into reality.

Listen, I was blessed. I was truly blessed. God gave me an opportunity to go all the way to the top of the mountain and see what it was really all about. I met a lot of good friends. I met a lot of good people whom I still associate with to this day. And I am not disappointed about anything that happened to me in my career. I was truly blessed. I hold no grudges against anybody. I don't say anybody did me wrong. Everything that happened to me happened to me for a reason. And I thank God for it to this day.

HERB TRAVENIO, KICKER

College: Texas College
Years with the Chargers: 1964, 1965

Herb Travenio was one of the first true specialists in professional football. He had kicked for the Marine Corps Recruit Depot and at Camp Pendleton before coming to the Chargers for four games in 1964 and all of 1965.

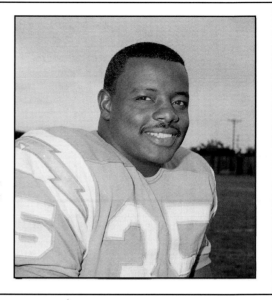

I was working here in the U.S. Postal Service. I did a hitch in the Marine Corps and I was working in the U.S. Post Office when the Vietnam War got nasty. Being an ex-Marine, I chose to go back in to help train troops in this specialty that I had, which was tanks and stuff like that. I decided to go back in and do that because a lot of the guys were doing it and they were asked, "Would you come back and do this?" So I volunteered and did that. I was an instructor.

My first hitch I was wounded in Korea, a young man, 17 years old. I came back and didn't want to get out, but I decided to get out and I wound up in the post office. But in the mean time I went back in and trained troops for Vietnam and I decided to play football too, at MCRD. They requested that I come down and play football. I was up at Camp Del Mar and Scotty Harris was coach at that time. So he requested I come down and play, which I did. I became All-Marine down there. So in the mean time the pros were checking me out. I never kicked a football, but I'd go out and practice every evening because I was a fourth string full back. So I said, "I might as well do something to help this ball team. Because I'm never going to do it as a fourth string full back, because we had some great backs."

So in the mean time I went out and started practicing placekicking. And Jesus, I didn't know I was going to become that good where pro scouts would be coming out to talk to me. So I said, "Boy, I guess I got something here." So in the meantime Dallas came out, and that's my hometown. I said, "Boy, it would be great to play for the Cowboys." But Bob Beathard came around and he was convinced that I should come to Kansas City. That's where he signed me and when I got out I went to Kansas City. I took another leave of absence from the post office, for a year. And I went back to Kansas City and I made the ball team. They wanted me to taxi and I said, "Well, no. I can't do that. I'll go back to work in San Diego and if you need me, call me." We all agreed, Hank Stram, Steadman, we all agreed to that. I came back home and went back to the post office to work and I didn't lose any time because that's all federal time. Going back in the service is all federal time, so I didn't lose any time. It's just like transferring from one federal job to another job.

In the mean time I'm working mail and somebody came to the back dock and says, "Hey, hey, hey, you gotta get out of here and tomorrow get on a plane out to New York City." I says, "Who are you?" She says, "I'm Sid Gillman's secretary. You're Travenio?" I said, "Yeah." She had come to the back dock and asked for Travenio. I said, "I'm Travenio." She said, "You've been traded." I said, "Boy, they sure don't let you know." So I knew it was cold back there and I said, "I'll stall for about three or four days because I was in condition. I practiced every day." I caught that late flight out of here to New Your City, flew up to L.A. and right out to New York City. Bobby Hood was waiting for me at the airport and took me up to Bear Mountain. This is where they were in New York, at Bear Mountain practicing. So I checked in and Sid asked me how was the flight? And I said, "fine." And I had a press conference that afternoon. But I went out and at the time Tobin Rote was quarterback and Hadl was setting behind Tobin. We practiced. I hit about eight out of ten and we were ready. We were ready for Boston. Because we were going up to Boston and New York, then Buffalo. We made that circuit and I had three good games. We came back to San Diego and that's where it started...

Playing for the Chargers in Balboa Stadium, I just looked around one day and looked at the area where I used to sit, to watch them. And then I said, "Now here I am." But the amazing thing about that was Earl Faison, I'll tell you what. We used to work out at Lincoln (High School), the Chargers, guys that lived here from other teams, NFL, AFL, we'd all meet; it was predominantly black in this area. So we'd all meet down at Lincoln and work out. Well, I was working out down there with the pros and kicking. Then Earl Faison teased me one day, he said, "Old man, what are you down here working out for? What are you kicking for?" I said, "I gotta get ready like you guys get ready." He said, "Aw, you're too damn old to be playing football." I said, "Well, if you think so." So we were all friends, though. So two years later I said, "Earl, here's this old man in the locker room, playing ball with you." So everybody just cracked up.

Jim Allison, Running Back
College: San Diego State
Years with the Chargers: 1965-1968

Jim Allison came to the Chargers in 1965 after leading the nation with 1,186 rushing yards as a senior at San Diego State. With the Chargers he played some fullback, halfback and tight end, but was also known as a valuable special teams player. He led the Chargers with 6.9 yards-per-carry in 1966.

My experiences coming into the AFL... When I entered into it, it was the "other" league. It was the lesser, the inferior league compared to the NFL. I made my decision. I was the last year of the double draft. So I was drafted by the Minnesota Vikings in the NFL, and the San Diego Chargers in the AFL. I felt having played my first year there that the quality of the league, all of the players were there, maybe the depth was a little bit different because the NFL had so many years of stockpiling talent and our league was just starting out. I think one-on-one our first teams were very equal, but then after that I think it dropped off a little bit. That's basically my comparisons of the leagues.

Stories upon stories of things we have done. I just think, without getting into all the stories, the camaraderie, the group of guys that we had, was something that you would never trade in your life. You know, all of us go to high school and whether you played sports or not, just the friends we have in high school is so special and you always remember that. It is a time that you can never duplicate. And then all of a sudden you get into pro football and you get the camaraderie and you know it is really neat. Everybody, when you played pro football in our years, I'm not saying it's that way in current times, but there was no prejudice, no racial differences, no economical differences. It was 40 guys there to play a football game. And we didn't see color, and we didn't see all these things. Speedy Duncan would call me and say, "Hey Jimmy, do you need a ride to the airport?" "Oh yes I do." It was just a brotherhood that was so special that even when we meet up today for reunions, it is just so special. We may not hang around each other, but the respect and love that all of us have is so special...

Well, to be honest with you, at San Diego State we played at Aztec Bowl, which is one heck of a nice old, outdoor stadium and Balboa Stadium is not much of a cut above it. I'm very fortunate because I came into the league in 1965, so I got to play two years at old Balboa Stadium and three years in the new San Diego Stadium. So I got to see the difference between, I mean the locker rooms down there were like two-and-a-half feet wide and then when you get your shoulder pads on, I'm between Keith Lincoln and John Hadl and I'm bumping into all those guys. The locker room was just really bad. The linemen had it worse than we had it. I remember Ernie Ladd would have to dress sideways almost. He was so huge at 6'9" he just had no room.

Then we would go out there on that field and the fans are right behind you in that stadium. I remember Jacque MacKinnon, he had dropped a pass that would have been a first down for us and as he was coming off the fans were like 20 feet behind you. It's not like it is at the new stadium. Then some guy yelled out to Jacque that his hands belonged on a clock. That he should

have been out there catching the ball or something like that. I remember Jacque just flipping him off and yelling out unpleasantries and Sid Gillman running down and grabbing him. "C'mon, c'mon Jacque," and just that type of thing.

The field was always in O.K. shape, but I think it only held 31,000 fans or something like that. And then when we got to go to the Murph, you're talking about, in our time, a state-of-the-art facility for us. The locker rooms were huge. You could sit two people in one locker. You had all different room for different pairs of shoes and all the different gear, the whirlpool, the room where you got medical treatment and all that. The whole thing was just first class. The weight room, everything. When you compare that to Balboa Stadium, it's like an apple and an orange. And I believe that the team functioned better in a facility like that where... I've always believed that people work better in an environment that they're happy working in, and that you get better production out of people.

I remember Earl Faison, we went to an after-game deal, a big party and Earl Faison was in there and Ernie Ladd. And we were all dancing all the rhythm and blues dances and stuff like that. My wife is 5'3" and you've got big Earl at 6'5" and he says, "Do you mind if I dance with your wife, Jimmy?" And I said, "Yeah, go ahead." So he just picked her up and they were dancing but her feet weren't even touching the ground. There was no offense to that and none taken. It was just all, honest, straight-out good relationships.

Hank Schmidt, boy they called him Kilroy. I remember one time after practice they had the PSA stewardesses come up and they had these watermelons cut in half. The girls were serving us after we finished eating our evening meal. One of these girls, very nice looking, offered Hank, "Would you like some watermelon?" She was referring that she would take half this watermelon and cut it whatever slice he wanted. He said, "Yeah" and he took his hand and stuck it straight in this watermelon, tore the whole heart of it out, walked away with all of this watermelon all over his mouth with seeds and stuff. This girl was looking and we were standing there behind going, "Oh my God..."

Howard Kindig played at L.A. State against us. That's an interesting story too. Howard Kindig. Which starting defensive line in college football was made up of all number-one draft choices? Most people would say Notre Dame, Alabama, Oklahoma, but they would be wrong. This team that I am referring to was from Los Angeles State and had Howard Kindig, who was a number-one by the San Diego Chargers, Don Davis, who was number-one with the New York Giants, Jimmy Weatherwax, who was number-one with the Green Bay Packers and then the great Walter Johnson, for the Cleveland Browns. That was the starting defensive line.

STEVE DELONG, DEFENSIVE END

College: Tennessee
Years with the Chargers: 1965-1971

Steve DeLong came to the Chargers as a highly touted defensive end from the University of Tennessee. He had been a unanimous All-America selection in 1964 and won the Outland Trophy as the nation's top collegiate lineman. With the Chargers he was a dominant pass-rusher and a multiple Pro Bowl player.

Well, I don't know really who scouted me. Oh, it was a guy that played for the Chargers and played at Ole' Miss. Yeah, Charlie Flowers. I was a number one pick with San Diego and Chicago, back when they had the draft. When I was in Chicago, when I was just about drafted, (George) Halas kept hiding me out. He wouldn't let Charlie Flowers know where I was. So finally I got a hold of him and I just about signed then with San Diego. I told them I would go out to San Diego and look and see what was out there. That's basically how it got started. It was a lot of hiding guys out and we stayed up there for about four or five days. Back then the draft was right after the last game of the season, which was in November. That's a long time ago, I'm just trying to remember. The Bears had three number one picks. They took Butkus, Gale Sayers, and myself. And the Cowboys told me they were going to draft me. I had played under Landry in the Senior Bowl, down in Mobile. And they said they were going to draft me, but somehow Halas got in there. He did whatever he wanted. He wasn't in for the teams very much. That's kind of how it happened that I came out to San Diego. I liked the warm weather. Chicago in November, it was freezing back there. My wife was pregnant with our first child and it was real cold and I didn't like it. I thought San Diego would be a better place for me. And the money was about the same.

I had a personal guarantee from the Hiltons to go along with my contract. See, there weren't any agents back then. There weren't any agents to speak of that were any good. So we just kind of did it on our own. Charlie Flowers, he helped me some. And I had a lawyer back here in Knoxville, but they were all kind of crooks then. We didn't know what they were. I mean, somebody strange coming in, that we thought was making a lot of money. And we were, for them, I guess...

Practicing most of the time in warm weather, I think that probably gave me a couple years. Cold weather is real hard on you. I think it is. And then I got traded and I really knew. Then I was really glad that I went to San Diego. I got traded back to the Bears for the last year that I played, and it was cold. That was the coldest winter they had had in about 20 years in Chicago. Well, you know, I decided to move out to San Diego, and I did for about four years after I retired. Then I moved back East again. But San Diego is a great town. I really enjoyed it...

Well, I signed a four-year deal as my first contract. When that was about to run out, I was living back in Tennessee then. Sid called me up and said, "What are we going to do about this contract. Come on out here and we'll talk about it." I said, "I don't know what I want, I will have to think about it." I didn't have an agent or nothing. So I went out there and went to talk to him. I told him that I was making about $28,000 and I wanted

$10,000 more each year. He said, "Who do you think you are. You're just crazy, thinking you're some kind of player." He'd just knock you down.

Well, I'd had 16 or 17 sacks that year. I made the Pro Bowl. So it was time for a raise. So he says, "Get out of here. I don't even want to talk to you." So I went back to the hotel and was packing my stuff, getting ready to head back to Tennessee. He called me up again three times and said, "Now are we going to work this contract out?" Here his coaching hat and his general manager hat was two different deals. So he gave us a hard time, he really did. But he finally came around to basically what I wanted. I'd come down about a thousand dollars. So the last couple years I made $39,000 or something. But it wasn't a whole lot. We thought it was pretty good. They had you pretty much. Because you couldn't just transfer. That came along a little later. You couldn't play your option out. You had to take pay cuts. They had a pretty complicated deal. And then the NFL owners and the AFL owners decided to quit battling each other and merge. It is kind of ridiculous the kind of money these guys are getting now. I don't knock them for it, but it seems like it was out of whack. In just this short period of time. I talked to guys like Doug Atkins, and in the best year he ever had with the Bears he only made $50,000. And that's a Hall of Fame guy, and he had to go to New Orleans to make $75,000, I think...

You know Sweeney, if anybody should be in the Hall of Fame, that guy should be in the Hall of Fame. He's the only player that I ever played against that I never could beat. I'd say, "Give me a couple shots today." He'd say, "You can't beat me. I don't feel like it today. Maybe I'll do it tomorrow." He'd play against somebody that pass rushed like me then he'd come and say, "Give me about four or five reps." Then he said, "He'll still never beat me." He never did. He was a good guy...

I went through three coaches in high school, three head coaches at Tennessee, and I guess I had three and one with the Bears, three different head coaches in San Diego. It was different. I thought for a while I needed three coaches for every football team I played with, just to find out what a good coach was, I guess. Maybe I never got one. Sid Gillman was a very smart coach. And Bum Phillips. He had a defensive coach named Jackie Simpson, played at Ole' Miss. Old Bum, he was about as good as you can get. He really was. He was a good coach, a good guy. He was kind of like a father, you know. You could talk to him, but just like your father, you're going to get some bad answers. And that's the way Bum was. He was fair, but if you didn't do it his way, you were going to sit out.

Joe Madro, he was short. He would go up to them big ol' offensive tackles and say, "We're going to throw you in the ocean." That's how those tiny little short guys would dictate to us. I think now it is probably worse than it has ever been. When the guy is making more money that you are, how can you tell him what to do? I think that's getting to be a problem. I just think when the whole team's operational budget was about $3,000,000, and now they're paying one guy $3-or $4,000,000. That's something right there. But that's the way it goes. We were happy as hell to make that kind of money. I'd say we 'd probably play for nothing just to get in there. But that's about it.

RICK REDMAN, LINEBACKER

College: Washington
Years with the Chargers: 1965-1973

Rick Redman came to the Chargers in 1965. He was a tough defender and was also able to fill in as a punter or kicker when needed. In his last year with the team, Redman was actually a player-coach, in charge of playing with and coaching the linebackers.

Well, I got drafted by Philadelphia in the NFL and the Chargers in the AFL. And so those are the teams I got to negotiate with. At the time, Joe Kuharich was at Philadelphia and I had had a chance to go to Notre Dame when I selected a college, and decided not to go there. He was at Notre Dame at the time, and I had always kind of thought about staying on the west coast if I had an opportunity. I probably would have looked harder at a Rams situation or a 49ers situation, but since it was a choice between Philly and the Chargers, I was much more enamored with the Chargers. They had just come off a championship season and had done pretty well. Chuck Allen, who was down there, was a former Washington guy, and so I had kind of followed the Chargers a little bit just watching him. He was a linebacker who played at Washington and then down there…

I was playing with a really good team that had just come off a couple championship seasons and so there was a strong commitment to winning and Sid Gillman was a well-respected coach. They had a great coaching staff. In retrospect, we didn't know how good it was at the time. When you look back historically, we had some really solid coaches on that staff and probably the guy who gave me my foundation in the game, because I got to work with him a lot my first year, was Chuck Noll, who obviously went on to a great career in Pittsburgh. He was the linebacker coach and defensive coordinator. I got to spend a lot of time with Chuck and I had a knee injury for a segment of my rookie year, so if I was not suited up for a game, he would always have me come up to the press box. I would sit next to him and watch him call the defenses and figure out what other people were trying to do against us, and it was a great learning experience…

Well, there are some guys that were just unbelievably great natural players. Guys like Lance (Alworth). John (Hadl) had a fine career. Some guys on defense like Ernie (Ladd) and Earl (Faison) that could make a difference and control a ball game. Then you also had other guys who were more journeymen-type of guys, but they worked their tails off and just got a lot out of their capabilities. People like Ron Mix, who was a very bright guy, and was kind of a student of his position, and was very successful as a result of that. You appreciate guys for different reasons that made them successful.

You take a guy like Gary Garrison who was a wide receiver an didn't have nearly the speed that Lance did, but he was just unbelievably effective because he had learned how to be a great move man and got his talents honed a little more by having the opportunity to work around a guy like Don Norton, who was there before him and there for Gary's first few years. Don did a great job of schooling Gary while he was there. You appreciate different guys for different reasons. Some of them just end up with a lot more talent than others and are naturally going to be successful and others are working their tails off every day to be successful, and you can appreciate both of them.

A guy like Keith Lincoln, who was a great all-around natural athlete, but he was a guy that I gained a lot of respect for just because he worked real hard in practice and he would run his stuff out. He was just unbelievably effective in terms of being an all-around running back. Out of the same kind of mold as some of the Green Bay running backs…

It was my rookie year and we were going to play Houston in Little Rock, Arkansas. And as a result of Arkansas' attitudes towards blacks at the time, we had to leave our place kicker, Herbie Travenio, at home. Because we only could travel with so many blacks and stay in the hotel we were staying in. So Herbie stayed home and as a result of that. Dick Van Raaphorst had been drafted that year and he was our place-kicker. But we needed a back up place-kicker, so Chuck Noll… I had been punting. I punted for my first couple of years with the Chargers. And so Chuck Noll asked me if I could placekick. I said that I hadn't ever placekicked. And he said, "Well, why don't you just go out and try it so we have a back up guy." So I put the kicking shoe on and placekicked during the week while we were getting ready to go play this exhibition game.

Well, early in the fourth quarter, or late in the third quarter, Van Raaphorst gets knocked out of the game because Houston had this attitude that they were always trying to take specialists

101

out of the game. So they had a game plan to try to take kickers out. And they ended up hitting him after he kicked a field goal and he had a hyper-extended knee and couldn't kick. So we get down to the end of the game with about three minutes to go in the game and we drive down and I've got to go in and kick a 17-yard field goal to go ahead. So I go and kick it and I came to the sidelines and the Noll was yelling at me that I've got to get back in the game because somebody has to kick off now. I didn't know that was part of the deal. So I go out there. Well, they had devised a deal and one of the ways they took out kickers was they had a guy that was like the guy that lines up right in front of the kicker. And when you started running at the ball, they had him running right at you. So you would get about one step to make a move and the guy would just deck you. He'd go after your legs. So we had a guy, our L-1, the guy on my left. His responsibility was to do nothing but go after the guy that was coming after the kicker.

So I'm lining up, and we had seen this in all the films and everything, what they did and everything. So I yelled over to the guy, "You got him, don't you?" And he said, "Yeah, don't worry, I got him." So I go kick the ball. I take two steps and they both meet on my left knee. And that's how I tore the cartilage in the last exhibition game of my rookie year. I probably missed a third of the games that year with a torn cartilage. At that time they waited until the end of the year to operate. Nobody scoped knees at that time, which I could have done if it was today. But they didn't then, so I was kind of on and off the rest of the season. But that's how I ended up tearing me knee up and ended up eventually having about three operations on that knee. I tore it up because Herbie Travenio couldn't travel to Little Rock…

Well, there are some great Sid Gillman stories. I happened to go down there. It was between my rookie year and my second year, and I was going down there just to have the doctors check up on my knee after I had my knee operated on. This was kind of the middle of the off-season. It was maybe two or three weeks after the draft. I happened to go in the office and I was watching some film or something and I saw some guy come through and somebody pointed out that he was one of our draft choices. And he had this guy with him. He went into Sid's office, kind of the outer-office and Sid was in watching film. Somebody notified Sid that the guy was there. He was like a third round draft pick or fourth round draft pick or something like that, and he was there with his agent. Sid walked in the deal in his entry room there where his receptionist was and the kid stood up and introduced his agent to the guy and Sid said, "Just a minute, I'll be right with you." He went in the back room and came back out in about five minutes and said "Hi" to the kid again and the guy says, "Well, we're here to talk." And Sid says, "I'm not dealing with any agents. You've been traded to Buffalo." And that was kind of Sid's reaction to dealing with agents, in the early stages. But that's a true story. I was right there. I was in the hallway right across the room. The guy couldn't believe it. And at the time, Buffalo was not the place that people wanted to go play because it was kind of the end of the world, it seemed like. Anyway, I thought that was an interesting story…

The thing I remember about Dickie Harris is about the third road trip we took, we had to sit alongside each other and he wanted to know if I played gin rummy. And I said, "Sure." And we sat down and he had taken about $30 off of me in about 30 minutes. I couldn't get a card. He just slammed me. I said, "I think I better go figure out my gin game before I play anymore with these veterans."

I am absolutely amazed at how many [football cards] I get [in the mail]. I get probably three a week. I just can't believe it. There's a funny story about one of those cards. I don't know if you remember a guy that was drafted the same time I was, by the Houston Oilers. He was a guy from Baylor and his name was Larry Elkins. He was an all-American at Baylor. In fact, we played against each other and were on several All-American teams at the same time. Well, Topps screwed up on the bubble gum cards and got our pictures mixed up on the cards. So every once in a while I'll get a card that has his picture on it. And I'll send it to him and let people know that they have something that they should really hang onto… Yeah, that's not my picture. Every time we saw each other before a game we'd say, "You never looked so good."

JOE BEAUCHAMP, CORNERBACK

College: Iowa State
Years with the Chargers: 1966-1975

Joe Beauchamp was the Chargers' sixth-round draft choice in 1966 and went on to have a 10-year pro football career, all of which was spent in San Diego. His career spanned the later years of the AFL, the AFL-NFL merger and the 1973 Chargers team that was fined by the NFL for drug use. When Beauchamp retired in 1975, he had played in 117 games and had 23 career interceptions.

Sid was frugal. I really liked him. I didn't for a few years, but I learned to appreciate his style of coaching and his style of management. When I was a rookie, I made a cardinal mistake, which could have been a terminal mistake, actually. Terminal in terms of career because the veterans told me it was OK. We played a game in L.A. or somewhere and we were training in Escondido. There were no women allowed in training camp. We went to a party after we played the Rams in preseason and guys got hooked up. I was one of those guys. I'm from Wisconsin and went to school in Iowa and I'm suddenly in L.A. and anyway... So they said, "Hey, bring her back to camp. No problem. Make sure she gets out tomorrow morning," which was Sunday morning. No problem, no problem. Well, she came back with me to training camp, spent the night, and somebody snitched on me in the interim. Sid found out and called everybody to his office. I'm just a rookie. He told me he was going to fine my ass off. I was scared to death. But I figured that the only way he could fine me, really, was to keep me on the roster. Otherwise, if he cuts me, he won't ever get his money. So he indeed fined me. I was on the roster, and really the rest in history, I guess.

I got to play for a really fine head coach. I don't know if that would have happened elsewhere. I got to play with a subtle, and not-so-subtle motivator. This isn't the Sid Gillman show. He did a couple things in my career that stuck with me and probably were the main reasons that I had a lengthy pro career. Besides that fine that I told you about when I was a rookie, for the first three years of my career... I went back to Iowa State my first year. Then I went back to Milwaukee, which is my hometown, and I taught high school during the off-season. Back in those days it snowed like Hell. The weather has changed significantly. But in Wisconsin in December, January, February, March, you may not get a break until May.

So Sid called a mini-camp, unexpectedly. No scheduled "camps" for us. It's 20-below in Wisconsin and I have been playing basketball and trying to run indoors on a little track there. He calls a mini-camp and in the letter he sent out he said, just come on out, casual mini-camp, etc. The very first day we get out, he pulls out the stopwatch and says, "I'm timing everybody." Well, the guys that live out here had a little advantage. I said, "Hey coach." And he said, "I don't care." I was a starting defensive back. I didn't run as well as I previously had. So not only did he do it one time, he did it three times. He made you run it again and then made me run it again in front of everybody. Then at the end of that practice session he calls everybody up. We all circled around Sid and he says, "I want to make damn sure that everybody knows what I'm talking about. I'm not gonna have my defensive backs in

such Goddamn-poor shape, running the way they're running. And if they can't do any better than that, I'll find myself another one or two defensive backs, whatever I have got to do." In front of the squad. Was I humbled, humiliated, embarrassed? Yeah. So I went back to Milwaukee. We went back after that weekend, and I ran in the snow. I ran in the snow for a good part of May. As soon as it got warm I ran with gloves. I was running in mud. And every time that I felt that I was getting tired, I thought about him embarrassing me. I used that every year. Every year of my career I remembered what he said. I subsequently moved out here after that year, just so I could make sure I trained right. But every year, every hill that I ran, every weight that I lifted, everything that I did, I had his face and that statement. "I won't have my ..." So to that extent, he motivated me. And that's all he ever had to do...

I remember a game that I had three interceptions, but that wasn't necessarily my best game. Best game is really an extremely subjective thing. Statistically the game I had three interceptions. But that wasn't my best game for a couple of reasons. I missed a tackle. It's sick how you remember these things. I missed a tackle on a kickoff, the opening kickoff of the game, actually. I was the safety and they ran in back for a score, Denver did. For the rest of the game I was pissed off. We ended up beating them pretty badly, 37-14 or 12 or something like that. But that wasn't my best game. If there was a best game, I think it maybe was against the Cincinnati Bengals, of all people. They got no net yards passing. It was something that my teammates and I kind of relished the fact that we could shut these guys out. No net yards passing...

Biggest collision? You're always getting knocked dizzy. I was under the misconception that because I was a very big defensive back... In fact, on this team, I was the only one that lifted weights. I thought of myself as a bad ass. On top of being just a corner or defensive back. I was under the misconception that I could hurt people. It didn't make any difference what size they were, I could hurt them. So I had a friend named Sam Cunningham. Sam "the Bam" Cunningham. He played for the Patriots. Randall Cunningham's older brother, actually. Sam was a fullback, 245 or 250 pounds. They used to run a lot of tosses to Sam, which is unusual for a fullback. But he had a lot of speed for a guy that was that big. Back in those days I had some friends on the Patriots and Sam was one of them. We'd work out here Saturday morning before a game and I'd take those guys down to Mexico with me. They'd want to do some shopping and buy some stuff to take back with them. So it would be me and three or four Patriots or whatever. Sam was always one of them. So we're jawing about tomorrow's game and I told Sam, "I saw you run over somebody the week before.

Don't try that shit with me, Sam." So he says, "You're too little to talk like that." That's the kind of stuff that went on. This is the day before the game. So we're playing them and they run a toss to Sam. I've got a run at Sam that's 10 yards. Just before he could turn up field. I hit Sam chest-high and Sam screamed. AAAARGH! The ball goes flying one way and I see the ball go. We're on the sidelines. I was flying the other way. I can remember the fans on the field level jumping up and yelling and screaming and then everything goes into super slow motion. I saw Sam on the ground. I got to my knees. I looked at Sam. He looked at me kind of confused, and I fell over backwards. So I'm lying on the ground and I remember Sam coming over and saying, "Beau, you OK? You OK?" So I got up again. I got to my knees, and I fell over backwards again. They ran it back in the film sessions about 20 times. "Hey, that's a pretty good move, Joe. Yeah." And I never lived that down with Sam. Big hit, hilarious? Yeah. Part of the game...

Well, they don't have road trips the way we used to have them. We used to go on an Eastern swing. We'd be gone for almost two weeks or a little more. We'd play either New England, the Jets and then go down to Miami. So we'd stay in Niagara Falls, Canada when we played the Jets, Patriots or Buffalo Bills, for a week. So we all had these "friends" that were in that part of the country. But my fondest memory, the one that you can print... We were in Michael's Inn in Canada. This was my rookie year or second year. We were getting ready to play the Buffalo Bills. Maybe it was my third year. I'm facing a guy named Elbert Dubenion. Elbert Dubenion's nickname was

Golden Wheels because he was so fast. The old vets would all get together on a Saturday night before the game and they'd play cards and have a few toddies. This was after curfew. We had adjoining rooms. I got my playbook after our meeting and I am thinking, "Shit. Oh Jesus. I've got Elbert Dubenion tomorrow." Bed check was at 10:30, lights out at 11:00. I got lights out. I don't know who my roommate was. Lights out, everything's good.

At 11:20 there's a bang on the door. "Get up. Get the fuck up." I think they said rookie. It might have been my rookie year. "Get up rookie!" So I get up. I'm wiping my eyes and I walk over there and unlock the adjoining door. These guys have a travel bar. Dominoes and cards. They've got poker going. "Come on in here and have a drink." I said, "Sorry guys." "Oh you big pussy." I said, "Listen, I have work to do tomorrow." "Yeah? Well so do we." So I closed the door and they're going at it. I finally fell asleep at midnight or whatever. We have breakfast at 8:30. I'm up at 6:00 thinking about Golden Wheels. I get up, open the door, and all these guys are passed out. The travel bar is empty. They're all laid out on the floor, my teammates who I've go to go to battle with in about six hours. I went down and went for a walk down by the Niagara Falls. I come back for breakfast at 8:30. By 8:30 the guys who were just knocked out were banging on tables about how we're gonna kick the Buffalo Bills' ass. This is breakfast. So I thought, "My God. This is a helluva transformation." From being comatose to where they are. Anyway, we got in the game and we beat the crap out of Buffalo.

GARY GARRISON, SPLIT END

College: San Diego State
Years with the Chargers: 1966-1976

Garrison came out of a pass-oriented offense at San Diego State and quickly became an impact player for the Chargers with his sure hands and precision route running. He complimented Lance Alworth beautifully for the latter half of the AFL, and played into the 1970s.

Y ou know when I was drafted, I was drafted number one by the Philadelphia Eagles and number one by the San Diego Chargers. And at that time, I really wasn't worried about the AFL or the NFL, but I was worried about not playing on the West Coast. I didn't want to go to the East Coast because I had never been there and I knew it was cold and snowy and that. So I really wanted to stay on the West Coast. So the Chargers were the ideal choice. But when Philadelphia found out that I didn't want to play with them, they traded my rights to San Francisco. So then it became a challenge and back then we had an attorney. His name was Robert Brockway of La Jolla. And he put together the deal where he was negotiating for me with the San Francisco 49ers and the San Diego Chargers. And so it was really what would do the best for me, how that would work. Would I be better off in San Francisco as far as playing,

or would I be better off in San Diego? And money-wise was a factor, so we just played one another against each other and San Diego came up with the most money...

Without Sid, I probably wouldn't have lasted as long as I did in the NFL. His scheme is still used today. People don't understand, but he helped the Washington Redskins, he helped Dick Vermeil with the Philadelphia Eagles, and he helped Dick Vermeil with the St. Louis Rams. They still use his playbook today. In other words, his theory of passing is still used in the NFL today. He's well respected. You talk to any coach and they'll always bring his name up. He was so far ahead of everybody, and that's one of the reasons that I thought I'd like to play for him, because he was just a genius about the pass offense.

Probably my best friend was a guy from Arkansas and his name was Chuck Dicus. He was a receiver from the University of Arkansas and he came to play with us. He was a young kid and we were thrown together as roommates and stuff like that. And he was probably one of the guys that I was very close to. But then after he got cut, it kind of bounced around to where we got switched with roommates and then one of my other roommates, after he left, was Mike Garrett. And that's when we got him from Kansas City. And then after that was when Keith Lincoln came to us that last year here. So I was kind of friends with Mike Garrett, and then at the end I ended up rooming with Keith Lincoln. So I've seen the young rookie, I've seen the middle of the track and then I had Keith Lincoln who was Mr. San Diego as far as football was. So I had a lot of good trips around here.

Well I think my favorite road trip story was in Houston when... it kind of tells you a little bit about Sid. Our windshield cracked on our plane and they were gonna say, "OK, were gonna be delayed until they fix this windshield." So everybody took off to the bars and to the places. And they said it'll take about four or five hours or whatever. And so everybody took off and was out drinking and everything like that. Well, what happened was they got another plane. And so we were taking off and so everybody started scouring around, trying to round up the people and everything. So we took off and George Pernicano

and John Hadl were coming to get the plane and they were bringing them out in a car and Sid said, "hit it." We left George Pernicano and Hadl in Houston. True story. So he's determined. When he says, "we're going," we're going and it doesn't matter who's left behind...

I think the thing that I learned about being with the Chargers is we really were a family. After the game there was places like George Pernicano's Casa di Baffi. We would all go up there and have a dinner. And you'd go in there and there might be 20 other players in there. After that we'd go to John Mabee's house in Alvarado Estates and we would have a party up there. There'd be half or more of the team up there. So I think the camaraderie that we had, that we always did things together. After that I started coming down to certain games and everything like that. I was with a couple of the players and I said, "Well, what do you guys want to do? Are we going to go meet there? Or I'll meet you later?" And they said, "No. We just do our own thing." So basically the players started being so independent that they started going to their own places and there might be one or two players here and one or two players over there. So I think my fondest memory is the friendships that I acquired and still have to this day.

TERRY OWENS, TACKLE
College: Jacksonville State
Years with the Chargers: 1966-1975

Terry Owens came to San Diego as an 11th round draft choice and stayed with the Chargers for the next 10 seasons. A durable lineman, Owens played in 116 consecutive games. He retired after the 1975 season and entered into the insurance business on a fulltime basis.

Well to be honest with you, I don't remember who scouted me. When I was a freshman at Alabama, all I know is a lot of pro scouts came to Alabama in those days because of the great things they had and of course, Bear Bryant. And the line that was told to me by my line coach, Joe Madro, years ago, was that... See, I played at Alabama my freshman and sophomore year. Then I left after my sophomore year; I transferred to Jacksonville State. Jacksonville State in Alabama. I went to a smaller school. And really and truly, I played football and basketball there. I have no idea who scouted or drafted me. I just read the paper one day and it said I had been drafted really, really late. I think I was drafted in maybe the twelfth or thirteenth round. In those days, and Coach Madro told me later on, "We really took a look at you when you were a freshman at Alabama, but then we kind of lost touch." But I was 6'6", weighed about 240, so they knew I had a big frame. He told me that they just drafted me late. In those days they drafted everybody and then they would bring everybody in and just kind of thin the ranks, as they got closer to the season...

The Chargers pretty much were one of the dominant teams in the AFL. Then of course, when the merger came along, then we became not a bad team, but not a great team. Just an average team. We would win about half of our games and I don't believe we ever made a playoff in my ten years there. I don't believe we did. The competition, though, was very good. I remember Earl Faison used to take me apart about ten times every afternoon. I think he was Most Valuable Player in the AFL Championship Game the year before, if I am not mistaken. Ernie Ladd had just been traded, I think. Of course Ron Mix, I kind of tried to pattern myself after him, he was so great. I played the left tackle side. He played the right tackle. Of course, he is in the Hall of Fame today and deserves to be there. But anyway, to answer your question, I felt, of course as a rookie you don't know what the competition level is going to be like, but everybody out there was a pretty doggone good football player.

He (Sid Gillman) was an outstanding coach and negotiating contracts with him was very difficult. He really was a bottom-liner. I used to think he felt like with the team, he was the owner.

I don't know if he had any kind of incentive from the owners to keep the salaries down, but he was very, very tough to negotiate a contract with. Very tough. I'll be honest with you, I could have probably played two or three more years, but I got out at the end of ten year and it was the smartest thing I ever did. I started making damn near as much money selling insurance as I did playing football. I was motivated to get on out. Of course, I had a good run. Ten years is a pretty good run. Coach Gillman though was a real good coach. He really was a wonderful man. He was always very good to me. I really can't say anything bad about him. You have got to understand that as a rookie, I came as probably one of the last picks in the whole draft. I didn't have an especially great college career. We won the little conference we played in. At Jackson State we played in a little conference here in the Southeast. But frankly, I didn't care if I played or not. It just wasn't that important to me. The only reason I went out there is because they gave me a new car and $10,000. They said that if I came out they would give me that and I said, "OK." So I went out there and stayed ten years, which I did not intend to do.

Joe Madro was a fiery little guy. I'll tell you one thing, if you listened to him; he really, really knew how to deal with professional athletes. He knew when to get in your face and when to get after you. I had a good relationship with Joe. I really enjoyed working with him. Of course, I can just see those sarcastic words coming out of his mouth. He was a very animated guy. He was only 5'3', maybe 5'4". He never wore a shirt, and had a little potbelly. He just kind of got up in your face. It was almost hilarious. But I had a very good relationship with him. He was a very good coach. I don't know. I never expected to play as long as I did. But he kept telling me and encouraging me. But the biggest influence in me staying there was John Hadl. I tried to quit twice the first year, but he wouldn't let me. John talked me out of it. John was a super guy. I don't know what he saw, but he just told me one day that they were expecting big things out of me and just to hang in there. That made me feel kind of good.

Lance was incredible. He was a superstar, and of course you think he would be untouchable, and unapproachable, but gosh, he used to always give me encouragement. We were both from the south. He was a Southern boy. He also gave me a lot of encouragement. But John was definitely my favorite. I'd jump off of a building for John Hadl. He was always positive. When I'd let my man beat me and take him down, he'd just give you that stare that meant, "Don't let it happen again." But he was really, really a class act. I really miss John…

Lyle (Alzado) was a lefty and he just gave me fits. He's dead now. The thing about Lyle, when he was a rookie we squared up and a couple years later he looked like a Godzilla. I think he got into the steroid business. Of course it's public knowledge. But he really built up, and I think that probably had something to do with his health. Believe it or not, Fred Dryer used to give me a rough day. He wasn't a real big guy, but he was like a snake. You couldn't find him. He was quick as a cat. He gave me a lot of trouble. Ben Davidson was an awfully good football player, but you know what I think? Ben didn't give me an especially tough time. He wasn't real quick; he was just a big, strong, burly guy. But we had some good battles. But I didn't dread matching up with him. But I sure didn't like going to Denver. Alzado just had a knack of coming up the field and hooking you with that left arm. He was so good with it. I don't know. In those days, believe it or not, they would usually put the most outstanding defensive player over the right tackle. I used to enjoy watching Ron (Mix). Ron was not a physical guy. He didn't have the size to physically run over people. He just out-finessed everybody. He was just so good with his footwork and his timing and everything. Of course, he'd knock your jock off if he got the chance. He wasn't physically a huge guy, but anyway, I remember Elvin Bethea just gave me holy Hell. I hated playing him. But those are the ones that jump out at me.

I never will forget this. We played Buffalo and we were going to stay over in Niagara Falls for the week. It had snowed and the snow must have been about four or five feet deep. I remember when the first guy stepped off the bus; he went up to his waist in snow. I never will forget that, going out to the practice field. But in those days I guess it was cheaper to put up the team in the east for a two-game swing. We played Buffalo and of course that was the field that Dickie Post almost drowned on. Remember old War Memorial Stadium? He actually got his face, almost his entire helmet pushed into the mud, submerged. We had to get everyone off of him so he could breathe. The next week we played the Jets and then after that we flew home. But that was the road trip that I remember.

JEFF STAGGS, LINEBACKER

College: San Diego State
Years with the Chargers: 1966-1971, 1974

Jeff Staggs is one of the rare athletes that plays high school, college and professional football in his hometown. A graduate of Point Loma High School and San Diego State, Staggs was drafted as a future by the Chargers in 1965. He played in San Diego until 1972, when he went from the Chargers to the Rams and then to the St. Louis Cardinals where he was reunited with his college coach, Don Coryell.

I had no aspirations of being a professional football player. As a matter of fact, when I was a senior at San Diego State, I remember going to an AFL All-Star practice being held here in San Diego. Standing between Earl Faison and Ernie Ladd, looking up and saying, "Oh, there's no way I could play on the same field as these guys." But the Chargers drafted me as a third round, future draft choice, my junior year, and said they thought I could play in the AFL. I said, "Well, if you think I can, I'll certainly try." And then of course I got to spring training and decided that I was just as good, if not better than most. That's basically how it began...

I don't have a real good recollection of my days with the Chargers. Game days are like days out of my life. You get up in the morning, you start concentrating, you start building yourself up, you start that adrenaline pumping. You are so focused on what's going on, on the field, and then afterwards you go out and have a few cocktails to try and come back down again. When you wake up the next morning, it's like a blur. Like it was a dream that you had the day before. If you weren't so sore, you wouldn't know.

I'll tell you what; my biggest remembrance was that I was drafted as a linebacker. In junior college I had been a Junior College All-American as a tight end, but I had always played linebacker also. As a linebacker at San Diego State, I also played tight end in short yardage and goal line situations. When I got to the Chargers, I was a linebacker through most of training camp. About two-thirds of the way through training camp, Sid came to me and told me that he was unhappy with either Jacque MacKinnon or Willie Frazier, who were the tight ends at the time. And he wanted to get rid of one and wanted me to make the transition to tight end. So I was kind of frustrated. Here I thought I am going to be destined to be the third or fourth string tight end, and I really wanted to play linebacker. So we were going into our last exhibition game of the season and we'd had about five linebackers go down within about a five-minute period through freak injuries. So they came running over to me and said, "Staggs, do you remember the defensive signals?" I said, "Well I remember the defensive signals O.K., but I won't know who to cover if they go in motion or if the pass coverage changes." So they said, "Don't worry about that. Kenny Graham will stand behind you and he'll tell you exactly where to go or who to cover." So I said O.K., so they threw me in there. I started for them for five years after that game. So a lot of young players come and go without ever getting a chance, depending upon a ball club's needs.

You know, I remember things like we went to Palm Springs because it was raining real heavily here and we were going to play the Oakland Raiders. So we could get some good weather over in Palm Springs, so they loaded us all on a bus and took us over to Palm Springs for a week. Well on the way over, I got into playing gin rummy with Lance Alworth. When we started we were playing for 50 cents if you knocked, a dollar if you ginned. I wasn't really experienced at cards, but I thought how much money could I lose on the way over there. By the time we got there we were playing for 50 dollars in you knocked, 100 dollars if you ginned, and I owed Lance something like $1,200. He came to me and said, "Rookie, take this as a lesson. You give me $600 today and we're even." I couldn't hardly get in my pocket fast enough. Then I remember playing card games with some of the veterans. I didn't realize until later, but they were passing cards to each other under the table. I'd have what I thought was a great hand and it always turned out to be second best. I just couldn't understand it. Shortly thereafter they laughed at me and told me, "Hey rookie, you have got to stay out of those card games with veterans."

Then I remember the veterans teasing me. They called me "Super-Rook." They were always teasing me about one thing or another. I remember Sid Gillman had quite a temper when aroused. One time we were in a hotel somewhere in Washington or New York. My roommate was Joe Beauchamp. We had gotten on the elevator and we had gotten on the wrong elevator. It was on its way up and then we had to ride it back down. To make a long story short, we were three minutes late to the meeting. Well, if you were late to a meeting, it was supposed to be a $100 fine. But Sid was steaming and stewing because we were the only two guys that were not there on time. He said, "It's going to be $100 a minute for every minute you were late." We went, "Whoa." Well as it turned out, we complained to the players association and they went to bat for us and they ended up with a $100 fine. But he had really worked himself up into a lather by the time we had gotten there. He didn't mind chewing some ass when it needed to be chewed. And you didn't say much and didn't complain much...

You know, one thing that always amazed me was his ability to take in the whole picture. I was up at La Costa. I had just gotten married and Sid and I ran into each other at a convenience store up at La Costa. And of course, Sid always has lived up there. So he asked me what I was doing for the Super Bowl, which was the next day. I said I didn't have any plans, I was here with my new wife and we were just getting away for a couple of days and he says, "Would you like to come over to my house?" I said that would be great. So I get to Sid's house and he's got a huge coffee table, and on the table he had about eight of the legal pads and a good dozen pencils and a pencil sharpener. I'm watching the game on TV and I'm following the ball, just like you would and I look over at Sid and he's diagramming the play that was just run with the pass patterns that the receivers ran, the blocking schemes that the blockers did and where everybody on the field went. And he's taking down names of anybody that made a good play on special teams or any of that stuff. So his ability to look at football and take in the big picture just amazed me.

There were a couple, three plays that stand out in my mind. They stand out in my mind more because of the hit that was put upon me, rather than the hit that I put on somebody else. One was a blitz, up in Oakland. Daryl Lamonica had taken the ball, reverse-pivoted, was rolling to his left. I was the linebacker on the far side. I came in on a blitz with a clear shot at him, just thinking in my mind, "I'm gonna knock this guy out." At the very last second, Jim Otto, the center, drop-steps, sees me coming and caught me right under the chin with the top of his helmet. Well it didn't knock me unconscious, but it knocked me coo-coo. I tried to go and line up in the Oakland Raider huddle after the play. And of course the Raiders are laughing at me and they take me and push me back in the direction of my own huddle. The next couple of plays I played on instinct alone, until the team realized what had happened, took me out and I took a breather for a few plays and went right back in. But that was probably the best hit that was ever put on me.

The best hit I ever put on somebody else turned out to be about a 20-yard gain for them. Linebackers are always on special teams. So I'm flying down in the middle of the pack, going full speed and I run into this Kansas City return man, probably 5'11", 180-pounds. And I hit him full speed. I go down in a heap and I jump back up and brush myself off and I'm looking down for this guy because I really believed in my head that this kid was probably laying there unconscious because of the impact. Well, when you saw the films from the side on Monday, it literally knocked him back about 10 yards. I mean he left the ground, everything, and flew back about 10 yards, but he kept his feet. And when he gathered himself, he kept on going. Well I think not only myself, but all of my teammates thought he was done for too, because everybody kind of relaxed because he turned out to make another 15 or 20 yards after that.

One of the other most memorable moments was…When I was a young player I was one of those guys that really threw my body around. I was one of these kind of guys that hated, literally hated to run across the field, chasing a play and get there too late to get a hit. So I used to hit offensive linemen who were standing around, just to be hitting somebody. Well, in those days it was $100 for the first time you got thrown out of a game. It was $300 the second time and $500 the third time. So I had already been thrown out of two games for fisticuffs. And we were playing the New York Jets and Joe Namath the last game of the season. There was about 30 seconds left on the clock and they were on about our four-yard line. Namath tried to go with a staggered count to draw us off sides. It worked, because Ron Billingsley jumps off sides, goes flying by the guard. Their fullback steps up, takes him on to protect Namath. Then the guard who he flew by turns around and runs up behind Billingsley and forearms him across the back of the head. I'm standing over here on the side of the line and I'm looking around and none of the referees saw it or didn't say anything. So I thought, "Well shoot, I'm gonna protect my teammate." So I go running over and I grab this guard and I throw an elbow that catches him right under the chin and he goes down in a heap. The referee comes running over to me and says, "What did you do that for?" And I said, "Well, you weren't doing anything." And he says "I am now." Had I been smarter, I'd have save myself $500 with 30 seconds left to go in the season. So I always remember that.

Then I remember a preseason game against the Minnesota Vikings where Carl Eller had hit John Hadl late on a pass play. Both benches had emptied and throughout the course of the game I think there were two or three bench-clearing things where tempers were always on edge because of this particular play. But the second time that we had gone into a bench-clearing brawl out in the middle of the field, my helmet got knocked off. There's a big difference between throwing blows when you've got your helmet on and when you don't. So I worked my way out to the edge of this crowd of guys and I grabbed this rookie. And I said, "Rookie. Did you see my helmet in there? Go get it." So he goes in and grabs my helmet and I put it back on, snap it up and jump back in there.

Harold Akin, Tackle

College: Oklahoma State
Years with the Chargers: 1967, 1968

Harold Akin came to the Chargers from Oklahoma State where his primary job had been to block for future Dallas Cowboy, Walt Garrison. Sid Gillman's wide-open passing style was a big change for Akin, as all his previous team had run was "Walt Garrison to the right, Walt Garrison to the left, Walt Garrison up the middle."

Coach Gillman was very, very, what I call, a "brainy-type" coach. He knew the business very, very well at the time I was there, and had already been around it for several years of coaching. So I highly respected him and his knowledge. Certainly we got along very well. He, from all aspects, has become the person that has put out lots and lots of head coaches over the years, throughout the NFL and college…

He was considered kind of an offensive coach genius, and I was in a system at Oklahoma State where we were mostly defensively inclined. So actually, we had very little offense designed and very little numbers of plays, compared to going out there. Because of his offensive-minded coaching, I thought it was unbelievable from the very first day I went to practice. As far as a more ingenious way to play offense, since I was an offensive tackle, I think I recognized most of it right then, that he really knew what he was doing…

Well, I think like most teams, when you get a group together, you always have some people that are the born teachers and leaders. For instance, Ron Mix was one of those. I really considered him a great mentor for me, as far as understanding the game and learning the game. He was quite a technician, and not so much a muscle guy. But he basically just out-tactically worked almost everybody that we played. Like I say, he was a very good teacher for me.

Without a doubt, I had the good fortune of being there when Lance Alworth was there. He, too, was an awfully good mentor for young rookies coming in. I think he paid attention to everybody, not just me. But that's what you find a lot of times in high-quality athletes. But Lance, certainly, was one of the most outstanding players I have ever seen play the game. We had a couple of guys. Sam Gruneisen, that was a center, that I felt was one of the all-time centers, probably not recognized enough. But he was a very, very good center…

We went to what we called the Eastern Swing, where we would go up to and stay around Buffalo, New York. Then we would play Buffalo, and what was then the Boston Patriots, now New England Patriots, and then also the Jets. I happened to be there in '67 to see Mr. Namath with his fur coat. We were in the game, I don't know if you recall that. He wore a fur coat; I think it was maybe three or four home games before they finally asked him to take it off. It was a full-length fur coat. You see some runners on that now. I remember being on the field there and we were thinking, "What in the heck is he doing on the other side?" Of course, we were kind of in awe of him anyway because of what he had done in college. Obviously he was a great, great player, he just didn't have the knees to hold up. But that was one of the neatest and funniest moments of all time. Then probably just being in New York City for the first

time. I think that was one of those things that was a real eye-opener for a little Oklahoma boy. We're not used to those big tall skyscrapers. So that was awesome to spend time there. We stayed two weeks and played three Sunday games…

Deacon Jones. He taught me a lesson. He was already a six-year pro. We played against him; I believe that was an exhibition game because we were just starting to cross over. If you remember those first couple of three years. But anyway, he gave me a real lesson in how not to be able to block somebody. He was obviously very, very good. And me being brand new, he took me to school that day. I found out what a great defensive end he was. So you remember those, and then probably the most interesting and psychic time I had was playing against Ben Davidson with Oakland. Big handlebar mustache, he was kind of a long, goosy guy. I think he's about 6'6", 6'7" maybe. He wasn't real heavy, but he was quick as a cat. And all he did was kind of grumble and get that real deep voice. So you never knew where you stood with him. You couldn't talk to him because he wouldn't answer. He'd just kind of grumble. But he was a very good player, obviously. He took me to school… Davidson never let up. Today in this time, he would have a penalty on every play. Hitting the quarterback late, hitting him in the head, grabbing their jersey, kicking him in the crotch when he was down… He was definitely on the edge of being a tough, tough player. Talented in his own right, but he didn't much care about how much he hurt you or what he did to you anytime. He was one to take you out. Of course you see him in those beer ads from time to time. He seems to be such a nice guy. I never figured him out because he wouldn't talk about the game. He just put himself into motion on every play and you didn't know where he was coming from. But a good ball player. But most quarterbacks didn't like him.

I think that I would probably just have one really, really important thought. This is the type of thing that whether it be in business or in pro football or pro whatever, playing at that level brought me to the knowledge and awareness of how good a person can be. Whether that was me or someone else, or people around you, because you saw excellence everywhere. You saw people get beat, but you really saw the best of the best. And I think without that, I probably would have gone on in life and just assumed that there wasn't an excellence higher than college football. But there is a whole other tier up there that's to be the very, very best. And to enjoy those times, I think that was one of the open-your-eye type things for my wife and I. I was married at the time. In fact, we had Jeff, my second son, was born in San Diego. And that would certainly be a highlight. He was on the scoreboard, "Jeff, 7.1 pounds, born to Sally and Harold Akin." I thought that was exciting, and that was spontaneous on their part. I thought that was really neat. I don't know if they do that today, but that was pretty impressive. We had that big electronic board. But I think just the situation of being in that kind of environment and be-

ing around a team is just one of those real highs that you don't want to miss if there's a chance you can be there as a player, as an assistant, as a coach, whatever. I think it's an extremely high rush of adrenaline. It was just a great, great experience in my lifetime. Even though it was short.

DICKIE POST, RUNNING BACK

College: Houston
Years with the Chargers: 1967-1970

Dickie Post was a small running back at 5'10" and 195 pounds. He had a scatterback style and was often seen changing direction and running opposite his blocking. But what his style lacked in convention it made up for in production. He left the team as the Chargers third all-time leading rusher with 2,519 yards in four seasons. In 1969 he led the AFL in rushing with 873 yards and a 4.8 average.

Actually, that was Bum Phillips. You know Bum, right? The year that I got drafted, Bum, Sid Gillman hired him as a defensive coordinator. So when my name came up in the draft...of course that was before little running backs. I think, who was that guy from L.A? That was the time before small running backs. But anyway, Bum put in a plug for me. He said, "Boy, you can't go wrong with the kid." So that's what happened. But actually what happened, of course I had been a running back through high school and college, but they put me at flanker behind Lance. Yeah, that's what happened. I actually made the team as a flanker behind Lance Alworth.

But then another interesting story that goes along with that... What happened was that we went through training camp and everything and I made the team as a flanker behind Lance. Then, you've heard of Paul Lowe? He was the Player of the Year a couple of years before. So he got hurt. He pulled a hamstring or something or other. Then it was the weekend before we were going to play the Houston Oilers, and we had an off day that weekend. So they called me in and said, "Dick, just learn the running back's spot because you have done this before and we're running short." But basically that's exactly what happened. Of course I just sat on the bench and there was another kid that was my roommate, by the name of Jim Allison, who could play fullback or halfback. Anyway, Paul re-injured his leg and then Jim Allison went in the next play. That's when we were playing the Houston Oilers. He just got knocked out. Old Sid just looked up and down the bench. I was the only guy there that could play running back. That's how it all started. I think I gained, on kick off returns and pass receiving and all that; I think I gained, 66 or 70 yards in rushing and everything.

Anyway, that's how that all started. Then Brad Hubbert, remember Brad? He and I were in. Then the next week, I don't know who in the Hell we were playing, but I had a good game. I gained like 110 yards rushing and kick off returns and that sort of thing. So back in those days, that was just normal. Naïve me, I thought that's just how you were supposed to do it. Then Sid, he and Paul never got along. Paul Lowe. It was really too bad. I was such a naïve kid then. I thought that's just the way it

works. I had no idea this guy was an all-pro. That's Paul Lowe I'm talking about. Sid, he just hung that shit out on you. It was really too bad. But there again, that's what I am saying. Your job could be taken that quickly. I just thought, well Hell, if you do better than the next guy, then you're supposed to get it. But I had no idea. I had absolutely no idea that you had to play for several years before you got that sort of credibility. So anyway, that's how I started and then all of a sudden it became a pretty flared-up thing. Brad and I were the rookies and he just kept us in there. Then poor Paul, he just got put by the sideline. He eventually got traded to Kansas City. But I don't know. Looking back on it, I just thought that wasn't a good thing to do. In fact, the other teammates, I guess they were sort of going... Well, everybody was looking out for their own jobs. But there again, that's exactly what I am saying that Sid could do. He could hang that shit over you, and that's what he would do. There was no way in Hell I should have been playing, because Paul had earned his credentials and everything. Here I am, just a damn kid out of nowhere that made the team as a flanker, and all of a sudden I am the star running back. But I made it. I was Co-Rookie of the Year. But anyway, that's sort of what happened...

For me, college was probably harder for me actually than it was in the pros. I know that sounds a bit weird. But in college I was expected to do that *every* week and I did it *every* week. I was expected to do that. But things were so different. I ran a little heavy in college and didn't have the moves that I did in the pros. But honestly, after my first knee operation, I got together with this Dr. Carter at San Diego State. That was way before all of the muscle balance and all of that. That's where it happened and that's what really changed my whole deal. I happened to be living next to San Diego State and this Dr. Carter; he came out with the Chargers. That was back when everybody was trying to experiment with different things. He experimented on us in two-a-days and everything. He was able to evaluate if you were going to pull a hamstring. It's muscle balance; the difference between your quadriceps and your hamstrings. Mine was totally out of balance. Totally. Anyway, to make a long story short, it was serious. Now they fix those things all together. But I had a torn up knee. So I went to him on my own. It had nothing to do with the Chargers. I said, "God, can you help me?" He said, "Yeah, if you will really go with me on this thing, I can really help you." So, I put my faith in him and he made me stretch as long as I worked out. I worked out with really, really light weights, trying to coordinate the hamstring. My hamstrings were way weaker than my quadriceps, and it was totally out of balance. So after I went through this whole thing, I said, "OK, I'm going to go with it." So that's what happened. Then my speed increased and that's what happened when I got all that damn speed. Because I was muscle balanced. My God, I could run like a deer. To me, it was just incredible. So anyway, that's how I started.

Sid Gillman and I just didn't get along. I just didn't see eye-to-eye with what he was doing. Of course, I was a kid and this guy had been well respected, and certainly had earned that. However, his camaraderie with the players left something to be desired. I felt a little bad. Here I am nearly 60 years old. He just died. I feel bad about saying that, but the truth was that it didn't matter if you were Lance or me or any of our linemen or anybody. He kept you under pressure at all times. I just didn't think that was conducive to running a football team. I'm certainly not the one in charge of that, but basically that's what it was. I always thought we had the talent to really go all the way, but Sid just kept you under... Do you understand what I'm saying? He just kept you under the damn gun all the time. You were just scared to death all the damn time.

Of course they wanted control of you. That was the whole trip, especially Gillman. He never mentioned it to me, but it was just understood that you don't do anything like that (running Dick Post LTD. clothing stores) outside of football. You can't take your attention away from football. So basically that was it. There was nothing really said. It was just understood that's just the way that it was. But Hell, I was just a young kid. I thought I was on top of the world. I thought this shit was going to go on forever. That was just being stupid and young. Honestly for me, I was never that way. I just tried to fit in. I got totally sidetracked with who I was.

I was just a little kid from Oklahoma. I lived with my grandparents when I was a kid and we lived in a little two-room house with a bunch of kids. I got carried away. I absolutely got carried away. Kind of not too hard to look at, had all the women in the world and I was running good. Hell, I just lost it. I had no idea. Especially California from Oklahoma back in those days. My God, you have got to be kidding. We don't do that shit here in Oklahoma. But there was a lot of stuff I wasn't very proud of. I just tried to fit in. It was such a shallow life, really. It was a shallow life compared to the way it is now. My God. But back in those days we didn't have any advisors; we didn't have any counseling. What the Hell would you do? If they threw open a candy store out there for you, what the Hell would you do when you never had a damn thing in your life?

There's a lot of stuff I'm really embarrassed about; that whole damn thing. Because that was never me. That was just never me. I just tried to be somebody I wasn't. At that time, it was just a few years. I look back on it now and I'm approaching 60. I'll be 59 soon. But my God, you look back and you go, "Oh my God. That's a little embarrassing." Getting a look at all that shit. But I played it for all it was worth. You gotta give yourself a break. It was just the times... You can't beat yourself up for it because it just happened and that is the way it was. I couldn't control it, and I just went for it. But I had a lot of great experiences. I just loved it all. That will always be part, just a tiny little part of my life. That's part of life. That's what you do. You live and learn. The only thing kids have now is you have all the advantages that we didn't have when I was going through it. Guys are so damn much smarter than we were. They really are. They have so much more information. And that's a good thing. But Hell, back then you just sort of went for it. But hey man, it was a trip. It was a trip.

A lot of people have asked me, "Would you do it again?" I say, "Well shit, how in the Hell can you say?" It made me be who I am today. Yeah, I would do it again. I would like to have a little more information, but Hell yeah, shit. If not, what in the Hell would you be doing? So all in all it was a trip. It was just a damn trip. But Lance helped me immensely. He just took me under his wing. I just idolized him and tried to be just like him. He's from Arkansas and I'm from Oklahoma. So we hooked up pretty good. He helped me as much as he could. But we all just went through it. It was amazing what you don't know as you look back from today's level, from whatever is going on in pro football. You just look back on Sid and whatever happened. You know, Bum (Phillips) was such a great guy. He was there the entire time I was there, as defensive coordinator. It would have really been fun to play for someone that was really in touch with you. And I don't mean to put Sid down or anything. He just wasn't good for me. Bum would have been great. I would have loved to play for him. Or Al Davis. Those guys, my God. All those old guys are with Al and are Raiders forever. We just didn't get that opportunity. It's just too damn bad you couldn't hook up with the right team to your personality. But basically once you're done, you're done. When he calls you in and says you're traded to the Denver Broncos, I just couldn't believe it. Anyway, that's the way that whole trip pretty much went.

Martin Baccaglio,
Defensive End
College: San Jose State
Years with the Chargers: 1968

Most professional football careers are short-lived. Such was the case for Martin Baccaglio. But in just three years in the American Football League, Baccaglio played for two of the greatest coaches the game has ever known, Sid Gillman and Paul Brown.

When I first was drafted, they flew me down to San Diego and I met Sid Gillman. I guess he wasn't in a good mood that day. I came in there and he said, "Here, I have your contract. I want you to sign it." And I said, "Well, I'd like to take it home." I said I had an advisor, which Sid didn't like. Anyway, at that point he just flew into an absolute tirade, and started yelling and screaming at me that the players have had their way with the two leagues, but now things were different. I had better sign the thing right now. This was all I was going to get.

Anyway, he ranted and raved for about five minutes and I forget who was the player personnel guy at the time (Tom Miner), but he was sitting next to me and he was sort of aghast. So anyway, Sid finally shut up and we got up and walked out. And that was it. That was my first meeting with him. We never did get together on a contract, so I didn't go my first year, and I played in a minor league in San Jose. We never were able to get together on a contract, so then the next year I did go to camp. But Sid and I got along great after that. I liked the guy. They used to call him the "Lion that Roared." Two or three times a week he would just flip his lid and start ranting and raving. But the guy had a heart of gold. He and I got to be what I would say... we had good mutual respect and enjoyed one another. He liked me and I liked him. So it turned into a nice relationship. Most of the players liked Sid...

The Chargers were a flamboyant team. Sid Gillman liked everybody to have a good time. It was kind of a circus atmosphere all the time. The Bengals were old-style football. Paul Brown was a very, very conservative guy.

With the Chargers, after every game they'd bring a cooler full of beer in the locker room and everybody would start partying. You could drink at the airports, and smoke in public. With the Bengals, there was absolutely no liquor anywhere around the organization. You were not allowed to go buy a drink at the airport; you were not allowed to smoke in public. If you had a

real flamboyant girlfriend with the Bengals, Paul Brown didn't like that. If you got in trouble with the law, you were pretty much off the team.

In San Diego, all that sort of stuff was just looked over. So it was a completely different atmosphere. It was the Midwest versus California. I really enjoyed the Chargers. Sid liked to have fun, and he felt that when you're playing football, you should be having fun. With the Bengals it was just like this is a coalminers job, and you're only here for one thing, and that is to play football. Anyway, it was a completely different atmosphere.

I guess the funniest was when we went to New York. We stayed a week in East Orange when we played the Jets. I think we played Boston and then we went up to New York. Anyway, I had a roommate, Brian Bernard, I think his name was. He was a linebacker; he was a rookie too. He was from the Bible Belt, and he didn't drink or anything. So he and I decided to go tour the town of New York one day. So we ended up down by the waterfront and we just were wandering around. I was getting kind of thirsty. It was hot that day, so I said, "Let's go get a beer." And he kind of turned up his eyebrows at me. We walked into this bar and there were these rough, old salts in there. Just a rough and tumble bunch. So anyway, the bartender comes up, and they were kind of eyeing us. He said, "What are you going to have?" And I said, "Well, I'll have a beer." And Brian, he didn't want a beer, he didn't want to drink anything, but he was just so intimidated by all these things that he ordered a beer too, and drank it. I just thought that was kind of funny.

Football was a wonderful experience. I did it for three years, and that was enough. The Chargers were a wonderful organization to play for, and I enjoyed myself when I was there. I wish I could have finished my career there, but that's not the way things worked out.

JIM SCHMEDDING, GUARD

College: Weber State
Years with the Chargers: 1968-1970

After a successful college career that included being named as a division All-American, the Chicago Bears drafted Jim Schmedding. Schmedding had no desire to begin his career on the Bears' taxi squad, so he left the team and was picked up by the Chargers where he made significant contributions for more than two years.

As a young man who just really enjoyed playing, who never really had any great aspirations or overwhelming aspirations to be a professional football player, it's kind of like the opportunity showed up. If I can say it that way.

The NFL was, I was kind of oriented that way rather than the AFL. The AFL was this run-and-gun basketball-in-the-grass kind of a program. I didn't know much about it. Television didn't cover them nearly as well as the NFL. I had just been an NFL guy, but it wasn't because of anything other than the environment I grew up in. The AFL was this other group of guys and the fact that when the circumstances, when it became clear that I was at least gonna get an opportunity to play professional football, it was the first year of the combined draft. So there were just more guys they were gonna take and there were more places you could go. It really didn't matter from my perspective. They were all gonna be the same. Sure there were some teams that were better than others, and I'd like to have been this place or that place more but it really didn't matter. I was just grateful for the opportunity to go try. And that's what continued to puzzle me...

Joe Madro was a line coach and he was a funny little old guy. After getting out and seeing a lot of things, he's the closest thing to Yoda I've ever met. The guy's amazing. He was a brilliant man in understanding football and understanding really basic technical movements in football. For people who wanted to take advantage of what he could do, he'd put up this caustic thing at times. He loved pushing you as far as you'd go, and then a little further. He was an interesting guy. He really helped me out a lot. I made things almost too complicated and he helped me to get past that, to get it very simple. He showed me some secrets and some things from his perspective that I'd never heard anybody say and 20 years later I've never heard anybody say. There's things I teach kids right now about pulling that I still haven't heard guys talk about that's still the most efficient way I've seen the move. They're Joe, just Joe. But they're little gems, little jewels...

What are some memorable moments of your time with the Chargers? There's probably time on the field and time off the field. When I think of playing professional football, and I think about a moment in time with the Chargers, the one that sticks out as bright and clear as today, I shut my eyes and I can see the whole thing again. It was playing in Shea Stadium against Joe Namath, the New York Jets. The last two minutes of, I think it was a Monday Night Football game. If it wasn't, it was a Saturday night. It was a nationally televised deal. There were 60 or 70,000 screaming people and that stadium goes straight up. It doesn't go back. I'm standing on the sidelines looking up at this, and for the first time in my life, realizing, "I really am

here. I really am in this place." Joe Namath, taking their team down, it was a classic battle, who's gonna have the ball last. Whether we're gonna beat them or they're gonna beat us. I can't tell you today who won that game. I just remember in the last two minutes, stopping and realizing where I was. The impact of that has never left me. The magnitude was probably the first realization that I ever had of, "Man, I'm really in here." The rest of it was just playing. It's kind of like you play from sideline to sideline and that's it. Yeah, there's people in the stands, there's a lot of noise and this and that. That was the most memorable for me. That was an interesting one.

I remember being on special teams on a regular basis and we were not doing well. The first half of the game, we were getting going. Something happened and I took off. You usually had a guy who was coming from the other side, hitting you. Normally what would happen is I'd get hit, knocked down, roll, and get up, and go. I found that if I did that correctly, about the time I'd show up at the wedge, the guys would have usually just committed themselves to somebody else who was there ahead of me who hadn't been hit. I went flying up into that wedge as hard as I could and the back came in the other way. There was a collision. Stars and everything else going up in my head. I heard 50,000 people in San Diego Stadium go, "Ooh." It was one of those kind of collisions. I got mobbed by the guys. I got up and was kind of dazed, walking around. The other guy was still laying on the ground. It was ugly. It was one of those deals where I hit him and we just went right over. I went right on top of him. We were both going full blast at each other. How we kept from killing each other, I don't know. Other than that, there were games and people I played against that were...

I remember Ben Davidson jumping over the top of me, literally jumping over me. How did he do that? Buck Buchanan, the Kansas City Chiefs. He was like 6'8" and a good 320 pounds at that time. I was only 280. Buck Buchanan could get to the quarterback any play he wanted to. And it really didn't matter who he was playing against. When he teed off and he wanted to go, it'd take four guys to hold onto him. But he didn't do it very often, which I found very interesting. There were times when I could handle guys and there were times when, "Is this the same guy? What happened here?" It was incredible. I think it was as much, on the field stuff was gaining the respect of the other people and people you had respect for and doing the best you could with your job and working as hard as you could and recognizing that it wasn't always perfect. If we didn't have to hurry the ball off, and you kept your hands off John, and I'd done the job, I was okay. I'd get to the next play and get on.

There's the time in Oakland when John Hadl called an audible that we hadn't used for 6 weeks, that everybody on the team got but me. I hesitated, just a fraction of a second. We were on the goal line. And that fraction of a second hesitation almost cost Dickie Post his life. He came flying up in the air and just got crucified because I blew it. I absolutely went blank on what the play was. And we had like 70 or 80 audibles. We had almost every one of our regular plays had an audible number to it. They weren't always tied together, so that the relationships weren't real good. And we normally would go through the audibles that we would use, that we'd expect to use during that game. This was one we hadn't used for quite a while. And I was absolutely blank. So that's why some weeks I started and some weeks I didn't start.

Off the field, I think probably the most memorable event was the trip to New York. I'm walking through downtown New York, Time Square with three other offensive linemen who were all a lot bigger than I was. And just watching the people watch us. We were clearly something unique. Getting in and out of cabs, we'd have to take two cabs for all of us to get to the place we were going.

I was a guy who had been a pretty crazy kind of a guy and then got married. When I got married, kind of changed my whole program. Quit drinking and quit doing a lot of things. So when I'm out running around with a bunch of guys who enjoy the beer, I go right along with them, but I'd get to the point where, they'd just order 7-Up for me and it wasn't even an issue. Initially, it was like, "What's the problem? What's wrong with you?" They found out I was okay and I wasn't a bad guy. I wasn't a spy. Just that I'd made some changes. So I'd gained the respect of the guys and their acceptance.

PHIL TUCKETT, WIDE RECEIVER
College: Weber State
Years with the Chargers: 1968

Phil Tuckett's AFL playing career consisted of just one regular-season game. It was after his retirement as a player that Tuckett made his greatest contribution to the game as a Vice President for NFL Films. He has written and edited many of NFL Films' greatest pieces. Tuckett's work as a writer, producer and director is highly acclaimed and has received more than 30 Emmy Awards.

I was a senior at Weber State College in Ogden, Utah. Then I had received quite a few inquiries from about 12 different teams. They sent letters and questionnaires that I filled out. They had expressed interest in drafting me. I think the team that I heard from the most was the Dallas Cowboys. They were indicating that they were going to draft me in the seventh or eighth round. Back then I think there were 16 rounds. There were more than there are today. So I had my mind set on going to camp with Dallas in Thousand Oaks, California. So it was a good learning experience for me because I had actually told a bunch of people that that is what I thought was going to happen. My father, who was very interested in my athletic career, was telling his friends that I was going to be drafted by the Dallas Cowboys. So the first day came and went. They went through about seven or eight rounds in the first day and I didn't get drafted. It was pretty humiliating to me but I had done it to myself by telling people. Then I got some calls from people asking what had happened. I was just semi-humiliated as it turned out, because the next day the next seven or eight rounds went by and I still hadn't been drafted. I guess I found out later that in the NFL they send out thousands of those letters and promise all kinds of stuff that never happens. I was just naïve enough to believe it. So I kind of went into hiding. I was pretty embarrassed, myself. I just made up my mind that there would be no post-graduate football for me.

As soon as the draft ended, I got a telegram. In those days you actually sent telegrams. There was no email or anything. It was from the Chargers, a team that had never sent me a letter at all. I had never had any contact with them whatsoever. It said, we're interested in signing you as a free agent, and they gave me an offer right there on the telegram. It was a bonus of $1,500 to sign a contract with them. I believe the contract was for $28,000 a season, or something like that. And since I didn't have any other offers, it sounded pretty good to me. I didn't even need an agent to figure that one out. But when I did go to camp, I found out that everybody drafted from the sixth round on, didn't get a signing bonus at all because they were obligated to the Chargers and nobody had leverage to go anywhere else. So it turned out that at least financially, back in those days my wife and I really put the $1,500 to good use. So it turned out that except for the embarrassment that is caused for me not to be drafted, it turned out to be a better deal for me right off the bat with that $1,500 bonus. So I responded and said I would sign. They sent me a contract in the mail, I signed it and sent it back and I was on my way to camp…

Sid was obviously a master of the grand design of the passing game. I knew that right away. It was something like sitting in a class at Princeton, Albert Einstein teaching the theory of relativity or something. He impressed me a great deal that way. Also his intensity; Sid was always on edge. When he was talking about players on other teams, they were either brilliant or they were horseshit. But there didn't seem to be anything in between. He was just an extremist that way. He analyzed things so minutely, that if he saw a flaw, he knew how to attack it. And that's why he would say, " This guy is awful. We can kill them right here, because here are his flaws." If he couldn't find a flaw, then he just assumed that this guy was brilliant, that we should stay away from him. And the way his analytical mind worked, that's the way it turned out most of the time. And those Charger offenses of that era reflected that. He was less interested in the defense. Personally, and this is just my opinion from being around him for a year-and-a-half, he sort of had a distaste for defense in general. Even almost subliminally for his own defense. Because his life was all based around attacking defenses. So I think he was the polar opposite of George Allen, who had very little interest in the offense of his team and had an intense interest in the defense, to the point of maybe neglecting that part of the equation, on the offense. All he wanted to do was have a team up there that didn't make mistakes and put his defense in a bad position. I think Sid maybe felt a little bit the same way. I know that he was often disgusted with his own defense, to the point where he couldn't even really deal with them. So he delegated a lot of that authority to his defensive coaches, just turned that white-hot glare of his intellect onto the passing game and stretching the field, as he used to say. Stretching it to the sidelines and to the end zones, and making these poor bastards in the secondary cover us. So he impressed me that way, of course.

I have been impressed my whole career at NFL Films with his influence. It's just so obvious that he invented the West Coast Passing Game. His offense was running up 600 yards of passing offense in 1958 with the Los Angeles Rams. So he started way back when nobody was doing this kind of thing, and he perfected it. And after I was cut, I ran into Sid many times. He was always really happy to see that I had succeeded in the career that I had taken on after I left the Chargers. And probably, in sort of a wishful-thinking kind of way, took a little credit for my career in that he was smart enough to cut me at the right time that I could go and get this other job. It seemed to me to be a little auspicious, but I understood also, that he had probably cut a lot of people in his career and never knew what happened to them. And there was a little bit of feeling bad in telling someone that they are not good enough to do their job. At least here was one case where he knew that the person went on and actually benefited from being cut. So we always had a fun relationship that way whenever I saw him...

I had a B.A. in English from Weber State. So during the off-season, because that $28,000 contract became $1,000-a-week during the season when I was on the taxi squad. I was activated right at the end of the season and got my "full salary" for that one week. The other weeks I was making $1,000-a-week, and that was just for the football season. So during the off-season, I did a lot of scrambling just to pay the rent and provide food and clothing for my family. So I worked construction, I was a substitute teacher, and then I was a reporter and columnist for the *Daily Californian*. And in the process of doing that, I kind of got that job just by going and applying. Even though I was a periphery player on the Chargers, the *Californian* was a local paper out in El Cajon, so they were kind of proud that they had an actual San Diego Charger on their staff writing sports. It was a good, little concern. I enjoyed every minute of it. I still have the column that I wrote, talking about a sophomore basketball player for Helix who was doing such a great job. But I predicted that he didn't have much of a career ahead of him because his knees, he had two knee operations as a sophomore. That was Bill Walton. So I picked that one pretty well. I didn't think he was going to go anywhere. But it was fun. I didn't make much money, but it was good experience for me, as I say. It kind of crystallized this interest I had in observing my fellow human beings and didn't have any outlet for that.

I had just been a jock my whole life growing up, and in high school and in college. But I wrote in the *Daily Californian*, and then Jerry Wynn, who was the Charger P.R. guy at the time. He would be a great guy to talk to, because as the P.R. Director, if he's interested in talking about it, he knows where all the bodies are buried. Who ran the front office, and then he put his stamp on what the public should know and all of the other things. And somebody gave him a copy of the *Daily Californian*. He saw it and he called me at my apartment. He said, "I didn't even know you were a writer." I explained my background to him and he said, "This is good. It is very interesting; you have a nice point of view. Diaries are big right now." It was the time of *Instant Replay*, it was a best seller. That was Jerry Kramer's book. He said, "Did you keep a diary of your season last year? It may be interesting. Here's an all-pro, and here's the flip side of the coin, a free agent, taxi squad guy." So I said, "Yeah, yeah, I did keep a diary." So he said, "Well, I could take that to New York, and I have a good friend there named Al Silverman, who is the publisher of *Sport Magazine*. They're always looking for first-person account kind of things. So he says, "Why don't you bring it by the office?" I said, "OK." And that's where the scraps of paper came in because I had actually told a falsehood. I had not kept a diary. It just seemed like when he said that, that the right thing to say was, "Yes, I had." So in a very stream-of-conscious way, I told my wife to go get a bunch of paper. I didn't want it to look all neat and tidy, like I had written it in a little book. So I just got a bunch of scraps of paper and started over one weekend, doing a stream of conscious remembering of things that had happened. It wasn't very well structured, but there were a lot of ideas of conscious that stuck in my brain and surprisingly it all came flooding back pretty easily. I think I wrote like 70-80 pages. Once I got started I couldn't stop. Maybe it was good therapy, too. I hadn't thought of it that way until just now. But it might have been helping me get through my struggles during the off-season there.

So I came and gave it to Jerry Wynn and I apologized for it being such a mess. I said, "Do you want me to go back and organize it better?" He said, "No, no. They have editors at *Sport Magazine* that could do that." So he took it up to New York and right as summer camp opened the next year, it was on the newsstand, "How I won my Lightning Bolts," in *Sport Magazine*. It was a first-person account of my rookie free-agent season with the Chargers. That article was what I presented Ed Sabol with when I met him at camp one day. I knew that he had something to do with football and television, but I wasn't sure what. But I approached him with the magazine in his hand and said, "This is my article, I'm a writer. I was wondering if you hired football-playing writers." And Ed Sabol's comment to me was, "I didn't think there were any football-playing writers." He was falling back on the old stereotype of jocks. But I think that right there he looked at that and made up his mind that if I looked for a job, that he was interested in hiring me. He knew I had no experience...

I remember having spent the whole year suffering up in the stands, watching my team, the team I was supposed to be on, playing on the field. It was brutal, psychologically. It was just horrifying. I remember it was kind of a thrill to make the team and be on the taxi squad because I had come from so far away, being a free agent. But I found out that if you're not playing, and especially if you're not even dressing for the games, it is so different from if you were on the bench in high school or anyplace else. You develop all this feeling of teamwork that football gives you. You work for that goal during the week in practice, and then your role is to sit up in the stands in street clothes. It was really quite brutal.

The other thing I didn't like about it is that you can help and hope that something happens to one of the people ahead of you. In this case it was a fellow named Ken Dyer and Lane Fenner. They were two wide receiver rookies that were backing up Alworth and Garrison. I didn't want to feel this way. I didn't want to think this way, but I couldn't help thinking that if somebody took them out on a coverage or something and they were injured, that I would get a chance. As soon as I would think that, I would say, "Oh Jeez, what a jerk you are for feeling that way. These guys are your teammates." But then I noticed that every time someone was hurt during a game and all the taxi squad guys sat together, everybody would lean forward and all of a sudden be paying really strict attention. Seeing if the number of the guy on the field corresponded with their position. So really, everybody felt the same way. It wasn't something we discussed, but it was psychologically sort of devastating to be put in that position. Because of that, and then the fact that that happened all year, when I finally got the chance to dress, I can remember very clearly every aspect of that day.

Getting up in the morning, going to the stadium and going into the players' entrance. And even though I had been with the team all year, I had never experienced that. Realizing that I was going to go and put on my own uniform and go out on the field. I can remember very clearly dressing. I can remember Lance Alworth coming by and congratulating me on being activated. He was a good guy. And also Ron Mix took a special interest in me. They both made a point to come by and say that they were proud of the fact that I had hung in there all year and hadn't given in to the obvious opportunity to be depressed about everything. I just felt proud of all the hard work that had gone into it. I felt proud that my dad was in the stands. He came in that day to see me run out on the field with the team. Even though I knew that there was a slim chance that I would get in on offense, I probably was just as proud as any rookie that's ever gone onto the field to play their first game in the history of the NFL. I can't imagine it meaning more to anybody than it meant to me that day.

I had also had a very vivid dream of scoring a touchdown. This dream puzzled me because I didn't score a touchdown on a pass play; I had scored a touchdown on recovering a fumble in the end zone. It was so vivid that I had that in my mind. So in the second quarter I was covering a punt and Rodger Bird was the punt returner for the Raiders. He fumbled the ball, but the way he fumbled it, it popped out of his arms and rolled right towards me. I was coming down as the right contain man, R1 in the terminology of special teams. My job was to keep containment. But as soon as I saw that ball pop out, I can just remember my brain kicking in and thinking that this is what my dream was. That ball was coming and I was just going to pick it up and run it right in. He was at about the 30-yard line. So the ball came right at me and even though you are supposed to just fall on the ball, I had no intention of doing that because I was going to fulfill my dream. Whatever my destiny was through that dream, I was going to fulfill it. So I leaned over to pick up the ball and as soon as I touched, whoever on the Raiders was behind me came and he saw that I was about to pick it up, so he pushed me from behind. That push gave my momentum a surge and I went over the top of the ball. I touched, but I overshot it. The ball popped in the air, and I still have the play. When I got here to NFL Films, I went and got a copy of it. It is in my private archives. The ball popped up in the air. It turned out to be one of the great football follies that ever came out of the AFL because the ball was touched by about 10 different people and fumbled several times and pushed all the way back into the end one where it is recovered for a touchdown, but not by me unfortunately. That would have been the perfect end to the story. And actually I got up and I had another shot at it at about the five-yard line, but by then both teams were in like a rugby scrum. I think it was Ken Dyer, the guy that was ahead of me on the depth chart, who actually recovered the ball. So that's what I remember most vividly about the action in the game is how close I came to living that dream that I had. It was a thrill from start to finish and something that I will never forget. I would say that it was worth all the hard work just to have that one opportunity to be a pro football player on the field with my team that I had been working with all year and contributing what little I could.

1960 CHARGERS TEAM STATISTICS
(10-4 OVERALL) FIRST PLACE IN THE AFL WEST

Team Statistics	Chargers	Opponent
TOTAL FIRST DOWNS	273	259
Rushing	106	97
Passing	141	138
Penalty	26	24
TOTAL NET YARDS	4,713	4,258
Avg. Per Game	336.6	304.1
Avg. Per Play	5.4	4.7
NET YARDS RUSHING	1,900	1,705
Avg. Per Game	135.7	121.8
NET YARDS PASSING	2,813	2,553
Avg. Per Game	200.9	182.4
Gross Yards	3,177	2,851
Completions/Attempts	229/441	227/467
Completion Pct.	.519	.486
Had Intercepted	29	28
PUNTS/AVERAGE	58/39.7	62/38.6
PENALTIES/YARDS	70/648	59/569
FUMBLES/BALL LOST	30/16	39/17
TOUCHDOWNS	48	42
Rushing	23	20
Passing	21	21
Returns	4	1
QUARTERBACK SACKS	36.0	40.0

Rushing	No.	Yds.	Avg.	TD
Lowe	136	855	6.3	8
Ferguson	126	438	3.5	4
Kemp	45	238	4.4	8
Ford	20	154	7.7	2
Flowers	39	161	4.1	1
Martin	6	23	3.8	0
Laraba	3	13	4.3	0
Clatterbuck	3	11	3.7	0
Waller	9	5	0.6	0
Norton	1	2	2.0	0
Totals	**397**	**1,900**	**5.0**	**23**

Receiving	No.	Yds.	Avg.	TD
R. Anderson	44	614	14.0	5
Kocourek	40	662	16.6	1
Womble	32	316	9.9	2
Clark	27	431	16.0	0
Norton	25	414	16.6	5
Lowe	23	377	16.4	2
Ferguson	21	168	8.0	2
Flowers	12	153	12.8	1
Martin	2	18	9.0	1
Waller	3	24	8.0	0
Totals	**229**	**3,177**	**14.0**	**19**

Passing	Att.	Comp.	Yds.	Comp.%	TD	Int.
Kemp	406	211	3,018	.520	20	25
Clatterbuck	23	15	112	.652	1	1
Laraba	7	2	23	.286	0	2
Lowe	3	1	24	.333	0	0
Ford	1	0	0	.000	0	0
Waller	1	0	0	.000	0	1
Totals	**441**	**229**	**3,177**	**.519**	**21**	**29**

Interceptions	No.	Yds.	TD
D. Harris	5	56	1
Nix	4	30	1
McNeil	3	47	0
Maguire	3	37	0
Loudd	3	17	0
Sears	2	73	0
Zeman	2	25	0
Botchan	2	8	0
Garner	2	2	0
Laraba	1	17	0
Schleicher	1	5	0
Totals	**28**	**317**	**2**

Kicking	FG	Att.	PAT	Att.	Pts.
Agajanian	13	23	46	47	85

Punting	No.	Avg.
Maguire	43	40.5
Laraba	15	37.2

Punt Returns	No.	FC	Yds.	Avg.	TD
D. Harris	13	0	105	8.1	0
Sears	9	0	101	11.2	0
Garner	6	0	85	14.2	0
Ford	2	0	6	3	0
Lowe	1	0	0	0	0

Kickoff Returns	No.	Yds.	Avg.	TD
Lowe	28	611	21.8	0
Ford	13	294	22.6	0
Norton	8	153	19.1	0
Sears	8	155	19.4	0
DeLuca	1	0	0	0

Above: The 1960 Los Angeles Chargers.

Left: May 18, 1960 - The Chargers offensive line from left to right, Ron Mix, Fred Cole, Joe Amstutz, Orlando Ferrante and Sam DeLuca.

SEPTEMBER 10, 1960
Memorial Coliseum - Los Angeles, California
Attendance - 17,724

					Total
Chargers	0	7	0	14	21
Texans	6	14	0	0	20

Texans	Davidson 12-yard pass to Burford for the touchdown.
Texans	Spikes 1-yard run for the touchdown. Spikes kicks the extra point.
Chargers	Kemp 46-yard pass to Anderson for the touchdown. Agajanian kicks the extra point.
Texans	Davidson 17-yard pass to Haynes for the touchdown. Spikes kicks the extra point.
Chargers	Kemp 7-yard run for the touchdown. Agajanian kicks the extra point.
Chargers	Kemp 4-yard pass to Ferguson for the touchdown. Agajanian kicks the extra point.

	Chargers	Texans
First Downs	22	21
Rushing Yards	55	64
Passing Yards	299	230
Punts-Average	4-40.0	5-47.5
Fumbles-Lost	2-1	1-0
Penalties-Yards	2-13	7-50

Chargers' Leaders
Rushing	Kemp 8-26, Ferguson 8-22, Lowe 8-20, Waller 3-3
Passing	Kemp 24-41-0-275, Lowe 1-1-0-24
Receiving	Womble 7-92, Anderson 5-103, Lowe 3-14, Clark 3-42, Flowers 2-25
Interceptions	Sears 1-26

Texans' Leaders
Rushing	Spikes 9-62, Robinson 8-27, Swink 6-16, Davidson 5-7, Haynes 3-15
Passing	Davidson 22-40-1-230, Haynes 0-1-0-0
Receiving	Haynes 7-62, Robinson 5-52, Boydston 3-45, Burford 3-31, Swink 2-10
Interceptions	None

Week 1 Games
Los Angeles 21, Dallas 20
Denver 13, Boston 10
Houston 37, Oakland 22
New York 27, Buffalo 3

Week 1 Standings
East	W	L	T	West	W	L	T
Houston	1	0	0	Los Angeles	1	0	0
Boston	0	1	0	Denver	1	0	0
New York	1	0	0	Oakland	0	1	0
Buffalo	0	1	0	Dallas	0	1	0

Jack Kemp threw the first touchdown pass in Chargers' history, a 46-yard strike to Ralph Anderson.

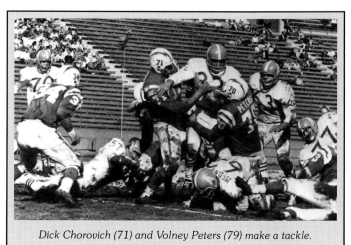

Dick Chorovich (71) and Volney Peters (79) make a tackle.

SEPTEMBER 18, 1960
Jeppesen Stadium - Houston, Texas
Attendance – 20,156

					Total
Chargers	7	7	0	14	28
Oilers	14	7	17	0	38

Chargers	Kemp 25-yard pass to Womble for the touchdown. Agajanian kicks extra point.
Oilers	Smith 47-yard run for the touchdown. Blanda kicks the extra point.
Oilers	Blanda 1-yard run for the touchdown. Blanda kicks the extra point.
Oilers	Blanda 1-yard run for the touchdown. Blanda kicks the extra point.
Oilers	Blanda kicks a 13-yard field goal.
Oilers	Tolar 1-yard run for the touchdown. Blanda kicks the extra point.
Chargers	Kemp 18-yard pass to Womble for the touchdown. Agajanian kicks the extra point.
Chargers	Kemp 55-yard pass to Flowers for the touchdown. Agajanian kicks the extra point.

	Chargers	Oilers
First Downs	22	22
Rushing Yards	43	295
Passing Yards	337	111
Punts-Average	5-43.2	6-40.6
Fumbles-Lost	3-2	2-1
Penalties-Yards	5-40	10-88

Chargers' Leaders
Rushing	Ferguson 7-25, Waller 6-14, Flowers 1-3, Lowe 1-1, Kemp 1-0
Passing	Kemp 27-44-1-337, Waller 1-0-1-0
Receiving	Anderson 8-50, Womble 5-65, Clark 4-94, Ferguson 3-14, Flowers 2-70
Interceptions	Maguire 1-0

Oilers' Leaders
Rushing	Smith 14-80, Tolar 11-51, Cannon 8-68, Cline, 8-62, Blanda 7-20
Passing	Blanda 6-17-0-101, Lee 0-3-1-0, Milstead 1-1-0-10
Receiving	Carson 3-54, Tolar 1-21, J. White 1-18, Cline 1-10, Groman 1-8
Interceptions	Johnston 1-33, Norton 1-20

Week 2 Games
Houston 38, Los Angeles 28
Dallas 34, Oakland 16
Boston 28, New York 24
Denver 27, Buffalo 21

Week 2 Standings
East	W	L	T	West	W	L	T
Houston	2	0	0	Denver	2	0	0
New York	1	1	0	Los Angeles	1	1	0
Boston	1	1	0	Dallas	1	1	0
Buffalo	0	2	0	Oakland	0	2	0

September 25, 1960
Cotton Bowl - Dallas, Texas
Attendance – 42,000

					Total
Chargers	0	0	0	0	0
Texans	0	7	0	10	17

Texans	Davidson 6-yard pass to Robinson for the touchdown. Davidson kicks the extra point.
Texans	Johnson 1-yard run for the touchdown. Davidson kicks the extra point.
Texans	Davidson kicks a 12-yard field goal.

	Chargers	Texans
First Downs	16	20
Rushing Yards	122	91
Passing Yards	89	167
Punts-Average	3-41.3	4-41.0
Fumbles-Lost	5-2	2-1
Penalties-Yards	7-52	6-55

Chargers' Leaders

Rushing	Ferguson 16-93, Flowers 6-49, Kemp 6-(-28), Lowe 1-8
Passing	Kemp 11-30-4-89
Receiving	Clark 4-44, Ferguson 3-13, Norton 2-21, Anderson 2-11
Interceptions	Loudd 1-12, Garner 1-2

Texans' Leaders

Rushing	Robinson 9-45, Haynes 8-9, Dickinson 6-19, Spikes 4-10, Johnson 3-4
Passing	Davidson 17-37-2-167
Receiving	Boydston 4-52, Burford 4-43, Haynes 4-41, Robinson 4-36, Swink 1-(-5)
Interceptions	Corey 2-13, Stover 1-10, Headrick 1-6

Week 3 Games
Dallas 17, Los Angeles 0
Oakland 14, Houston 13
New York 28, Denver 24
Buffalo 13, Boston 0

Week 3 Standings

East	W	L	T	West	W	L	T
Houston	2	1	0	Denver	2	1	0
New York	2	1	0	Dallas	2	1	0
Boston	1	2	0	Los Angeles	1	2	0
Buffalo	1	2	0	Oakland	1	2	0

Charlie Flowers was highly sought after by teams in both leagues after coming out of college in 1959.

Royce Womble

October 2, 1960
War Memorial Stadium – Buffalo, New York
Attendance – 15,821

					Total
Chargers	0	7	7	10	24
Bills	0	3	7	0	10

Bills	Harper kicks a 27-yard field goal.
Chargers	Clatterbuck 11-yard pass to Kocourek for the touchdown. Agajanian kicks the extra point.
Chargers	Ferguson 2-yard run for the touchdown. Agajanian kicks the extra point.
Bills	Lucas 36-yard pass to Dubenion for the touchdown. Atkins kicks the extra point.
Chargers	Flowers 7-yard run for the touchdown. Agajanian kicks the extra point.
Chargers	Agajanian kicks an 8-yard field goal.

	Chargers	Bills
First Downs	12	18
Rushing Yards	89	89
Passing Yards	70	149
Punts-Average	5-43.8	4-39
Fumbles-Lost	2-1	0-0
Penalties-Yards	8-66	4-74

Chargers' Leaders

Rushing	Ferguson 15-40, Flowers 10-60, Clatterbuck 3-(-6), Lowe 1-(-5)
Passing	Clatterbuck 9-15-1-70
Receiving	Lowe 3-32, Flowers 3-8, Kocourek 1-11, Ferguson 1-10, Anderson 1-9
Interceptions	Maguire 2-37, Harris 1-14, Sears 1-47

Bills' Leaders

Rushing	Carlton 12-25, Brodhead 9-0, Kulbacki 8-35, O'Connell 4-(-12), Lucas 3-0
Passing	O'Connell 8-14-3-53, Brodhead 4-10-1-60, Lucas 1-1-0-36
Receiving	Dubenion 6-88, Rychelec 2-27, Chamberlin 2-18, Carlton 2-8, Lucas 1-8
Interceptions	McCabe 1-0

Week 4 Games
Los Angeles 24, Buffalo 10
New York 37, Dallas 35
Denver 31, Oakland 14
Houston and Boston - Bye

Week 4 Standings

East	W	L	T	West	W	L	T
New York	3	1	0	Denver	3	1	0
Houston	2	1	0	Dallas	2	2	0
Boston	1	2	0	Los Angeles	2	2	0
Buffalo	1	3	0	Oakland	1	3	0

Ben Agajanian had already played for nine professional football teams before coming to the Chargers in 1960.

OCTOBER 8, 1960
Memorial Coliseum – Los Angeles, California
Attendance – 18,226

					Total
Chargers	0	0	0	0	0
Patriots	18	7	10	0	35

Patriots	Cappalletti kicks a 23-yard filed goal.
Patriots	Burton 4-yard run for the touchdown. Cappalletti 2-yard pass to Crawford for the 2-point conversion.
Patriots	Songin 19-yard pass to Colclough for the touchdown. Cappalletti kicks the extra point.
Patriots	Crawford 1-yard run for the touchdown. Cappalletti kicks the extra point.
Patriots	Miller 1-yard run for the touchdown. Cappalletti kicks the extra point.
Patriots	Cappalletti kicks a 35-yard field goal.

	Chargers	Patriots
First Downs	14	17
Rushing Yards	18	171
Passing Yards	182	182
Punts-Average	6-40.5	4-36.5
Fumbles-Lost	4-3	3-0
Penalties-Yards	2-10	4-44

Chargers' Leaders
Rushing	Lowe 5-14, Flowers 5-3, Ferguson 3-9, Clatterbuck 3-0, Kemp 2-(-8)
Passing	Kemp 6-8-0-42, Clatterbuck 15-28-2-140
Receiving	Anderson 7-73, Clark 5-65, Womble 3-22, Ferguson 2-13, Flowers 2-12
Interceptions	Laraba 1-17

Patriots' Leaders
Rushing	Crawford 19-93, Christy 9-29, Burton 8-28, Miller 4-14, White 3-11
Passing	Songin 7-15-0-182, Christy 0-1-1-0
Receiving	Colclough 3-40, Wells 2-89, Lofton 2-39, Miller 1-11, Burton 1-3
Interceptions	Jacobs 1-12, Washington 1-0

Week 5 Games
Boston 35, Los Angeles 0
Oakland 20, Dallas 19
Houston 27, New York 21
Buffalo and Denver - Bye

Week 5 Standings
East	W	L	T	West	W	L	T
Houston	3	1	0	Denver	3	1	0
New York	3	2	0	Dallas	2	3	0
Boston	2	2	0	Los Angeles	2	3	0
Buffalo	1	3	0	Oakland	2	3	0

OCTOBER 16, 1960
Bears Stadium - Denver, Colorado
Attendance – 19,141

					Total
Chargers	7	3	13	0	23
Broncos	6	3	0	10	19

Broncos	Mingo kicks a 17-yard field goal
Chargers	Lowe 12-yard run for the touchdown. Agajanian kicks the extra point.
Broncos	Mingo kicks a 13-yard field goal.
Chargers	Agajanian kicks an 11-yard field goal.
Broncos	Mingo kicks a 38-yard field goal.
Chargers	Agajanian kicks a 26-yard field goal.
Chargers	Agajanian kicks a 46-yard field goal.
Chargers	Lowe 44-yard run for the touchdown. Agajanian kicks the extra point.
Broncos	Mingo kicks a 45-yard field goal.
Broncos	Carmichael 1-yard run for the touchdown. Mingo kicks the extra point.

	Chargers	Broncos
First Downs	16	14
Rushing Yards	75	72
Passing Yards	243	155
Punts-Average	5-39.6	3-41
Fumbles-Lost	2-2	3-3
Penalties-Yards	7-91	2-10

Chargers' Leaders
Rushing	Ferguson 15-63, Lowe 11-72, Kemp 7-(-62) Flowers 6-2
Passing	Kemp 16-29-1-243
Receiving	Lowe 4-95, Womble 4-57, Anderson 3-50, Clark 2-22, Kocourek 2-11
Interceptions	Nix 1-0, Loudd 1-5

Broncos' Leaders
Rushing	Rolle 10-11, Carmichael 4-11, Bell 3-73, Tripucka 2-(-26)
Passing	Tripucka 16-32-2-155, Mingo 0-1-0-0
Receiving	Taylor 7-54, Rolle 3-27, Carmichael 2-24, McNamara 1-21, Greer 1-17
Interceptions	Gonsoulin 1-19

Week 6 Games
Los Angeles 23, Denver 19
New York 17, Buffalo 13
Houston 20, Dallas 10
Oakland 27, Boston 14

Week 6 Standings
East	W	L	T	West	W	L	T
Houston	4	1	0	Denver	3	2	0
New York	4	2	0	Oakland	3	3	0
Boston	2	3	0	Los Angeles	3	3	0
Buffalo	1	4	0	Dallas	2	4	0

After his football career, Ernie Barnes became a highly accomplished artist.

Week 7 Games
Buffalo 38, Oakland 9
Houston 42, New York 28
Denver 31, Boston 24
Los Angeles and Dallas - Bye

Week 7 Standings

East	W	L	T	West	W	L	T
Houston	5	1	0	Denver	4	2	0
New York	4	3	0	Los Angeles	3	3	0
Boston	2	4	0	Oakland	3	4	0
Buffalo	2	4	0	Dallas	2	4	0

Orlando Ferrante

Paul Lowe had the Chargers first 100-yard rushing game.

OCTOBER 28, 1960
Boston University Field – Boston, Massachusetts
Attendance – 13,988

					Total
Chargers	7	21	7	10	45
Patriots	0	0	14	2	16

Chargers	Ferguson 1-yard run for the touchdown. Agajanian kicks the extra point.
Chargers	Kemp 1-yard run for the touchdown. Agajanian kicks the extra point.
Chargers	Harris intercepts Songin pass, returns it 42 yards for the touchdown. Agajanian kicks the extra point.
Chargers	Lowe 66-yard run for the touchdown. Agajanian kicks the extra point.
Chargers	Greene punt blocked, recovered in the end zone for the touchdown by Maguire. Agajanian kicks the extra point.
Patriots	Songin 59-yard pass to Beach for the touchdown. Cappalletti kicks the extra point.
Patriots	Songin 14-yard pass to Lofton for the touchdown. Cappalletti kicks the extra point.
Chargers	Agajanian kicks an 18-yard field goal.
Chargers	Kemp 38-yard pass to Anderson for the touchdown. Agajanian kicks the extra point.
Patriots	Laraba fumbles in the end zone, recovered by the Chargers for a safety.

	Chargers	Patriots
First Downs	18	13
Rushing Yards	199	31
Passing Yards	250	202
Punts-Average	3-39.3	4-45.25
Fumbles-Lost	2-0	2-2
Penalties-Yards	14-142	3-29

Chargers' Leaders

Rushing	Ferguson 13-50, Lowe 8-137, Kemp 5-6, Flowers 4-4, Martin 3-18
Passing	Kemp 13-23-1-234, Laraba 1-3-1-16
Receiving	Anderson 6-135, Clark 4-72, Kocourek 4-43
Interceptions	Harris 1-42, Garner 1-0

Patriots' Leaders

Rushing	Miller 11-45, Beach 3-(-3), Songin 2-(-13), Wells 1-12, Burton 1-3
Passing	Songin 11-23-2-140, White 3-7-0-43, Greene 3-3-0-19
Receiving	Beach 6-79, Colclough 4-38, Miller 3-19, Stephens 1-23, Lofton 1-21
Interceptions	Soltis 1-0, Cappalletti 1-21

Week 8 Games
Los Angeles 45, Boston 16
Buffalo 25, Houston 24
Dallas 17, Denver 14
Oakland 28, New York 27

Week 8 Standings

East	W	L	T	West	W	L	T
Houston	5	2	0	Denver	4	3	0
New York	4	4	0	Oakland	4	4	0
Boston	2	5	0	Los Angeles	4	3	0
Buffalo	3	4	0	Dallas	3	4	0

NOVEMBER 4, 1960
Polo Grounds – New York City, New York
Attendance – 19,402

					Total
Chargers	0	7	7	7	21
Titans	0	0	7	0	7

Chargers	Ferguson 1-yard run for the touchdown. Agajanian kicks the extra point.
Chargers	Lowe 62-yard run for the touchdown. Agajanian kicks the extra point.
Titans	Dorow 19-yard pass to Bohling for the touchdown. Shockley kicks the extra point.
Chargers	Kemp 1-yard run for the touchdown. Agajanian kicks the extra point.

	Chargers	Titans
First Downs	16	12
Rushing Yards	151	47
Passing Yards	186	169
Punts-Average	5-33	5-39.8
Fumbles-Lost	7-3	1-1
Penalties-Yards	2-20	1-7

Chargers' Leaders
Rushing	Lowe 10-80, Ferguson 10-29, Kemp 6-33
Passing	Kemp 13-33-1-186
Receiving	Clark 4-72, Kocourek 2-7, Lowe 2-28, Womble 2-15
Interceptions	Botchan 1-0, Zeman 1-0, Nix 1-8

Titans' Leaders
Rushing	Mathis 10-43, Burton 2-18
Passing	Dorow 12-32-3-169
Receiving	Bohling 4-42, Maynard 4-41, Powell 3-65
Interceptions	Donahoo 1-19

Week 9 Games
Los Angeles 21, New York 7
Boston 34, Oakland 28
Houston 45, Denver 25
Dallas 45, Buffalo 28

Week 9 Standings

East	W	L	T	West	W	L	T
Houston	6	2	0	Los Angeles	5	3	0
New York	4	5	0	Denver	4	4	0
Boston	3	5	0	Dallas	4	4	0
Buffalo	3	5	0	Oakland	4	5	0

Ron Waller runs through the Titans' defense.

Paul Lowe (23), Sid Gillman, Chuck Noll and Sam DeLuca (72) check out the action from the sidelines.

NOVEMBER 13, 1960
Memorial Coliseum – Los Angeles, California
Attendance – 21,805

					Total
Chargers	14	7	3	0	24
Oilers	0	14	0	7	21

Chargers	Kemp 34-yard pass to Anderson for the touchdown. Agajanian kicks the extra point.
Chargers	Kemp 4-yard pass to Anderson for the touchdown. Agajanian kicks the extra point.
Oilers	Blanda 6-yard pass to Carson for the touchdown. Blanda kicks the extra point.
Chargers	Lowe 3-yard run for the touchdown. Agajanian kicks the extra point.
Oilers	Blanda 3-yard pass to Groman for the touchdown. Blanda kicks the extra point.
Chargers	Agajanian kicks a 22-yard field goal.
Oilers	Blanda 4-yard pass to Cannon for the touchdown. Blanda kicks the extra point.

	Chargers	Oilers
First Downs	26	24
Rushing Yards	116	20
Passing Yards	296	366
Punts-Average	2-39.5	1-38.0
Fumbles-Lost	2-2	2-1
Penalties-Yards	7-74	4-44

Chargers' Leaders
Rushing	Kemp 15-15, Lowe 12-85, Ferguson 5-16
Passing	Kemp 18-37-2-296, Lowe 0-1-0-0
Receiving	Kocourek 7-105, Anderson 5-85, Lowe 2-53, Ferguson 2-27, Clark 1-20
Interceptions	Harris 1-0, Nix 1-5, Loudd 1-0, Zeman 1-25

Oilers' Leaders
Rushing	D. Smith 11-31, Cannon 6-18, Blanda 4-(-29)
Passing	Blanda 31-55-4-366
Receiving	Hennigan 8-110, D. Smith 8-73, Groman 7-88, Carson 4-57, Cannon 4-38
Interceptions	Spence 1-0, Kendall 1-10

Week 10 Games
Los Angeles 24, Houston 21
Oakland 20, Buffalo 7
Boston 38, New York 21
Dallas 34, Denver 7

Week 10 Standings

East	W	L	T	West	W	L	T
Houston	6	3	0	Los Angeles	6	3	0
Boston	4	5	0	Dallas	5	4	0
New York	4	6	0	Oakland	5	5	0
Buffalo	3	6	0	Denver	4	5	0

NOVEMBER 20, 1960
Memorial Coliseum – Los Angeles, California
Attendance – 16,161

					Total
Chargers	0	3	0	0	3
Bills	6	13	0	13	32

Bills	O'Connell 17-yard pass to Lucas for the touchdown.
Chargers	Agajanian kicks a 31-yard field goal.
Bills	Carlton 1-yard run for the touchdown. Atkins kicks the extra point.
Bills	Matsos intercepts Kemp pass, returns it 20 yards for the touchdown.
Bills	Carlton 7-yard run for the touchdown. Atkins kicks the extra point.
Bills	Green 49-yard pass to Chamberlin for the touchdown.

	Chargers	Bills
First Downs	11	14
Rushing Yards	-11	69
Passing Yards	196	179
Punts-Average	5-44.0	8-39.37
Fumbles-Lost	4-2	1-1
Penalties-Yards	1-3	3-28

Chargers' Leaders
Rushing	Kemp 9-(-75), Lowe 5-35, Ferguson 5-17, Ford 3-16, Laraba 2-(-6)
Passing	Kemp 13-30-5-189, Laraba 1-4-1-7, Ford 0-1-0-0
Receiving	Anderson 7-109, Kocourek 3-53, Lowe 2-1, Ferguson 1-26, Martin 1-7
Interceptions	Harris 1-0

Bills' Leaders
Rushing	C. Smith 8-24, Fowler 7-14, Dubenion 4-18, Lucas 4-3, Carlton 3-9
Passing	O'Connell 8-16-1-92, Green 6-12-0-87
Receiving	C. Smith 3-40, Chamberlin 2-66, Crockett 2-7, Lucas 1-17, Rychlec 1-15
Interceptions	Wagstaff 2-24, Matsos 2-23, Shaffer 1-19, McCabe 1-0

Week 11 Games
Buffalo 32, Los Angeles 3
Boston 42, Dallas 14
Houston 20, Denver 10
Oakland and New York - Bye

Week 11 Standings
East	W	L	T		West	W	L	T
Houston	7	3	0		Los Angeles	6	4	0
Boston	5	5	0		Dallas	5	5	0
New York	4	6	0		Oakland	5	5	0
Buffalo	4	6	0		Denver	4	6	0

Jim Sears

Howie Ferguson gets wrapped up by the Oakland Raiders' defense.

NOVEMBER 27, 1960
Memorial Coliseum – Los Angeles, California
Attendance – 15,075

					Total
Chargers	14	17	7	14	52
Raiders	7	0	7	14	28

Chargers	Kemp 69-yard pass to Norton for the touchdown. Agajanian kicks the extra point.
Raiders	Smith 1-yard run for the touchdown. Barnes kicks the extra point.
Chargers	Kemp 63-yard pass to Lowe for the touchdown. Agajanian kicks the extra point.
Chargers	Ferguson 1-yard run for the touchdown. Agajanian kicks the extra point.
Chargers	Kemp 1-yard run for the touchdown. Agajanian kicks the extra point.
Chargers	Agajanian kicks a 28-yard field goal.
Chargers	Lowe 2-yard run for the touchdown. Agajanian kicks the extra point.
Raiders	Flores 11-yard pass to Teresa for the touchdown. Barnes kicks the extra point.
Raiders	Lott 7-yard run for the touchdown. Lott 2-yard run for the 2-point conversion.
Chargers	Ford 4-yard run for the touchdown. Agajanian kicks the extra point.
Chargers	Nix intercepts Parilli pass, returns it 17 yards for the touchdown. Agajanian kicks the extra point.
Raiders	Parilli 8-yard pass to Asad for the touchdown.

	Chargers	Raiders
First Downs	31	22
Rushing Yards	232	93
Passing Yards	307	187
Punts-Average	3-40.66	6-46.0
Fumbles-Lost	0-0	4-1
Penalties-Yards	5-47	5-52

Chargers' Leaders
Rushing	Lowe 26-149, Ferguson 11-41, Ford 7-19, Kemp 7-10, Laraba 2-13
Passing	Kemp 13-24-2-307
Receiving	Kocourek 5-81, Norton 4-119, Lowe 2-96, Womble 2-11
Interceptions	Nix 1-17

Raiders' Leaders
Rushing	Lott 8-77, Teresa 6-13, Smith 2-4, Larschied 2-0, Reynolds 1-6
Passing	Flores 13-24-0-119, Parilli 6-17-1-45, Teresa 2-3-0-23
Receiving	Lott 5-51, Teresa 5-50, Goldstein 3-33, Hardy 3-21, Prebola 3-21
Interceptions	Louderback 1-2, Cannavino 1-0

Week 12 Games
Los Angeles 52, Oakland 28
Buffalo 38, Denver 38
Houston 24, Boston 10
New York 41, Dallas 35

Week 12 Standings
East	W	L	T		West	W	L	T
Houston	8	3	0		Los Angeles	7	4	0
Boston	5	6	0		Dallas	5	6	0
New York	5	6	0		Oakland	5	6	0
Buffalo	4	6	1		Denver	4	6	1

Chargers vs. Raiders

DECEMBER 4, 1960
Candlestick Park – San Francisco, California
Attendance – 12,061

					Total
Chargers	0	14	0	27	41
Raiders	0	14	3	0	17

Chargers	Kemp 3-yard pass to Womble for the touchdown. Agajanian kicks the extra point.
Raiders	Lott 3-yard run for the touchdown. Barnes kicks the extra point.
Raiders	Flores 12-yard pass to Hardy for the touchdown. Barnes kicks the extra point.
Chargers	Kemp 21-yard pass to Norton for the touchdown. Agajanian kicks the extra point.
Raiders	Barnes kicks a 25-yard field goal.
Chargers	Kemp 49-yard pass to Lowe for the touchdown. Agajanian kicks the extra point.
Chargers	Kemp 7-yard run for the touchdown. Agajanian kicks the extra point.
Chargers	Kemp 9-yard run for the touchdown. Agajanian kicks the extra point.
Chargers	Loudd recovers fumble and returns it 49 yards for the touchdown.

	Chargers	Raiders
First Downs	16	21
Rushing Yards	110	158
Passing Yards	289	251
Punts-Average	5-32.6	3-38.7
Fumbles-Lost	0-0	4-3
Penalties-Yards	1-14	3-44

Chargers' Leaders
Rushing	Lowe 18-90, Ferguson 10-21, Kemp 6-(-1)
Passing	Kemp 17-25-0-289
Receiving	Kocourek 7-144, Norton 6-84, Womble 3-12, Lowe 1-49
Interceptions	Harris 1-0

Raiders' Leaders
Rushing	Teresa 14-67, Lott 10-47, Larschied 5-30, Flores 2-7, Smith 2-7
Passing	Flores 16-27-1-219, Parilli 2-7-0-23, Larscheid 1-1-0-9, Teresa 0-1-0-0
Receiving	Lott 6-32, Prebola 5-62, Hardy 4-123, Reynolds 1-24, Larscheid 1-7
Interceptions	None

Week 13 Games
Los Angeles 41, Oakland 17
Buffalo 38, Boston 14
Dallas 24, Houston 0
New York 30, Denver 27

Week 13 Standings
East	W	L	T	West	W	L	T
Houston	8	4	0	Los Angeles	8	4	0
New York	6	6	0	Dallas	6	6	0
Buffalo	5	6	1	Oakland	5	7	0
Boston	5	7	0	Denver	4	7	1

DECEMBER 10, 1960
Memorial Coliseum – Los Angeles, California
Attendance – 9,928

					Total
Chargers	14	10	3	14	41
Broncos	10	13	7	3	33

Broncos	Mingo kicks a 41-yard field goal.
Broncos	Tripucka 49-yard pass to Taylor for the touchdown. Mingo kicks the extra point.
Chargers	Kemp 39-yard pass to Ferguson for the touchdown. Agajanian kicks the extra point.
Chargers	Lowe 3-yard run for the touchdown. Agajanian kicks the extra point.
Broncos	Mingo 1-yard run for the touchdown. Mingo kicks the extra point.
Broncos	Mingo kicks a 12-yard field goal.
Chargers	Kemp 12-yard pass to Womble for the touchdown. Agajanian kicks the extra point.
Chargers	Agajanian kicks a 23-yard field goal.
Broncos	Mingo kicks a 13-yard field goal.
Broncos	Tripucka 21-yard pass to Greer for the touchdown. Mingo kicks the extra point.
Chargers	Agajanian kicks a 40-yard field goal.
Broncos	Mingo kicks a 28-yard field goal.
Chargers	Kemp 1-yard run for the touchdown. Agajanian kicks the extra point.
Chargers	Kemp 15-yard pass to Norton for the touchdown. Agajanian kicks the extra point.

	Chargers	Broncos
First Downs	22	20
Rushing Yards	142	100
Passing Yards	205	291
Punts-Average	5-41.0	3-29.0
Fumbles-Lost	0-0	2-2
Penalties-Yards	3-36	3-20

Chargers' Leaders
Rushing	Lowe 19-106, Kemp 9-8, Ferguson 5-18
Passing	Kemp 15-32-2-205
Receiving	Norton 5-81, Ferguson 3-53, Kocourek 3-49, Womble 3-20, Lowe 1-2
Interceptions	Schleicher 1-5, Botchan 1-8

Broncos' Leaders
Rushing	Rolle 17-68, Mingo 12-37, Allen 1-5, Tripucka 1-(-10)
Passing	Tripucka 17-35-2-291
Receiving	Taylor 9-171, Carpenter 3-70, Greer 3-40, Mingo 2-10
Interceptions	King 1-3, McNamara 1-19

Week 14 Games
Los Angeles 41, Denver 33
Houston 31, Buffalo 23
New York 31, Oakland 28
Dallas 34, Boston 0

Week 14 Standings
East	W	L	T	West	W	L	T
Houston	9	4	0	Los Angeles	9	4	0
New York	7	6	0	Dallas	7	6	0
Buffalo	5	7	1	Oakland	5	8	0
Boston	5	8	0	Denver	4	8	1

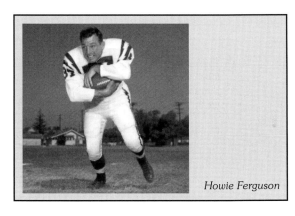

Howie Ferguson

DECEMBER 18, 1960
Memorial Coliseum – Los Angeles, California
Attendance – 11,457

					Total
Chargers	10	6	17	17	50
Titans	7	14	15	7	43

Chargers	Lowe 25-yard run for the touchdown. Agajanian kicks the extra point.
Titans	Mathis 1-yard run for the touchdown. Shockley kicks the extra point.
Chargers	Agajanian kicks a 41-yard field goal.
Titans	Dorow 6-yard pass to Herndon for the touchdown. Shockley kicks the extra point.
Chargers	Kemp 11-yard pass to Norton for the touchdown.
Titans	Dorow 34-yard pass to Powell for the touchdown. Shockley kicks the extra point.
Chargers	Agajanian kicks a 37-yard field goal.
Chargers	Kemp 31-yard pass to Norton for the touchdown. Agajanian kicks the extra point.
Titans	Dorow 1-yard run for the touchdown. Jamieson 2-yard pass to Cooper for the 2-point conversion.
Chargers	Ford 53-yard run for the touchdown. Agajanian kicks the extra point.
Titans	Dorow 42-yard pass to Shockley for the touchdown. Shockley kicks the extra point.
Titans	Burton 11-yard run for the touchdown. Shockley kicks the extra point.
Chargers	Kemp 11-yard pass to Martin for the touchdown. Agajanian kicks the extra point.
Chargers	Kemp 5-yard run for the touchdown. Agajanian kicks the extra point.
Chargers	Agajanian kicks a 27-yard field goal.

	Chargers	Titans
First Downs	24	18
Rushing Yards	200	132
Passing Yards	239	200
Punts-Average	2-34.0	5-44.4
Fumbles-Lost	2-0	1-1
Penalties-Yards	5-65	2-16

Chargers' Leaders

Rushing	Lowe 11-63, Ford 7-109, Kemp 7-(-7), Flowers 4-31, Ferguson 2-2
Passing	Kemp 16-29-4-239, Lowe 0-1-0-0
Receiving	Kocourek 5-92, Norton 4-64, Flowers 3-38, Womble 2-16, Lowe 1-18
Interceptions	McNeil 3-47

Titans' Leaders

Rushing	Burton 12-90, Dorow 9-(-3), Mathis 6-2, Shockley 3-18, Pagliei 1-25
Passing	Dorow 12-28-3-200
Receiving	Powell 5-82, Maynard 3-49, Shockley 2-43, Cooper 1-20, Herndon 1-6
Interceptions	Julian 1-0, Donahoo 1-0, Bell 1-12, Felt 1-7

Week 15 Games
Los Angeles 50, New York 43
Dallas 24, Buffalo 7
Oakland 48, Denver 10
Houston 37, Boston 21

Week 15 Standings

East	W	L	T	West	W	L	T
Houston	10	4	0	Los Angeles	10	4	0
New York	7	7	0	Dallas	8	6	0
Buffalo	5	8	1	Oakland	6	8	0
Boston	5	9	0	Denver	4	9	1

JANUARY 1, 1961
American Football League Championship Game
Jeppesen Stadium – Houston, Texas
Attendance – 32,183

					Total
Chargers	6	3	7	0	16
Oilers	0	10	7	7	24

Chargers	Agajanian kicks a 38-yard field goal.
Chargers	Agajanian kicks a 22-yard field goal.
Oilers	Blanda 17-yard pass to Smith for the touchdown. Blanda kicks the extra point.
Oilers	Blanda kicks an 18-yard field goal.
Chargers	Agajanian kicks a 27-yard field goal.
Oilers	Blanda 7-yard pass to Groman for the touchdown. Blanda kicks the extra point.
Chargers	Lowe 2-yard run for the touchdown. Agajanian kicks the extra point.
Oilers	Blanda 88-yard pass to Cannon for the touchdown. Blanda kicks the extra point.

	Chargers	Oilers
First Downs	21	17
Rushing Yards	208	107
Passing Yards	171	301
Punts-Average	4-41.0	5-34.0
Fumbles-Lost	2-0	0-0
Penalties-Yards	3-15	4-54

Chargers' Leaders

Rushing	Lowe 21-174, Kemp 6-19, Ferguson 4-14, Ford 2-1
Passing	Kemp 21-41-2-171
Receiving	Norton 6-55, Womble 6-29, Kocourek 3-57, Lowe 3-5, Ferguson 2-19
Interceptions	None

Oilers' Leaders

Rushing	Smith 19-51, Cannon 18-51, Hall 3-5
Passing	Blanda 16-31-0-301, Cannon 0-1-0-0
Receiving	Smith 5-52, Hennigan 4-71, Cannon 3-128, Groman 3-37, Carson 1-13
Interceptions	Dukes 1-8, Gordon 1-27

Houston's rookie running back, Billy Cannon, was selected as the game's Most Valuable Player in the first AFL Championship.

BILLY CANNON
HALFBACK
HOUSTON OILERS

Dave Kocourek hurdles the New York Titans' would-be tacklers.

Team Statistics	Chargers	Opponent
TOTAL FIRST DOWNS	208	224
Rushing	81	79
Passing	110	124
Penalty	17	21
TOTAL NET YARDS	4,328	3,726
Avg. Per Game	309.1	266.1
Avg. Per Play	5.1	4.0
NET YARDS RUSHING	1,481	1,363
Avg. Per Game	105.8	97.4
NET YARDS PASSING	2,847	2,363
Avg. Per Game	203.4	168.8
Gross Yards	3,121	2,736
Completions/Attempts	190/423	224/485
Completion Pct.	.449	.462
Had Intercepted	25	49
PUNTS/AVERAGE	62/42.3	70/40.1
PENALTIES/YARDS	88/683	54/501
FUMBLES/BALL LOST	32/19	33/17
TOUCHDOWNS	52	27
Rushing	24	7
Passing	17	16
Returns	11	4
QUARTERBACK SACKS	42.0	28.0

Rushing	No.	Yds.	Avg.	TD
Lowe	175	767	4.4	9
Roberson	58	275	4.7	3
Flowers	51	177	3.5	3
Lincoln	41	150	3.7	0
Kemp	43	105	2.4	6
Enis	16	13	0.8	2
Laraba	5	5	1.0	1
Maguire	1	-11	-11.0	0
Totals	**390**	**1,481**	**3.8**	**24**

Receiving	No.	Yds.	Avg.	TD
Kocourek	55	1,055	19.2	4
Norton	47	816	17.4	6
Lowe	17	103	6.1	0
Flowers	16	175	10.9	0
Hayes	14	280	20.0	3
Lincoln	12	208	17.3	2
Clark	11	182	16.5	0
Scarpitto	9	163	18.1	2
Roberson	6	81	13.5	0
MacKinnon	3	58	19.3	0
Totals	**190**	**3,121**	**16.4**	**17**

Passing	Att.	Comp.	Yds.	Comp. %	TD	Int.
Kemp	364	165	2,868	.453	15	22
Enis	55	23	365	.418	2	3
Lowe	4	2	70	.500	0	0
Totals	**423**	**190**	**3,121**	**.449**	**17**	**25**

Interceptions	No.	Yds.	TD
McNeil	9	349	2
D. Harris	7	140	3
Zeman	8	89	0
Laraba	5	151	2
Allen	5	111	1
Gibson	5	43	0
Karas	3	21	0
Faison	2	14	0
Blair	2	4	0
Hudson	1	5	1
Maguire	1	2	0
Whitehead	1	0	0
Totals	**49**	**929**	**9**

Kicking	FG	Att.	PAT	Att.	Pts.
Blair	13	25	42	47	81
Laraba	0	1	1	2	1

Punting	No.	Avg.
Maguire	62	42.3

Punt Returns	No.	FC	Yds.	Avg.	TD
Gibson	14	0	209	14.9	0
Lincoln	7	0	150	21.4	1
Scarpitto	4	0	47	11.8	0
Lowe	1	0	0	0.0	0
Zeman	1	0	12	12.0	0

Kickoff Returns	No.	Yds.	Avg.	TD
Roberson	11	189	17.2	0
Lowe	10	240	24.0	0
Lincoln	4	98	24.5	0
Gibson	3	17	5.7	0
Scarpitto	3	50	16.7	0
Kemp	2	18	9.0	0
Blair	1	2	2.0	0
Ferrante	1	0	0.0	0
Karas	1	5	5.0	0
Mix	1	0	0.0	0
Schmidt	1	22	22.0	0
Selawski	1	1	1.0	0

The coaching staff of the new San Diego Chargers clowns around, from left; Joe Madro, Chuck Noll, Jack Faulkner, Al Davis. Sid Gillman, seated.

A new way to sell tickets.

September 10, 1961
Cotton Bowl – Dallas, Texas
Attendance – 24,500

				Total	
Chargers	6	6	0	14	26
Texans	0	0	0	10	10

Chargers	Lowe 87-yard run for the touchdown.
Chargers	Blair kicks an 18-yard field goal.
Chargers	Blair kicks a 17-yard field goal.
Texans	Spikes kicks a 27-yard field goal.
Chargers	Laraba 1-yard run for the touchdown. Blair kicks the extra point.
Chargers	Roberson 59-yard run for the touchdown. Blair kicks the extra point.
Texans	Spikes 74-yard run for the touchdown. Spikes kicks the extra point.

	Chargers	Texans
First Downs	17	16
Rushing Yards	198	209
Passing Yards	169	83
Punts-Average	3-42.3	3-37.3
Fumbles-Lost	4-2	2-2
Penalties-Yards	5-25	5-55

Chargers' Leaders
Rushing	Lowe 13-100
Passing	Kemp 15-32-0-162
Receiving	Kocourek 6-67, Norton 4-57, Clark 2-29
Interceptions	Allen 1-4, Faison 1-10, McNeil 1-0, Gibson 1-5

Texans' Leaders
Rushing	Spikes 7-109
Passing	Davidson 7-16-3-78, Duncan 3-8-1-19
Receiving	Boydston 3-35, Jackson 3-17, Robinson 2-23, Romeo 1-19
Interceptions	None

Week 1 Games
San Diego 26, Dallas 0
Denver 22, Buffalo 10
New York 21, Boston 20
Houston 55, Oakland 0

Week 1 Standings
East	W	L	T	West	W	L	T
Houston	1	0	0	San Diego	1	0	0
New York	1	0	0	Denver	1	0	0
Boston	0	1	0	Dallas	0	1	0
Buffalo	0	1	0	Oakland	0	1	0

Dave Kocourek

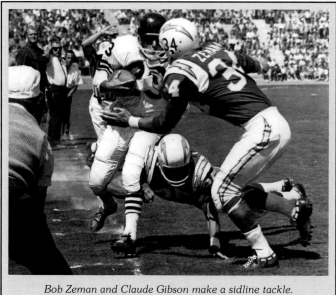

Bob Zeman and Claude Gibson make a sideline tackle.

September 17, 1961
Balboa Stadium – San Diego, California
Attendance – 20,216

					Total
Chargers	14	16	0	14	44
Raiders	0	0	0	0	0

Chargers	Harris intercepts Flores pass, returns it 41 yards for the touchdown. Blair kicks the extra point.
Chargers	Lowe 2-yard run for the touchdown. Blair kicks the extra point.
Chargers	Roberson 31-yard run for the touchdown. Blair kicks the extra point.
Chargers	Flowers 1-yard run for the touchdown.
Chargers	Blair kicks a 23-yard field goal.
Chargers	Flowers 1-yard run for the touchdown. Blair kicks the extra point.
Chargers	Roberson 17-yard run for the touchdown. Blair kicks the extra point.

	Chargers	Raiders
First Downs	23	13
Rushing Yards	208	82
Passing Yards	183	21
Punts-Average	2-45.0	4-43.8
Fumbles-Lost	0-0	2-0
Penalties-Yards	7-55	2-20

Chargers' Leaders
Rushing	Lowe 17-72, Roberson 7-90, Flowers 7-17, Lincoln 3-12, Enis 1-7
Passing	Kemp 11-20-0-130, Enis 6-9-0-53
Receiving	Roberson 4-45, Kocourek 3-33, Norton 3-30, Lowe 3-4, Clark 2-54
Interceptions	Harris 2-48, Maguire 1-2, Karas 1-11, Blair 1-4

Raiders' Leaders
Rushing	Fuller 13-65, Larscheid 5-2, Miller 4-15, Flores 1-3
Passing	Flores 14-23-3-94, Fuller 0-1-0-0, Papac 0-3-2-0
Receiving	Asad 3-27, Miller 3-5, Coolbaugh 2-23, Fuller 2-19, Larscheid 2-11
Interceptions	None

Week 2 Games
San Diego 44, Oakland 0
Boston 45, Denver 17
Buffalo 41, New York 31
Dallas and Houston – Bye

Week 2 Standings
East	W	L	T	West	W	L	T
Houston	1	0	0	San Diego	2	0	0
New York	1	1	0	Denver	1	1	0
Buffalo	1	1	0	Dallas	0	1	0
Boston	1	1	0	Oakland	0	2	0

Jack Kemp throws a deep one.

SEPTEMBER 24, 1961
Balboa Stadium – San Diego, California
Attendance – 29,210

					Total
Chargers	3	28	3	0	34
Oilers	3	0	7	14	24

Chargers	Blair kicks a 44-yard field goal.
Oilers	Blanda kicks a 28-yard field goal.
Chargers	Kemp 7-yard pass to Kocourek for the touchdown. Blair kicks the extra point.
Chargers	Lowe 2-yard run for the touchdown. Blair kicks the extra point.
Chargers	McNeil intercepts Blanda pass, returns it 74 yards for the touchdown. Blair kicks the extra point.
Chargers	Kemp 37-yard pass to Hayes for the touchdown. Blair kicks the extra point.
Oilers	Blanda 13-yard pass to Hall for the touchdown. Blanda kicks the extra point.
Chargers	Blair kicks a 14-yard field goal.
Oilers	Lee 40-yard pass to White for the touchdown. Blanda kicks the extra point.
Oilers	Lee 3-yard pass to Tolar for the touchdown. Blanda kicks the extra point.

	Chargers	Oilers
First Downs	7	19
Rushing Yards	50	72
Passing Yards	108	300
Punts-Average	8-38.6	6-30.0
Fumbles-Lost	3-1	3-1
Penalties-Yards	6-70	6-60

Chargers' Leaders
Rushing	Lowe 17-23, Roberson 5-6, Flowers 4-19, Kemp 4-11, Enis 3-(-3)
Passing	Kemp 6-17-0-101, Enis 1-5-0-15
Receiving	Kocourek 3-27, Flowers 2-25, Hayes 1-37, Norton 1-27
Interceptions	McNeil 3-177, Allen 1-9, Faison 1-8, Karas 1-0

Oilers' Leaders
Rushing	Tolar 13-32, Cannon 7-17, Smith 3-(-1), Lee 2-14, Hall 2-10
Passing	Blanda 15-29-4-131, Lee 10-25-2-190, Cannon 0-1-0-0
Receiving	White 6-112, Hennigan 6-109, Cannon 6-31, Groman 2-53, Tolar 2-9
Interceptions	None

Week 3 Games
San Diego 34, Houston 24
Boston 23, Buffalo 21
Dallas 42, Oakland 35
New York 35, Denver 28

Week 3 Standings
East	W	L	T	West	W	L	T
New York	2	1	0	San Diego	3	0	0
Boston	2	1	0	Dallas	1	1	0
Houston	1	1	0	Denver	1	2	0
Buffalo	1	2	0	Oakland	0	3	0

SEPTEMBER 30, 1961
War Memorial Stadium – Buffalo, New York
Attendance – 20,742

					Total
Chargers	13	0	6	0	19
Bills	0	11	0	0	11

Chargers	Harris intercepts Reynolds pass, returns it 56 yards for the touchdown. Blair kicks the extra point.
Chargers	Lowe 30 yard run for the touchdown.
Bills	Hergert kicks a 16-yard filed goal.
Bills	Reynolds 29-yard pass to Dubenion for the touchdown. Lucas runs 2 yards for the 2-point conversion.
Chargers	Blair kicks a 38-yard field goal.
Chargers	Blair kicks an 11-yard field goal.

	Chargers	Bills
First Downs	15	15
Rushing Yards	162	102
Passing Yards	140	137
Punts-Average	4-43.8	3-41.3
Fumbles-Lost	0-0	1-1
Penalties-Yards	6-50	3-25

Chargers' Leaders
Rushing	Lowe 22-128, Kemp 4-19, Flowers 3-17, Roberson 2-(-2)
Passing	Kemp 14-26-1-146
Receiving	Hayes 4-49, Flowers 3-48, Norton 3-35, Lowe 3-6, Kocourek 1-108
Interceptions	Harris 1-56

Bills' Leaders
Rushing	Brown 13-40, Reynolds 8-65, Baker 7-(-3)
Passing	Reynolds 15-28-1-177
Receiving	Rychlec 5-57, Dubenion 4-52, Bass 3-36, Carlton 3-32
Interceptions	McCabe 1-17

Week 4 Games
San Diego 19, Buffalo 11
Dallas 26, Houston 21
Oakland 33, Denver 19
New York 37, Boston 30

Week 4 Standings
East	W	L	T	West	W	L	T
New York	3	1	0	San Diego	4	0	0
Boston	2	2	0	Dallas	2	1	0
Houston	1	2	0	Denver	1	3	0
Buffalo	1	3	0	Oakland	1	3	0

Ernie Ladd (helmet #77) and Don Rogers (52) at practice.

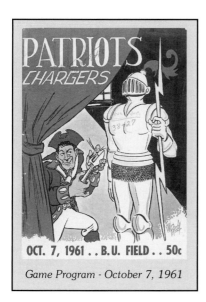

Game Program - October 7, 1961

OCTOBER 7, 1961
Boston University Stadium – Boston, Massachusetts
Attendance – 17,748

					Total
Chargers	7	24	0	7	38
Patriots	0	14	7	6	27

Chargers	Kemp 13-yard pass to Hayes for the touchdown. Blair kicks the extra point.
Patriots	Lott 1-yard run for the touchdown. Cappalletti kicks the extra point.
Chargers	Yewcic punt blocked, recovered by Zeman and returned 65 yards for the touchdown. Blair kicks the extra point.
Chargers	Blair kicks a 17-yard field goal.
Patriots	Yewcic punts to Lowe who fumbles. Ball recovered by Stephens and returned 10 yards for the touchdown. Cappalletti kicks the extra point.
Chargers	Kemp 75-yard pass to Kocourek for the touchdown. Blair kicks the extra point.
Chargers	Kemp 30-yard pass to Norton for the touchdown. Blair kicks the extra point.
Patriots	Parilli 18-yard pass to Colclough for the touchdown. Cappalletti kicks the extra point.
Chargers	Kemp 4-yard run for the touchdown. Blair kicks the extra point.
Patriots	Parilli 47-yard pass to Cappalletti for the touchdown.

	Chargers	Patriots
First Downs	19	17
Rushing Yards	84	105
Passing Yards	315	174
Punts-Average	2-43.0	6-45.5
Fumbles-Lost	2-1	1-1
Penalties-Yards	6-40	7-53

Chargers' Leaders
Rushing	Lowe 12-31, Flowers 8-25, Roberson 7-24
Passing	Kemp 12-24-2-315, Lowe 0-1-0-0
Receiving	Norton 4-84, Kocourek 3-160, Hayes 3-56
Interceptions	Harris 1-0, Zeman 1-19

Patriots' Leaders
Rushing	Garron 7-40, Lott 6-61, Crawford 6-16
Passing	Songin 6-17-1-46, Parilli 9-15-1-128
Receiving	Cappalletti 5-86, Garron 4-42, Colclough 2-27
Interceptions	Addison 1-4, Washington 1-9

Week 5 Games
San Diego 38, Boston 27
Dallas 19, Denver 12
Buffalo 22, Houston 12
New York and Oakland – Bye

Week 5 Standings
East	W	L	T	West	W	L	T
New York	3	1	0	San Diego	5	0	0
Boston	2	3	0	Dallas	3	1	0
Buffalo	2	3	0	Oakland	1	3	0
Houston	1	3	0	Denver	1	4	0

OCTOBER 15, 1961
Polo Grounds – New York City, New York
Attendance – 25,136

					Total
Chargers	7	10	0	8	25
Titans	0	7	3	0	10

Chargers	Kemp 1-yard run for the touchdown. Blair kicks the extra point.
Titans	Dorow 4-yard pass to Mathis for the touchdown. Shockley kicks the extra point.
Chargers	Blair kicks a 20-yard field goal.
Chargers	Kemp 1-yard run for the touchdown. Blair kicks the extra point.
Titans	Shockley kicks a 31-yard field goal.
Chargers	Lowe 25-yard run for the touchdown. Gibson runs 2 yards for the 2-point conversion.

	Chargers	Titans
First Downs	19	14
Rushing Yards	123	62
Passing Yards	299	140
Punts-Average	7-37.7	7-47.6
Fumbles-Lost	5-4	2-1
Penalties-Yards	10-79	1-5

Chargers' Leaders
Rushing	Lowe 14-58, Flowers 11-49, Kemp 4-(-2)
Passing	Kemp 15-38-1-302
Receiving	Norton 5-111, Lowe 4-55, Flowers 3-63
Interceptions	Zeman 1-7, Laraba 1-6, Harris 2-0

Titans' Leaders
Rushing	Mathis 10-47, Dorow 4-19
Passing	Dorow 18-40-1-186, Scrabis 0-3-0-0
Receiving	Powell 8-88, Maynard 5-80, Mathis 4-15, Christy 1-3
Interceptions	Bobo 1-19

Week 6 Games
San Diego 25, New York 10
Buffalo 27, Dallas 24
Houston 31, Boston 31
Denver 27, Oakland 24

Week 6 Standings
East	W	L	T	West	W	L	T
New York	3	2	0	San Diego	6	0	0
Buffalo	3	3	0	Dallas	3	2	0
Boston	2	3	1	Denver	2	4	0
Houston	1	3	1	Oakland	1	4	0

Linebackers Emil Karas (56) and Bob Laraba (53) both died young. Cancer claimed Karas' life in 1974, while Laraba was killed in a 1962 auto accident.

OCTOBER 22, 1961
Candlestick Park – San Francisco, California
Attendance – 12,014

					Total
Chargers	20	14	7	0	41
Raiders	7	0	3	0	10

Raiders	Flores 28-yard pass to Coolbaugh for the touchdown. Fleming kicks the extra point.
Chargers	Lowe 35-yard run for the touchdown.
Chargers	Lowe 46-yard run for the touchdown. Blair kicks the extra point.
Chargers	Kemp 15-yard pass to Norton for the touchdown. Blair kicks the extra point.
Chargers	Flowers 1-yard run for the touchdown. Blair kicks the extra point.
Chargers	Kemp 1-yard run for the touchdown. Blair kicks the extra point.
Raiders	Fleming kicks a 44-yard field goal.
Chargers	Enis 2-yard run for the touchdown. Blair kicks the extra point.

	Chargers	Raiders
First Downs	26	6
Rushing Yards	213	2
Passing Yards	116	56
Punts-Average	2-16.5	6-31.3
Fumbles-Lost	3-2	3-2
Penalties-Yards	1-5	2-20

Chargers' Leaders
Rushing	Lowe 11-106, Roberson 11-51, Flowers 9-27, Enis 8-21
Passing	Kemp 5-17-0-65, Enis 5-16-1-63
Receiving	Clark 3-23, Kocourek 2-24, Norton 2-40, Lincoln 1-16, Roberson 1-13
Interceptions	McNeil 1-21, Zeman 1-21, Gibson 2-0,

Raiders' Leaders
Rushing	Crow 10-7, Fleming 3-15, Miller 2-(-3), Flores 2-(-9), Kowalczyk 1-(-1)
Passing	Flores 9-20-3-96, Papac 1-5-1-4
Receiving	Asad 3-44, Coolbaugh 2-32, Miller 2-7, Kowalczyk 1-7, Burch 1-7
Interceptions	Cannavino 1-0

Week 7 Games
San Diego 41, Oakland 10
Houston 38, Dallas 7
Denver 27, New York 10
Boston 52, Buffalo 21

Week 7 Standings
East	W	L	T	West	W	L	T
New York	3	3	0	San Diego	7	0	0
Houston	2	3	1	Dallas	3	3	0
Boston	3	3	1	Denver	3	4	0
Buffalo	3	4	0	Oakland	1	5	0

Howard Clark

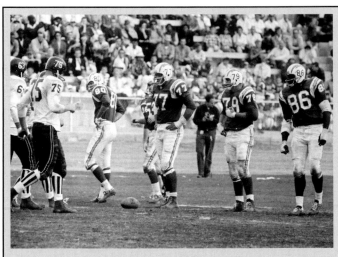

The Fearsome Foursome, Ron Nery (80), Ernie Ladd (77), Bill Hudson (79) and Earl Faison (86).

OCTOBER 29, 1961
Balboa Stadium – San Diego, California
Attendance – 32,584

					Total
Chargers	3	14	10	10	37
Broncos	0	0	0	0	0

Chargers	Blair kicks a 16-yard field goal.
Chargers	Laraba intercepts Herring pass, returns it 57 yards for the touchdown. Blair kicks the extra point.
Chargers	Allen intercepts Herring pass, returns it 59 yards for the touchdown. Blair kicks the extra point.
Chargers	Blair kicks a 13-yard field goal.
Chargers	Kemp 33-yard pass to Norton for the touchdown. Blair kicks the extra point.
Chargers	Blair kicks a 42-yard field goal.
Chargers	Enis 34-yard pass to Lincoln for the touchdown. Blair kicks the extra point.

	Chargers	Broncos
First Downs	13	14
Rushing Yards	101	76
Passing Yards	211	228
Punts-Average	2-51.0	4-40.7
Fumbles-Lost	1-1	3-3
Penalties-Yards	11-75	4-50

Chargers' Leaders
Rushing	Lowe 10-27, Roberson 5-38, Lincoln 5-9, Kemp 4-16, Flowers 1-11
Passing	Kemp 11-28-4-162, Enis 2-5-0-63
Receiving	Norton 5-103, Kocourek 4-57, Clark 2-34, Lincoln 2-31
Interceptions	Allen 1-59, Laraba 1-57, McNeil 1-58, Blair 1-0

Broncos' Leaders
Rushing	Stone 12-42, Sturm 6-20, Bukaty 4-11, Herring 1-3
Passing	Tripucka 15-30-1-110, Herring 6-15-3-124
Receiving	Stone 7-74, Taylor 7-68, Prebola 2-62, Bukaty 2-16, Frazier 2-11
Interceptions	McNamara 1-20, Nugent 2-11, Lambert 1-5

Week 8 Games
San Diego 37, Denver 0
New York 14, Oakland 6
Boston 18, Dallas 17
Houston 28, Buffalo 16

Week 8 Standings
East	W	L	T	West	W	L	T
New York	4	3	0	San Diego	8	0	0
Boston	4	3	1	Dallas	3	4	0
Houston	3	3	1	Denver	3	5	0
Buffalo	3	5	0	Oakland	1	6	0

November 5, 1961
Balboa Stadium – San Diego, California
Attendance – 33,391

					Total
Chargers	0	7	28	14	48
Titans	7	6	0	0	13

Titans	Mathis 5-yard run for the touchdown. Guesman kicks the extra point.
Titans	Dorow 1-yard run for the touchdown.
Chargers	Kemp 1-yard run for the touchdown. Blair kicks the extra point.
Chargers	Lowe 67-yard run for the touchdown. Blair kicks the extra point.
Chargers	Kemp 13-yard pass to Norton for the touchdown. Blair kicks the extra point.
Chargers	McNeil intercepts Dorow pass, returns it 41 yards for the touchdown. Blair kicks the extra point.
Chargers	Enis 1-yard run for the touchdown.
Chargers	Enis 17-yard pass to Hayes for the touchdown. Blair kicks the extra point.

	Chargers	Titans
First Downs	17	16
Rushing Yards	184	90
Passing Yards	169	111
Punts-Average	3-43.7	6-41.7
Fumbles-Lost	2-2	4-1
Penalties-Yards	8-63.5	4-32

Chargers' Leaders
Rushing Lincoln 11-42, Lowe 9-110, Kemp 5-11, Roberson 4-20, Enis 2-1
Passing Kemp 8-18-2-127, Enis 4-5-0-59
Receiving Kocourek 4-71, Norton 3-46, Lincoln 2-14, Roberson 1-24, Hayes 1-17
Interceptions Allen 2-39, McNeil 1-41, Gibson 1-13, Zeman 1-4

Titans' Leaders
Rushing Mathis 16-39, Dorow 9-31, Christy 9-7, West 3-10, Apple 2-1
Passing Dorow 12-24-3-127, Scrabis 0-6-2-0
Receiving Powell 5-80, Renn 5-30, Christy 2-17
Interceptions Bookman 2-0

Week 9 Games
San Diego 48, New York 13
Houston 55, Denver 13
Oakland 31, Buffalo 22
Boston 28, Dallas 21

Week 9 Standings

East	W	L	T	West	W	L	T
Boston	5	3	1	San Diego	9	0	0
Houston	4	3	1	Dallas	3	5	0
New York	4	4	0	Denver	3	6	0
Buffalo	3	6	0	Oakland	2	6	0

Linemen Sam DeLuca (left), Don Rogers (52) and Sherman Plunkett (70) watch the game with the halftime entertainment.

Game Program - November 12, 1961

November 12, 1961
Bears Stadium – Denver, Colorado
Attendance – 7,859

					Total
Chargers	0	0	12	7	19
Broncos	7	2	0	7	16

Broncos	Bukaty 1-yard run for the touchdown. Hill kicks the extra point.
Broncos	Maguire to punt, ball centered out of the end zone for a safety.
Chargers	Kemp 91-yard pass to Lincoln for the touchdown.
Chargers	Harris intercepts Tripucka pass, returns it 30 yards for the touchdown.
Broncos	Tripucka 87-yard pass to Frazier for the touchdown. Hill kicks the extra point.
Chargers	Kemp 16-yard pass to Scarpitto for the touchdown. Laraba kicks the extra point.

	Chargers	Broncos
First Downs	13	19
Rushing Yards	71	86
Passing Yards	153	272
Punts-Average	3-59.6	6-46.1
Fumbles-Lost	1-0	0-0
Penalties-Yards	10-71	5-34

Chargers' Leaders
Rushing Lowe 18-15, Lincoln 4-36, Kemp 3-20
Passing Kemp 11-31-3-201
Receiving Lincoln 3-97, Kocourek 3-51, Scarpitto 2-28, Norton 2-24, Lowe 1-1
Interceptions Karas 1-10, McNeil 1-32, Harris 1-30, Laraba 1-7, Zeman 1-21

Broncos' Leaders
Rushing Bukaty 18-6, Ames 10-62, Stone 4-18
Passing Tripucka 23-49-5-285
Receiving Taylor 10-119, Frazier 5-125, Ames 5-17, Bukaty 2-18, Hill 1-6
Interceptions Gonsoulin 1-0, Nugent 1-30, Hudson 1-3

Week 10 Games
San Diego 19, Denver 16
Houston 27, Boston 15
New York 23, Oakland 12
Buffalo 30, Dallas 20

Week 10 Standings

East	W	L	T	West	W	L	T
Houston	5	3	1	San Diego	10	0	0
Boston	5	4	1	Dallas	3	6	0
New York	5	4	0	Denver	3	7	0
Buffalo	4	6	0	Oakland	2	7	0

NOVEMBER 19, 1961
Balboa Stadium – San Diego, California
Attendance – 33,788

					Total
Chargers	0	17	0	7	24
Texans	0	0	7	7	14

Chargers	Blair kicks a 10-yard field goal.
Chargers	Kemp 61-yard pass to Kocourek for the touchdown. Blair kicks the extra point.
Chargers	Laraba intercepts Davidson pass, returns it 30 yards for the touchdown. Blair kicks the extra point.
Texans	Davidson 1-yard run for the touchdown. Davidson kicks the extra point.
Chargers	Kemp 53-yard pass to Scarpitto for the touchdown. Blair kicks the extra point.
Texans	Davidson 34-yard pass to Robinson for the touchdown. Davidson kicks the extra point.

	Chargers	Texans
First Downs	13	17
Rushing Yards	3	108
Passing Yards	335	180
Punts-Average	3-59.6	6-46.1
Fumbles-Lost	3-2	2-0
Penalties-Yards	2-10	5-55

Chargers' Leaders

Rushing Roberson 10-(-19), Lincoln 6-24, Lowe 2-(-1), Kemp 2-(-1)

Passing Kemp 15-27-1-357, Enis 0-1-0-0

Receiving Kocourek 7-169, Norton 6-120, Scarpitto 2-68

Interceptions Laraba 1-40, Zeman 1-2, McNeil 1-0

Texans' Leaders

Rushing Haynes 12-76, Jackson 4-15, Davidson 4-11, Robinson 4-8, Dickinson 3-0

Passing Davidson 14-33-3-165, Duncan 1-2-0-18, Jackson 1-1-0-9

Receiving Robinson 3-53, Burford 3-44, Haynes 3-36, Dickinson 3-32, Romeo 3-28

Interceptions Grayson 1-0

Week 11 Games
San Diego 24, Dallas 14
Houston 49, New York 13
Buffalo 23, Denver 10
Boston 20, Oakland 17

Week 11 Standings

East	W	L	T	West	W	L	T
Houston	6	3	1	San Diego	11	0	0
Boston	6	4	1	Dallas	3	7	0
New York	5	5	0	Denver	3	8	0
Buffalo	5	6	0	Oakland	2	8	0

Week 12 Games
San Diego and Boston - Bye
New York 21, Buffalo 14
Dallas 43, Oakland 11
Houston 45, Denver 14

Week 12 Standings

East	W	L	T	West	W	L	T
Houston	7	3	1	San Diego	11	0	0
Boston	6	4	1	Dallas	4	7	0
New York	6	5	0	Denver	3	9	0
Buffalo	5	7	0	Oakland	2	9	0

Chargers' end, Dave Kocourek, fights Dallas defenders for the ball.

Paul Lowe (23) and Jack Kemp (15)

Sid Gillman (kneeling), Bo Roberson (26) and Joe Madro (rear).

DECEMBER 3, 1961
Jeppesen Stadium – Houston, Texas
Attendance – 37,845

					Total
Chargers	7	0	0	6	13
Oilers	13	6	14	0	33

Chargers	Kemp 10-yard pass to Norton for the touchdown. Blair kicks the extra point.
Oilers	Blanda 17-yard pass to McLeod for the touchdown.
Oilers	Blanda 31-yard pass to Hennigan. Blanda kicks the extra point.
Oilers	Blanda kicks a 55-yard field goal.
Oilers	Blanda kicks a 23-yard field goal.
Oilers	Blanda 15-yard pass to Hennigan. Blanda kicks the extra point.
Oilers	Blanda 32-yard pass to Hennigan. Blanda kicks the extra point.
Chargers	Kemp 4-yard pass to Norton for the touchdown.

	Chargers	Oilers
First Downs	14	22
Rushing Yards	35	122
Passing Yards	271	351
Punts-Average	6-37.3	3-40.3
Fumbles-Lost	2-1	3-2
Penalties-Yards	2-30	3-25

Chargers' Leaders
Rushing	Lowe 9-20, Kemp 4-8, Flowers 4-7
Passing	Kemp 22-39-2-242, Enis 2-3-1-63
Receiving	Kocourek 8-69, Norton 5-92, MacKinnon 4-76, Scarpitto 4-62, Flowers 2-15
Interceptions	Laraba 1-5

Oilers' Leaders
Rushing	Tolar 12-59, Cannon 11-46, Smith 6-13, Blanda 1-7
Passing	Blanda 20-33-1-351, Tolar 0-1-0-0
Receiving	Hennigan 10-214, Cannon 5-37, McLeod 3-48, White 1-49, Tolar 1-3
Interceptions	Banfield 2-11, Norton 1-25

Week 13 Games
Houston 33, San Diego 13
Buffalo 26, Oakland 21
Boston 28, Denver 24
New York 28, Dallas 7

Week 13 Standings
East	W	L	T	West	W	L	T
Houston	8	3	1	San Diego	11	1	0
Boston	7	4	1	Dallas	4	8	0
New York	7	5	0	Denver	3	10	0
Buffalo	6	7	0	Oakland	2	10	0

DECEMBER 10, 1961
Balboa Stadium – San Diego, California
Attendance – 24,486

					Total
Chargers	0	14	14	0	28
Bills	10	0	0	0	10

Bills	Shockley kicks a 20-yard field goal.
Bills	McDonald recovers a fumble and returns it 24 yards for the touchdown. Atkins kicks the extra point.
Chargers	Lincoln returns a punt 57 yards for the touchdown. Blair kicks the extra point.
Chargers	Hudson intercepts Reynolds pass, returns it 5 yards for the touchdown. Blair kicks the extra point.
Chargers	Lowe 4-yard run for the touchdown. Blair kicks the extra point.
Chargers	Kemp 76-yard pass to Kocourek for the touchdown. Blair kicks the extra point.

	Chargers	Bills
First Downs	7	18
Rushing Yards	47	99
Passing Yards	190	180
Punts-Average	6-47.8	6-46.8
Fumbles-Lost	2-0	2-1
Penalties-Yards	7-54	2-25

Chargers' Leaders
Rushing	Lowe 14-57, Kemp 4-2, Enis 1-(-12)
Passing	Kemp 11-21-2-213, Enis 0-4-0-0
Receiving	Kocourek 3-175, Norton 3-19, Lowe 2-17, Flowers 2-(-3), Scarpitto 1-5
Interceptions	Whitehead 1-0, Hudson 1-5, Zeman 1-17

Bills' Leaders
Rushing	Baker 31-117, Carlton 3-9, Bohling 2-6, Carlton 1-9, Green 1-(-15)
Passing	Green 11-25-0-152, Reynolds 2-9-3-61
Receiving	Dubenion 3-69, Rychlec 3-45, Bohling 3-37, Bass 2-21, Crockett 1-21
Interceptions	Barber 1-5, Atkins 1-24

Week 14 Games
San Diego 28, Buffalo 10
Boston 35, Oakland 21
Dallas 49, Denver 21
Houston 48, New York 21

Week 14 Standings
East	W	L	T	West	W	L	T
Houston	9	3	1	San Diego	12	1	0
Boston	8	4	1	Dallas	5	8	0
New York	7	6	0	Denver	3	11	0
Buffalo	6	8	0	Oakland	2	11	0

Bob Zeman hauls in an interception.

December 17, 1961
Balboa Stadium – San Diego, California
Attendance – 21,339

					Total
Chargers	0	0	0	0	0
Patriots	17	10	7	7	41

Patriots	Cappalletti kicks a 40-yard field goal.
Patriots	Parilli 33-yard pass to Colclough for the touchdown. Cappalletti kicks the extra point.
Patriots	Webb intercepts Kemp pass, returns it 31 yards for the touchdown. Cappalletti kicks the extra point.
Patriots	Lott 5-yard run for the touchdown. Cappalletti kicks the extra point.
Patriots	Cappalletti kicks a 40-yard field goal.
Patriots	Parilli 7-yard pass to Cappalletti for the touchdown. Cappalletti kicks the extra point.
Patriots	Maguire punt blocked, recovered by Webb and returned 20 yards for the touchdown. Cappalletti kicks the extra point.

	Chargers	Patriots
First Downs	11	18
Rushing Yards	2	139
Passing Yards	190	151
Punts-Average	7-38.1	4-35.5
Fumbles-Lost	4-1	1-1
Penalties-Yards	7-55	5-42

Chargers' Leaders

Rushing	Lowe 7-21, Lincoln 5-11, Kemp 2-(-17), Maguire 1-(-11), Flowers 1-(-2)
Passing	Kemp 9-26-4-163, Enis 3-7-1-49, Lowe 1-1-0-36
Receiving	Kocourek 5-98, Hayes 3-100, Lincoln 3-45, Lowe 1-8, Flowers 1-(-8)
Interceptions	Zeman 1-0, Harris 1-8

Patriots' Leaders

Rushing	Lott 20-94, Schwedes 7-9, Burton 5-10, Garron 3-9, Yewcic 2-13
Passing	Parilli 9-20-2-178, Yewcic 2-3-0-7
Receiving	Cappalletti 4-88, Lott 3-2, Colclough 2-78, Shonta 1-9, Burton 1-8
Interceptions	Bruney 2-20, Webb 1-31, Washington 1-33, Addison 1-3

Week 15 Games
Boston 41, San Diego 0
Houston 47, Oakland 16
Dallas 35, New York 24
Denver and Buffalo - Bye

Week 15 Standings

East	W	L	T	West	W	L	T
Houston	10	3	1	San Diego	12	2	0
Boston	9	4	1	Dallas	6	8	0
New York	7	7	0	Denver	3	11	0
Buffalo	6	8	0	Oakland	2	12	0

Game Program - December 17, 1961

Luther Hayes leaps high for a reception in the Chargers' second championship loss to Houston.

December 24, 1961
American Football League Championship Game
Balboa Stadium – San Diego, California
Attendance – 29,556

					Total
Chargers	0	0	0	3	3
Oilers	0	3	7	0	10

Oilers	Blanda kicks a 46-yard field goal.
Oilers	Blanda 35-yard pass to Cannon for the touchdown. Blanda kicks the extra point.
Chargers	Blair kicks a 12-yard field goal.

	Chargers	Oilers
First Downs	15	18
Rushing Yards	92	96
Passing Yards	177	160
Punts-Average	6-33.3	4-41.5
Fumbles-Lost	2-2	5-1
Penalties-Yards	10-106	5-68

Chargers' Leaders

Rushing	Roberson 8-37, Lowe 5-30, Lincoln 3-7
Passing	Kemp 17-32-4-226
Receiving	Kocourek 7-123, Norton 3-48, Flowers 2-17, Roberson 1-11, Lowe 1-10
Interceptions	Whitehead 2-45, McNeil 2-15, Zeman 2-0

Oilers' Leaders

Rushing	Tolar 16-52, Cannon 15-48, Blanda 2-(-4)
Passing	Blanda 18-40-5-160, Groman 0-1-1-0
Receiving	Hennigan 5-43, Cannon 5-35, Groman 3-32, Dewveall 2-10, Tolar 2-2
Interceptions	Cline 1-7, Glick 1-0, Banfield 1-0, Spence 1-0

1962 CHARGERS TEAM STATISTICS
(4-10 OVERALL) THIRD PLACE IN THE AFL WEST

Team Statistics	Chargers	Opponent
TOTAL FIRST DOWNS	217	248
Rushing	82	105
Passing	113	120
Penalty	22	23
TOTAL NET YARDS	4,106	4,518
Avg. Per Game	293.3	322.7
Avg. Per Play	4.8	5.1
NET YARDS RUSHING	1,672	1,903
Avg. Per Game	119.4	135.9
NET YARDS PASSING	2,434	2,615
Avg. Per Game	173.9	186.8
Gross Yards	2,686	2,926
Completions/Attempts	168/416	196/402
Completion Pct.	.404	.488
Had Intercepted	34	29
PUNTS/AVERAGE	79/41.6	68/40.7
PENALTIES/YARDS	88/768	65/709
FUMBLES/BALL LOST	24/14	30/13
TOUCHDOWNS	38	48
Rushing	13	16
Passing	23	29
Returns	2	3
QUARTERBACK SACKS	41.0	28.0

Rushing	No.	Yds.	Avg.	TD
Lincoln	117	574	4.9	2
B. Jackson	106	411	3.9	5
MacKinnon	55	224	4.1	0
McDougall	43	197	4.6	3
Hadl	40	139	3.5	1
Braxton	17	35	2.1	1
Kemp	8	28	3.5	1
Alworth	1	17	17.0	0
Coan	12	10	0.8	0
Robinson	2	10	5.0	0
Gillett	2	8	4.0	0
Keckin	1	3	3.0	0
Wood	1	0	0.0	0
Totals	**409**	**1,672**	**4.1**	**13**

Receiving	No.	Yds.	Avg.	TD
Norton	48	771	16.1	7
Kocourek	39	688	17.6	4
Robinson	21	391	18.6	3
Lincoln	16	214	13.4	1
B. Jackson	13	136	10.5	2
Alworth	10	226	22.6	3
MacKinnon	9	125	13.9	2
McDougall	4	27	6.8	0
Braxton	4	17	4.3	0
Carolan	3	39	13.0	1
Coan	1	52	52.0	0
Totals	**168**	**2,686**	**16.0**	**23**

Passing	Att.	Comp.	Yds.	Comp. %	TD	Int.
Hadl	260	107	1,632	.412	15	25
Wood	97	41	655	.423	4	7
Kemp	45	13	292	.289	2	2
Keckin	9	5	64	.556	0	1
Lincoln	5	2	43	.400	2	0
Totals	**416**	**168**	**2,686**	**.404**	**23**	**34**

Interceptions	No.	Yds.	TD
Gibson	8	85	1
D. Harris	5	52	0
Buncom	4	49	0
Bethune	3	6	0
Blair	2	36	0
Karas	2	8	0
McNeil	1	36	0
Faison	1	30	0
Whitehead	1	18	0
Maguire	1	13	0
Allen	1	7	0
Totals	**29**	**340**	**1**

Kicking	FG	Att.	PAT	Att.	Pts.
Blair	17	20	31	34	82

Punting	No.	Avg.
Maguire	79	41.6

Punt Returns	No.	FC	Yds.	Avg.	TD
Lincoln	11	0	94	8.5	0
Gibson	10	0	89	8.9	0
D. Harris	7	0	95	13.6	0
Braxton	1	0	0	0.0	0

Kickoff Returns	No.	Yds.	Avg.	TD
Robinson	32	748	23.4	0
Lincoln	14	398	28.4	1
Bethune	12	251	20.9	0
McDougall	3	71	23.7	0
Coan	2	31	15.5	0
Gibson	2	55	27.5	0
B. Jackson	1	16	16.0	0
Klotz	1	15	15.0	0

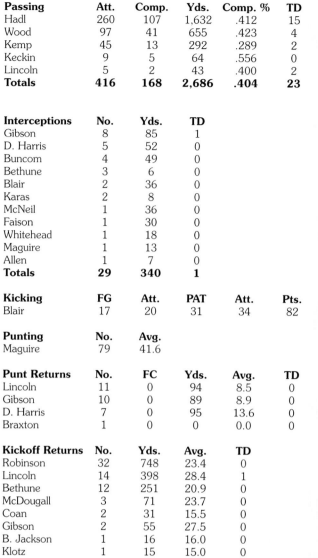

Above: *The Chargers often socialized away from the football field, such as this pool party at the Gillman's home on Mt. Helix.*

Left: *Teammates Chuck Allen and Bill Hudson (79) enjoy a post-practice chat.*

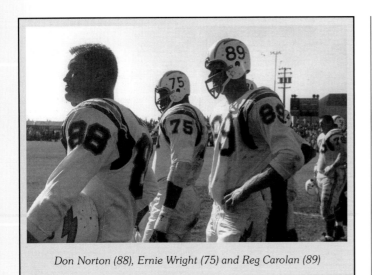

Don Norton (88), Ernie Wright (75) and Reg Carolan (89)

SEPTEMBER 7, 1962
Denver University Stadium – Denver, Colorado
Attendance – 28,000

					Total
Chargers	0	7	7	7	21
Broncos	10	14	6	0	30

Broncos	Mingo 5-yard run for the touchdown. Mingo kicks the extra point.
Broncos	Mingo kicks a 12-yard field goal.
Chargers	Kemp 7-yard pass to Norton for the touchdown. Blair kicks the extra point.
Broncos	Tripucka 49-yard pass to Scarpitto for the touchdown. Mingo kicks the extra point.
Broncos	Tripucka 2-yard pass to Dickinson for the touchdown. Mingo kicks the extra point.
Broncos	Mingo kicks a 14-yard field goal.
Broncos	Mingo kicks a 53-yard field goal.
Chargers	Gibson intercepts Mingo pass, returns it 37 yards for the touchdown. Blair kicks the extra point.
Chargers	Hadl 15-yard pass to Jackson for the touchdown. Blair kicks the extra point.

	Chargers	Broncos
First Downs	14	28
Rushing Yards	96	121
Passing Yards	112	384
Punts-Average	6-43	3-35.3
Fumbles-Lost	0	0
Penalties-Yards	6-56	4-45

Chargers' Leaders
Rushing	Jackson 9-51, Coan 6-15, MacKinnon 4-16, Kemp 4-2, Hadl 1-12
Passing	Kemp 8-27-1-108, Hadl 1-1-0-15
Receiving	Kocourek 4-66, Norton 3-25, Alworth 1-17, Jackson 1-15
Interceptions	Gibson 1-37, Karas 1-8, McNeil 1-36

Broncos' Leaders
Rushing	Frazier 12-72, Mingo 9-25, Dickinson 5-16, Stinnette 1-8
Passing	Tripucka 28-47-2-384, Enis 0-1-0-0, Mingo 0-1-1-0
Receiving	Taylor 7-79, Prebola 7-69, Dickinson 5-50, Frazier 3-50, Stinnette 3-37
Interceptions	Gonsoulin 1-0

Week 1 Games
Denver 30, San Diego 21
Houston 28, Buffalo 23
New York 28, Oakland 17
Dallas 42, Boston 28

Week 1 Standings
East	W	L	T	West	W	L	T
New York	1	0	0	Denver	1	0	0
Houston	1	0	0	Dallas	1	0	0
Boston	0	1	0	San Diego	0	1	0
Buffalo	0	1	0	Oakland	0	1	0

SEPTEMBER 16, 1962
Balboa Stadium – San Diego, California
Attendance – 22,003

					Total
Chargers	7	14	10	9	40
Titans	0	0	0	14	14

Chargers	Kemp 1-yard run for the touchdown. Blair kicks the extra point.
Chargers	Lincoln 23-yard pass to Alworth for the touchdown. Blair kicks the extra point.
Chargers	Jackson 5-yard run for the touchdown. Blair kicks the extra point.
Chargers	Kemp 67-yard pass to Alworth for the touchdown. Blair kicks the extra point.
Chargers	Blair kicks a 44-yard field goal.
Titans	Grosscup 10 –yard pass to Powell for the touchdown. Guesman kicks the extra point.
Chargers	Lincoln returns the kickoff 103 yards for the touchdown.
Chargers	Blair kicks a 30-yard field goal.
Titans	Grosscup 14 –yard pass to Powell for the touchdown. Guesman kicks the extra point.

	Chargers	Titans
First Downs	13	20
Rushing Yards	110	83
Passing Yards	187	165
Punts-Average	5-46.8	3-53.7
Fumbles-Lost	1-0	5-3
Penalties-Yards	7-59	5-31

Chargers' Leaders
Rushing	Lincoln 13-48, Jackson 7-29, Kemp 4-26, MacKinnon 4-4, Coan 4-1
Passing	Kemp 5-18-1-184, Lincoln 1-1-0-23, Hadl 0-1-1-0
Receiving	Alworth 2-90, Coan 1-52, Jackson 1-33, Norton 1-24, MacKinnon 1-8
Interceptions	Karas 1-0, Harris 1-36, Gibson 1-0

Titans' Leaders
Rushing	Flowers 13-42, Grosscup 4-31, Christy 4-10
Passing	Grosscup 20-41-3-216
Receiving	Powell 5-75, Flowers 5-43, Christy 5-25, Maynard 3-47, Richards 1-22
Interceptions	Atkins 1-0, Hynes 1-2

Week 2 Games
San Diego 40, New York 14
Denver 23, Buffalo 20
Boston 34, Houston 21
Oakland and Dallas - Bye

Week 2 Standings
East	W	L	T	West	W	L	T
New York	1	1	0	Denver	2	0	0
Houston	1	1	0	Dallas	1	0	0
Boston	1	1	0	San Diego	1	1	0
Buffalo	0	2	0	Oakland	0	1	0

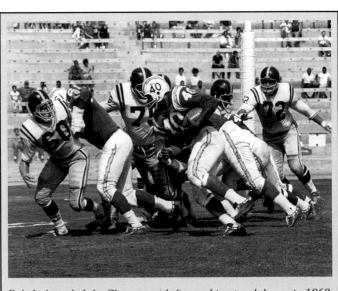

Bob Jackson led the Chargers with five rushing touchdowns in 1962.

Lance Alworth wore number 24 during his rookie season.

SEPTEMBER 23, 1962
Balboa Stadium – San Diego, California
Attendance – 28,061

					Total
Chargers	7	3	0	7	17
Oilers	14	14	7	7	42

Oilers	Blanda 75-yard pass to Hennigan for the touchdown. Blanda kicks the extra point.
Oilers	Cannon 1-yard run for the touchdown. Blanda kicks the extra point.
Chargers	Wood 7-yard pass to Norton for the touchdown. Blair kicks the extra point.
Oilers	Cannon 10-yard run for the touchdown. Blanda kicks the extra point.
Chargers	Blair kicks a 29-yard field goal.
Oilers	Blanda 13-yard pass to Cannon for the touchdown. Blanda kicks the extra point.
Oilers	Tolar 21-yard run for the touchdown. Blanda kicks the extra point.
Oilers	Lee 4-yard pass to Dewveall for the touchdown. Blanda kicks the extra point
Chargers	Wood 22-yard pass to Norton for the touchdown. Blair kicks the extra point.

	Chargers	Oilers
First Downs	15	27
Rushing Yards	45	277
Passing Yards	292	155
Punts-Average	5-45.2	2-53
Fumbles-Lost	1-1	0-0
Penalties-Yards	11-79	7-45

Chargers' Leaders
Rushing	Lincoln 10-18, Jackson 4-10, Alworth 1-17, Hadl 1-0, Wood 1-0
Passing	Wood 16-33-1-294, Hadl 1-4-1-6, Lincoln 0-1-0-0
Receiving	Kocourek 5-140, Norton 4-78, Alworth 4-53, Lincoln 3-25, Jackson 1-4
Interceptions	Allen 1-7

Oilers' Leaders
Rushing	Tolar 18-142, Cannon 12-70, Smith 9-66, Babb 2-(-1), Lee 1-0
Passing	Blanda 11-20-1-164, Smith 0-1-0-0, Lee 1-1-0-4
Receiving	McLeod 3-40, Dewveall 3-19, Tolar 2-33, Groman 1-31, Hennigan 1-25
Interceptions	Banfield 1-11, Johnston 1-27

Week 3 Games
Houston 42, San Diego 17
New York 17, Buffalo 6
Boston 41, Denver 16
Dallas 26, Oakland 16

Week 3 Standings
East	W	L	T	West	W	L	T
New York	2	1	0	Dallas	2	0	0
Houston	2	1	0	Denver	2	1	0
Boston	2	1	0	San Diego	1	2	0
Buffalo	0	3	0	Oakland	0	3	0

SEPTEMBER 30, 1962
Frank Youell Field – Oakland, California
Attendance – 13,000

					Total
Chargers	7	21	14	0	42
Raiders	7	7	3	10	33

Chargers	Wood 10-yard pass to Jackson for the touchdown. Blair kicks the extra point.
Raiders	Roberson returns the kickoff 87 yards for the touchdown. Simpson kicks the extra point.
Raiders	Williamson intercepts Hadl pass, returns it 91 yards for the touchdown. Simpson kicks the extra point.
Chargers	Hadl 30-yard pass to Kocourek for the touchdown. Blair kicks the extra point.
Chargers	Hadl 13-yard pass to Horton for the touchdown. Blair kicks the extra point.
Chargers	Hadl 53-yard pass to Alworth for the touchdown. Blair kicks the extra point.
Raiders	Simpson kicks a 25-yard field goal.
Chargers	Jackson 6-yard run for the touchdown. Blair kicks the extra point.
Chargers	Lincoln 86-yard run for the touchdown. Blair kicks the extra point.
Raiders	Gallegos 35-yard pass to Craig for the touchdown. Roberson runs 2 yards for the 2-point conversion.
Raiders	Gallegos 32-yard pass to Roberson for the touchdown. Gallegos 8-yard pass to White for the 2-point conversion.

	Chargers	Raiders
First Downs	15	14
Rushing Yards	205	141
Passing Yards	179	125
Punts-Average	7-42.9	7-36.3
Fumbles-Lost	0-0	1-1
Penalties-Yards	3-14	7-84

Chargers' Leaders
Rushing	Jackson 16-43, Lincoln 12-106, Coan 2-(-6), MacKinnon 1-2
Passing	Hadl 7-14-3-161, Wood 3-7-0-31
Receiving	Alworth 3-66, Norton 3-39, Kocourek 2-48, Lincoln 1-29, Jackson 1-10
Interceptions	Blair 1-19, Maguire 1-13

Raiders' Leaders
Rushing	Daniels 11-55, Roberson 9-38, Gallegos 2-29, Davidson 2-9, Miller 1-10
Passing	Davidson 10-24-2-95, Gallegos 4-7-0-89
Receiving	Miller 4-46, Craig 3-59, Boydston 3-16, Roberson 1-32, Hardy 1-15
Interceptions	Williamson 1-91, Morrow 1-1, Simpson 1-0

Week 4 Games
San Diego 42, Oakland 33
Denver 32, New York 10
Dallas 41, Buffalo 21
Boston and Houston - Bye

Week 4 Standings
East	W	L	T	West	W	L	T
Boston	2	1	0	Dallas	3	0	0
Houston	2	1	0	Denver	3	1	0
New York	2	2	0	San Diego	2	2	0
Buffalo	0	4	0	Oakland	0	3	0

Keith Lincoln (22) and Maury Schleicher (81) tackle Oakland's Clem Daniels.

OCTOBER 7, 1962
Balboa Stadium – San Diego, California
Attendance – 23,092

					Total
Chargers	9	14	3	6	**32**
Texans	0	14	0	14	**28**

Chargers	Blair kicks a 10-yard field goal.
Chargers	Hadl 4-yard run for the touchdown.
Chargers	Hadl 14-yard pass to Norton for the touchdown. Blair kicks the extra point.
Texans	Jackson 1-yard run for the touchdown. Brooker kicks the extra point.
Chargers	Hadl 33-yard pass to Robinson for the touchdown. Blair kicks the extra point.
Texans	Dawson 46-yard pass to Haynes for the touchdown. Brooker kicks the extra point.
Chargers	Blair kicks a 27-yard field goal.
Texans	Dawson 14-yard pass to Haynes for the touchdown. Brooker kicks the extra point.
Chargers	Lincoln 2-yard run for the touchdown.
Texans	Dawson 12-yard pass to Burford for the touchdown. Brooker kicks the extra point.

	Chargers	Texans
First Downs	22	10
Rushing Yards	138	74
Passing Yards	233	139
Punts-Average	6-41.8	6-39.5
Fumbles-Lost	1-1	3-1
Penalties-Yards	9-134	8-70

Chargers' Leaders
Rushing Lincoln 19-85, Jackson 13-32, Hadl 8-21
Passing Hadl 14-29-0-208, Wood 1-1-0-36, Lincoln 0-1-0-0
Receiving Kocourek 5-41, Robinson 3-86, Norton 3-60, Lincoln 3-42, MacKinnon 1-15
Interceptions Buncon 1-11, Gibson 1-0

Texans' Leaders
Rushing Haynes 6-33, Jackson 3-21, Spikes 3-16, Dawson 2-5, McClinton 1-(-1)
Passing Dawson 12-24-2-156
Receiving Haynes 5-92, Arbanas 3-30, Burford 2-19, Spikes 2-15
Interceptions None

Week 5 Games
San Diego 32, Dallas 28
Houston 17, Buffalo 14
Boston 43, New York 14
Denver 44, Oakland 7

Week 5 Standings

East	W	L	T	West	W	L	T
Boston	3	1	0	Denver	4	1	0
Houston	3	1	0	Dallas	3	1	0
New York	2	3	0	San Diego	3	2	0
Buffalo	0	5	0	Oakland	0	4	0

Game Program - October 7, 1962

Reg Carolan

OCTOBER 13, 1962
War Memorial Stadium - Buffalo, New York
Attendance – 20,074

					Total
Chargers	0	3	0	7	**10**
Bills	7	14	7	7	**35**

Bills	Rabb 19-yard pass to Dubenion for the touchdown. Yoho Kicks the extra point.
Bills	Rabb 24-yard pass to Bass for the touchdown. Yoho kicks the extra point.
Chargers	Blair kicks a 27-yard field goal.
Bills	Gilchrist 1-yard run for the touchdown. Yoho kicks the extra point.
Bills	Rabb 7-yard pass to Gilchrist for the touchdown. Yoho kicks the extra point.
Bills	Crow 1-yard run for the touchdown. Yoho kicks the extra point.
Chargers	Braxton 5-yard run for the touchdown. Blair kicks the extra point.

	Chargers	Bills
First Downs	12	17
Rushing Yards	68	303
Passing Yards	72	136
Punts-Average	5-45.6	5-39
Fumbles-Lost	0-0	2-2
Penalties-Yards	4-20	7-105

Chargers' Leaders
Rushing Lincoln 10-32, Jackson 6-17, Braxton 2-11, MacKinnon 2-8
Passing Hadl 2-12-2-17, Wood 8-20-2-70
Receiving Lincoln 3-16, Kocourek 2-31, Jackson 2-4, Robinson 1-18, Norton 1-11
Interceptions Gibson 1-0

Bills' Leaders
Rushing Gilchrist 25-124, Carlton 11-43, Crow 6-115, Rabb 2-9, Wheeler 3-3
Passing Rabb 5-13-1-81, Crow 0-0-0-0
Receiving Dubenion 2-45, Gilchrist 2-23, Bass 1-76, Carlton 1-14
Interceptions Charon 2-51, West 2-0

Week 6 Games
Buffalo 35, San Diego 10
Houston 56, New York 17
Dallas 27, Boston 7
Denver 23, Oakland 6

Week 6 Standings

East	W	L	T	West	W	L	T
Houston	4	1	0	Denver	5	1	0
Boston	3	2	0	Dallas	4	1	0
New York	2	4	0	San Diego	3	3	0
Buffalo	1	5	0	Oakland	0	5	0

OCTOBER 19, 1962
Boston University Stadium – Boston, Massachusetts
Attendance – 20,888

					Total
Chargers	10	10	0	0	20
Patriots	3	0	14	7	24

Patriots	Cappalletti kicks a 13-yard field goal.
Chargers	Wood 36-yard pass to Kocourek for the touchdown. Blair kicks the extra point.
Chargers	Blair kicks a 43-yard field goal.
Chargers	Jackson 2-yard run for the touchdown. Blair kicks the extra point.
Chargers	Blair kicks a 27-yard field goal.
Patriots	Parilli 9-yard pass to Colclough for the touchdown.
Patriots	Parilli 25-yard pass to Colclough for the touchdown. Parilli 2-yard pass to Crawford for the 2-point conversion.
Patriots	Crawford 1-yard run for the touchdown. Cappalletti kicks the extra point.

	Chargers	Patriots
First Downs	11	20
Rushing Yards	90	175
Passing Yards	206	166
Punts-Average	7-39.6	8-37.5
Fumbles-Lost	0-0	0-0
Penalties-Yards	7-55	3-35

Chargers' Leaders
Rushing	Lincoln 12-48, Jackson 4-8, Hadl 2-14, Robinson 2-10, MacKinnon 2-8
Passing	Wood 8-23-3-162, Hadl 4-8-1-44
Receiving	Norton 4-107, Kocourek 4-65, Robinson 2-18, Lincoln 2-16
Interceptions	Gibson 1-9, Harris 1-1

Patriots' Leaders
Rushing	Crawford 11-61, Burton 11-32, Garron 8-34, King 6-6, Parilli 5-42
Passing	Parilli 14-26-2-166
Receiving	Burton 5-54, Crawford 5-53, Colclough 2-39, Cappalletti 1-16, Garron 1-9
Interceptions	Addison 2-16, Bouniconti 1-3, O'Hanley 1-15

Week 7 Games
Boston 24, San Diego 20
Buffalo 14, Oakland 6
Denver 20, Houston 10
Dallas 20, New York 17

Week 7 Standings
East	W	L	T	West	W	L	T
Houston	4	2	0	Denver	6	1	0
Boston	4	2	0	Dallas	5	1	0
New York	2	5	0	San Diego	3	4	0
Buffalo	2	5	0	Oakland	0	6	0

Sid Gillman

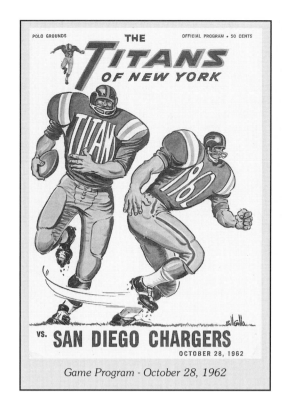

Game Program - October 28, 1962

OCTOBER 28, 1962
Polo Grounds – New York City, New York
Attendance – 21,467

					Total
Chargers	0	3	0	0	3
Titans	0	3	20	0	23

Titans	Shockley kicks an 18-yard field goal.
Chargers	Blair kicks a 43-yard field goal.
Titans	Green 63-yard pass to Maynard for the touchdown.
Chargers	Maguire punts to Christy, returned 73 yards for the touchdown. Shockley kicks the extra point.
Titans	Green 18-yard pass to Maynard for the touchdown. Shockley kicks the extra point.

	Chargers	Titans
First Downs	10	13
Rushing Yards	38	70
Passing Yards	168	320
Punts-Average	8-41.5	7-36.3
Fumbles-Lost	2-1	4-3
Penalties-Yards	6-71	5-52

Chargers' Leaders
Rushing	MacKinnon 12-36, Hadl 5-7, Braxton 4-(-8), Jackson 1-3
Passing	Hadl 9-27-1-106, Wood 5-13-1-62
Receiving	Norton 6-74, Jackson 3-16, MacKinnon 2-29, Kocourek 1-21, Robinson 1-18
Interceptions	Harris 1-0

Titans' Leaders
Rushing	Tiller 10-(-1), Christy 9-71, Green 1-0
Passing	Green 17-30-1-295, Stephens 1-1-0-7
Receiving	Maynard 6-157, Powell 6-105, Christy 4-45, Tiller 1-7, Johnson 1-6
Interceptions	Kovac 1-21, Cooke 1-20

Week 8 Games
New York 23, San Diego 3
Buffalo 45, Denver 38
Boston 26, Oakland 16
Dallas 31, Houston 7

Week 8 Standings
East	W	L	T	West	W	L	T
Boston	5	2	0	Dallas	6	1	0
Houston	4	3	0	Denver	6	2	0
New York	3	5	0	San Diego	3	5	0
Buffalo	3	5	0	Oakland	0	7	0

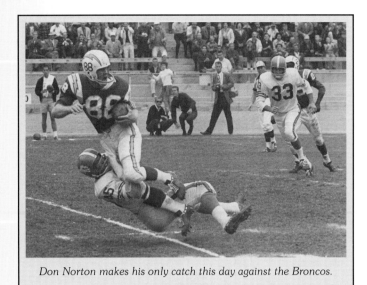
Don Norton makes his only catch this day against the Broncos.

NOVEMBER 4, 1962
Balboa Stadium – San Diego, California
Attendance – 20,827

					Total
Chargers	0	17	3	0	20
Broncos	7	0	7	9	23

Broncos	Stone 1-yard run for the touchdown. Mingo kicks the extra point.
Chargers	Blair kicks a 27-yard field goal.
Chargers	Hadl 72-yard pass to Robinson for the touchdown. Blair kicks the extra point.
Chargers	Hadl 9-yard pass to MacKinnon for the touchdown. Blair kicks the extra point.
Chargers	Blair kicks a 15-yard field goal.
Broncos	Stone 5-yard run for the touchdown. Mingo kicks the extra point.
Broncos	Tripucka 14-yard pass to Stone for the touchdown. Mingo kicks the extra point.
Broncos	Maguire to punt, ball centered out of the end zone for a safety.

	Chargers	Broncos
First Downs	16	21
Rushing Yards	151	51
Passing Yards	162	200
Punts-Average	5-44.2	7-50
Fumbles-Lost	3-2	2-1
Penalties-Yards	8-70	5-77

Chargers' Leaders
Rushing	MacKinnon 11-48, Hadl 10-60, Jackson 7-32, Braxton 5-11
Passing	Hadl 10-26-2-198
Receiving	Robinson 3-125, MacKinnon 2-29, Kocourek 2-24, Braxton 2-5, Norton 1-15
Interceptions	Gibson 1-20, Bethune 1-2

Broncos' Leaders
Rushing	Stone 15-9, Mingo 6-18, Stinnette 5-17, Dickinson 2-9, Frazier 2-(-2)
Passing	Tripucka 17-32-1-202, Shaw 1-3-1-16
Receiving	Prebola 5-73, Dickinson 5-31, Stone 4-67, Taylor 2-18, Scarpitto 1-16
Interceptions	Gonsoulin 1-0, Zeman 1-0

Week 9 Games
Denver 23, San Diego 20
New York 31, Oakland 21
Buffalo 28, Boston 28
Houston 14, Dallas 6

Week 9 Standings
East	W	L	T	West	W	L	T
Boston	5	2	1	Denver	7	2	0
Houston	5	3	0	Dallas	6	2	0
New York	4	5	0	San Diego	3	6	0
Buffalo	3	5	1	Oakland	0	8	0

NOVEMBER 11, 1962
Balboa Stadium – San Diego, California
Attendance – 22,204

					Total
Chargers	0	0	6	14	20
Bills	17	20	3	0	40

Bills	Gilchrist 22-yard run for the touchdown. Gilchrist kicks the extra point.
Bills	Gilchrist kicks an 18-yard field goal.
Bills	Carlton 12-yard run for the touchdown. Gilchrist kicks the extra point.
Bills	Carlton 14-yard run for the touchdown. Gilchrist kicks the extra point.
Bills	Rabb 68-yard pass to Dubenion for the touchdown. Gilchrist kicks the extra point.
Bills	Rabb 13-yard pass to Bass for the touchdown.
Chargers	Hadl 15-yard pass to Kocourek for the touchdown.
Bills	Gilchrist kicks a 5-yard field goal.
Chargers	Jackson 1-yard run for the touchdown.
Chargers	Jackson 3-yard run for the touchdown. Braxton 2-yard run for the 2-point conversion.

	Chargers	Bills
First Downs	21	20
Rushing Yards	164	211
Passing Yards	206	124
Punts-Average	2-37.5	3-43.6
Fumbles-Lost	5-2	2-0
Penalties-Yards	6-60	5-48

Chargers' Leaders
Rushing	MacKinnon 17-102, Jackson 10-37, Braxton 4-18, Gillett 2-8, Hadl 1-(-1)
Passing	Hadl 15-28-3-217
Receiving	Kocourek 7-126, Norton 3-43, Robinson 3-20, Jackson 1-26, Braxton 1-2
Interceptions	Harris 1-16, Buncom 1-26

Bills' Leaders
Rushing	Gilchrist 14-46, Carlton 12-90, Crow 6-66, Rabb 6-8, Jones 2-1
Passing	Rabb 6-16-2-124
Receiving	Dubenion 3-89, Rychelec 1-13, Bass 1-13, Warlick 1-9
Interceptions	Edgerson 1-40, Stratton 2-59

Week 10 Games
Buffalo 40, San Diego 20
Dallas 52, New York 31
Boston 33, Denver 29
Houston 28, Oakland 20

Week 10 Standings
East	W	L	T	West	W	L	T
Boston	6	2	1	Dallas	7	2	0
Houston	6	3	0	Denver	7	3	0
Buffalo	4	5	1	San Diego	3	7	0
New York	4	6	0	Oakland	0	9	0

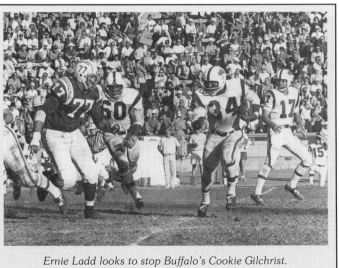
Ernie Ladd looks to stop Buffalo's Cookie Gilchrist.

The Chargers "practice" against Sid Gillman's Huddle Club, a youth fan club.

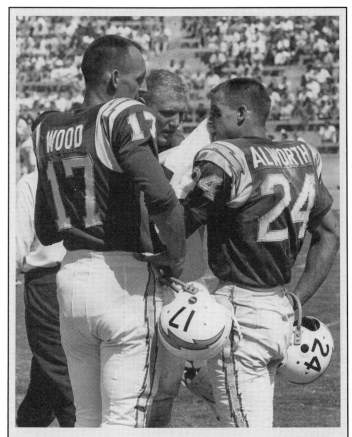

Dick Wood (17) and Lance Alworth (24) discuss strategy on the sideline.

Week 11 Games
San Diego and New York - Bye
Dallas 24, Denver 3
Houston 21, Boston 17
Buffalo 10, Oakland 6

Week 11 Standings

East	W	L	T	West	W	L	T
Houston	7	3	0	Dallas	8	2	0
Boston	6	3	1	Denver	7	4	0
Buffalo	5	5	1	San Diego	3	7	0
New York	4	6	0	Oakland	0	10	0

NOVEMBER 25, 1962
Jeppesen Stadium – Houston, Texas
Attendance – 28,235

					Total
Chargers	14	7	3	3	27
Oilers	0	12	7	14	33

Chargers	Hadl 32-yard pass to MacKinnon for the touchdown. Blair kicks the extra point.
Chargers	Hadl 26-yard pass to Kocourek for the touchdown. Blair kicks the extra point.
Oilers	Lee 98-yard pass to Dewveall for the touchdown. Lee kicks the extra point.
Oilers	Robinson tackled in the end zone on the kickoff for a safety.
Oilers	Blanda kicks a 42-yard field goal.
Chargers	Hadl 12-yard pass to Carolan for the touchdown. Blair kicks the extra point.
Oilers	Cannon 1-yard run for the touchdown. Blanda kicks the extra point.
Chargers	Blair kicks a 17-yard field goal.
Chargers	Blair kicks an 11-yard field goal.
Oilers	Blanda 16-yard pass to Dewveall for the touchdown. Blanda 2-yard pass to Cannon for the 2-point conversion.
Oilers	Blanda kicks a 22-yard field goal.
Oilers	Blanda kicks a 39-yard field goal.

	Chargers	Oilers
First Downs	18	10
Rushing Yards	153	47
Passing Yards	241	228
Punts-Average	6-35.7	4-44.8
Fumbles-Lost	0-0	3-2
Penalties-Yards	4-21	1-33

Chargers' Leaders

Rushing	Jackson 17-86, MacKinnon 6-17, Lincoln 5-14, McDougall 4-35, Hadl 4-1
Passing	Hadl 15-39-3-261
Receiving	Robinson 4-48, Norton 3-59, Lincoln 2-49, Kocourek 2-42, Carolan 2-21
Interceptions	Gibson 2-17, Harris 1-0, Bethune 1-4, Whitehead 1-18

Oilers' Leaders

Rushing	Tolar 12-40, Cannon 8-5, Smith 3-1, Lee 1-4, Blanda 1-1
Passing	Blanda 5-18-2-76, Lee 7-13-3-164
Receiving	Tolar 4-18, Dewveall 3-139, Groman 2-30, Cannon 2-25, McLeod 1-28
Interceptions	Johnston 1-0, Cline 1-14, Norton 1-10

Week 12 Games
Houston 33, San Diego 27
New York 46, Denver 45
Dallas 35, Oakland 7
Boston 21, Buffalo 10

Week 12 Standings

East	W	L	T	West	W	L	T
Houston	8	3	0	Dallas	9	2	0
Boston	7	3	1	Denver	7	5	0
Buffalo	5	6	1	San Diego	3	8	0
New York	5	6	0	Oakland	0	11	0

December 2, 1962
Balboa Stadium- San Diego, California
Attendance – 17,874

					Total
Chargers	14	0	7	10	31
Raiders	0	0	7	14	21

Chargers	McDougall 7-yard run for the touchdown. Blair kicks the extra point.
Chargers	McDougall 24-yard run for the touchdown. Blair kicks the extra point.
Raiders	Daniels 2-yard run fort he touchdown. Agajanian kicks the extra point.
Chargers	Hadl 17-yard pass to Lincoln for the touchdown. Blairkicks the extra point.
Raiders	Davidson 65-yard pass to Dorsey for the touchdown. Agajanian kicks the extra point.
Raiders	Davidson 90-yard pass to Dorsey for the touchdown. Agajanian kicks the extra point.
Chargers	Blair kicks a 12-yard field goal.

	Chargers	Raiders
First Downs	23	12
Rushing Yards	185	76
Passing Yards	150	296
Punts-Average	8-38.4	5-38.0
Fumbles-Lost	1-1	4-1
Penalties-Yards	7-57	2-20

Chargers' Leaders
Rushing	McDougall 22-108, Lincoln 15-57, Jackson 5-18, Hadl 2-2
Passing	Hadl 11-24-1-161
Receiving	Norton 5-71, Lincoln 2-37, Robinson 2-30, Carolan 1-18, MacKinnon 1-5
Interceptions	Bethune 1-0, Faison 1-30

Raiders' Leaders
Rushing	Daniels 16-85, Roberson 3-(-9), Miller 1-0, Davidson 1-0
Passing	Davidson 10-25-2-273, Enis 4-8-0-32, Daniels 0-1-0-0
Receiving	Roberson 3-80, Boydston 3-20, Dorsey 2-155, Craig 2-23, Miller 2-7
Interceptions	Morrow 1-0

Week 13 Games
San Diego 31, Oakland 21
Boston 24, New York 17
Houston 34, Denver 17
Buffalo 23, Dallas 14

Week 13 Standings
East	W	L	T	West	W	L	T
Houston	9	3	0	Dallas	9	3	0
Boston	8	3	1	Denver	7	6	0
Buffalo	6	6	1	San Diego	4	8	0
New York	5	7	0	Oakland	0	12	0

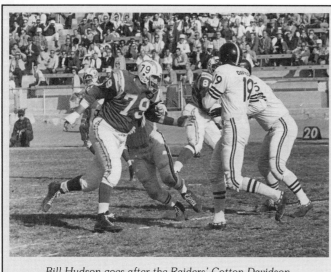

Bill Hudson goes after the Raiders' Cotton Davidson.

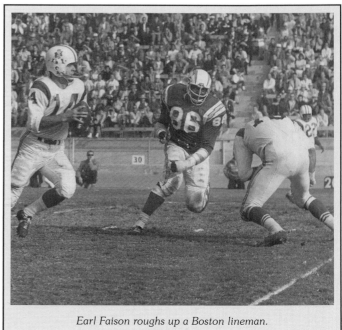

Earl Faison roughs up a Boston lineman.

December 9, 1962
Balboa Stadium – San Diego, California
Attendance – 19,887

					Total
Chargers	0	3	3	8	14
Patriots	7	10	0	3	20

Patriots	Yewcic 43-yard pass to Crawford for the touchdown. Cappalletti kicks the extra point.
Chargers	Blair kicks a 42-yard field goal.
Patriots	Cappalletti kicks an 18-yard field goal.
Patriots	Yewcic 12-yard pass to Colclough for the touchdown. Cappalletti kicks the extra point.
Chargers	Blair kicks a 42-yard field goal.
Patriots	Cappalletti kicks a 9-yard field goal.
Chargers	McDougall 4-yard run for the touchdown. Keckin 2-yard pass to Kocourek for the 2-point conversion.

	Chargers	Patriots
First Downs	10	15
Rushing Yards	86	140
Passing Yards	101	147
Punts-Average	6-40.3	5-38.6
Fumbles-Lost	3-3	2-1
Penalties-Yards	4-20	2-20

Chargers' Leaders
Rushing	McDougall 13-38, Lincoln 10-32, Hadl 4-16
Passing	Hadl 7-18-0-86, Keckin 3-4-0-44, Lincoln 0-1-0-0
Receiving	Norton 5-79, Kocourek 3-42, McDougall 2-9
Interceptions	Buncom 1-9

Patriots' Leaders
Rushing	Burton 19-83, Crawford 16-26, Yewcic 9-31
Passing	Yewcic 7-22-1-147
Receiving	Crawford 2-61, Romeo 2-57, Cappalletti 1-15, Colclough 1-12, Burton 1-2
Interceptions	None

Week 14 Games
Boston 20, San Diego 14
Houston 32, Oakland 17
Dallas 17, Denver 10
Buffalo 20, New York 3

Week 14 Standings
East	W	L	T	West	W	L	T
Houston	10	3	0	Dallas	10	3	0
Boston	9	3	1	Denver	7	7	0
Buffalo	7	6	1	San Diego	4	9	0
New York	5	8	0	Oakland	0	13	0

DECEMBER 16, 1962
Cotton Bowl – Dallas, Texas
Attendance – 18,384

					Total
Chargers	7	0	10	0	17
Texans	3	20	0	3	26

Texans	Brooker kicks a 30-yard field goal.
Chargers	Lincoln 20-yard pass to Robinson for the touchdown. Blair kicks the extra point.
Texans	Brooker kicks a 28-yard field goal.
Texans	Dawson 5-yard run for the touchdown. Brooker kicks the extra point.
Texans	Dawson 13-yard pass to Spikes for the touchdown. Brooker kicks the extra point.
Texans	Brooker kicks a 34-yard field goal.
Chargers	Hadl 13-yard pass to Norton for the touchdown. Blair kicks the extra point.
Chargers	Blair kicks a 35-yard field goal.
Texans	Brooker kicks a 13-yard field goal.

	Chargers	Texans
First Downs	17	19
Rushing Yards	143	134
Passing Yards	192	154
Punts-Average	3-41.3	3-37.7
Fumbles-Lost	3-1	1-0
Penalties-Yards	7-71	3-25

Chargers' Leaders

Rushing	Lincoln 11-73, Jackson 7-46, McDougall 4-16, Hadl 1-5, Keckin 1-3
Passing	Hadl 11-29-5-152, Keckin 2-5-1-20, Lincoln 1-1-0-20
Receiving	Norton 6-86, Jackson 3-28, Kocourek 2-42, Robinson 2-28, McDougall 1-8
Interceptions	Buncom 1-3, Blair 1-17

Texans' Leaders

Rushing	Haynes 20-82, Spikes 5-24, Dawson 5-18, McClinton 4-5, Saxton 1-5
Passing	Dawson 13-21-2-126, Wilson 2-6-0-28
Receiving	McClinton 6-68, Arbanas 3-21, Haynes 2-35, Saxton 2-13, Spikes 1-13
Interceptions	Ply 4-108, Headrick 1-19, Grayson 1-0

Week 15 Games
Dallas 26, San Diego 17
Oakland 20, Boston 0
Houston 44, New York 10
Buffalo and Denver - Bye

Week 15 Standings

East	W	L	T	West	W	L	T
Houston	11	3	0	Dallas	11	3	0
Boston	9	4	1	Denver	7	7	0
Buffalo	7	6	1	San Diego	4	10	0
New York	5	9	0	Oakland	1	13	0

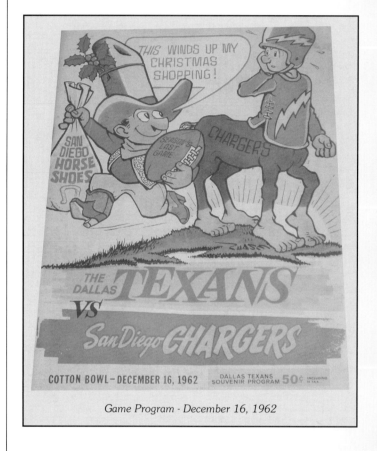

Game Program - December 16, 1962

1963 CHARGERS TEAM STATISTICS
(11-3 OVERALL) FIRST PLACE IN THE AFL WEST

Team Statistics	Chargers	Opponent
TOTAL FIRST DOWNS	252	241
Rushing	112	85
Passing	124	135
Penalty	16	21
TOTAL NET YARDS	5,153	4,161
Avg. Per Game	368.1	297.2
Avg. Per Play	6.7	4.7
NET YARDS RUSHING	2,203	1,468
Avg. Per Game	157.4	104.9
NET YARDS PASSING	2,950	2,693
Avg. Per Game	210.7	192.4
Gross Yards	3,138	2,976
Completions/Attempts	202/357	231/472
Completion Pct.	.566	.489
Had Intercepted	24	29
PUNTS/AVERAGE	60/38.6	50/43.7
PENALTIES/YARDS	77/773	69/771
FUMBLES/BALL LOST	16/12	22/17
TOUCHDOWNS	50	28
Rushing	20	10
Passing	28	17
Returns	2	1
QUARTERBACK SACKS	31.0	20.0

Rushing	No.	Yds.	Avg.	TD
Lowe	177	1,010	5.7	8
Lincoln	128	826	6.5	5
McDougall	39	201	5.2	1
B. Jackson	18	64	3.6	4
Rote	24	62	2.6	2
Hadl	8	26	3.3	0
Alworth	2	14	7.0	0
Totals	**396**	**2,203**	**5.6**	**20**

Receiving	No.	Yds.	Avg.	TD
Alworth	61	1,205	19.8	11
Lowe	26	191	7.3	2
Lincoln	24	325	13.5	3
Kocourek	23	359	15.6	5
Norton	21	281	13.4	1
Robinson	18	315	17.5	2
MacKinnon	11	262	23.8	4
McDougall	10	115	11.5	0
B. Jackson	8	85	10.6	0
Totals	**202**	**3,138**	**15.5**	**28**

Passing	Att.	Comp.	Yds.	Comp. %	TD	Int.
Rote	286	170	2,510	.594	20	17
Hadl	64	28	502	.438	6	6
Lowe	4	2	100	.500	1	1
Lincoln	1	0	0	.000	0	0
McDougall	1	1	11	100.0	1	0
Norton	1	1	15	100.0	0	0
Totals	**357**	**202**	**3,138**	**.566**	**28**	**24**

Interceptions	No.	Yds.	TD
D. Harris	8	83	1
Allen	5	37	0
Maguire	4	47	0
McNeil	4	23	0
Mitinger	3	26	0
Karas	2	30	0
Blair	1	40	0
Glick	1	13	0
Whitehead	1	0	0
Totals	**29**	**299**	**1**

Kicking	FG	Att.	PAT	Att.	Pts.
Blair	17	28	44	47	95

Punting	No.	Avg.
Maguire	58	38.6
Hadl	2	37.5

Punt Returns	No.	FC	Yds.	Avg.	TD
Alworth	11	0	120	10.9	0
Lincoln	7	0	98	14.0	0
D. Harris	4	0	43	10.8	0

Kickoff Returns	No.	Yds.	Avg.	TD
Lincoln	17	439	25.8	0
Alworth	10	216	21.6	0
Westmoreland	10	204	20.4	0
Lowe	5	132	26.4	0
McDougall	3	77	25.7	0
D. Harris	2	34	17.0	0
Robinson	2	27	13.5	0
B. Jackson	1	16	16.0	0
Maguire	1	5	5.0	0
Sweeney	1	18	18.0	0

Above: Playing cards was one of the few ways to spend free time at the Rough Acres Ranch.

Left: The AFL Champion San Diego Chargers.

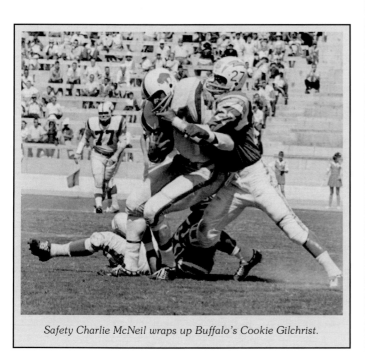

Safety Charlie McNeil wraps up Buffalo's Cookie Gilchrist.

SEPTEMBER 8, 1963
Balboa Stadium – San Diego, California
Attendance – 22,344

					Total
Chargers	0	7	7	0	14
Bills	0	3	0	7	10

Chargers	Jackson 1-yard run for the touchdown. Blair kicks the extra point.
Bills	Yoho kicks a 17-yard field goal.
Chargers	Lowe 48-yard run for the touchdown. Blair kicks the extra point.
Bills	Brown 4-yard run for the touchdown. Yoho kicks the extra point.

	Chargers	Bills
First Downs	17	19
Rushing Yards	131	116
Passing Yards	239	192
Punts-Average	4-41.0	3-48.0
Fumbles-Lost	0-0	1-1
Penalties-Yards	7-100	5-45

Chargers' Leaders
Rushing	Lowe 10-96, Jackson 8-15, Lincoln 3-9, McDougall 1-6, Rote 1-5
Passing	Rote 18-29-1-260
Receiving	Jackson 4-56, Kocourek 2-60, Robinson 2-45, Lincoln 2-38, Alworth 2-35
Interceptions	Whitehead 1-0, Mitinger 1-3, Maguire 1-38

Bills' Leaders
Rushing	Carlton 10-41, Saimes 10-40, Kemp 2-19, Gilchrist 2-4, Crow 2-0
Passing	Kemp 17-33-3-220
Receiving	Miller 5-60, Bass 4-34, Warlick 3-68, Saimes 3-1, Dubenion 1-17
Interceptions	Jacobs 1-8

Week 1 Games
San Diego 14, Buffalo 10
Boston 38, New York 14
Oakland 24, Houston 13
Kansas City 59, Denver 7

Week 1 Standings
East	W	L	T	West	W	L	T
Boston	1	0	0	San Diego	1	0	0
Houston	0	1	0	Oakland	1	0	0
New York	0	1	0	Kansas City	1	0	0
Buffalo	0	1	0	Denver	0	1	0

SEPTEMBER 14, 1963
Balboa Stadium – San Diego, California
Attendance – 26,097

					Total
Chargers	0	14	0	3	17
Patriots	3	7	0	3	13

Patriots	Cappalletti kicks a 35-yard field goal.
Chargers	Rote 43-yard pass to Alworth for the touchdown. Blair kicks the extra point.
Chargers	Lowe 29-yard pass to Robinson for the touchdown. Blair kicks the extra point.
Patriots	Yewcic 1-yard run for the touchdown. Cappalletti kicks the extra point.
Patriots	Cappalletti kicks a 36-yard field goal.
Chargers	Blair kicks a 31-yard field goal.

	Chargers	Patriots
First Downs	11	19
Rushing Yards	76	164
Passing Yards	172	139
Punts-Average	6-39.0	4-40.0
Fumbles-Lost	1-1	2-0
Penalties-Yards	8-65	3-25

Chargers' Leaders
Rushing	Lincoln 8-39, McDougall 7-31, Lowe 4-6, Rote 1-0, Hadl 1-0
Passing	Rote 5-12-1-105, Lowe 1-1-0-71, Hadl 2-8-0-17
Receiving	Alworth 4-76, Robinson 2-83, McDougall 1-21
Interceptions	McNeil 1-21, Maguire 1-4

Patriots' Leaders
Rushing	Garron 19-69, Crawford 14-47, Yewcic 6-38, Parilli 3-10, Lott 1-0
Passing	Parilli 8-20-2-74, Yewcic 7-14-0-59, Crawford 1-1-0-15
Receiving	Garron 5-45, Graham 4-36, Cappalletti 3-29, Romeo 2-19, Crawford 2-19
Interceptions	Addison 1-17

Week 2 Games
San Diego 17, Boston 13
Oakland 35, Buffalo 17
Houston 20, Denver 14
Kansas City and New York - Bye

Week 2 Standings
East	W	L	T	West	W	L	T
Boston	1	1	0	San Diego	2	0	0
Houston	1	1	0	Oakland	2	0	0
New York	0	1	0	Kansas City	1	0	0
Buffalo	0	2	0	Denver	0	2	0

Game Program - September 14, 1963

Earl Faison (86), Bud Whitehead (47), Gerry McDougall (20) and George Blair (39)

Week 3 Games
San Diego and Denver - Bye
Kansas City 27, Buffalo 27
New York 24, Houston 17
Boston 20, Oakland 14

Week 3 Standings

East	W	L	T	West	W	L	T
Boston	2	1	0	San Diego	2	0	0
New York	1	1	0	Oakland	2	1	0
Houston	1	2	0	Kansas City	1	0	1
Buffalo	0	2	1	Denver	0	2	0

SEPTEMBER 29, 1963
Balboa Stadium – San Diego, California
Attendance – 22,654

					Total
Chargers	7	14	0	3	24
Chiefs	0	3	0	7	10

Chargers	Rote 20-yard pass to Kocourek for the touchdown. Blair kicks the extra point.
Chargers	Rote 35-yard pass to Kocourek for the touchdown. Blair kicks the extra point.
Chargers	Rote 16-yard pass to Lincoln for the touchdown. Blair kicks the extra point.
Chiefs	Brooker kicks a 22-yard field goal.
Chargers	Blair kicks a 38-yard field goal.
Chiefs	Dawson 2-yard pass to Arbanas for the touchdown. Brooker kicks the extra point.

	Chargers	Chiefs
First Downs	17	12
Rushing Yards	154	27
Passing Yards	140	137
Punts-Average	5-35.0	4-51.0
Fumbles-Lost	0-0	1-1
Penalties-Yards	7-48	4-52

Chargers' Leaders
Rushing	Lowe 17-91, Lincoln 14-59, Rote 2-4
Passing	Rote 10-16-1-127, Hadl 2-3-0-41
Receiving	Lincoln 4-28, Kocourek 3-71, Robinson 2-40, Alworth 2-16, MacKinnon 1-13
Interceptions	Maguire 1-5, McNeil 1-0, Allen 1-8

Chiefs' Leaders
Rushing	Haynes 8-9, McClinton 5-11, Dawson 1-7
Passing	Dawson 18-34-3-152
Receiving	Haynes 5-49, Arbanas 4-41, McClinton 4-21, Jackson 3-25, Burford 1-8
Interceptions	Holub 1-24

Week 4 Games
San Diego 24, Kansas City 10
Houston 31, Buffalo 20
New York 10, Oakland 7
Denver 14, Boston 10

Week 4 Standings

East	W	L	T	West	W	L	T
New York	2	1	0	San Diego	3	0	0
Boston	2	2	0	Kansas City	1	1	1
Houston	2	2	0	Oakland	2	2	0
Buffalo	0	3	1	Denver	1	2	0

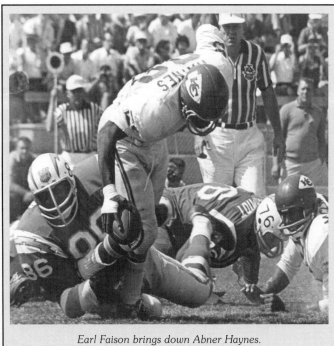

Earl Faison brings down Abner Haynes.

OCTOBER 6, 1963
Bears Stadium – Denver, Colorado
Attendance – 18,428

					Total
Chargers	13	7	0	14	34
Broncos	3	14	9	24	50

Broncos	Mingo kicks a 37-yard field goal.
Chargers	Rote 39-yard pass to Lincoln for the touchdown. Blair kicks the extra point.
Chargers	Rote 31-yard pass to Lowe for the touchdown. Blair kicks the extra point.
Broncos	McCormick 12-yard pass to Prebola for the touchdown. Mingo kicks the extra point.
Chargers	Rote 85-yard pass to Alworth for the touchdown. Blair kicks the extra point.
Broncos	McCormick 23-yard pass to Taylor for the touchdown. Mingo kicks the extra point.
Broncos	Mingo kicks a 41-yard field goal.
Broncos	Mingo kicks a 26-yard field goal.
Broncos	Mingo kicks a 13-yard field goal.
Chargers	Hadl 19-yard pass to Lincoln for the touchdown. Blair kicks the extra point.
Broncos	McCormick 49-yard pass to Taylor for the touchdown. Mingo kicks the extra point.
Broncos	Stone 39-yard run for the touchdown. Mingo kicks the extra point.
Broncos	Gonsoulin intercepts Hadl pass, returns it 42 yards for the touchdown. Mingo kicks the extra point.
Chargers	Hadl 54-yard pass to MacKinnon for the touchdown. Blair kicks the extra point.
Broncos	Mingo kicks a 21-yard field goal.

	Chargers	Broncos
First Downs	15	24
Rushing Yards	95	205
Passing Yards	317	229
Punts-Average	4-38.0	3-53.0
Fumbles-Lost	4-4	1-1
Penalties-Yards	8-76	9-95

Chargers' Leaders

Rushing	Lincoln 8-62, Lowe 6-42, Rote 1-(-2), Alworth 1-(-7)
Passing	Rote 11-17-2-230, Hadl 3-6-1-87, Lincoln 0-1-0-0
Receiving	Alworth 4-114, Lincoln 4-73, MacKinnon 2-68, Lowe 2-28, Robinson 1-26
Interceptions	McNeil 1-17

Broncos' Leaders

Rushing	Stone 17-104, Joe 16-69, Dickinson 4-28, Mingo 2-7, McCormick 1-(-3)
Passing	McCormick 18-36-1-265, Stone 0-1-0-0
Receiving	Taylor 7-142, Groman 3-42, Prebola 3-36, Joe 3-33, Scarpitto 1-13
Interceptions	Gonsoulin 2-52, Janik 1-1

Week 5 Games
Denver 50, San Diego 34
Buffalo 12, Oakland 0
New York 31, Boston 24
Kansas City 28, Houston 7

Week 5 Standings

East	W	L	T	West	W	L	T
New York	3	1	0	San Diego	3	1	0
Boston	2	3	0	Kansas City	2	1	1
Houston	2	3	0	Denver	2	2	0
Buffalo	1	3	1	Oakland	2	3	0

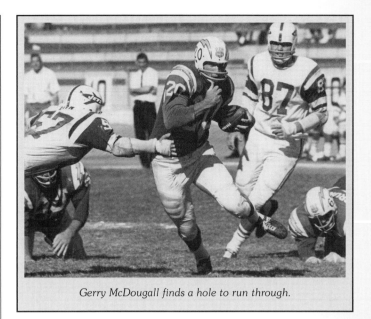

Gerry McDougall finds a hole to run through.

OCTOBER 13, 1963
Balboa Stadium – San Diego, California
Attendance – 27,189

					Total
Chargers	3	0	14	7	24
Jets	7	3	10	0	20

Jets	Wood 51-yard pass to Turner for the touchdown. Guesman kicks the extra point.
Chargers	Blair kicks a 28-yard field goal.
Jets	Guesman kicks a 44-yard field goal.
Chargers	Hadl 9-yard pass to Kocourek for the touchdown. Blair kicks the extra point.
Chargers	McDougall 11-yard pass to Alworth for the touchdown. Blair kicks the extra point.
Jets	Guesman kicks a 32-yard field goal.
Jets	Smolinsky 2-yard run for the touchdown. Guesman kicks the extra point.
Chargers	Lowe 7-yard run for the touchdown. Blair kicks the extra point.

	Chargers	Jets
First Downs	22	16
Rushing Yards	287	63
Passing Yards	223	203
Punts-Average	4-34.0	4-44.0
Fumbles-Lost	1-1	0-0
Penalties-Yards	7-148	4-70

Chargers' Leaders

Rushing	Lowe 16-161, Lincoln 13-33, McDougall 6-56, Hadl 4-38, Rote 1-(-1)
Passing	Rote 10-13-1-78, Hadl 8-12-0-134, McDougall 1-1-0-11, Lowe 0-1-1-0
Receiving	Alworth 4-54, Robinson 4-26, Lowe 4-18, Kocourek 3-42, Lincoln 2-40
Interceptions	None

Jets' Leaders

Rushing	Mathis 10-26, Smolinsky 10-26, Christy 4-11
Passing	Wood 15-31-0-220
Receiving	Smolinski 4-34, Turner 3-68, Maynard 2-59, Christy 2-22, Mathis 2-10
Interceptions	Baird 1-0, Jamerette 1-6

Week 6 Games
San Diego 24, New York 20
Buffalo 35, Kansas City 26
Houston 33, Denver 24
Boston 20, Oakland 14

Week 6 Standings

East	W	L	T	West	W	L	T
New York	3	2	0	San Diego	4	1	0
Boston	3	3	0	Kansas City	2	2	1
Houston	3	3	0	Denver	2	3	0
Buffalo	2	3	1	Oakland	2	4	0

147

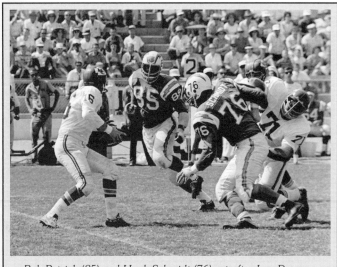

Bob Petrich (85) and Hank Schmidt (76) get after Len Dawson.

OCTOBER 20, 1963
Municipal Stadium – Kansas City, Missouri
Attendance – 30,107

					Total
Chargers	0	3	14	21	38
Chiefs	0	7	3	7	17

Chargers	Blair kicks a 29-yard field goal.
Chiefs	Dawson 73-yard pass to Haynes for the touchdown. Brooker kicks the extra point.
Chargers	Rote 44-yard pass to Alworth for the touchdown. Blair kicks the extra point.
Chiefs	Brooker kicks a 36-yard field goal.
Chargers	Lowe runs 7 yard for the touchdown. Blair kicks the extra point.
Chargers	Rote 72-yard pass to Alworth for the touchdown. Blair kicks the extra point.
Chiefs	Dawson 7-yard pass to Arbanas for the touchdown. Brooker kicks the extra point.
Chargers	Lincoln 76-yard run for the touchdown. Blair kicks the extra point.
Chargers	Lowe 21-yard run for the touchdown. Blair kicks the extra point.

	Chargers	Chiefs
First Downs	18	17
Rushing Yards	147	78
Passing Yards	281	253
Punts-Average	3-45.0	3-46.0
Fumbles-Lost	2-0	3-1
Penalties-Yards	3-41	3-54

Chargers' Leaders

Rushing	Lowe 11-24, Lincoln 10-127, Rote 3-9, Hadl 1-(-4), McDougall 1-(-9)
Passing	Rote 16-22-0-266, Hadl 1-4-0-15
Receiving	Alworth 9-232, Robinson 3-36, Lowe 3-11, Lincoln 2-2
Interceptions	Allen 1-26, Blair 1-40

Chiefs' Leaders

Rushing	McClinton 15-60, Haynes 14-24, Spikes 4-(-6)
Passing	Dawson 16-24-2-225, Wilson 2-5-0-28
Receiving	Haynes 8-149, Burford 5-53, Jackson 4-44, Arbanas 1-7
Interceptions	None

Week 7 Games
San Diego 38, Kansas City 17
Oakland 49, New York 26
Houston 28, Buffalo 14
Boston 40, Denver 21

Week 7 Standings

East	W	L	T	West	W	L	T
Houston	4	3	0	San Diego	5	1	0
Boston	4	3	0	Oakland	3	4	0
New York	3	3	0	Kansas City	2	3	1
Buffalo	2	4	1	Denver	2	4	0

OCTOBER 27, 1963
Balboa Stadium – San Diego, California
Attendance – 30,182

					Total
Chargers	10	7	9	7	33
Raiders	7	7	7	13	34

Raiders	Flores 20-yard pass to Powell for the touchdown. Mercer kicks the extra point.
Chargers	Blair kicks a 23-yard field goal.
Chargers	Rote 32-yard pass to Alworth for the touchdown. Blair kicks the extra point.
Raiders	Flores 5-yard pass to Miller for the touchdown. Mercer kicks the extra point.
Chargers	Hadl 69-yard pass to MacKinnon for the touchdown. Blair kicks the extra point.
Chargers	Harris intercepts Davidson pass, returns it 22 yards for the touchdown.
Raiders	Davidson 39-yard pass to Craig for the touchdown. Mercer kicks the extra point.
Raiders	Davidson 9-yard pass to Shaw for the touchdown.

	Chargers	Raiders
First Downs	18	13
Rushing Yards	234	179
Passing Yards	146	115
Punts-Average	3-41.0	5-46.0
Fumbles-Lost	1-1	0-0
Penalties-Yards	5-55	4-31

Chargers' Leaders

Rushing	Lincoln 15-130, Lowe 12-82, McDougall 3-16, Rote 1-6
Passing	Rote 6-14-4-67, Hadl 2-6-1-82, Lowe 1-1-0-29
Receiving	MacKinnon 3-111, Alworth 3-50, Lincoln 2-11, Robinson 1-6
Interceptions	Harris 2-26, McNeil 1-6

Raiders' Leaders

Rushing	Daniels 19-125, Miller 7-13, Davidson 5-27, Shaw 4-7, Flores 1-7
Passing	Flores 3-11-2-31, Davidson 5-10-1-115
Receiving	Powell 3-77, Craig 1-39, Herock 1-10, Shaw 1-9, Daniels 1-6
Interceptions	Williamson 2-15, Matsos 1-13, Krakoski 1-3, Gibson 1-18

Week 8 Games
Oakland 34, San Diego 33
Buffalo 28, Boston 21
Houston 28, Kansas City 7
New York 35, Denver 35

Week 8 Standings

East	W	L	T	West	W	L	T
Houston	5	3	0	San Diego	5	2	0
Boston	4	4	0	Oakland	4	4	0
New York	3	3	1	Kansas City	2	4	1
Buffalo	3	4	1	Denver	2	4	1

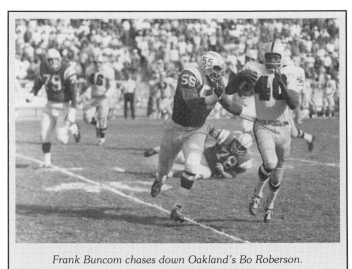

Frank Buncom chases down Oakland's Bo Roberson.

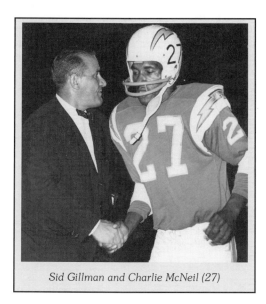

Sid Gillman and Charlie McNeil (27)

NOVEMBER 2, 1963
Polo Grounds – New York City, New York
Attendance – 18,336

					Total
Chargers	7	17	14	15	53
Jets	0	0	0	7	7

Chargers	Rote 11-yard pass to Lowe for the touchdown. Blair kicks the extra point.
Chargers	Rote 14-yard pass to Kocourek for the touchdown. Blair kicks the extra point.
Chargers	Lowe 11-yard run for the touchdown. Blair kicks the extra point.
Chargers	Blair kicks an 18-yard field goal.
Chargers	Rote 28-yard pass to Alworth for the touchdown. Blair kicks the extra point.
Chargers	Rote 1-yard run for the touchdown. Blair kicks the extra point.
Chargers	McDougall 3-yard run for the touchdown. Blair kicks the extra point.
Jets	Wood 4-yard run for the touchdown. Guesman kicks the extra point.
Chargers	Hadl 8-yard pass to Robinson for the touchdown. Hadl 2-yard pass to Kocourek for the 2-point conversion.

	Chargers	Jets
First Downs	25	15
Rushing Yards	157	39
Passing Yards	371	196
Punts-Average	2-32.5	3-35.3
Fumbles-Lost	1-1	3-3
Penalties-Yards	10-84	5-82

Chargers' Leaders
Rushing	Lowe 16-79, Lincoln 11-62, Rote 2-10, McDougall 2-6
Passing	Rote 21-29-0-369, Hadl 1-2-0-8
Receiving	Alworth 5-180, Norton 4-41, Lowe 4-24, Kocourek 3-34, Lincoln 2-44
Interceptions	Harris 2-14

Jets' Leaders
Rushing	Smolinski 8-29, Mathis 4-7, Wood 2-3
Passing	Wood 15-30-1-173, Hall 4-11-1-47
Receiving	Turner 5-70, Smolinski 4-32, Mackey 3-49, Christy 3-21, Gregory 2-29
Interceptions	None

Week 9 Games
San Diego 53, New York 7
Boston 45, Houston 3
Oakland 10, Kansas City 7
Buffalo 30, Denver 28

Week 9 Standings
East	W	L	T	West	W	L	T
Houston	5	4	0	San Diego	6	2	0
Boston	5	4	0	Oakland	5	4	0
Buffalo	4	4	1	Kansas City	2	5	1
New York	3	4	1	Denver	2	5	1

NOVEMBER 10, 1963
Balboa Stadium – San Diego, California
Attendance – 20,827

					Total
Chargers	7	0	0	0	7
Patriots	0	0	6	0	6

Chargers	Rote 23-yard pass to Alworth for the touchdown. Blair kicks the extra point.
Patriots	Cappalletti kicks a 36-yard field goal.
Patriots	Cappalletti kicks a 25-yard field goal.

	Chargers	Patriots
First Downs	12	15
Rushing Yards	32	103
Passing Yards	242	188
Punts-Average	7-33.8	3-30.5
Fumbles-Lost	1-1	3-3
Penalties-Yards	4-30	6-54

Chargers' Leaders
Rushing	Lincoln 11-37, Lowe 9-0, Rote 1-1, Hadl 1-(-5)
Passing	Rote 17-29-1-246, Hadl 1-3-0-6, Lincoln 0-0-0-(-7)
Receiving	Alworth 13-210, Norton 4-37, Lowe 1-11
Interceptions	Allen 2-3

Patriots' Leaders
Rushing	Garron 23-88, Lott 3-5, Parilli 2-7, Crump 1-2
Passing	Parilli 14-30-2-188
Receiving	Cappalletti 4-40, Graham 3-64, Colclough 3-47, Crump 2-10, Romeo 1-26
Interceptions	Suci 1-15

Week 10 Games
San Diego 7, Boston 6
Buffalo 27, Denver 17
Oakland 22, Kansas City 7
Houston 31, New York 27

Week 10 Standings
East	W	L	T	West	W	L	T
Houston	6	4	0	San Diego	7	2	0
Buffalo	5	4	1	Oakland	6	4	0
Boston	5	5	0	Kansas City	2	6	1
New York	3	5	1	Denver	2	6	1

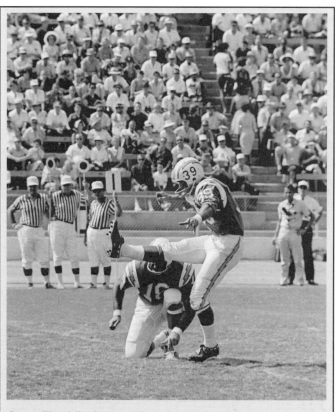

George Blair follow's Alworth's touchdown with the game-winning extra point.

149

November 17, 1963
War Memorial Stadium – Buffalo, New York
Attendance – 38,592

					Total
Chargers	10	0	7	6	23
Bills	7	3	3	0	13

Bills	Gilchrist 1-yard run for the touchdown. Yoho kicks the extra point.
Chargers	Lincoln 46-yard run for the touchdown. Blair kicks the extra point.
Chargers	Blair kicks a 39-yard field goal.
Bills	Yoho kicks a 27-yard field goal.
Chargers	Rote 17-yard pass to Alworth for the touchdown. Blair kicks the extra point.
Bills	Yoho kicks a 9-yard field goal.
Chargers	Blair kicks a 15-yard field goal.
Chargers	Blair kicks a 45-yard field goal.

	Chargers	Bills
First Downs	16	22
Rushing Yards	199	119
Passing Yards	156	239
Punts-Average	3-38.7	4-33.7
Fumbles-Lost	0-0	1-0
Penalties-Yards	5-38	6-50

Chargers' Leaders

Rushing	Lowe 14-65, Lincoln 10-101, Rote 2-12, Alworth 1-21
Passing	Rote 10-22-2-156
Receiving	Alworth 4-79, Lincoln 3-31, Norton 2-20, Kocourek 1-26
Interceptions	Harris 3-25

Bills' Leaders

Rushing	Gilchrist 17-95, Rutkowski 5-12, Kemp 1-12
Passing	Kemp 23-36-3-278, Rutkowski 0-1-0-0
Receiving	Rutkowski 7-49, Dubenion 6-112, Gilchrist 5-36, Miller 4-52, Warlick 1-29
Interceptions	West 1-0, Saimes 1-16

Week 11 Games
San Diego 23, Buffalo 13
New York 14, Denver 9
Kansas City 24, Boston 24
Oakland and Houston - Bye

Week 11 Standings

East	W	L	T		West	W	L	T
Houston	6	4	0		San Diego	8	2	0
Buffalo	5	5	1		Oakland	6	4	0
Boston	5	5	1		Kansas City	2	6	2
New York	4	5	1		Denver	2	7	1

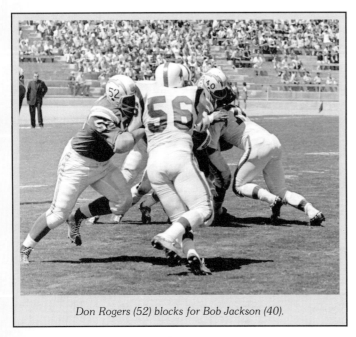

Don Rogers (52) blocks for Bob Jackson (40).

Keith Lincoln breaks the tackle of Houston's Ed Husmann.

December 1, 1963
Balboa Stadium – San Diego, California
Attendance – 31,713

					Total
Chargers	7	13	0	7	27
Oilers	0	0	0	0	0

Chargers	Lincoln 15-yard run for the touchdown. Blair kicks the extra point.
Chargers	Blair kicks a 42-yard field goal.
Chargers	Lowe 2-yard run for the touchdown. Blair kicks the extra point.
Chargers	Blair kicks a 20-yard field goal.
Chargers	Rote 22-yard pass to Alworth for the touchdown. Blair kicks the extra point.

	Chargers	Oilers
First Downs	24	14
Rushing Yards	224	104
Passing Yards	143	141
Punts-Average	4-45.0	4-40.0
Fumbles-Lost	1-0	2-1
Penalties-Yards	5-40	4-35

Chargers' Leaders

Rushing	Lowe 21-80, Lincoln 13-102, McDougall 1-16, Jackson 1-11, Rote 1-3
Passing	Rote 13-24-2-134, Hadl 0-7-0-2, Norton 1-1-0-15
Receiving	Alworth 4-56, Kocourek 3-40, Lowe 3-25, Norton 2-16, MacKinnon 1-7
Interceptions	Karas 1-30, Mitinger 1-5, Glick 1-13

Oilers' Leaders

Rushing	Tolar 13-74, Tobin 8-28
Passing	Blanda 9-26-2-110, Lee 4-6-1-41
Receiving	Dewveall 5-62, Tobin 2-19, Frazier 2-18, Tolar 2-16, McLeod 1-22
Interceptions	Norton 2-59, Banfield 1-0, Dukes 1-4

Week 12 Games
San Diego 27, Houston 0
Oakland 26, Denver 10
New York 17, Kansas City 0
Boston 17, Buffalo 7

Week 12 Standings

East	W	L	T		West	W	L	T
Houston	6	5	0		San Diego	9	2	0
Boston	6	5	1		Oakland	7	4	0
New York	5	5	1		Kansas City	2	7	2
Buffalo	5	6	1		Denver	2	8	1

DECEMBER 8, 1963
Frank Youell Field – Oakland, California
Attendance – 20,249

					Total
Chargers	7	13	7	0	27
Raiders	3	7	0	31	41

Chargers	Rote 32-yard pass to Norton for the touchdown. Blair kicks the extra point.
Raiders	Mercer kicks a 37-yard field goal.
Chargers	Jackson 14-yard run for the touchdown. Blair kicks the extra point.
Raiders	Flores 45-yard pass to Powell for the touchdown. Mercer kicks the extra point.
Chargers	Rote 5-yard pass to MacKinnon for the touchdown. Blair kicks the extra point.
Chargers	Rote 15-yard pass to Alworth for the touchdown. Blair kicks the extra point.
Raiders	Davidson 10-yard pass to Powell for the touchdown. Mercer kicks the extra point.
Raiders	Mercer kicks a 30-yard field goal.
Raiders	Davidson 9-yard run for the touchdown. Mercer kicks the extra point.
Raiders	Davidson 40-yard pass to Powell for the touchdown. Mercer kicks the extra point.
Raiders	Miller 2-yard run for the touchdown. Mercer kicks the extra point.

	Chargers	Raiders
First Downs	17	24
Rushing Yards	45	154
Passing Yards	304	278
Punts-Average	5-34.0	3-39.0
Fumbles-Lost	2-2	0-0
Penalties-Yards	2-20	8-101

Chargers' Leaders
Rushing	Lowe 6-5, Jackson 5-33, Rote 5-7, Lincoln 2-0
Passing	Rote 17-25-0-284, Hadl 2-6-1-20
Receiving	Norton 6-119, Kocourek 4-34, Alworth 3-71, Jackson 2-29, Lowe 2-12
Interceptions	None

Raiders' Leaders
Rushing	Daniels 17-90, Miller 10-34, Davidson 7-41, Flores 3-(-11)
Passing	Flores 11-23-0-173, Davidson 6-17-0-95, Daniels 1-1-0-10
Receiving	Daniels 7-90, Powell 6-132, Miller 3-34, Roberson 2-22
Interceptions	Osborne 1-48

Week 13 Games
Oakland 41, San Diego 27
Kansas City 52, Denver 21
Boston 46, Houston 28
Buffalo 45, New York 14

Week 13 Standings
East	W	L	T	West	W	L	T
Boston	7	5	1	San Diego	9	3	0
Houston	6	6	0	Oakland	8	4	0
Buffalo	6	6	1	Kansas City	3	7	2
New York	5	6	1	Denver	2	9	1

Barron Hilton and George Pernicano

Paul Lowe evades a Houston tackler.

DECEMBER 15, 1963
Jeppesen Stadium – Houston, Texas
Attendance – 18,540

					Total
Chargers	0	17	3	0	20
Oilers	0	7	0	7	14

Chargers	Rote 1-yard run for the touchdown. Blair kicks the extra point.
Chargers	Jackson 1-yard run for the touchdown. Blair kicks the extra point.
Oilers	Blanda 24-yard pass to Dewveall for the touchdown. Blanda kicks the extra point.
Chargers	Blair kicks a 22-yard field goal.
Chargers	Blair kicks a 10-yard field goal.
Oilers	Dickinson 1-yard run for the touchdown. Blanda kicks the extra point.

	Chargers	Oilers
First Downs	14	13
Rushing Yards	162	26
Passing Yards	85	259
Punts-Average	5-42.2	4-46.5
Fumbles-Lost	2-1	1-1
Penalties-Yards	0-0	2-20

Chargers' Leaders
Rushing	Lowe 19-96, McDougall 15-56, Rote 3-8, Jackson 2-2
Passing	Rote 9-17-1-81, Hadl 1-1-0-4
Receiving	Alworth 3-28, McDougall 3-23, Lowe 3-21, Kocourek 1-13
Interceptions	Karas 1-0, Allen 1-0, Maguire 1-0

Oilers' Leaders
Rushing	Tolar 5-24, Tobin 5-13, Smith 4-(-4), Lee 1-8, Dickinson 1-1
Passing	Blanda 17-32-2-247, Lee 1-7-1-12
Receiving	Dickinson 4-34, Smith 4-23, Dewveall 3-44, McLeod 2-45, Hennigan 2-95
Interceptions	Glick 1-0

Week 14 Games
San Diego 20, Houston 14
Kansas City 35, Boston 3
Oakland 35, Denver 31
Buffalo 19, New York 10

Week 14 Standings
East	W	L	T	West	W	L	T
Boston	7	6	1	San Diego	10	3	0
Buffalo	7	6	1	Oakland	9	4	0
Houston	6	7	0	Kansas City	4	7	2
New York	5	7	1	Denver	2	10	1

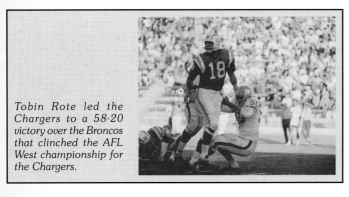

Tobin Rote led the Chargers to a 58-20 victory over the Broncos that clinched the AFL West championship for the Chargers.

DECEMBER 22, 1963
Balboa Stadium – San Diego, California
Attendance – 31,312

					Total
Chargers	10	16	24	8	58
Broncos	7	10	3	0	20

Chargers	Lowe 10-yard run for the touchdown. Blair kicks the extra point.
Broncos	Joe 1-yard run for the touchdown. Mingo kicks the extra point.
Chargers	Blair kicks a 17-yard field goal.
Chargers	Jackson 2-yard run for the touchdown.
Broncos	Breaux 18-yard pass to Stone for the touchdown. Mingo kicks the extra point.
Chargers	Rote 26-yard pass to Kocourek for the touchdown.
Broncos	Mingo kicks a 12-yard field goal.
Chargers	Blair kicks a 28-yard field goal.
Chargers	Lowe 66-yard run for the touchdown. Blair kicks the extra point.
Broncos	Mingo kicks a 15-yard field goal.
Chargers	Blair kicks a 13-yard field goal.
Chargers	Lincoln 29-yard run for the touchdown. Blair kicks the extra point.
Chargers	Allen recovers a fumble and returns it 32 yards for the touchdown. Blair kicks the extra point.
Chargers	Hadl 5-yard pass to MacKinnon for the touchdown. Hadl 2-yard pass to Faison for the 2-point conversion.

	Chargers	Broncos
First Downs	23	16
Rushing Yards	270	77
Passing Yards	187	154
Punts-Average	3-44.0	4-53.0
Fumbles-Lost	0-0	4-4
Penalties-Yards	6-30	7-68

Chargers' Leaders
Rushing	Lowe 17-183, Lincoln 10-66, McDougall 2-21, Jackson 2-3, Hadl 1-(-3)
Passing	Rote 7-17-1-109, Hadl 5-7-1-94, Lowe 0-1-0-0
Receiving	Norton 3-48, Robinson 2-46, MacKinnon 2-40, Lincoln 1-19, Lowe 1-12
Interceptions	Mitinger 1-18, Harris 1-19

Broncos' Leaders
Rushing	Mingo 6-30, Dixon 6-22, Breaux 4-17, Stone 4-7, Joe 3-1
Passing	Breaux 16-31-2-192, Mingo 0-1-0-0
Receiving	Taylor 5-79, Dixon 3-44, Stone 3-42, Groman 2-16, Prebola 1-8
Interceptions	Janik 1-31, Zeman 1-23

Week 15 Games
San Diego 58, Denver 20
Oakland 52, Houston 49
Kansas City 48, New York 0
Boston and Buffalo – Bye

Week 15 Standings
East	W	L	T	West	W	L	T
Boston	7	6	1	San Diego	11	3	0
Buffalo	7	6	1	Oakland	10	4	0
Houston	6	8	0	Kansas City	5	7	2
New York	5	8	1	Denver	2	11	1

* On December 28, Boston beat Buffalo 26-8 in the Eastern Division Playoff and went on to represent the East in the AFL Championship against the Chargers on January 5, 1964.

JANUARY 5, 1964
American Football League Championship Game
Balboa Stadium – San Diego, California
Attendance – 30,127

					Total
Chargers	21	10	7	13	51
Patriots	7	3	0	0	10

Chargers	Rote 2-yard run for the touchdown. Blair kicks the extra point.
Chargers	Lincoln 67-yard run for the touchdown. Blair kicks the extra point.
Patriots	Garron 7-yard run for the touchdown. Cappalletti kicks the extra point.
Chargers	Lowe 58-yard run for the touchdown. Blair kicks the extra point.
Chargers	Blair kicks an 11-yard field goal.
Patriots	Cappalletti kicks a 15-yard field goal.
Chargers	Rote 14-yard pass to Norton for the touchdown. Blair kicks the extra point.
Chargers	Rote 48-yard pass to Alworth for the touchdown. Blair kicks the extra point.
Chargers	Hadl 25-yard pass to Lincoln for the touchdown.
Chargers	Hadl 1-yard run for the touchdown. Blair kicks the extra point.

	Chargers	Patriots
First Downs	21	14
Rushing Yards	309	75
Passing Yards	292	186
Punts-Average	2-44.0	7-47.0
Fumbles-Lost	1-1	1-0
Penalties-Yards	6-30	1-18

Chargers' Leaders
Rushing	Lincoln 13-206, Lowe 12-94, Rote 3-6, McDougall 1-2, Hadl 1-1
Passing	Rote 10-15-0-173, Hadl 6-10-0-112, Lincoln 1-1-0-20
Receiving	Lincoln 7-123, Alworth 4-77, MacKinnon 2-53, Norton 2-44, Kocourek 1-5
Interceptions	Mitinger 1-5, Maguire 1-10

Patriots' Leaders
Rushing	Crump 7-18, Garron 3-15, Lott 3-15, Yewcic 1-14, Parilli 1-10
Passing	Parilli 14-29-1-189, Yewcic 3-8-1-39
Receiving	Burton 4-12, Colclough 3-26, Cappalletti 2-72, Graham 2-68, Crump 2-28
Interceptions	None

Keith Lincoln on one of his many long runs of the day.

1964 Chargers Team Statistics
(8-5-1 Overall) First Place in the AFL West

Team Statistics	Chargers	Opponent
TOTAL FIRST DOWNS	250	244
Rushing	85	78
Passing	153	146
Penalty	12	20
TOTAL NET YARDS	4,706	4,040
Avg. Per Game	336.1	288.6
Avg. Per Play	5.5	4.4
NET YARDS RUSHING	1,564	1,522
Avg. Per Game	111.7	108.7
NET YARDS PASSING	3,142	2,518
Avg. Per Game	224.4	179.9
Gross Yards	3,363	2,926
Completions/Attempts	224/445	240/484
Completion Pct.	.503	.496
Had Intercepted	30	30
PUNTS/AVERAGE	63/39.3	62/43.0
PENALTIES/YARDS	88/709	55/528
FUMBLES/BALL LOST	30/15	32/14
TOUCHDOWNS	44	36
Rushing	14	10
Passing	28	22
Returns	2	4
QUARTERBACK SACKS	38.0	22.0

Rushing	No.	Yds.	Avg.	TD
Lincoln	155	632	4.1	4
Lowe	130	496	3.8	3
MacKinnon	24	124	5.2	2
Kinderman	24	111	4.6	0
McDougall	23	73	3.2	2
Hadl	20	70	3.5	1
Alworth	3	60	20.0	2
Robinson	1	10	10.0	0
Rote	10	-12	-1.2	0
Totals	**390**	**1,564**	**4.0**	**14**

Receiving	No.	Yds.	Avg.	TD
Alworth	61	1,235	20.2	13
Norton	49	669	13.7	6
Lincoln	34	302	8.9	2
Kocourek	33	593	18.0	5
Lowe	14	182	13.0	2
MacKinnon	10	177	17.7	0
Robinson	10	93	9.3	0
McDougall	8	106	13.3	0
Kinderman	3	21	7.0	0
Whitehead	1	-4	-4.0	0
Rote	1	-11	-11.0	0
Totals	**224**	**3,363**	**15.0**	**28**

Passing	Att.	Comp.	Yds.	Comp. %	TD	Int.
Hadl	274	147	2,157	.536	18	15
Rote	163	74	1,156	.454	9	15
Lincoln	4	2	61	.500	1	0
Lowe	2	0	0	.000	0	0
Alworth	1	1	-11	100.0	0	0
Kinderman	1	0	0	.000	0	0
Totals	**445**	**224**	**3,363**	**.503**	**28**	**30**

Interceptions	No.	Yds.	TD
Westmoreland	6	51	0
Allen	4	75	0
Graham	4	24	0
D. Harris	3	82	0
Whitehead	3	43	0
McNeil	2	30	0
Warren	2	28	0
Schmidt	1	58	1
Faison	1	42	1
Carpenter	1	29	0
Buncom	1	11	0
Petrich	1	11	0
Duncan	1	3	0
Totals	**30**	**487**	**2**

Kicking	FG	Att.	PAT	Att.	Pts.
Blair	3	5	5	6	14
Lincoln	5	12	16	17	31
Travenio	2	5	10	12	16
Agajanian	2	4	8	8	14

Punting	No.	Avg.
Hadl	62	39.5
Whitehead	1	30.0

Punt Returns	No.	FC	Yds.	Avg.	TD
Alworth	18	0	189	10.5	0
Robinson	7	0	41	5.9	0
Duncan	4	0	19	4.8	0
Graham	2	0	24	12.0	0
Westmoreland	2	0	10	5.0	0
Warren	1	0	0	0.0	0

Kickoff Returns	No.	Yds.	Avg.	TD
Westmoreland	18	360	20.0	0
Warren	13	353	27.2	0
Duncan	9	318	35.3	0
Graham	7	172	24.6	0
Robinson	3	70	23.3	0
Carpenter	1	15	15.0	0
Norton	1	0	0.0	0
Wright	1	0	0.0	0

Above: *The Chargers' defensive linemen, Hank Schmidt (76), Fred Moore (71), George Gross (79), Ernie Ladd (77), Bob Petrich (85) and Earl Faison (86).*

Left: *Sid Gillman and Alvin Roy supervise weight training during training camp.*

SEPTEMBER 12, 1964
Balboa Stadium – San Diego, California
Attendance – 22,632

					Total
Chargers	7	0	14	6	27
Oilers	0	7	7	7	21

Chargers	Rote 1-yard pass to Kocourek for the touchdown. Blair kicks the extra point.
Oilers	Blanda 2-yard pass to Frazier for the touchdown. Blanda kicks the extra point.
Chargers	McDougall 3-yard run for the touchdown. Blair kicks the extra point.
Oilers	Blanda 5-yard pass to McLeod for the touchdown. Blanda kicks the extra point.
Chargers	Rote 19-yard pass to Norton for the touchdown. Blair kicks the extra point.
Chargers	Rote 27-yard pass to Alworth for the touchdown.
Oilers	Jackson 1-yard run for the touchdown. Blanda kicks the extra point.

	Chargers	Oilers
First Downs	22	28
Rushing Yards	93	121
Passing Yards	235	240
Punts-Average	4-30.0	4-39.7
Fumbles-Lost	0-0	2-1
Penalties-Yards	5-42	8-75

Chargers' Leaders
Rushing	Lincoln 10-52, McDougall 8-23, Lowe 6-18
Passing	Rote 15-26-1-235
Receiving	Alworth 6-119, McDougall 4-57, Norton 3-41, Lowe 1-17, Kocourek 1-1
Interceptions	None

Oilers' Leaders
Rushing	Tolar 20-67, Blanks 11-53, Jackson 2-1
Passing	Blanda 27-47-0-254
Receiving	Blanks 13-131, Hennigan 7-104, McLeod 2-18, Dewveall 1-9, Craig 1-7
Interceptions	Jaquess 1-0

Week 1 Games
San Diego 27, Houston 20
Boston 17, Oakland 14
Buffalo 34, Kansas City 17
New York 30, Denver 6

Week 1 Standings
East	W	L	T	West	W	L	T
Buffalo	1	0	0	San Diego	1	0	0
Boston	1	0	0	Oakland	0	1	0
New York	1	0	0	Kansas City	0	1	0
Houston	0	1	0	Denver	0	1	0

Game Program - September 12, 1964

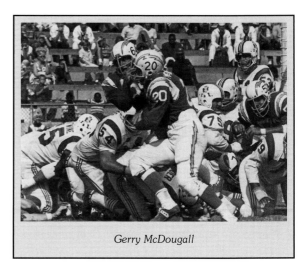

Gerry McDougall

SEPTEMBER 20, 1964
Balboa Stadium – San Diego, California
Attendance – 20,568

					Total
Chargers	0	10	0	18	28
Patriots	10	3	10	10	33

Patriots	Parilli 17-yard pass to Cappalletti for the touchdown. Cappalletti kicks the extra point.
Patriots	Cappalletti kicks a 41-yard field goal.
Chargers	Hadl 8-yard pass to Alworth for the touchdown. Blair kicks the extra point.
Patriots	Cappalletti kicks a 32-yard field goal.
Chargers	Blair kicks a 30-yard field goal.
Patriots	Cappalletti kicks a 37-yard field goal.
Patriots	Parilli 17-yard pass to Graham for the touchdown. Cappalletti kicks the extra point.
Chargers	McDougall 2-yard run for the touchdown. Blair kicks the extra point.
Patriots	Capalletti kicks a 37-yard field goal.
Patriots	Parilli 13-yard pass to Garron for the touchdown.
Chargers	Hadl 15-yard pass to Norton for the touchdown. Hadl 2-yard pass to McDougall for the 2-point conversion.
Chargers	Blair kicks a 12-yard field goal.

	Chargers	Patriots
First Downs	13	13
Rushing Yards	84	116
Passing Yards	196	97
Punts-Average	5-36.8	4-42.0
Fumbles-Lost	5-2	2-2
Penalties-Yards	7-65	4-40

Chargers' Leaders
Rushing	Lincoln 12-29, McDougall 9-44, Hadl 1-11
Passing	Rote 7-16-2-42, Hadl 11-19-1-177, Lincoln 0-1-0-0
Receiving	Alworth 5-67, Norton 5-55, McDougall 4-37, Lincoln 2-22, Kocourek 1-24
Interceptions	None

Patriots' Leaders
Rushing	Garron 22-93, Garrett 5-9, Burton 2-11, Parilli 2-2, Yewcic 2-1
Passing	Parilli 15-32-0-174, Garron 0-1-0-0
Receiving	Graham 4-51, Cappalletti 3-31, Romeo 2-31, Garron 2-21, Burton 2-18
Interceptions	Hall 3-47

Week 2 Games
Boston 33, San Diego 28
Buffalo 30, Denver 13
Houston 42, Oakland 28
New York and Kansas City - Bye

Week 2 Standings
East	W	L	T	West	W	L	T
Buffalo	2	0	0	San Diego	1	1	0
Boston	2	0	0	Kansas City	0	1	0
New York	1	0	0	Oakland	0	2	0
Houston	1	1	0	Denver	0	2	0

SEPTEMBER 26, 1964
War Memorial Stadium – Buffalo, New York
Attendance – 40,167

					Total
Chargers	0	3	0	0	3
Bills	7	7	3	13	30

Bills	Byrd intercepts Rote pass, returns it 75 yards for the touchdown. Gogolak kicks the extra point.
Chargers	Blair kicks a 12-yard field goal.
Bills	Hadl punts to Clarke, returned 47 yards for the touchdown.
Bills	Gogolak kicks a 13-yard field goal.
Bills	Auer 2-yard run for the touchdown. Gogolak kicks the extra point.
Bills	Lamonica 40-yard pass to Dubenion for the touchdown.

	Chargers	Bills
First Downs	15	14
Rushing Yards	128	109
Passing Yards	118	163
Punts-Average	5-44.8	2-47.5
Fumbles-Lost	2-1	2-1
Penalties-Yards	2-25	1-15

Chargers' Leaders

Rushing	Lincoln 21-94, MacKinnon 7-32, McDougall 2-4, Rote 1-(-2)
Passing	Rote 9-21-1-137, Hadl 4-12-1-50
Receiving	Norton 4-96, MacKinnon 4-39, Lincoln 2-21, Robinson 1-21, McDougall 1-14
Interceptions	Graham 1-6

Bills' Leaders

Rushing	Gilchrist 23-81, Auer 6-16, Lamonica 3-21, Kemp 1-(-9)
Passing	Kemp 8-19-1-95, Lamonica 2-2-0-68
Receiving	Dubenion 5-123, Gilchrist 3-15, Warlick 1-19, Auer 1-6
Interceptions	Byrd 1-75, Saimes 1-32

Week 3 Games
Buffalo 30, San Diego 3
Boston 33, New York 10
Houston 38, Denver 17
Kansas City 21, Oakland 9

Week 3 Standings

East	W	L	T	West	W	L	T
Buffalo	3	0	0	Kansas City	1	1	0
Boston	3	0	0	San Diego	1	2	0
Houston	2	1	0	Oakland	0	3	0
New York	1	1	0	Denver	0	3	0

Bob Petrich (85) and Hank Schmidt (76) lift weights as Chuck Noll (left) and Walt Hackett (right) supervise.

Sid Gillman and John Hadl

OCTOBER 3, 1964
Shea Stadium – New York City, New York
Attendance – 47,746

					Total
Chargers	3	7	0	7	17
Jets	0	3	7	7	17

Chargers	Lincoln kicks a 47-yard field goal.
Chargers	Rote 30-yard pass to Kocourek for the touchdown. Lincoln kicks the extra point.
Jets	J. Turner kicks a 34-yard field goal.
Jets	Wood 23-yard pass to B. Turner for the touchdown. J. Turner kicks the extra point.
Chargers	Rote 17-yard pass to Lowe for the touchdown. Lincoln kicks the extra point.
Jets	Wood 68-yard pass to Maynard for the touchdown. J. Turner kicks the extra point.

	Chargers	Jets
First Downs	17	14
Rushing Yards	88	47
Passing Yards	205	273
Punts-Average	4-38.8	4-45.7
Fumbles-Lost	3-2	1-0
Penalties-Yards	6-41	1-5

Chargers' Leaders

Rushing	Lowe 19-64, Lincoln 8-26
Passing	Rote 15-29-2-225
Receiving	Lincoln 6-94, Kocourek 4-64, Lowe 3-31, Norton 1-30
Interceptions	Allen 1-16, McNeil 1-17

Jets' Leaders

Rushing	Mathis 7-22, Snell 7-17, Wood 1-6, Smolinski 1-2
Passing	Wood 19-43-2-302
Receiving	Snell 8-79, Maynard 4-113, Heeter 3-56, B. Turner 2-34
Interceptions	Paulson 2-0

Week 4 Games
San Diego 17, New York 17
Boston 39, Denver 10
Kansas City 28, Houston 17
Buffalo 23, Oakland 20

Week 4 Standings

East	W	L	T	West	W	L	T
Buffalo	4	0	0	Kansas City	2	1	0
Boston	4	0	0	San Diego	1	2	1
Houston	2	2	0	Oakland	0	4	0
New York	1	1	1	Denver	0	4	0

Alvin Roy watches as Emil Karas works out.

OCTOBER 9, 1964
Fenway Park – Boston, Massachusetts
Attendance – 35,095

					Total
Chargers	0	10	13	3	26
Patriots	3	0	7	7	17

Patriots	Cappalletti kicks a 48-yard field goal.
Chargers	Travenio kicks a 16-yard field goal.
Chargers	Hadl 2-yard pass to Alworth for the touchdown. Travenio kicks the extra point.
Chargers	Hadl 15-yard pass to Norton for the touchdown. Travenio kicks the extra point.
Patriots	Garron 1-yard run for the touchdown. Cappalletti kicks the extra point.
Chargers	Hadl 13-yard pass to Alworth for the touchdown. Travenio kicks the extra point.
Patriots	Parilli 9-yard pass to Garron for the touchdown. Cappalletti kicks the extra point.
Chargers	Travenio kicks a 17-yard field goal.

	Chargers	Patriots
First Downs	21	18
Rushing Yards	133	93
Passing Yards	252	168
Punts-Average	4-46.0	4-34.25
Fumbles-Lost	2-1	3-1
Penalties-Yards	5-41	4-27

Chargers' Leaders

Rushing	Lowe 15-69, Lincoln 10-28, Hadl 3-24, MacKinnon 2-5, Rote 1-(-3)
Passing	Rote 3-8-1-24, Hadl 17-29-0-228
Receiving	Alworth 8-124, Kocourek 5-71, Lincoln 3-(-1), Norton 2-21, MacKinnon 1-20
Interceptions	Allen 1-11, Westmoreland 1-0, Graham 1-0, McNeil 1-13

Patriots' Leaders

Rushing	Garron 23-79, Burton 3-14, Parilli 2-0
Passing	Parilli 17-35-4-205
Receiving	Cappalletti 6-101, Graham 6-62, Garron 3-16, Burton 2-26
Interceptions	Webb 1-11

Week 5 Games
San Diego 26, Boston 17
Buffalo 48, Houston 17
Denver 33, Kansas City 27
New York 35 Oakland 13

Week 5 Standings

East	W	L	T	West	W	L	T
Buffalo	5	0	0	Kansas City	2	2	0
Boston	4	1	0	San Diego	2	2	1
Houston	2	3	0	Denver	1	4	0
New York	2	1	1	Oakland	0	5	0

OCTOBER 18, 1964
Balboa Stadium – San Diego, California
Attendance – 23,332

					Total
Chargers	7	14	14	7	42
Broncos	7	0	0	7	14

Broncos	Lee 11-yard pass to Scarpitto for the touchdown. Mingo kicks the extra point.
Chargers	Lincoln 5-yard run for the touchdown. Travenio kicks the extra point.
Chargers	Hadl 4-yard pass to Alworth for the touchdown. Travenio kicks the extra point.
Chargers	Lincoln 2-yard run for the touchdown. Travenio kicks the extra point.
Chargers	Hadl 46-yard pass to Kocourek for the touchdown. Travenio kicks the extra point.
Chargers	Hadl 18-yard run for the touchdown. Travenio kicks the extra point
Broncos	Lee 8-yard pass to Scarpitto for the touchdown. Mingo kicks the extra point.
Chargers	MacKinnon 1-yard run for the touchdown. Travenio kicks the extra point.

	Chargers	Broncos
First Downs	26	14
Rushing Yards	272	107
Passing Yards	214	79
Punts-Average	3-34.0	7-46.7
Fumbles-Lost	0-0	0-0
Penalties-Yards	5-32	1-15

Chargers' Leaders

Rushing	Lowe 15-83, Kinderman 9-57, MacKinnon 7-74, Lincoln 6-35, Hadl 2-23
Passing	Hadl 18-28-0-216, Rote 1-4-1-14
Receiving	Alworth 5-44, Kocourek 4-113, Norton 4-42, Robinson 2-15, Lincoln 2-18
Interceptions	Graham 1-9, Whitehead 1-0

Broncos' Leaders

Rushing	Mitchell 15-52, Joe 9-44, Lee 3-11
Passing	Lee 16-32-2-100
Receiving	Taylor 6-54, Scarpitto 5-37, Dixon 2-13, Mitchell 2-(-12), Stone 1-10
Interceptions	McGeever 1-19

Week 6 Games
San Diego 42, Denver 14
Oakland 43, Boston 43
Buffalo 35, Kansas City 22
New York 24, Houston 21

Week 6 Standings

East	W	L	T	West	W	L	T
Buffalo	6	0	0	San Diego	3	2	1
Boston	4	1	1	Kansas City	2	3	0
New York	3	1	1	Denver	1	5	0
Houston	2	4	0	Oakland	0	5	1

Chuck Allen

Lance Alworth and Sid Gillman

OCTOBER 25, 1964
Jeppesen Stadium – Houston, Texas
Attendance – 21,671

					Total
Chargers	0	20	0	0	20
Oilers	7	10	0	0	17

Oilers	Blanda 8-yard pass to Hennigan for the touchdown. Blanda kicks the extra point.
Chargers	Hadl 13-yard pass to Kocourek for the touchdown. Travenio kicks the extra point.
Chargers	Alworth 35-yard run for the touchdown.
Chargers	Schmidt intercepts Blanda pass, returns it 58 yards for the touchdown. Travenio kicks the extra point.
Oilers	Blanda 21-yard pass to Hennigan for the touchdown. Blanda kicks the extra point.
Oilers	Blanda kicks a 36-yard field goal.

	Chargers	Oilers
First Downs	20	22
Rushing Yards	102	94
Passing Yards	237	304
Punts-Average	3-38.0	4-44.3
Fumbles-Lost	3-0	0-0
Penalties-Yards	7-57	4-40

Chargers' Leaders
Rushing	Lincoln 12-65, Lowe 9-3, Rote 3-(-4), Alworth 1-35, Hadl 1-3
Passing	Hadl 19-31-1-226, Rote 1-2-1-22
Receiving	Alworth 5-76, Kocourek 5-70, Norton 3-40, Robinson 3-35, Lincoln 3-29
Interceptions	Schmidt 1-58, Warren 1-0

Oilers' Leaders
Rushing	Blanks 14-40, Tolar 10-48, Trull 3-6
Passing	Blanda 22-37-2-312, Trull 1-2-0-11, Blanks 1-1-0-8
Receiving	Hennigan 8-145, Tolar 6-61, Dewveall 5-83, Blanks 4-31, Frazier 1-11
Interceptions	Odom 1-0, Jaquess 1-0

Week 7 Games
San Diego 20, Houston 17
Buffalo 34, New York 24
Boston 24, Kansas City 7
Oakland 40, Denver 7

Week 7 Standings
East	W	L	T	West	W	L	T
Buffalo	7	0	0	San Diego	4	2	1
Boston	5	1	1	Kansas City	2	4	0
New York	3	2	1	Oakland	1	5	1
Houston	2	5	0	Denver	1	6	0

NOVEMBER 1, 1964
Balboa Stadium – San Diego, California
Attendance – 25,557

					Total
Chargers	14	0	3	14	31
Raiders	3	7	0	7	17

Raiders	Mercer kicks a 33-yard field goal.
Chargers	Hadl 76-yard pass to Alworth for the touchdown. Agajanian kicks the extra point.
Chargers	Lincoln 9-yard run for the touchdown. Agajanian kicks the extra point.
Raiders	Davidson 14-yard pass to Powell for the touchdown. Mercer kicks the extra point.
Chargers	Agajanian kicks a 32-yard field goal.
Chargers	Lincoln 12-yard run for the touchdown. Agajanian kicks the extra point.
Raiders	Davidson 41-yard pass to Barrett for the touchdown. Mercer kicks the extra point.
Chargers	Rote 47-yard pass to Alworth for the touchdown. Agajanian kicks the extra point.

	Chargers	Raiders
First Downs	20	18
Rushing Yards	99	61
Passing Yards	331	270
Punts-Average	6-42.3	5-42.0
Fumbles-Lost	1-1	3-1
Penalties-Yards	11-76	3-25

Chargers' Leaders
Rushing	Lincoln 10-44, Lowe 7-26, Kinderman 7-29
Passing	Hadl 15-29-2-261, Rote 2-10-1-83, Lincoln 1-1-0-8
Receiving	Alworth 8-203, Kocourek 3-71, Norton 3-43, Lincoln 3-17, Lowe 1-18
Interceptions	Harris 2-82, Westmoreland 2-51, Allen 1-12, Graham 1-0

Raiders' Leaders
Rushing	Daniels 9-55, Cannon 9-13, Davidson 1-(-3), Roberson 1-(-4)
Passing	Davidson 19-45-6-317
Receiving	Powell 6-89, Daniels 4-96, Roberson 3-32, Cannon 3-31, Herlock 2-28
Interceptions	Morrow 2-5, Birdwell 1-16

Week 8 Games
San Diego 31, Oakland 17
New York 35, Boston 14
Kansas City 49, Denver 39
Buffalo 24, Houston 10

Week 8 Standings
East	W	L	T	West	W	L	T
Buffalo	8	0	0	San Diego	5	2	1
Boston	5	2	1	Kansas City	3	4	0
New York	4	2	1	Oakland	1	6	1
Houston	2	6	0	Denver	1	7	0

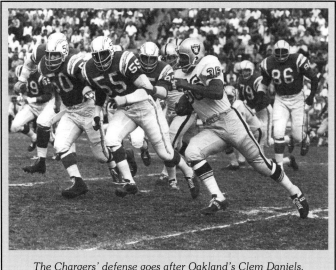

The Chargers' defense goes after Oakland's Clem Daniels.

November 8, 1964
Bears Stadium – Denver, Colorado
Attendance – 19,670

					Total
Chargers	7	3	7	14	31
Broncos	0	9	11	0	20

Chargers	Hadl 5-yard pass to Alworth for the touchdown. Agajanian kicks the extra point.
Chargers	Agajanian kicks a 15-yard field goal.
Broncos	Lee 8-yard run for the touchdown. Guesman kicks the extra point.
Broncos	Hadl tackled in the end zone by Brown for a safety.
Broncos	Hadl fumbles, recovered in the end zone by McMillan for the touchdown. Slaughter 2-yard run for the 2-point conversion.
Broncos	Guesman kicks a 44-yard field goal.
Chargers	Rote 20-yard pass to Norton for the touchdown. Agajanian kicks the extra point.
Chargers	Rote 2-yard pass to Lincoln for the touchdown. Agajanian kicks the extra point.
Chargers	MacKinnon 7-yard run for the touchdown. Agajanian kicks the extra point.

	Chargers	Broncos
First Downs	19	13
Rushing Yards	70	121
Passing Yards	127	158
Punts-Average	6-44.2	4-50.0
Fumbles-Lost	2-1	2-2
Penalties-Yards	3-23	6-45

Chargers' Leaders

Rushing	Lincoln 20-100, MacKinnon 4-6, Hadl 3-7, Kinderman 2-(-1)
Passing	Hadl 9-24-1-79, Rote 5-12-1-84
Receiving	Norton 7-78, Alworth 4-54, MacKinnon 1-17, Kocourek 1-12, Lincoln 1-2
Interceptions	Harris 1-0, Buncom 1-0, Petrich 1-11

Broncos' Leaders

Rushing	Mitchell 18-63, Joe 10-29, Lee 4-24, Stone 1-5
Passing	Lee 12-23-3-171
Receiving	Denson 4-83, Scarpitto 2-49, Mitchell 2-16, Dixon 2-10, Joe 1-10
Interceptions	Fraser 1-1, Brown 1-0

Week 9 Games
San Diego 31, Denver 20
Buffalo 20, New York 7
Boston 25, Houston 24
Kansas City 42, Oakland 7

Week 9 Standings

East	W	L	T	West	W	L	T
Buffalo	9	0	0	San Diego	6	2	1
Boston	6	2	1	Kansas City	4	4	0
New York	4	3	1	Oakland	1	7	1
Houston	2	7	0	Denver	1	8	0

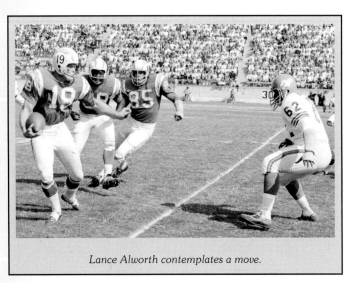
Lance Alworth contemplates a move.

Len Dawson gets off a pass as Bob Petrich tries to bring him down.

November 15, 1964
Municipal Stadium – Kansas City, Missouri
Attendance – 19,792

					Total
Chargers	0	28	0	0	28
Chiefs	0	7	0	7	14

Chargers	Lowe 50-yard run for the touchdown. Lincoln kicks the extra point.
Chargers	Hadl 38-yard pass to Kocourek for the touchdown. Lincoln kicks the extra point.
Chargers	Hadl 47-yard pass to Alworth for the touchdown. Lincoln kicks the extra point.
Chargers	Alworth 19-yard run for the touchdown. Lincoln kicks the extra point.
Chiefs	Westmoreland intercepts Dawson pass, fumbles in end zone and is recovered by Haynes for the touchdown. Brooker kicks the extra point.
Chiefs	Dawson 1-yard run for the touchdown. Brooker kicks the extra point.

	Chargers	Chiefs
First Downs	12	19
Rushing Yards	95	72
Passing Yards	238	176
Punts-Average	7-36.0	5-38.8
Fumbles-Lost	3-2	9-3
Penalties-Yards	11-79	2-28

Chargers' Leaders

Rushing	Lincoln 20-35, Lowe 7-41, Alworth 2-25
Passing	Hadl 11-19-0-283
Receiving	Alworth 5-168, Lincoln 4-29, Kocourek 2-41
Interceptions	Whitehead 1-33, Westmoreland 1-0

Chiefs' Leaders

Rushing	Dawson 11-27, Hill 8-36, Haynes 5-12
Passing	Dawson 17-34-2-176
Receiving	Haynes 7-70, Jackson 5-57, Hill 3-29, Burford 2-20
Interceptions	None

Week 10 Games
San Diego 28, Kansas City 14
Boston 36, Buffalo 28
Oakland 20, Houston 10
Denver 20, New York 16

Week 10 Standings

East	W	L	T	West	W	L	T
Buffalo	9	1	0	San Diego	7	2	1
Boston	7	2	1	Kansas City	4	5	0
New York	4	4	1	Oakland	2	7	1
Houston	2	8	0	Denver	2	8	0

Week 11 Games

San Diego and Buffalo – Bye
Boston 12, Denver 7
Kansas City 28, Houston 19
Oakland 35, New York 26

Week 11 Standings

East	W	L	T	West	W	L	T
Buffalo	9	1	0	San Diego	7	2	1
Boston	8	2	1	Kansas City	5	5	0
New York	4	5	1	Oakland	3	7	1
Houston	2	9	0	Denver	2	9	0

Tom Denman packs for a road game.

Ernie Ladd gets a hand on Jack Kemp.

NOVEMBER 26, 1964

Balboa Stadium – San Diego, California
Attendance – 31,860

					Total
Chargers	10	0	7	7	24
Bills	0	14	0	13	27

Chargers	Lincoln kicks a 27-yard field goal.
Chargers	Hadl 63-yard pass to Alworth for the touchdown. Lincoln kicks the field goal.
Bills	Auer 1-yard run for the touchdown. Gogolak kicks the extra point.
Bills	Kemp 1-yard run for the touchdown. Gogolak kicks the extra point.
Chargers	Hadl 17-yard pass to Norton for the touchdown. Lincoln kicks the extra point.
Chargers	Lincoln 53-yard pass to Alworth for the touchdown. Lincoln kicks the extra point.
Bills	Hadl tackled in the end zone for a safety.
Bills	Lamonica 1-yard run for the touchdown. Lamonica 2-yard run for the 2-point conversion.
Bills	Gogolak kicks a 33-yard field goal.

	Chargers	Bills
First Downs	11	18
Rushing Yards	52	146
Passing Yards	282	133
Punts-Average	4-40.5	6-42.7
Fumbles-Lost	3-2	2-1
Penalties-Yards	6-37	5-50

Chargers' Leaders

Rushing	Lowe 9-5, Lincoln 8-34, Hadl 2-13
Passing	Hadl 10-20-3-209, Rote 1-3-2-20, Lincoln 1-1-0-53
Receiving	Norton 5-65, Alworth 4-185, Lincoln 3-32
Interceptions	Warren 1-28

Bills' Leaders

Rushing	Gilchrist 21-87, Auer 15-46, Lamonica 6-6, Kemp 2-1
Passing	Kemp 8-20-1-136, Lamonica 4-7-0-40
Receiving	Warlick 3-79, Dubenion 3-55, Gilchrist 3-9, Auer 2-19, Bass 1-14
Interceptions	Jacobs 1-13, Tracey 1-6, Stratton 1-0, Sykes 1-36, Byrd 1-0

Week 12 Games

Buffalo 27, San Diego 24
Oakland 20, Denver 20
New York 27, Kansas City 14
Boston 34, Houston 17

Week 12 Standings

East	W	L	T	West	W	L	T
Buffalo	10	1	0	San Diego	7	3	1
Boston	9	2	1	Kansas City	5	6	0
New York	5	5	1	Oakland	3	7	2
Houston	2	10	0	Denver	2	9	1

159

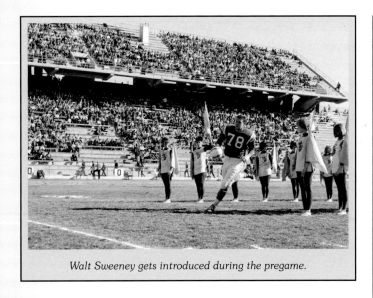

Walt Sweeney gets introduced during the pregame.

December 6, 1964
Balboa Stadium – San Diego, California
Attendance – 25,753

					Total
Chargers	10	14	7	7	38
Jets	0	3	0	0	3

Chargers	Hadl 8-yard pass to Norton for the touchdown. Lincoln kicks the extra point.
Chargers	Lincoln kicks a 19-yard field goal.
Chargers	Lowe 1-yard run for the touchdown. Lincoln kicks the extra point.
Jets	J. Turner kicks a 37-yard filed goal.
Chargers	Hadl 5-yard pass to Lincoln for the touchdown. Lincoln kicks the extra point.
Chargers	Faison intercepts Wood pass, returns it 42 yards for the touchdown. Lincoln kicks the extra point.
Chargers	Rote 82-yard pass to Alworth for the touchdown. Lincoln kicks the extra point.

	Chargers	Jets
First Downs	23	9
Rushing Yards	144	33
Passing Yards	322	80
Punts-Average	3-35.0	8-44.5
Fumbles-Lost	2-0	4-1
Penalties-Yards	12-101	5-36

Chargers' Leaders
Rushing	Lowe 18-96, Lincoln 13-42, McDougall 3-1, Hadl 2-(-5), Robinson 1-10
Passing	Hadl 15-27-2-240, Rote 1-2-0-82, Lincoln 0-1-0-0, Lowe 0-1-0-0
Receiving	Kocourek 4-76, Lincoln 4-45, Alworth 3-101, Norton 3-29, MacKinnon 2-71
Interceptions	Faison 1-42, Allen 1-33, Duncan 1-3

Jets' Leaders
Rushing	Snell 9-21, Smolinski 3-12, Mathis 2-14, Wood 1-0, Maynard 1-(-14)
Passing	Taliaferro 7-16-1-69, Wood 5-15-1-29, Liske 0-4-1-0
Receiving	B. Turner 4-26, Snell 3-2, Mackey 2-31, Maynard 2-27, Heeter 1-12
Interceptions	Johnston 1-3, Paulson 1-42

Week 13 Games
San Diego 38, New York 3
Boston 31, Kansas City 24
Oakland 16, Buffalo 13
Houston and Denver - Bye

Week 13 Standings
East	W	L	T	West	W	L	T
Buffalo	10	2	0	San Diego	8	3	1
Boston	10	2	1	Kansas City	5	7	0
New York	5	6	1	Oakland	4	7	2
Houston	2	10	0	Denver	2	9	1

December 13, 1964
Balboa Stadium – San Diego, California
Attendance – 26,562

					Total
Chargers	0	0	6	0	6
Chiefs	11	14	7	27	49

Chiefs	Dawson 64-yard pass to Jackson for the touchdown. Dawson 2-yard pass to McClinton for the 2-point conversion.
Chiefs	Brooker kicks a 27-yard field goal.
Chiefs	Dawson 5-yard pass to Jackson for the touchdown. Brooker kicks the extra point.
Chiefs	Dawson 21-yard pass to Jackson for the touchdown. Brooker kicks the extra point.
Chargers	Hadl 6-yard pass to Alworth for the touchdown.
Chiefs	Dawson 20-yard pass to Jackson for the touchdown. Brooker kicks the extra point.
Chiefs	Brooker kicks a 21-yard field goal.
Chiefs	Coan 1-yard run for the touchdown. Brooker kicks the extra point.
Chiefs	Coan 37-yard run for the touchdown. Brooker kicks the extra point.

	Chargers	Chiefs
First Downs	13	22
Rushing Yards	74	178
Passing Yards	110	213
Punts-Average	5-41.0	4-35.5
Fumbles-Lost	3-3	1-0
Penalties-Yards	3-36	4-39

Chargers' Leaders
Rushing	Lowe 12-16, Lincoln 5-48, Kinderman 2-12, Hadl 1-0, MacKinnon 1-(-2)
Passing	Rote 4-12-1-44, 8-20-2-108, Alworth 1-1-0-(-11)
Receiving	Alworth 6-80, Lowe 2-33, Norton 1-17, Kocourek 1-11, Robinson 1-9
Interceptions	Westmoreland 1-0

Chiefs' Leaders
Rushing	Hill 20-92, Coan 6-48, Haynes 6-20, McClinton 4-16, Dawson 2-3
Passing	Dawson 17-28-0-220, Beathard 0-2-1-0
Receiving	Jackson 8-142, Burford 4-46, Haynes 3-13, Hill 2-19
Interceptions	Mitchell 1-0, Wood 1-2, Grayson 1-40

Week 14 Games
Kansas City 49, San Diego 6
Houston 33, New York 17
Buffalo 30, Denver 19
Oakland and Boston - Bye

Week 14 Standings
East	W	L	T	West	W	L	T
Buffalo	11	2	0	San Diego	8	4	1
Boston	10	2	1	Kansas City	6	7	0
New York	5	7	1	Oakland	4	7	2
Houston	3	10	0	Denver	2	10	1

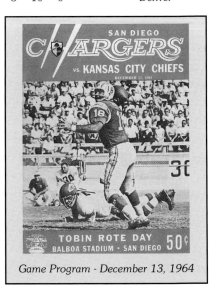

Game Program - December 13, 1964

Dave Kocourek pulls one in.

DECEMBER 20, 1964
Frank Youell Field – Oakland, California
Attendance – 20,124

					Total
Chargers	3	7	10	20	20
Raiders	0	14	0	7	21

Chargers	Lincoln kicks a 17-yard field goal.
Chargers	Hadl 41-yard pass to Lowe for the touchdown. Lincoln kicks the extra point.
Raiders	Flores 26-yard pass to Powell for the touchdown. Mercer kicks the extra point.
Raiders	Flores 10-yard pass to Mingo for the touchdown. Mercer kicks the extra point.
Chargers	Lowe 28-yard run for the touchdown. Lincoln kicks the extra point.
Chargers	Lincoln kicks a 33-yard field goal.
Raiders	Flores 13-yard pass to Cannon for the touchdown. Mercer kicks the extra point.

	Chargers	Raiders
First Downs	18	22
Rushing Yards	123	215
Passing Yards	259	242
Punts-Average	4-37.8	2-43.5
Fumbles-Lost	1-0	2-1
Penalties-Yards	5-54	7-88

Chargers' Leaders

Rushing	Lowe 12-85, MacKinnon 4-23, Kinderman 4-15
Passing	Hadl 10-16-2-129, Rote 11-18-1-126, Kinderman 0-1-0-0, Lowe 0-1-0-0
Receiving	Norton 8-98, Lowe 4-80, Kocourek 2-39, Alworth 2-14, Robinson 2-7
Interceptions	Carpenter 1-29, Whitehead 1-10, Robinson 1-0

Raiders' Leaders

Rushing	Daniels 16-144, Jackson 4-29, Cannon 3-27, Flores 2-15
Passing	Flores 21-39-3-242
Receiving	Jackson 5-48, Powell 4-60, Daniels 4-33, Roberson 3-31, Herock 2-35
Interceptions	Powers 2-33, F. Williamson 1-3

Week 15 Games
Oakland 21, San Diego 20
Buffalo 24, Boston 14
Houston 34, Denver 15
Kansas City 24, New York 7

Week 15 Standings

East	W	L	T	West	W	L	T
Buffalo	12	2	0	San Diego	8	5	1
Boston	10	3	1	Kansas City	7	7	0
New York	5	8	1	Oakland	5	7	2
Houston	4	10	0	Denver	2	11	1

DECEMBER 26, 1964
American Football League Championship Game
War Memorial Stadium – Buffalo, New York
Attendance – 40,242

					Total
Chargers	7	0	0	0	7
Bills	3	10	0	7	20

Chargers	Rote 26-yard pass to Kocourek for the touchdown. Lincoln kicks the extra point.
Bills	Gogolak kicks a 12-yard field goal.
Bills	Carlton 4-yard run for the touchdown. Gogolak kicks the extra point.
Bills	Gogolak kicks a 17-yard field goal. Gogolak kicks the extra point.
Bills	Kemp 1-yard run for the touchdown. Gogolak kicks the extra point.

	Chargers	Bills
First Downs	15	21
Rushing Yards	124	219
Passing Yards	135	168
Punts-Average	5-36.4	5-46.8
Fumbles-Lost	1-0	0-0
Penalties-Yards	3-20	3-45

Chargers' Leaders

Rushing	Lowe 7-34, Kinderman 4-14, Lincoln 3-47, MacKinnon 1-17, Hadl 1-13
Passing	Rote 10-26-2-118, Hadl 3-10-1-31
Receiving	Kinderman 4-52, MacKinnon 3-12, Kocourek 2-52, Lowe 2-9, Norton 1-13
Interceptions	None

Bills' Leaders

Rushing	Carlton 18-70, Gilchrist 16-122, Kemp 5-16, Dubenion 1-9, Lamonica 1-2
Passing	Kemp 10-20-0-188
Receiving	Dubenion 3-56, Bass 2-70, Warlick 2-41, Gilchrist 2-22, Ross 1-(-1)
Interceptions	Warner 1-8, Stratton 1-0, Byrd 1-0

George Pernicano and Sid Gillman on the plane trip to Buffalo for the 1964 AFL Championship Game.

1965 CHARGERS TEAM STATISTICS
(9-2-3 OVERALL) FIRST PLACE IN THE AFL WEST

Team Statistics	Chargers	Opponent
TOTAL FIRST DOWNS	268	188
Rushing	127	54
Passing	127	117
Penalty	14	17
TOTAL NET YARDS	5,154	3,268
Avg. Per Game	368.1	233.4
Avg. Per Play	5.7	4.0
NET YARDS RUSHING	2,081	1,094
Avg. Per Game	221.6	155.3
NET YARDS PASSING	3,103	2,174
Avg. Per Game	221.6	155.3
Gross Yards	3,379	2,486
Completions/Attempts	203/401	207/471
Completion Pct.	.506	.439
Had Intercepted	26	28
PUNTS/AVERAGE	70/40.0	80/43.2
PENALTIES/YARDS	84/929	62/665
FUMBLES/BALL LOST	20/12	18/10
TOUCHDOWNS	41	25
Rushing	12	7
Passing	23	17
Returns	6	1
QUARTERBACK SACKS	38.0	27.0

Rushing	No.	Yds.	Avg.	TD
Lowe	222	1,119	5.0	6
Foster	121	469	3.9	2
Lincoln	74	302	4.1	3
Allison	28	98	3.5	0
Hadl	28	91	3.3	1
MacKinnon	3	17	5.7	0
Sweeney	0	8	-	0
Breaux	1	-1	-1.0	0
Norton	1	-5	-5.0	0
Shea	1	-5	-5.0	0
Alworth	3	-12	-4.0	0
Totals	**482**	**2,081**	**4.3**	**12**

Receiving	No.	Yds.	Avg.	TD
Alworth	69	1,602	23.2	14
Norton	34	485	14.3	2
Kocourek	28	363	13.0	2
Lincoln	23	376	16.3	4
Lowe	17	126	7.4	1
Foster	17	199	11.7	0
Allison	8	109	13.6	0
MacKinnon	6	106	17.7	0
Taylor	1	13	13.0	0
Totals	**203**	**3,379**	**16.6**	**23**

Passing	Att.	Comp.	Yds.	Comp. %	TD	Int.
Hadl	348	174	2,798	.500	20	21
Breaux	43	22	404	.512	2	4
Lowe	4	3	81	.750	0	0
Foster	3	2	31	.667	0	0
Lincoln	3	2	65	.667	1	1
Totals	**401**	**203**	**3,379**	**.506**	**23**	**26**

Interceptions	No.	Yds.	TD
Whitehead	7	127	1
Graham	5	108	1
Warren	5	43	0
Duncan	4	30	0
Degan	2	6	0
Westmoreland	1	28	0
Faison	1	24	1
Redman	1	11	0
Allen	1	0	0
D. Harris	1	0	0
Totals	**28**	**377**	**3**

Kicking	FG	Att.	PAT	Att.	Pts.
Travenio	18	31	40	40	94

Punting	No.	Avg.
Hadl	38	40.6
Redman	29	39.5
Allison	2	36.0
Whitehead	1	40.0

Punt Returns	No.	FC	Yds.	Avg.	TD
Duncan	30	0	464	15.5	2
Graham	5	0	36	7.2	0
D. Harris	3	0	8	2.7	0

Kickoff Returns	No.	Yds.	Avg.	TD
Duncan	26	612	23.5	0
Farr	7	123	17.6	0
Foster	5	108	21.6	0
Allison	4	80	20.0	0
Carson	3	44	14.7	0
Lincoln	2	46	23.0	0
D. Harris	1	15	15.0	0
Kirner	1	0	0.0	0
MacKinnon	1	0	0.0	0

Above: *Chargers fans pack the stands at Balboa Stadium.*

Left: *Ron Mix (74), Earl Faison (86), Jacque MacKinnon (38) and Ernie Ladd (77) horsing around.*

SEPTEMBER 11, 1965
Balboa Stadium – San Diego, California
Attendance – 27,022

					Total
Chargers	3	24	0	7	34
Broncos	14	3	0	14	31

Broncos	Haynes 2-yard run for the touchdown. Kroner kicks the extra point.
Chargers	Travenio kicks a 32-yard field goal.
Broncos	Slaughter 31-yard pass to Scarpitto for the touchdown. Kroner kicks the extra point.
Chargers	Foster 2-yard run for the touchdown. Travenio kicks the extra point.
Chargers	Travenio kicks a 25-yard field goal.
Chargers	Lowe 41-yard run for the touchdown. Travenio kicks the extra point.
Chargers	Foster 17-yard run for the touchdown. Travenio kicks the extra point.
Broncos	Kroner kicks a 37-yard field goal.
Broncos	Slaughter 29-yard pass to Gilchrist for the touchdown. Kroner kicks the extra point.
Chargers	Hadl 38-yard pass to Alworth for the touchdown. Travenio kicks the extra point.
Broncos	Slaughter 13-yard pass to Scarptiio for the touchdown. Kropner kicks the extra point.

	Chargers	Broncos
First Downs	19	21
Rushing Yards	164	151
Passing Yards	293	179
Punts-Average	2-39.0	4-42.5
Fumbles-Lost	3-2	4-2
Penalties-Yards	5-96	7-148

Chargers' Leaders
Rushing	Lowe 18-122, Foster 11-49, Hadl 3-(-7)
Passing	Hadl 11-25-1-246, Lowe 1-1-0-42, Foster 1-1-0-21
Receiving	Alworth 7-211, Kocourek 2-41, Foster 2-31, Norton 1-14, Lowe 1-12
Interceptions	None

Broncos' Leaders
Rushing	Gilchrist 17-49, Haynes 8-43, Hayes 4-35, Slaughter 4-24
Passing	Slaughter 16-27-0-214
Receiving	Scarpitto 5-108, Taylor 3-38, Dixon 3-31, Hayes 2-9, Haynes 2-(-1)
Interceptions	Gonsoulin 1-31

Week 1 Games
San Diego 34, Denver 31
Houston 27, New York 21
Oakland 37, Kansas City 10
Buffalo 24, Boston 7

Week 1 Standings
East	W	L	T	West	W	L	T
Houston	1	0	0	San Diego	1	0	0
Buffalo	1	0	0	Oakland	1	0	0
Boston	0	1	0	Kansas City	0	1	0
New York	0	1	0	Denver	0	1	0

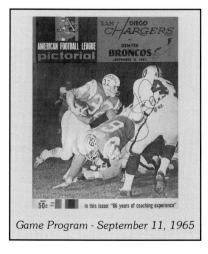

Game Program - September 11, 1965

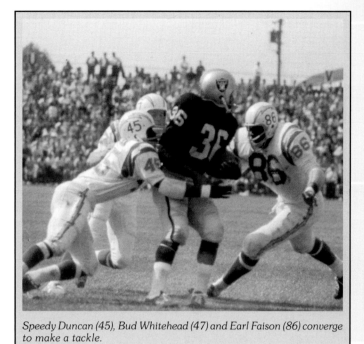

Speedy Duncan (45), Bud Whitehead (47) and Earl Faison (86) converge to make a tackle.

SEPTEMBER 19, 1965
Frank Youell Field - Oakland California
Attendance – 21,406

					Total
Chargers	7	3	0	7	17
Raiders	0	6	0	0	6

Chargers	Lowe 4-yard run for the touchdown. Travenio kicks the extra point.
Raiders	Mingo kicks a 48-yard field goal.
Chargers	Travenio kicks a 29-yard field goal.
Raiders	Mingo kicks a 35-yard field goal.
Chargers	Hadl 24-yard pass to Alworth for the touchdown. Travenio kicks the extra point.

	Chargers	Raiders
First Downs	18	12
Rushing Yards	178	36
Passing Yards	143	114
Punts-Average	8-39.4	4-55.3
Fumbles-Lost	1-1	0-0
Penalties-Yards	5-35	5-45

Chargers' Leaders
Rushing	Foster 21-104, Lowe 18-67, Hadl 1-15, Alworth 1-(-3), Shea 1-(-5)
Passing	Hadl 11-28-0-143
Receiving	Alworth 4-66, Norton 3-39, Foster 3-34, Lowe 1-4
Interceptions	Degen 1-0, Duncan 1-0, Graham 1-29

Raiders' Leaders
Rushing	Hagberg 8-14, Daniels 8-9, Flores 2-17, Roberson 1-(-4)
Passing	Flores 6-15-1-83, Wood 4-14-2-31
Receiving	Powell 5-72, Hagberg 3-9, Roberson 2-33
Interceptions	None

Week 2 Games
San Diego 17, Oakland 6
Buffalo 30, Denver 15
Kansas City 14, New York 10
Houston 31, Boston 10

Week 2 Standings
East	W	L	T	West	W	L	T
Houston	2	0	0	San Diego	2	0	0
Buffalo	2	0	0	Oakland	1	1	0
Boston	0	2	0	Kansas City	1	1	0
New York	0	2	0	Denver	0	2	0

Lance Alworth (19), noted hypnotist Dr. Dean, and Ernie Ladd (77)

SEPTEMBER 26, 1965
Balboa Stadium – San Diego, California
Attendance – 28,126

					Total
Chargers	0	3	0	7	10
Chiefs	0	0	7	3	10

Chargers	Travenio kicks a 19-yard field goal.
Chiefs	Dawson 12-yard pass to Taylor for the touchdown. Brooker kicks the extra point.
Chargers	Fraser punts to Duncan, returned 66 yards for the touchdown. Travenio kicks the extra point.
Chiefs	Brooker kicks a 28-yard field goal.

	Chargers	Chiefs
First Downs	12	8
Rushing Yards	93	127
Passing Yards	174	209
Punts-Average	8-41.5	8-48.9
Fumbles-Lost	2-1	2-0
Penalties-Yards	5-65	8-88

Chargers' Leaders
Rushing	Lowe 13-55, Foster 12-29, Hadl 1-1, Sweeney 0-8
Passing	Hadl 11-27-3-82, Breaux 0-3-0-0, Lowe 1-1-0-9, Foster 1-1-0-10
Receiving	Kocourek 4-35, Foster 4-29, Alworth 2-21, Lowe 2-3, Taylor 1-13
Interceptions	Warren 1-26, Whitehead 1-17, Duncan 1-4

Chiefs' Leaders
Rushing	McClinton 9-41, Hill 9-15, Coan 4-20, Dawson 3-46
Passing	Dawson 14-26-2-144, Beathard 0-2-1-0, McClinton 0-1-0-0
Receiving	McClinton 5-62, Taylor 2-30, Jackson 2-16, Burford 2-15, Hill 1-11
Interceptions	Williamson 2-32, Robinson 1-0

Week 3 Games
San Diego 10, Kansas City 10
Buffalo 33, New York 21
Denver 27, Boston 10
Oakland 21, Houston 17

Week 3 Standings
East	W	L	T	West	W	L	T
Buffalo	3	0	0	San Diego	2	0	1
Houston	2	1	0	Oakland	2	1	0
Boston	0	3	0	Kansas City	1	1	1
New York	0	3	0	Denver	1	2	0

OCTOBER 3, 1965
Balboa Stadium – San Diego, California
Attendance – 28,190

					Total
Chargers	0	10	14	7	31
Oilers	0	0	0	14	14

Chargers	Travenio kicks a 13-yard field goal.
Chargers	Hadl 69-yard pass to Alworth for the touchdown. Travenio kicks the extra point.
Chargers	Hadl 15-yard pass to Kocourek for the touchdown. Travenio kicks the extra point.
Oilers	Trull 9-yard pass to Hennigan for the touchdown. Blanda kicks the extra point.
Oilers	Trull 7-yard run for the touchdown. Blanda kicks the extra point.
Chargers	Hadl 57-yard pass to Alworth for the touchdown. Travenio kicks the extra point.

	Chargers	Oilers
First Downs	26	12
Rushing Yards	269	47
Passing Yards	222	146
Punts-Average	6-49.0	9-44.9
Fumbles-Lost	3-0	0-0
Penalties-Yards	6-83	1-5

Chargers' Leaders
Rushing	Lowe 20-157, Foster 10-73, Allison 9-34, MacKinnon 3-17, Norton 1-(-5)
Passing	Hadl 14-26-0-242
Receiving	Alworth 4-145, Norton 4-33, Kocourek 2-29, Allison 2-25, Foster 1-10
Interceptions	Faison 1-24

Oilers' Leaders
Rushing	Burrell 9-30, Tolar 5-8, Trull 2-9
Passing	Blanda 10-24-0-68, Trull 3-11-1-78
Receiving	Burrell 4-54, C. Frazier 2-32, Hennigan 2-22, W. Frazier 2-16, McLeod 1-31
Interceptions	None

Week 4 Games
San Diego 31, Houston 14
Kansas City 27, Boston 17
Denver 16, New York 13
Buffalo 17, Raiders 12

Week 4 Standings
East	W	L	T	West	W	L	T
Buffalo	4	0	0	San Diego	3	0	1
Houston	2	2	0	Kansas City	2	1	1
Boston	0	4	0	Oakland	2	2	0
New York	0	4	0	Denver	2	2	0

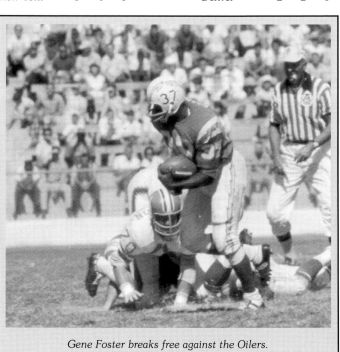

Gene Foster breaks free against the Oilers.

Lance Alworth

OCTOBER 10, 1965
War Memorial Stadium – Buffalo, New York
Attendance – 45,260

					Total
Chargers	0	14	17	3	34
Bills	3	0	0	0	3

Bills	Gogolak kicks a 38-yard field goal
Chargers	Hadl 14-yard pass to Alworth for the touchdown. Travenio kicks the extra point.
Chargers	Hadl 8-yard pass to Lincoln for the touchdown. Travenio kicks the extra point.
Chargers	Travenio kicks a 15-yard field goal.
Chargers	Hadl 52-yard pass to Alworth for the touchdown. Travenio kicks the extra point.
Chargers	Whitehead intercepts Kemp pass, returns it 35 yards for the touchdown. Travenio kicks the extra point.
Chargers	Travenio kicks a 19-yard field goal.

	Chargers	Bills
First Downs	18	8
Rushing Yards	89	57
Passing Yards	369	93
Punts-Average	4-35.0	6-45.0
Fumbles-Lost	1-1	2-2
Penalties-Yards	8-90	5-48

Chargers' Leaders
Rushing	Lowe 19-37, Foster 9-27, Lincoln 4-21, Hadl 1-5, Allison 1-(-1)
Passing	Hadl 18-29-1-314, Lincoln 1-1-0-31, Lowe 1-1-0-17, Breaux 1-1-0-7
Receiving	Alworth 8-168, Norton 6-107, Kocourek 3-54, Foster 2-24, Lincoln 2-16
Interceptions	Whitehead 3-66, Duncan 1-0

Bills' Leaders
Rushing	Carlton 6-11, Joe 4-22, Kemp 2-14, Stone 2-6, Auer 1-4
Passing	Kemp 7-23-2-48, Lamonica 8-14-2-60
Receiving	Rutkowski 4-44, Ferguson 3-37, Costa 2-15, Joe 2-10, Stone 2-5
Interceptions	Clarke 1-6

Week 5 Games
San Diego 34, Buffalo 3
Kansas City 31, Denver 23
Oakland 24, Boston 10
New York and Houston – Bye

Week 5 Standings
East	W	L	T	West	W	L	T
Buffalo	4	1	0	San Diego	4	0	1
Houston	2	2	0	Kansas City	3	1	1
Boston	0	5	0	Oakland	3	2	0
New York	0	4	0	Denver	2	3	0

OCTOBER 17, 1965
Fenway Park – Boston, Massachusetts
Attendance – 20,924

					Total
Chargers	3	10	0	0	13
Patriots	0	7	3	3	13

Chargers	Travenio kicks a 40-yard field goal.
Patriots	Parilli 73-yard pass to Burton for the touchdown. Cappalletti kicks the extra point.
Chargers	Hadl 85-yard pass to Alworth for the touchdown. Travenio kicks the extra point.
Chargers	Travenio kicks a 10-yard field goal.
Patriots	Cappalletti kicks a 21-yard field goal.
Patriots	Cappalletti kicks a 22-yard field goal.

	Chargers	Patriots
First Downs	15	7
Rushing Yards	161	37
Passing Yards	168	156
Punts-Average	8-35.0	7-31.0
Fumbles-Lost	2-2	0-0
Penalties-Yards	8-78	3-38

Chargers' Leaders
Rushing	Lowe 21-91, Lincoln 10-51, Foster 7-17, Hadl 2-2
Passing	Hadl 10-22-1-168
Receiving	Lowe 4-31, Alworth 3-109, Kocourek 1-12, Norton 1-9, Foster 1-7
Interceptions	Warren 2-6

Patriots' Leaders
Rushing	Burton 8-23, Garron 8-16, Nance 3-2, Parilli 1-5, Wilson 1-0
Passing	Parilli 6-25-1-136, Wilson 2-7-1-20
Receiving	Colclough 3-54, Burton 2-78, Romeo 2-20, Garron 1-4
Interceptions	Webb 1-45

Week 6 Games
San Diego 13, Boston 13
Buffalo 23, Kansas City 7
New York 24, Oakland 24
Denver 28, Houston 17

Week 6 Standings
East	W	L	T	West	W	L	T
Buffalo	5	1	0	San Diego	4	0	2
Houston	3	2	0	Kansas City	3	2	1
New York	0	4	1	Oakland	3	2	1
Boston	0	5	1	Denver	3	3	0

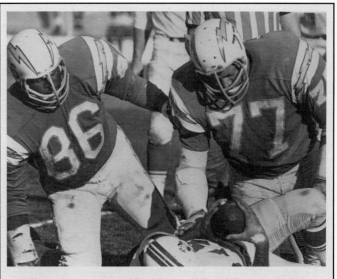
The mighty tandem of Earl Faison (86) and Ernie Ladd (77).

OCTOBER 23, 1965
Shea Stadium – New York City, New York
Attendance – 60,679

					Total
Chargers	0	10	14	10	34
Jets	3	3	0	3	9

Jets	J. Turner kicks a 12-yard field goal.
Chargers	Lowe 8-yard run for the touchdown. Travenio kicks the extra point.
Jets	J. Turner kicks a 24-yard field goal.
Chargers	Travenio kicks a 20-yard field goal.
Chargers	Hadl 2-yard pass to Alworth for the touchdown. Travenio kicks the extra point.
Chargers	Lowe 59-yard run for the touchdown. Travenio kicks the extra point.
Jets	J. Turner kicks a 40-yard field goal.
Chargers	Travenio kicks a 20-yard field goal.
Chargers	Breaux 57-yard pass to Alworth for the touchdown. Travenio kicks the extra point.

	Chargers	Jets
First Downs	17	15
Rushing Yards	152	79
Passing Yards	190	222
Punts-Average	4-29.5	5-41.8
Fumbles-Lost	1-1	6-4
Penalties-Yards	5-75	10-133

Chargers' Leaders
Rushing	Lowe 16-110, Lincoln 10-47, Foster 4-(-5)
Passing	Hadl 16-28-1-182, Breaux 2-2-0-56
Receiving	Alworth 7-142, Lincoln 4-30, Norton 4-38, Kocourek 3-29, Allison 1-(-1)
Interceptions	None

Jets' Leaders
Rushing	Snell 15-69, Mathis 3-8, Taliaferro 3-2
Passing	Taliaferro 17-35-0-205, Namath 2-5-0-21
Receiving	Mackey 4-53, Maynard 4-36, Sauer 4-22, Mathis 3-58, Snell 2-40
Interceptions	Paulson 1-23

Week 7 Games
San Diego 34, New York 9
Buffalo 31, Denver 13
Houston 38, Kansas City 36
Oakland 30, Boston 21

Week 7 Standings
East	W	L	T	West	W	L	T
Buffalo	6	1	0	San Diego	5	0	2
Houston	4	2	0	Oakland	4	2	1
New York	0	5	1	Kansas City	3	3	1
Boston	0	6	1	Denver	3	4	0

Don Norton answers questions for NBC's Paul Christman.

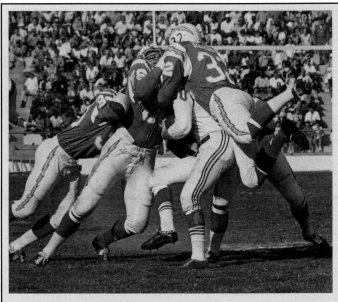

Steve DeLong (56) and Jim Allison (32) stop a Boston runner.

OCTOBER 31, 1965
Balboa Stadium – San Diego, California
Attendance – 33,366

					Total
Chargers	0	0	0	6	6
Patriots	9	0	3	10	22

Patriots	Duncan tackled in the end zone by Cunningham for a safety
Patriots	Parilli 29-yard pass to Cappalletti for the touchdown. Cappalletti kicks the extra point.
Patriots	Cappalletti kicks a 30-yard field goal.
Patriots	Parilli 46-yard pass to Cappalletti for the touchdown. Cappalletti kicks the extra point.
Patriots	Cappalletti kicks a 33-yard field goal.
Chargers	Lincoln 1-yard run for the touchdown.

	Chargers	Patriots
First Downs	17	10
Rushing Yards	80	133
Passing Yards	150	120
Punts-Average	8-43.5	7-44.4
Fumbles-Lost	1-0	3-1
Penalties-Yards	5-35	2-20

Chargers' Leaders
Rushing	Lowe 12-47, Lincoln 11-24, Hadl 1-6, Foster 1-3
Passing	Hadl 13-26-3-119, Breaux 6-13-1-109, Foster 0-1-0-0
Receiving	Alworth 5-59, Norton 5-106, Kocourek 3-30, Lincoln 3-20, Lowe 3-13
Interceptions	Whitehead 1-18, Harris 1-0

Patriots' Leaders
Rushing	Garron 11-87, Burton 9-11, Nance 6-21, Garrett 2-7, Parilli 1-7
Passing	Parilli 7-21-2-148
Receiving	Cappalletti 3-82, Colclough 4-66
Interceptions	Hennessey 1-14, Addison 1-13, Dukes 1-10, Webb 1-0

Week 8 Games
Boston 22, San Diego 6
Kansas City 14, Oakland 7
New York 45, Denver 10
Houston 19, Buffalo 17

Week 8 Standings
East	W	L	T	West	W	L	T
Buffalo	6	2	0	San Diego	5	1	2
Houston	4	3	0	Oakland	4	3	1
New York	1	5	1	Kansas City	4	3	1
Boston	1	6	1	Denver	3	5	0

NOVEMBER 7, 1965
Bears Stadium – Denver, Colorado
Attendance – 33,073

					Total
Chargers	0	14	7	14	35
Broncos	0	14	7	0	21

Broncos	Wilson intercepts Hadl pass, returns it 65 yards for the touchdown. Kroner kicks the extra point.
Chargers	Hadl 7-yard pass to Lincoln for the touchdown. Travenio kicks the extra point.
Chargers	Hadl 66-yard pass to Lincoln for the touchdown. Travenio kicks the extra point.
Broncos	Haynes 3-yard run for the touchdown. Kroner kicks the extra point.
Chargers	Lincoln 34-yard pass to Alworth for the touchdown. Travenio kicks the extra point.
Broncos	Gilchrist 1-yard run for the touchdown. Kroner kicks the extra point.
Chargers	Hadl 45-yard pass to Lowe for the touchdown. Travenio kicks the extra point.
Chargers	Lincoln 1-yard run for the touchdown. Travenio kicks the extra point.

	Chargers	Broncos
First Downs	21	22
Rushing Yards	176	74
Passing Yards	264	202
Punts-Average	5-41.0	5-41.8
Fumbles-Lost	0-0	1-0
Penalties-Yards	6-92	3-38

Chargers' Leaders
Rushing	Lowe 17-112, Lincoln 8-24, Foster 6-36, Allison 1-4
Passing	Hadl 13-23-2-256, Lincoln 1-1-0-34
Receiving	Kocourek 4-58, Lowe 4-57, Lincoln 2-73, MacKinnon 2-55, Alworth 2-47
Interceptions	Graham 2-28, Redman 1-11

Broncos' Leaders
Rushing	Gilchrist 14-27, Hayes 12-46, Haynes 1-1
Passing	McCormick 18-36-3-209, Slaughter 2-5-0-19
Receiving	Taylor 7-114, Haynes 4-19, Gilchrist 2-28, Hayes 2-23, Scarpitto 2-20
Interceptions	Wilson 1-65, Cooke 1-8

Week 9 Games
San Diego 35, Denver 21
Oakland 33, Houston 21
New York 13, Kansas City 10
Buffalo 23, Boston 7

Week 9 Standings
East	W	L	T	West	W	L	T
Buffalo	7	2	0	San Diego	6	1	2
Houston	4	4	0	Oakland	5	3	1
New York	2	5	1	Kansas City	4	4	1
Boston	1	7	1	Denver	3	6	0

Sid Gillman prepares for the upcoming game.

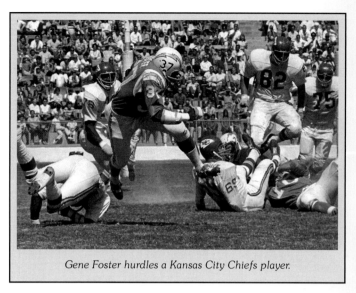

Gene Foster hurdles a Kansas City Chiefs player.

NOVEMBER 14, 1965
Municipal Stadium – Kansas City, Missouri
Attendance – 21,968

					Total
Chargers	0	7	0	0	7
Chiefs	10	7	0	14	31

Chiefs	Brooker kicks a 14-yard field goal.
Chiefs	McClinton 1-yard run for the touchdown. Brooker kicks the extra point.
Chargers	Hadl 51-yard pass to Alworth for the touchdown. Travenio kicks the extra point.
Chiefs	Dawson 20-yard pass to Burford for the touchdown. Brooker kicks the extra point.
Chiefs	Dawson 7-yard pass to McClinton for the touchdown. Brooker kicks the extra point.
Chiefs	Dawson 8-yard pass to Hill for the touchdown. Brooker kicks the extra point.

	Chargers	Chiefs
First Downs	14	14
Rushing Yards	78	149
Passing Yards	258	170
Punts-Average	5-39.0	5-44.6
Fumbles-Lost	1-1	1-1
Penalties-Yards	8-90	6-76

Chargers' Leaders
Rushing	Lowe 12-48, Lincoln 6-13, Foster 5-22
Passing	Hadl 7-18-4-152, Breaux 7-16-2-106
Receiving	Alworth 6-181, Kocourek 4-33, Lincoln 3-36
Interceptions	Warren 1-0

Chiefs' Leaders
Rushing	McClinton 14-43, Hill 11-76, Dawson 3-225
Passing	Dawson 13-22-1-170
Receiving	McClinton 5-51, Hill 4-57, Arbanas 2-35, Burford 1-20
Interceptions	Robinson 2-64, Williamson 2-51, Mitchell 1-7, Bell 1-4

Week 10 Games
Kansas City 31, San Diego 7
Buffalo 17, Oakland 14
Denver 31, Houston 21
New York 30, Boston 20

Week 10 Standings
East	W	L	T	West	W	L	T
Buffalo	8	2	0	San Diego	6	2	2
Houston	4	5	0	Oakland	5	4	1
New York	3	5	1	Kansas City	5	4	1
Boston	1	8	1	Denver	4	6	0

Roommates Ron Mix and Jacque MacKinnon

Balboa Stadium – San Diego, California
Attendance – 27,473

					Total
Chargers	0	10	0	10	20
Bills	7	0	10	3	20

Bills	Kemp 6-yard pass to Carlton for the touchdown. Gogolak kicks the extra point.
Chargers	Lowe 6-yard run for the touchdown. Travenio kicks the extra point.
Chargers	Travenio kicks a 9-yard field goal.
Bills	Lamonica 1-yard run for the touchdown. Gogolak kicks the extra point.
Bills	Gogolak kicks a 9-yard field goal.
Chargers	Travenio kicks a 14-yard field goal.
Chargers	Lowe recovers Hadl fumble in the end zone for the touchdown. Travenio kicks the extra point.
Bills	Gogolak kicks a 22-yard field goal.

	Chargers	Bills
First Downs	23	13
Rushing Yards	52	47
Passing Yards	306	184
Punts-Average	5-36.0	8-43.1
Fumbles-Lost	5-3	3-2
Penalties-Yards	5-37	8-78

Chargers' Leaders

Rushing Lowe 20-69, Foster 8-10, Hadl 5-12, Lincoln 1-3
Passing Hadl 18-37-2-312
Receiving Alworth 7-124, Norton 3-42, Foster 3-39, MacKinnon 3-39, Lincoln 2-68
Interceptions Westmoreland 1-28

Bills' Leaders

Rushing Joe 7-11, Carlton 6-14, Kemp 2-11, Smith 2-10, Lamonica 1-1
Passing Kemp 17-35-1-201, Lamonica 1-2-0-4
Receiving Roberson 5-59, Costa 3-70, Ferguson 3-39, Carlton 3-15, Joe 2-11
Interceptions Edgerson 1-16, Clark 1-0

Week 11 Games
San Diego and Buffalo – Bye
Kansas City 10, Boston 10
Oakland 28, Denver 20
New York 41, Houston 14

Week 11 Standings

East	W	L	T	West	W	L	T
Buffalo	8	2	0	San Diego	6	2	2
New York	4	5	1	Oakland	6	4	1
Houston	4	6	0	Kansas City	5	4	2
Boston	1	8	2	Denver	4	7	0

Week 12 Games
San Diego 20, Buffalo 20
Kansas City 52, Houston 21
Boston 27, New York 23
Oakland and Denver - Bye

Week 12 Standings

East	W	L	T	West	W	L	T
Buffalo	8	2	1	San Diego	6	2	3
New York	4	6	1	Oakland	6	4	1
Houston	4	7	0	Kansas City	6	4	2
Boston	2	8	2	Denver	4	7	0

Herb Travenio (35) attempts a field goal.

John Hadl (21) and Chuck Allen (50).

DECEMBER 4, 1965
Balboa Stadium – San Diego, California
Attendance – 32,169

					Total
Chargers	0	17	14	7	38
Jets	0	0	7	0	7

Chargers	Lincoln 1-yard run for the touchdown. Travenio kicks the extra point.
Chargers	Hadl 25-yard pass to Lincoln for the touchdown. Travenio kicks the extra point
Chargers	Travenio kicks a 26-yard field goal.
Chargers	Graham intercepts Namath pass, returns it 51 yards for the touchdown. Travenio kicks the extra point.
Jets	Namath 21-yard pass to Maynard for the touchdown. J. Turner kicks the extra point.
Chargers	Hadl 46-yard pass to Alworth for the touchdown. Travenio kicks the extra point.
Chargers	Hadl 36-yard pass to Alworth for the touchdown. Travenio kicks the extra point.

	Chargers	Jets
First Downs	23	12
Rushing Yards	174	41
Passing Yards	229	156
Punts-Average	3-40.7	3-43.7
Fumbles-Lost	1-1	1-1
Penalties-Yards	7-75	3-37

Chargers' Leaders
Rushing	Lowe 14-71, Lincoln 13-57, Foster 6-29, Hadl 3-6, Allison 2-19
Passing	Hadl 13-19-1-236, Breaux 1-1-0-15, Lincoln 0-1-1-0
Receiving	Alworth 7-147, Lincoln 2-46, Norton 2-18, Allison 1-15, Kocourek 1-13
Interceptions	Graham 2-51, Degan 1-6

Jets' Leaders
Rushing	Mathis 8-17, Snell 7-28, Namath 1-(-4)
Passing	Namath 18-34-3-179, Taliaferro 1-5-0-6
Receiving	Snell 7-34, Maynard 5-83, Sauer 4-28, B. Turner 2-23, Mathis 1-17
Interceptions	Paulson 1-21, West 1-2

Week 13 Games
San Diego 38, New York 7
Buffalo 29, Houston 18
Oakland 24, Denver 13
Kansas City and Boston - Bye

Week 13 Standings
East	W	L	T	West	W	L	T
Buffalo	9	2	1	San Diego	7	2	3
New York	4	7	1	Oakland	7	4	1
Houston	4	8	0	Kansas City	6	4	2
Boston	2	8	2	Denver	4	8	0

DECEMBER 12, 1965
Rice Stadium – Houston, Texas
Attendance – 24,120

					Total
Chargers	7	7	3	20	37
Oilers	2	10	7	7	26

Chargers	Norton punts to Duncan who returns it 63 yards for the touchdown.
Oilers	Hadl tackled in the end zone by Cutsinger for the safety.
Chargers	Hadl 5-yard pass to Alworth for the touchdown. Travenio kicks the extra point.
Oilers	Blanda kicks a 40-yard field goal.
Oilers	Blanda 10-yard pass to Hennigan for the touchdown. Blanda kicks the extra point.
Oilers	Blanda 30-yard pass to Compton for the touchdown. Blanda kicks the extra point.
Chargers	Travenio kicks a 32-yard field goal.
Oilers	Blanda 9-yard pass to Hennigan for the touchdown. Blanda kicks the extra point.
Chargers	Hadl 1-yard run for the touchdown. Travenio kicks the extra point.
Chargers	Travenio kicks a 32-yard field goal.
Chargers	Lowe 15-yard run for the touchdown. Travenio kicks the extra point.

	Chargers	Oilers
First Downs	18	13
Rushing Yards	225	19
Passing Yards	136	202
Punts-Average	4-39.0	6-41.0
Fumbles-Lost	1-1	0-0
Penalties-Yards	5-61	2-5

Chargers' Leaders
Rushing	Lowe 19-99, Lincoln 11-62, Hadl 6-48, Foster 4-21, Allison 2-(-5)
Passing	Hadl 11-25-1-146
Receiving	Lincoln 5-87, Norton 3-39, Alworth 2-14, Lowe 1-6
Interceptions	Warren 1-11, Duncan 1-26

Oilers' Leaders
Rushing	Burrell 10-13, Spikes 2-(-1), Trull 1-4, Jackson 1-3
Passing	Blanda 12-40-2-212, Trull 1-5-0-9
Receiving	McLeod 4-59, Burrell 4-42, Hennigan 3-44, Compton 2-45, Jackson 1-31
Interceptions	Hicks 1-14

Week 14 Games
San Diego 37, Houston 26
Buffalo 34, Kansas City 25
Boston 28, Denver 20
Oakland 24, New York 14

Week 14 Standings
East	W	L	T	West	W	L	T
Buffalo	10	2	1	San Diego	8	2	3
New York	4	8	1	Oakland	8	4	1
Boston	3	8	2	Kansas City	6	5	2
Houston	4	9	0	Denver	4	9	0

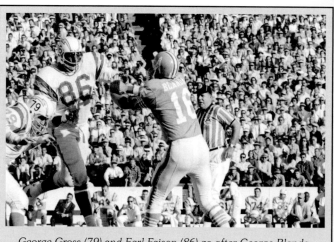

George Gross (79) and Earl Faison (86) go after George Blanda.

169

DECEMBER 19, 1965
Balboa Stadium – San Diego, California
Attendance – 26,056

					Total
Chargers	0	7	7	10	24
Raiders	7	7	0	0	14

Raiders	Flores 4-yard pass to Powell for the touchdown. Mercer kicks the extra point.
Raiders	Daniels 1-yard run for the touchdown. Mercer kicks the extra point.
Chargers	Hadl 22-yard pass to Norton for the touchdown. Travenio kicks the extra point.
Chargers	Hadl 10-yard pass to Norton for the touchdown. Travenio kicks the extra point.
Chargers	Breaux 66-yard pass to Alworth for the touchdown. Travenio kicks the extra point.
Chargers	Travenio kicks a 15-yard field goal.

	Chargers	Raiders
First Downs	18	20
Rushing Yards	147	102
Passing Yards	291	212
Punts-Average	1-39.0	3-31.0
Fumbles-Lost	1-1	0-0
Penalties-Yards	5-47	1-5

Chargers' Leaders

Rushing	Foster 17-55, Allison 13-47, Lowe 3-32, Hadl 2-14, Breaux 1-(-1)
Passing	Hadl 8-14-1-192, Breaux 4-6-1-99, Lowe 0-1-0-0
Receiving	Alworth 5-160, Allison 4-70, Norton 2-32, Kocourek 1-29
Interceptions	Allen 1-0, Whitehead 2-13

Raiders' Leaders

Rushing	Daniels 19-85, Miller 2-8, Hagberg 1-9
Passing	Flores 20-38-3-207, Mercer 1-1-0-14
Receiving	Daniels 7-61, Todd 2-35, Miller 2-28, Cannon 2-21, Powell 2-17
Interceptions	Powers 1-21, McCloughan 1-16

Week 15 Games
San Diego 24, Oakland 14
Kansas City 45, Denver 35
Boston 42, Houston 14
New York 14, Buffalo 12

Week 15 Standings

East	W	L	T	West	W	L	T
Buffalo	10	3	1	San Diego	9	2	3
New York	5	8	1	Oakland	8	5	1
Boston	4	8	2	Kansas City	7	5	2
Houston	4	10	0	Denver	4	10	0

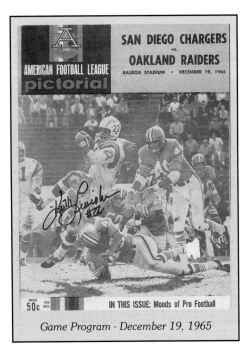

SAN DIEGO CHARGERS
vs.
OAKLAND RAIDERS
AMERICAN FOOTBALL LEAGUE
pictorial
BALBOA STADIUM · DECEMBER 19, 1965

PRICE 50¢ TAX INCL.   IN THIS ISSUE: Moods of Pro Football

Game Program - December 19, 1965

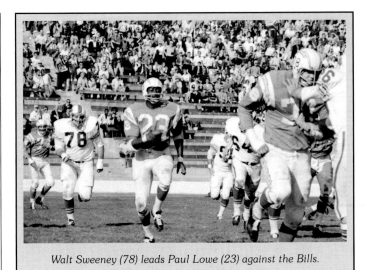

Walt Sweeney (78) leads Paul Lowe (23) against the Bills.

DECEMBER 26, 1965
American Football League Championship Game
War Memorial Stadium – Buffalo, New York
Attendance – 30,361

					Total
Chargers	0	0	0	0	0
Bills	0	14	6	3	23

Bills	Kemp 18-yard pass to Warlick for the touchdown. Gogolak kicks the extra point.
Bills	Hadl punts to Byrd, returned 74 yards for the touchdown. Gogolak kicks the extra point.
Bills	Gogolak kicks an 11-yard field goal.
Bills	Gogolak kicks a 39-yard field goal.
Bills	Gogolak kicks a 32-yard field goal.

	Chargers	Bills
First Downs	12	14
Rushing Yards	104	108
Passing Yards	119	152
Punts-Average	7-40.7	4-46.8
Fumbles-Lost	1-0	1-0
Penalties-Yards	3-41	2-21

Chargers' Leaders

Rushing	Lowe 12-57, Hadl 8-24, Lincoln 4-16, Foster 2-9, Breaux 1-(-2)
Passing	Hadl 11-23-2-140, Breaux 1-2-0-24
Receiving	Alworth 4-82, Lowe 3-3, Norton 1-35, Farr 1-24, MacKinnon 1-10
Interceptions	Warren 1-0

Bills' Leaders

Rushing	Carlton 16-63, Joe 16-35, Stone 3-5, Smith 1-5
Passing	Kemp 8-19-1-155, Lamonica 1-1-0-12
Receiving	Roberson 3-88, Warlick 3-35, Costa 2-32, Tracy 1-12
Interceptions	Byrd 1-24, Jacobs 1-12

1966 Chargers Team Statistics
(7-6-1 Overall) Third Place in the AFL West

Team Statistics	Chargers	Opponent
TOTAL FIRST DOWNS	230	260
Rushing	77	127
Passing	137	116
Penalty	16	17
TOTAL NET YARDS	4,553	4,558
Avg. Per Game	325.2	325.6
Avg. Per Play	5.5	5.0
NET YARDS RUSHING	1,537	2,403
Avg. Per Game	109.8	171.6
NET YARDS PASSING	3,016	2,155
Avg. Per Game	215.4	153.9
Gross Yards	3,347	2,386
Completions/Attempts	224/434	170/382
Completion Pct.	.516	.445
Had Intercepted	15	27
PUNTS/AVERAGE	66/37.0	52/43.0
PENALTIES/YARDS	68/667	60/527
FUMBLES/BALL LOST	17/7	17/8
TOUCHDOWNS	41	33
Rushing	9	19
Passing	29	13
Returns	3	1
QUARTERBACK SACKS	26.0	32.0

Rushing	No.	Yds.	Avg.	TD
Lowe	146	643	4.4	3
Foster	81	352	4.3	1
Lincoln	58	214	3.7	1
Allison	31	213	6.9	2
Hadl	38	95	2.5	2
Redman	2	14	7.0	0
Alworth	3	10	3.3	0
Tensi	1	-1	-1.0	0
Garrison	1	-3	-3.0	0
Totals	**361**	**1,537**	**4.3**	**9**

Receiving	No.	Yds.	Avg.	TD
Alworth	73	1,383	18.9	13
Garrison	46	642	14.0	4
MacKinnon	26	477	18.3	6
Foster	26	260	10.0	2
Lincoln	14	264	18.9	2
Allison	12	99	8.3	0
Lowe	12	41	3.4	0
Frazier	9	144	16.0	2
Norton	4	50	12.5	0
Hadl	2	-13	-6.5	0
Totals	**224**	**3,347**	**14.9**	**29**

Passing	Att.	Comp.	Yds.	Comp. %	TD	Int.
Hadl	375	200	2,846	.533	23	14
Tensi	52	21	405	.404	5	1
Lincoln	4	2	71	.500	1	0
Lowe	3	1	25	.333	0	0
Totals	**434**	**224**	**3,347**	**.516**	**29**	**15**

Interceptions	No.	Yds.	TD
Duncan	7	67	0
Graham	5	70	1
Farr	3	68	0
Matsos	1	6	0
Whitehead	2	89	0
Beauchamp	2	24	0
Redman	2	7	0
Milks	1	13	0
Allen	1	8	0
Degan	1	7	0
Kindig	1	0	0
Tolbert	1	0	0
Totals	**27**	**359**	**1**

Kicking	FG	Att.	PAT	Att.	Pts.
Van Raaphorst	16	31	39	40	87

Punting	No.	Avg.
Redman	66	37.0

Punt Returns	No.	FC	Yds.	Avg.	TD
Duncan	18	4	238	13.2	1
Graham	2	4	15	7.5	0
Plump	1	0	4	4.0	0

Kickoff Returns	No.	Yds.	Avg.	TD
Duncan	25	642	25.7	0
Plump	15	345	23.0	0
Lowe	7	167	23.9	0
Beauchamp	4	64	16.0	0
Farr	2	54	27.0	0
Gruneisen	1	0	0.0	0
Whitmyer	1	10	10.0	0

The Charger Horse

Lance Alworth (19) and Rick Redman (66)

Quarterbacks John Hadl (21) and Jack Kemp (15) talk before the game.

SEPTEMBER 4, 1966
Balboa Stadium – San Diego, California
Attendance – 27,572

					Total
Chargers	0	7	3	17	27
Bills	0	0	0	7	7

Chargers	Hadl 7-yard pass to Hadl for the touchdown. Van Raaphorst kicks the extra point.
Chargers	Van Raaphorst kicks a 30-yard field goal.
Chargers	Van Raaphorst kicks a 10-yard field goal.
Chargers	Hadl 3-yard pass to MacKinnon for the touchdown. Van Raaphorst kicks the extra point.
Chargers	Maguire punts to Duncan who returns it 81 yards for the touchdown. Van Raaphorst kicks the extra point.
Bills	Burnett 2-yard run for the touchdown. Lusteg kicks the extra point

	Chargers	Bills
First Downs	15	15
Rushing Yards	137	117
Passing Yards	153	150
Punts-Average	4-30.8	4-51.2
Fumbles-Lost	1-0	0-0
Penalties-Yards	3-38	3-15

Chargers' Leaders
Rushing	Lowe 15-36, Foster 12-58, Hadl 4-6, Allison 5-37
Passing	Hadl 14-18-0-169
Receiving	Alworth 5-46, MacKinnon 3-56, Lowe 3-7, Garrison 2-47, Hadl 1-4
Interceptions	Whitehead 1-61, Farr 1-33, Graham 1-21

Bills' Leaders
Rushing	Carlton 16-87, Burnett 9-22, Rutkowski 1-10, Spikes 1-(-2)
Passing	Kemp 4-20-3-74, Lamonica 5-7-0-76
Receiving	Ferguson 3-77, Costa 2-44, Carlton 1-16, Dubenion 1-14, O'Donnell 1-2
Interceptions	None

Week 1 Games
San Diego 27, Buffalo 7
Oakland 23, Miami 14
Houston 45, Denver 7
New York, Boston and Kansas City - Bye

Week 1 Standings
East	W	L	T	West	W	L	T
Houston	1	0	0	San Diego	1	0	0
Buffalo	0	1	0	Oakland	1	0	0
Miami	0	1	0	Denver	0	1	0
New York	0	0	0	Kansas City	0	0	0
Boston	0	0	0				

SEPTEMBER 10, 1966
Balboa Stadium – San Diego California
Attendance – 29,539

					Total
Chargers	3	14	0	7	24
Patriots	0	0	0	0	0

Chargers	Van Raaphorst kicks a 10-yard field goal.
Chargers	Graham intercepts Parilli pass, returns it 32 yards for the touchdown. Van Raaphorst kicks the extra point.
Chargers	Hadl 5-yard pass to Alworth for the touchdown. Van Raaphorst kicks the extra point.
Chargers	Allison 61-yard run for the touchdown. Van Raaphorst kicks the extra point.

	Chargers	Patriots
First Downs	12	15
Rushing Yards	138	130
Passing Yards	141	122
Punts-Average	11-37.4	9-40.8
Fumbles-Lost	1-0	1-0
Penalties-Yards	6-37	4-26

Chargers' Leaders
Rushing	Foster 12-23, Lowe 10-21, Hadl 6-30, Allison 3-64
Passing	Hadl 10-28-0-155
Receiving	Alworth 5-97, Garrison 2-46, Foster 2-14, Lowe 1-(-2)
Interceptions	Graham 1-32, Allen 1-8, Whitehead 1-8, Farr 1-0

Patriots' Leaders
Rushing	Nance 12-68, Garron 6-41, Garrett 2-9, Huarte 1-12
Passing	Parilli 13-39-4-137, Huarte 1-2-0-11
Receiving	Nance 4-67, Graham 4-36, Garron 2-21, Whalen 2-13, Garrett 1-7
Interceptions	None

Week 2 Games
San Diego 24, Boston 0
Kansas City 42, Buffalo 20
New York 19, Miami 14
Houston 31, Oakland 0
Denver - Bye

Week 2 Standings
East	W	L	T	West	W	L	T
Houston	2	0	0	San Diego	2	0	0
New York	1	0	0	Kansas City	1	0	0
Boston	0	1	0	Oakland	1	1	0
Buffalo	0	2	0	Denver	0	1	0
Miami	0	2	0				

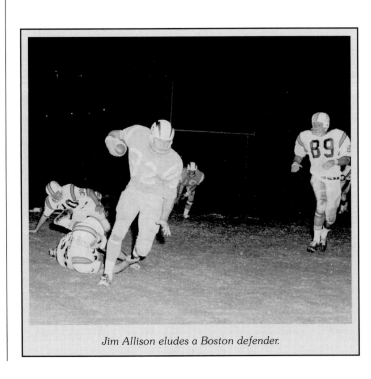

Jim Allison eludes a Boston defender.

John Hadl (21) calls the next play.

SEPTEMBER 25, 1966
Oakland-Alameda County Coliseum - Oakland, California
Attendance – 37,183

					Total
Chargers	3	9	10	7	29
Raiders	3	0	7	10	20

Chargers	Van Raaphorst kicks a 13-yard field goal.
Raiders	Eischeid kicks a 49-yard field goal.
Chargers	Birdwell centers the ball out of the end zone for a safety.
Chargers	Hadl 1-yard run for the touchdown. Van Raaphorst kicks the extra point.
Raiders	Daniels 1-yard run for the touchdown. Eischeid kicks the extra point.
Chargers	Hadl 19-yard pass to MacKinnon for the touchdown. Van Raaphorst kicks the extra point.
Chargers	Van Raaphorst kicks a 20-yard field goal.
Raiders	Flores 8-yard pass to Biletnikoff for the touchdown. Eischeid kicks the extra point.
Raiders	Eischeid kicks a 34-yard field goal.
Chargers	Foster 8-yard run for the touchdown. Van Raaphorst kicks the extra point.

	Chargers	Raiders
First Downs	12	18
Rushing Yards	133	109
Passing Yards	143	157
Punts-Average	5-33.2	3-47.5
Fumbles-Lost	2-1	0-0
Penalties-Yards	9-86	9-59

Chargers' Leaders

Rushing	Lowe 15-35, Allison 6-22, Foster 6-19, Hadl 4-39, Lincoln 4-18
Passing	Hadl 10-21-1-162
Receiving	Garrison 3-41, Alworth 2-50, MacKinnon 2-36, Lincoln 2-34, Foster 1-1
Interceptions	Duncan 3-32, Redman 1-7

Raiders' Leaders

Rushing	Daniels 16-49, Hagberg 8-45, Flores 1-15
Passing	Davidson 5-14-3-100, Flores 6-17-1-95
Receiving	Daniels 3-54, Powell 3-51, Hagberg 2-50, Mitchell 2-32, Biletnikof 1-8
Interceptions	Bird 1-23

Week 3 Games
San Diego - Bye
Kansas City 32, Oakland 10
Buffalo 58, Miami 24
Boston 24, Denver 10
New York 52, Houston 13

Week 3 Standings

East	W	L	T	West	W	L	T
New York	2	0	0	San Diego	2	0	0
Houston	2	1	0	Kansas City	2	0	0
Boston	1	1	0	Oakland	1	2	0
Buffalo	1	2	0	Denver	0	2	0
Miami	0	3	0				

Week 4 Games
San Diego 29, Oakland 20
Kansas City 43, Boston 24
New York 16, Denver 7
Buffalo 27, Houston 20
Miami - Bye

Week 4 Standings

East	W	L	T	West	W	L	T
New York	3	0	0	San Diego	3	0	0
Houston	2	2	0	Kansas City	3	0	0
Buffalo	2	2	0	Oakland	1	3	0
Boston	1	2	0	Denver	0	3	0
Miami	0	3	0				

Lance Alworth dives for the ball.

OCTOBER 2, 1966
Balboa Stadium – San Diego, California
Attendance – 26,444

					Total
Chargers	0	6	10	28	44
Dolphins	3	7	0	0	10

Dolphins	Mingo kicks a 27-yard field goal.
Dolphins	Wood 20-yard pass to Noonan for the touchdown.
Chargers	Redman recovers fumble and returns 54 yards for the touchdown.
Chargers	Van Raaphorst kicks a 9-yard field goal.
Chargers	Tensi 25-yard pass to Foster for the touchdown. Van Raaphorst kicks the extra point.
Chargers	Tensi 44-yard pass to Alworth for the touchdown. Van Raaphorst kicks the extra point.
Chargers	Tensi 63-yard pass to Foster for the touchdown. Van Raaphorst kicks the extra point.
Chargers	Lincoln 36-yard pass to Alworth for the touchdown. Van Raaphorst kicks the extra point.
Chargers	Tensi 30-yard pass to Frazier for the touchdown. Van Raaphorst kicks the extra point.

	Chargers	Dolphins
First Downs	14	16
Rushing Yards	40	187
Passing Yards	321	89
Punts-Average	4-35.7	5-36.4
Fumbles-Lost	1-1	2-2
Penalties-Yards	11-113	8-66

Chargers' Leaders

Rushing	Lowe 10-26, Lincoln 7-14, Foster 6-4, Hadl 1-(-1), Tensi 1-(-3)
Passing	Hadl 6-11-1-62, Tensi 9-12-0-223, Lincoln 1-1-0-36
Receiving	Foster 6-134, Alworth 119, Frazier 1-30, MacKinnon 1-17, Garrison 1-12
Interceptions	None

Dolphins' Leaders

Rushing	Casares 22-80, Auer 8-45, Joe 4-15, Price 4-11, Chesser 2-24
Passing	Wilson 2-5-0-12, Wood 7-22-0-84
Receiving	Noonan 2-30, Roderick 2-22, Twilley 1-20, Kocourek 1-9, Casares 1-6
Interceptions	Jaquess 1-0

Week 5 Games
San Diego 44, Miami 10
Boston 24, New York 24
Buffalo 29, Kansas City 14
Denver 40, Houston 38
Oakland - Bye

Week 5 Standings

East	W	L	T	West	W	L	T
New York	3	0	1	San Diego	4	0	0
Buffalo	3	2	0	Kansas City	3	1	0
Houston	2	3	0	Oakland	1	3	0
Boston	1	2	1	Denver	1	3	0
Miami	0	4	0				

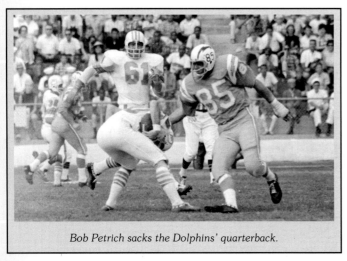

Bob Petrich sacks the Dolphins' quarterback.

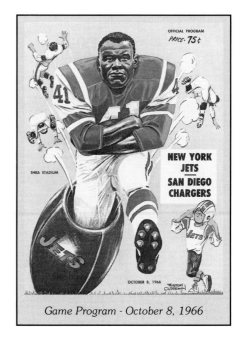

Game Program - October 8, 1966

OCTOBER 8, 1966
Shea Stadium – New York City, New York
Attendance – 63,497

					Total
Chargers	3	6	0	7	16
Jets	7	3	0	7	17

Chargers	Van Raaphorst kicks a 14-yard field goal.
Jets	Namath 17-yard pass to Snell for the touchdown. J. Turner kicks the extra point.
Chargers	Van Raaphorst kicks a 17-yard field goal.
Jets	J. Turner kicks a 33-yard field goal.
Chargers	Van Raaphorst kicks a 42-yard field goal.
Chargers	Hadl 67-yard pass to Lincoln for the touchdown. Van Raaphorst kicks the extra point.
Jets	Boozer runs 8-yards for the touchdown. J. Turner kicks the extra point.

	Chargers	Jets
First Downs	23	12
Rushing Yards	95	119
Passing Yards	350	129
Punts-Average	4-39.8	6-45.9
Fumbles-Lost	0-0	0-0
Penalties-Yards	6-88	7-62

Chargers' Leaders

Rushing	Lowe 11-26, Foster 5-42, Lincoln 5-24, Hadl 4-3
Passing	Hadl 22-41-0-331, Tensi 2-10-1-41
Receiving	Alworth 10-149, MacKinnon 4-68, Lincoln 3-71, Garrison 3-52, Foster 3-22
Interceptions	Graham 1-6, Farr 1-35, Duncan 1-0

Jets' Leaders

Rushing	Snell 18-28, Mathis 6-23, Boozer 1-20, Namath 1-(-2)
Passing	Namath 11-22-3-129
Receiving	Mathis 4-66, Sauer 2-23, Lammons 2-12, Snell 2-10, Maynard 1-18
Interceptions	Atkinson 1-10

Week 6 Games
New York 17, San Diego 16
Boston 20, Buffalo 10
Kansas City 37, Denver 10
Oakland 21, Miami 10
Houston - Bye

Week 6 Standings

East	W	L	T	West	W	L	T
New York	4	0	1	San Diego	4	1	0
Buffalo	3	3	0	Kansas City	4	1	0
Boston	2	2	1	Oakland	2	3	0
Houston	2	3	0	Denver	1	4	0
Miami	0	5	0				

OCTOBER 16, 1966
War Memorial Stadium – Buffalo, New York
Attendance – 45,169

					Total
Chargers	7	10	0	0	17
Bills	0	3	7	7	17

Chargers	Hadl 6-yard pass to Frazier for the touchdown. Van Raaphorst kicks the extra point.
Chargers	Van Raaphorst kicks a 23-yard field goal.
Chargers	Hadl 21-yard pass to Lincoln for the touchdown. Van Raaphorst kicks the extra point.
Bills	Lusteg kicks a 41-yard field goal.
Bills	Lamonica 3-yard pass to Burnetts for the touchdown. Lusteg kicks the extra point.
Bills	Lamonica 1-yard run for the touchdown. Lusteg kicks the extra point.

	Chargers	Bills
First Downs	12	22
Rushing Yards	50	213
Passing Yards	169	107
Punts-Average	5-38.2	3-36.7
Fumbles-Lost	0-0	3-0
Penalties-Yards	4-53	3-25

Chargers' Leaders
Rushing	Lowe 15-33, Lincoln 4-1, Allison 2-9, Hadl 2-7
Passing	Hadl 11-20-0-185, Lincoln 1-1-0-35
Receiving	Lincoln 5-123, Alworth 3-56, Frazier 3-36, Garrison 1-5
Interceptions	Graham 1-0, Kindig 1-0

Bills' Leaders
Rushing	Burnett 27-138, Carlton 12-61, Lamonica 2-11, Spikes 1-3
Passing	Kemp 6-18-2-75, Lamonica 5-8-0-49
Receiving	Dubenion 3-22, P. Costa 2-42, Crockett 2-34, Carlton 2-13, Burnett 2-13
Interceptions	None

Week 7 Games
San Diego 17, Buffalo 17
Oakland 34, Kansas City 13
Miami 24, Denver 7
Houston 24, New York 0
Boston - Bye

Week 7 Standings
East	W	L	T	West	W	L	T
New York	4	1	1	San Diego	4	1	1
Buffalo	3	3	1	Kansas City	4	2	0
Houston	3	3	0	Oakland	3	3	0
Boston	2	2	1	Denver	1	5	0
Miami	1	5	0				

Lance Alworth (19) and John Hadl (21)

Game Program - October 23, 1966

OCTOBER 23, 1966
Fenway Park – Boston, Massachusetts
Attendance – 32,371

					Total
Chargers	7	3	7	0	17
Patriots	0	14	7	14	35

Chargers	Hadl 42-yard pass to Alworth for the touchdown. Van Raaphorst kicks the extra point.
Chargers	Van Raaphorst kicks a 25-yard field goal.
Patriots	Parilli 53-yard pass to Garron for the touchdown. Cappalletti kicks the extra point.
Patriots	Parilli 14-yard pass to Cappalletti for the touchdown. Cappalletti kicks the extra point.
Patriots	Cappalletti kicks a 47-yard field goal.
Chargers	Hadl 66-yard pass to Alworth for the touchdown. Van Raaphorst kicks the extra point.
Patriots	Garron 2-yard run for the touchdown. Van Raaphorst kicks the extra point.
Patriots	Parilli 53-yard pass to Garron for the touchdown. Cappalletti kicks the extra point.
Patriots	Nance 2-yard run for the touchdown. Cappalletti kicks the extra point.

	Chargers	Patriots
First Downs	16	22
Rushing Yards	40	172
Passing Yards	289	250
Punts-Average	6-33.2	4-36.5
Fumbles-Lost	2-1	3-2
Penalties-Yards	1-15	5-29

Chargers' Leaders
Rushing	Lowe 9-25, Lincoln 4-11, Foster 3-10, Alworth 1-3, Allison 1-3
Passing	Hadl 19-36-2-289, Tensi 0-3-0-0
Receiving	Alworth 6-177, Garrison 4-56, Foster 3-17, Lowe 3-10, Allison 1-12
Interceptions	Degan 1-7, Graham 1-11

Patriots' Leaders
Rushing	Nance 25-108, Garron 12-38, Garrett 5-12, Cappadona 2-17, Parilli 2-(-1)
Passing	Parilli 13-22-1-250, Huarte 0-2-1-0
Receiving	Cappalletti 5-53, Garron 2-106, Wharton 2-44, Graham 2-26, Colclough 1-11
Interceptions	Bouniconti 1-41, Hall 1-34

Week 8 Games
Boston 35, San Diego 17
Oakland 24, New York 21
Kansas City 56, Denver 10
Miami 20, Houston 13
Buffalo - Bye

Week 8 Standings
East	W	L	T	West	W	L	T
New York	4	2	1	San Diego	4	2	1
Buffalo	3	3	1	Kansas City	5	2	0
Houston	3	4	0	Oakland	4	3	0
Boston	3	2	1	Denver	1	6	0
Miami	2	5	0				

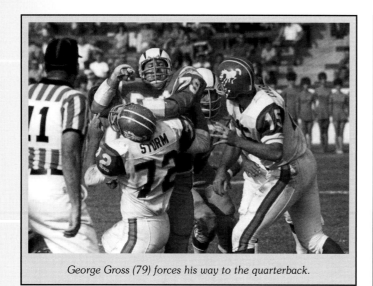
George Gross (79) forces his way to the quarterback.

OCTOBER 30, 1966
Balboa Stadium – San Diego, California
Attendance – 25,819

					Total
Chargers	7	14	0	3	24
Broncos	7	10	0	0	17

Broncos	Choboian 2-yard run for the touchdown. Kroner kicks the extra point.
Chargers	Lincoln 5-yard run for the touchdown. Van Raaphorst kicks the extra point.
Broncos	Scarpitto 63-yard run for the touchdown on a fake punt. Kroner kicks the extra point.
Chargers	Hadl 1-yard pass to Garrison for the touchdown. Van Raaphorst kicks the extra point.
Broncos	Kroner kicks a 23-yard field goal.
Chargers	Hadl 1-yard pass to MacKinnon for the touchdown. Van Raaphorst kicks the extra point.
Chargers	Van Raaphorst kicks a 26-yard field goal.

	Chargers	Broncos
First Downs	21	15
Rushing Yards	154	125
Passing Yards	180	156
Punts-Average	2-45.0	4-47.0
Fumbles-Lost	4-2	0-0
Penalties-Yards	6-24	3-56

Chargers' Leaders
Rushing	Lincoln 17-95, Foster 12-61, Hadl 3—(6), Alworth 1-4
Passing	Hadl 19-26-0-180
Receiving	Garrison 6-73, Alworth 5-47, MacKinnon 4-45, Foster 3-32, Hadl 1-(-17)
Interceptions	None

Broncos' Leaders
Rushing	Mitchell 11-25, Haynes 9-17, Lester 5-5, Choboian 3-5, Scarpitto 2-73
Passing	Choboian 6-13-0-71, McCormick 9-18-0-92
Receiving	Haynes 4-16, Denson 3-39, Taylor 3-38, Crabtree 1-38, Lester 1-21
Interceptions	None

Week 9 Games
San Diego 24, Denver 17
Buffalo 33, New York 23
Boston 24, Oakland 21
Kansas City 48, Houston 23
Miami - Bye

Week 9 Standings
East	W	L	T	West	W	L	T
Boston	4	2	1	Kansas City	6	2	0
Buffalo	4	3	1	San Diego	5	2	1
New York	4	3	1	Oakland	4	4	0
Houston	3	5	0	Denver	1	7	0
Miami	2	5	0				

NOVEMBER 6, 1966
Municipal Stadium – Kansas City, Missouri
Attendance – 40,986

					Total
Chargers	7	0	7	0	14
Chiefs	7	17	0	0	24

Chiefs	Coan 1-yard run for the touchdown. Mercer kicks the extra point.
Chargers	Hadl 46-yard pass to Alworth for the touchdown. Van Raaphorst kicks the extra point.
Chiefs	Dawson 27-yard pass to Taylor for the touchdown. Mercer kicks the extra point.
Chiefs	Mercer kicks a 50-yard field goal.
Chiefs	Dawson 10-yard pass to Burford for the touchdown. Merccer kicks the extra point.
Chargers	Hadl 7-yard pass to Alworth for the touchdown. Van Raaphorst kicks the extra point.

	Chargers	Chiefs
First Downs	14	24
Rushing Yards	84	159
Passing Yards	203	143
Punts-Average	5-40.6	3-52.3
Fumbles-Lost	1-0	1-0
Penalties-Yards	5-50	3-25

Chargers' Leaders
Rushing	Lincoln 9-20, Foster 8-54, Lowe 1-5, Allison 1-5, Hadl 1-0
Passing	Hadl 17-31-2-230
Receiving	Alworth 6-101, Allison 4-17, Garrison 3-35, MacKinnon 2-55, Norton 2-18
Interceptions	Duncan 1-0, Milks 1-13

Chiefs' Leaders
Rushing	McClinton 23-90, Garrett 14-53, Coan 5-16, Dawson 2-0
Passing	Dawson 12-24-2-153
Receiving	Burford 5-77, Taylor 3-54, Coan 2-0, McClinton 1-13, Arbanas 1-9
Interceptions	Robinson 1-29, Mitchell 1-30

Week 10 Games
Kansas City 24, San Diego 14
Denver 17, Boston 10
Buffalo 29, Miami 0
Oakland 38, Houston 23
New York - Bye

Week 10 Standings
East	W	L	T	West	W	L	T
Buffalo	5	3	1	Kansas City	7	2	0
Boston	4	3	1	San Diego	5	3	1
New York	4	3	1	Oakland	5	4	0
Houston	3	6	0	Denver	2	7	0
Miami	2	6	0				

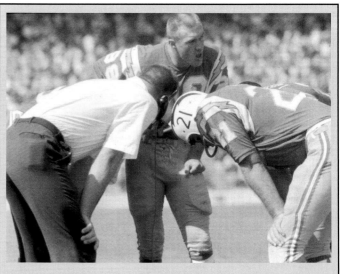
Sid Gillman, Don Norton (88) and John Hadl (21)

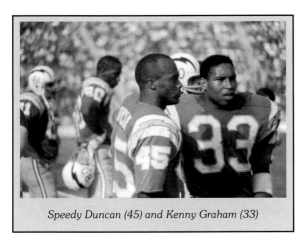

Speedy Duncan (45) and Kenny Graham (33)

November 13, 1966
Balboa Stadium – San Diego, California
Attendance – 26,230

					Total
Chargers	10	0	3	6	19
Raiders	7	21	7	6	41

Raiders	Flores 8-yard pass to Powell for the touchdown. Eischeid kicks the extra point.
Chargers	Hadl 2-yard pass to Garrison for the touchdown. Van Raaphorst kicks the extra point.
Chargers	Van Raaphorst kicks a 38-yard field goal.
Raiders	Flores 1-yard pass to Powell for the touchdown. Eischeid kicks the extra point.
Raiders	Dixon 3-yard run for the touchdown. Eischeid kicks the extra point.
Raiders	Flores 2-yard pass to Danies for the touchdown. Eischeid kicks the extra point.
Chargers	Van Raaphorst kicks a 39-yard field goal.
Raiders	Dixon 2-yard run for the touchdown. Eischeid kicks the extra point.
Raiders	Eischeid kicks a 22-yard field goal.
Raiders	Eischeid kicks a 23-yard field goal.
Chargers	Tensi 34-yard pass to MacKinnon for the touchdown.

	Chargers	Raiders
First Downs	16	20
Rushing Yards	151	219
Passing Yards	167	258
Punts-Average	2-41.5	2-36.5
Fumbles-Lost	1-1	1-0
Penalties-Yards	1-5	2-38

Chargers' Leaders
Rushing Lowe 10-125, Lincoln 3-13, Allison 3-3, Foster 2-28
Passing Hadl 8-16-1-91, Tensi 8-20-0-118, Lowe 0-1-0-0
Receiving Garrison 7-96, Allison 4-35, MacKinnon 3-65, Norton 1-9, Lowe 1-4
Interceptions None

Raiders' Leaders
Rushing Dixon 16-90, Daniels 11-104, Hagberg 5-22, Atkins 1-3
Passing Flores 14-29-0-279, Daniels 0-1-0-0
Receiving Powell 4-86, Daniels 3-74, Biletnikoff 3-37, Cannon 2-53, Mitchell 2-29
Interceptions McCloughan 1-0

Week 11 Games
Oakland 41, San Diego 19
Boston 27, Houston 21
Buffalo 13, New York 3
Kansas City 34, Miami 16
Denver - Bye

Week 11 Standings

East	W	L	T	West	W	L	T
Buffalo	6	3	1	Kansas City	8	2	0
Boston	5	3	1	Oakland	6	4	0
New York	4	4	1	San Diego	5	4	1
Houston	3	7	0	Denver	2	7	0
Miami	2	7	0				

Week 12 Games
San Diego – Bye
Boston 27, Kansas City 27
Oakland 17, Denver 3
New York 30, Miami 13
Buffalo 42, Houston 20

Week 12 Standings

East	W	L	T	West	W	L	T
Buffalo	7	3	1	Kansas City	8	2	1
Boston	5	3	2	Oakland	7	4	0
New York	5	4	1	San Diego	5	4	1
Houston	4	7	0	Denver	2	8	0
Miami	2	8	0				

Don Norton

NOVEMBER 27, 1966
Bears Stadium – Denver, Colorado
Attendance – 24,860

					Total
Chargers	0	0	3	14	17
Broncos	3	0	3	14	20

Broncos	Kroner kicks a 10-yard field goal.
Chargers	Van Raaphorst kicks a 10-yard field goal.
Broncos	Kroner kicks a 17-yard field goal.
Chargers	Hadl 27-yard pass to Alworth for the touchdown. Van Raaphorst kicks the extra point.
Broncos	Van Raaphorst kick blocked, recovered by Bramlett and run 72 yards for the touchdown. Kroner kicks the extra point.
Broncos	Hayes 56-yard run for the touchdown. Kroner kicks the extra point.
Chargers	Hadl 7-yard pass to Alworth for the touchdown. Van Raaphorst kicks the extra point.

	Chargers	Broncos
First Downs	16	16
Rushing Yards	86	170
Passing Yards	200	173
Punts-Average	4-33.5	1-45.0
Fumbles-Lost	2-1	2-1
Penalties-Yards	5-55	3-13

Chargers' Leaders
Rushing Lowe 12-66, Foster 5-11, Hadl 3-2, Lincoln 2-10, Garrison 1-(-3).
Passing Hadl 13-20-1-181, Tensi 1-2-0-7, Lowe 1-1-0-25
Receiving Alworth 6-111, Lowe 3-20, Garrison 2-28, MacKinnon 1-25, Allison 1-17
Interceptions Beauchamp 2-24

Broncos' Leaders
Rushing Hayes 12-87, Mitchell 12-58, Haynes 9-29, Choboian 3-3, Lester 1-2
Passing Choboian 12-25-1-173, McCormick 0-1-1-0
Receiving Haynes 4-54, Denson 3-73, Mitchell 2-21, Scarpitto 2-12, Taylor 1-13
Interceptions Wilson 1-2

Week 13 Games
Denver 20, San Diego 17
Boston 20, Miami 14
Kansas City 32, New York 24
Buffalo 31, Oakland 10
Houston - Bye

Week 13 Standings

East	W	L	T	West	W	L	T
Buffalo	8	3	1	Kansas City	9	2	1
Boston	6	3	2	Oakland	7	5	0
New York	5	5	1	San Diego	5	5	1
Houston	3	8	0	Denver	3	8	0
Miami	2	9	0				

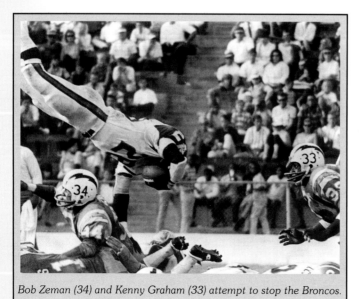

Bob Zeman (34) and Kenny Graham (33) attempt to stop the Broncos.

Ron Mix

DECEMBER 4, 1966
Rice Stadium – Houston, Texas
Attendance – 17,569

					Total
Chargers	7	7	0	14	28
Oilers	0	10	9	3	22

Chargers	Hadl 78-yard pass from Hadl for the touchdown. Van Raaphorst kicks the extra point.
Oilers	Johnson 1-yard run for the touchdown. Blanda kicks the extra point.
Chargers	Hadl 51-yard pass to Alworth for the touchdown. Van Raaphorst kicks the extra point.
Oilers	Blanda kicks a 51-yard field goal.
Oilers	Redman punts, ball hits upright for a safety.
Oilers	Trull 1-yard run for the touchdown. Blanda kicks the extra point.
Chargers	Hadl 24-yard pass to Garrison for the touchdown. Van Raaphorst kicks the extra point.
Oilers	Blanda kicks a 9-yard field goal.
Chargers	Hadl 12-yard pass to MacKinnon for the touchdown. Van Raaphorst kicks the extra point.

	Chargers	Oilers
First Downs	15	23
Rushing Yards	76	238
Passing Yards	302	157
Punts-Average	7-35.3	4-44.5
Fumbles-Lost	1-0	2-1
Penalties-Yards	4-26	7-55

Chargers' Leaders
Rushing Lowe 8-41, Foster 4-23, Lincoln 3-8, Hadl 1-3, Allison 1-1
Passing Hadl 20-35-3-341, Lincoln 0-1-0-0
Receiving Alworth 4-149, Frazier 4-71, Foster 4-14, MacKinnon 1-12, Allison 1-9
Interceptions Duncan 1-21

Oilers' Leaders
Rushing Granger 20-178, Burrell 11-40, Trull 6-10, Tolar 5-4, Johnson 4-6
Passing Trull 13-27-1-210
Receiving Frazier 4-62, Elkins 4-36, McLeod 3-36, Johnson 1-36, Poole 1-16
Interceptions Parrish 1-0, Jancik 1-35, Hicks 1-12

Week 14 Games
San Diego 28, Houston 22
Denver 17, Miami 7
Oakland 28, New York 28
Boston 14, Buffalo 3
Kansas City - Bye

Week 14 Standings

East	W	L	T	West	W	L	T
Buffalo	8	4	1	Kansas City	9	2	1
Boston	7	3	2	Oakland	7	5	1
New York	5	5	2	San Diego	6	5	1
Houston	3	9	0	Denver	4	8	0
Miami	2	10	0				

December 11, 1966
Balboa Stadium – San Diego, California
Attendance – 25,712

					Total
Chargers	0	14	14	14	42
Jets	9	3	7	8	27

Jets	J. Turner kicks a 36-yard field goal.
Jets	Snell 1-yard run for the touchdown.
Chargers	Hadl 8-yard pass to Garrison for the touchdown. Van Raaphorst kicks the extra point.
Chargers	Allison 9-yard run for the touchdown. Van Raaphorst kicks the extra point.
Jets	J. Turner kicks a 30-yard field goal.
Chargers	Lowe 1-yard run for the touchdown. Van Raaphorst kicks the extra point.
Jets	Namath 53-yard pass to Lammons for the touchdown. J. Turner kicks the extra point.
Chargers	Hadl 11-yard run for the touchdown. Van Raaphorst kicks the extra point.
Chargers	Hadl 3-yard pass to MacKinnon for the touchdown. Van Raaphorst kicks the extra point.
Chargers	Lowe 9-yard run for the touchdown. Van Raaphorst kicks the extra point.
Jets	Mathis 3-yard run for the touchdown. Taliaferro 2-yard run for the 2-point conversion.

	Chargers	Jets
First Downs	25	20
Rushing Yards	222	146
Passing Yards	203	189
Punts-Average	3-38.7	2-42.5
Fumbles-Lost	0-0	1-1
Penalties-Yards	4-30	3-14

Chargers' Leaders
Rushing	Lowe 14-126, Allison 6-58, Hadl 3-28, Foster 3-7, Alworth 1-3
Passing	Hadl 14-27-1-240, Tensi 1-5-0-12, Lowe 0-1-0-0
Receiving	Alworth 7-127, MacKinnon 4-90, Garrison 3-30, Foster 1-5
Interceptions	Matsos 1-6, Redman 1-0, Duncan 1-14

Jets' Leaders
Rushing	Snell 18-102, Boozer 10-37, Mathis 2-5, Smolinski 1-2
Passing	Namath 10-21-2-166, Taliaferro 4-9-1-39
Receiving	Maynard 5-56, Lammons 3-123, Snell 3-(-6), Mathis 1-17, Boozer 1-10
Interceptions	Atkinson 1-26

Week 15 Games
San Diego 42, New York 27
Oakland 28, Denver 0
Boston 38, Houston 14
Kansas City 19, Miami 18
Buffalo - Bye

Week 15 Standings
East	W	L	T	West	W	L	T
Buffalo	8	4	1	Kansas City	10	2	1
Boston	8	3	2	Oakland	8	5	1
New York	5	6	2	San Diego	7	5	1
Houston	3	10	0	Denver	4	9	0
Miami	2	11	0				

Lance Alworth leaps for a catch as Sid Gillman and Bud Whitehead (47) look on.

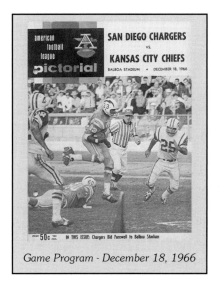

Game Program - December 18, 1966

December 18, 1966
Balboa Stadium – San Diego, California
Attendance – 28,548

					Total
Chargers	3	7	7	0	17
Chiefs	14	3	3	7	27

Chargers	Van Raaphorst kicks a 26-yard field goal.
Chiefs	McClinton 1-yard run for the touchdown. Mercer kicks the extra point.
Chiefs	Coan 15-yard run for the touchdown. Mercer kicks the extra point.
Chargers	Hadl 38-yard pass to Alworth for the touchdown. Van Raaphorst kicks the extra point.
Chiefs	Mercer kicks a 35-yard field goal.
Chargers	Lowe 6-yard run for the touchdown. Van Raaphorst kicks the extra point.
Chiefs	Mercer kicks a 25-yard field goal.
Chiefs	Garrett 4-yard run for the touchdown. Mercer kicks the extra point.

	Chargers	Chiefs
First Downs	19	22
Rushing Yards	131	294
Passing Yards	195	93
Punts-Average	4-44.0	2-41.0
Fumbles-Lost	1-0	1-1
Penalties-Yards	2-28	2-42

Chargers' Leaders
Rushing	Lowe 16-78, Foster 3-12, Hadl 3-(-2), Allison 2-11, Redman 1-32
Passing	Hadl 17-36-2-239
Receiving	Alworth 8-156, Garrison 5-50, Foster 2-16, Allison 1-9
Interceptions	Tolbert 1-0

Chiefs' Leaders
Rushing	Garrett 25-161, McClinton 10-53, Coan 5-30, Dawson 3-50
Passing	Dawson 9-15-1-121
Receiving	Taylor 3-90, Burford 2-21, Arbanas 1-10, Coan 1-5, McClinton 1-1
Interceptions	Hunt 1-30, Mitchell 1-6

Week 16 Games
Kansas City 27, San Diego 17
New York 38, Boston 28
Houston 38, Miami 29
Buffalo 38, Denver 21
Oakland - Bye

Week 16 Standings
East	W	L	T	West	W	L	T
Buffalo	9	4	1	Kansas City	11	2	1
Boston	8	4	2	Oakland	8	5	1
New York	6	6	2	San Diego	7	6	1
Houston	4	10	0	Denver	4	10	0
Miami	2	12	0				

1967 CHARGERS TEAM STATISTICS
(8-5-1 OVERALL) THIRD PLACE IN THE AFL WEST

Team Statistics	Chargers	Opponent
TOTAL FIRST DOWNS	259	251
Rushing	88	88
Passing	150	148
Penalty	21	15
TOTAL NET YARDS	5,125	4,705
Avg. Per Game	366.1	336.1
Avg. Per Play	5.8	5.0
NET YARDS RUSHING	1,715	1,553
Avg. Per Game	122.5	110.9
NET YARDS PASSING	3,410	3,152
Avg. Per Game	243.6	225.1
Gross Yards	3,517	3,455
Completions/Attempts	230/463	230/464
Completion Pct.	.497	.496
Had Intercepted	24	13
PUNTS/AVERAGE	63/37.5	75/45.2
PENALTIES/YARDS	72/817	61/666
FUMBLES/BALL LOST	18/10	22/10
TOUCHDOWNS	45	44
Rushing	14	17
Passing	26	26
Returns	5	1
QUARTERBACK SACKS	31.0	11.0

Rushing	No.	Yds.	Avg.	TD
Post	161	663	4.1	6
Hubbert	116	643	5.5	2
Smith	22	115	5.2	1
Hadl	37	107	2.9	3
Foster	28	78	2.1	0
Lowe	28	71	2.5	1
Allison	10	34	3.4	0
Stephenson	2	11	5.5	0
Alworth	1	5	5.0	0
Garrison	1	1	1.0	0
Redman	1	-13	-13.0	0
Totals	**417**	**1,715**	**4.1**	**14**

Receiving	No.	Yds.	Avg.	TD
Frazier	57	922	16.2	10
Alworth	52	1,010	19.4	9
Garrison	44	772	17.5	2
Post	32	278	8.7	1
Hubbert	19	214	11.3	2
Foster	9	46	5.1	0
MacKinnon	7	176	25.1	2
Newell	7	68	9.7	0
Lowe	2	25	12.5	0
Smith	1	6	6.0	0
Totals	**230**	**3,517**	**15.3**	**26**

Passing	Att.	Comp.	Yds.	Comp. %	TD	Int.
Hadl	427	217	3,365	.508	24	22
Stephenson	26	11	117	.423	2	2
Post	6	1	9	.167	0	0
Alworth	1	0	0	.000	0	0
Foster	1	0	0	.000	0	0
Lowe	1	1	26	100.0	0	0
Whitehead	1	0	0	.000	0	0
Totals	**463**	**230**	**3,517**	**.497**	**26**	**24**

Interceptions	No.	Yds.	TD
Beauchamp	3	44	0
Duncan	2	100	1
Graham	2	76	1
Redman	2	26	0
Allen	2	2	0
Erickson	1	17	0
Tolbert	1	9	0
Totals	**13**	**274**	**2**

Kicking	FG	Att.	PAT	Att.	Pts.
Van Raaphorst	15	30	45	45	90

Punting	No.	Avg.
Redman	58	37.0
Cordill	3	48.3
Hadl	2	35.0

Punt Returns	No.	FC	Yds.	Avg.	TD
Duncan	36	6	434	12.1	0
Graham	3	4	46	15.3	0
Smith	0	2	0	-	0

Kickoff Returns	No.	Yds.	Avg.	TD
Tolbert	18	441	24.5	0
Post	15	371	24.7	0
Duncan	9	231	25.7	0
Lowe	8	145	18.1	0
Smith	3	51	17.0	0
Erickson	1	0	0.0	0

Above: *The Chargers hired Bum Phillips (towards back, running projector) as their defensive line coach in 1967.*

Left: *Gary Garrison and other players gave tours of the new San Diego Stadium during construction.*

Ron Mix (74) and Gene Foster (37)

					Total
Chargers	7	7	0	14	28
Patriots	7	7	0	0	14

Chargers	Lowe 7-yard run for the touchdown. Van Raaphorst kicks the extra point.
Patriots	Parilli 30-yard pass to Whalen for the touchdown. Cappalletti kicks the extra point.
Patriots	Parilli 3-yard pass to Graham for the touchdown. Cappalletti kicks the extra point.
Chargers	Hadl 23-yard pass to Frazier for the touchdown. Van Raaphorst kicks the extra point.
Chargers	Hadl 11-yard pass to Frazier for the touchdown. Van Raaphorst kicks the extra point.
Chargers	Graham intercepts Parilli pass, returns it 68 yards for the touchdown. Van Raaphorst kicks the extra point.

	Chargers	Patriots
First Downs	14	17
Rushing Yards	62	106
Passing Yards	268	194
Punts-Average	5-30.6	6-38.5
Fumbles-Lost	1-1	2-2
Penalties-Yards	3-45	3-35

Chargers' Leaders

Rushing	Lowe 9-27, Foster 7-3, Allison 7-0, Hadl 4-28, Hubbert 1-4
Passing	Hadl 15-29-1-242, Lowe 1-1-0-26
Receiving	Frazier 5-105, Foster 4-29, Alworth 3-36, Lowe 2-25, MacKinnon 2-71
Interceptions	Redman 1-3, Graham 1-68

Patriots' Leaders

Rushing	Nance 18-61, Garron 11-42, Bellino 4-18, Huarte 2-5, Parilli 1-2
Passing	Parilli 17-32-2-187, Huarte 2-3-0-21
Receiving	Graham 9-116, Whalen 4-56, Garron 3-18, Nance 2-10, Cappalletti 1-8
Interceptions	Hall 1-4

Week 1 Games
Denver 26, Boston 21
Buffalo and Houston – Bye
Miami and New York – Bye
San Diego and Oakland - Bye
Kansas City - Bye

Week 1 Standings

East	W	L	T	West	W	L	T
Boston	0	1	0	Denver	1	0	0
Buffalo	0	0	0	San Diego	0	0	0
Houston	0	0	0	Oakland	0	0	0
Miami	0	0	0	Kansas City	0	0	0
New York	0	0	0				

Week 2 Games
San Diego 28, Boston 14
Oakland 51, Denver 0
Kansas City 25, Houston 20
Buffalo 20, New York 17
Miami - Bye

Week 2 Standings

East	W	L	T	West	W	L	T
Buffalo	1	0	0	San Diego	1	0	0
Houston	0	1	0	Oakland	1	0	0
New York	0	1	0	Kansas City	1	0	0
Boston	0	2	0	Denver	1	1	0
Miami	0	0	0				

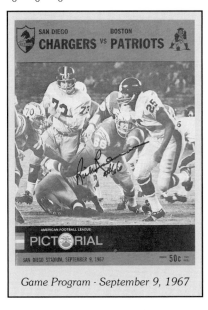

Game Program - September 9, 1967

Week 3 Games

San Diego, Kansas City and New York - Bye
Houston 20, Buffalo 3
Oakland 35, Boston 7
Miami 35, Denver 21

Week 3 Standings

East	W	L	T	West	W	L	T
Miami	1	0	0	Oakland	2	0	0
Buffalo	1	1	0	San Diego	1	0	0
Houston	1	1	0	Kansas City	1	0	0
New York	0	1	0	Denver	1	2	0
Boston	0	3	0				

San Diego Stadium, April 27, 1967

Scott Appleton pass rushes his former team, the Houston Oilers.

SEPTEMBER 24, 1967
San Diego Stadium – San Diego California
Attendance – 36,032

					Total
Chargers	3	3	0	7	13
Oilers	0	3	0	0	3

Chargers	Van Raaphorst kicks a 14-yard field goal.
Oilers	Wittenborn kicks a 31-yard field goal.
Chargers	Van Raaphorst kicks a 42-yard field goal.
Chargers	Hadl 44-yard pass to Alworth for the touchdown. Van Raaphorst kicks the extra point.

	Chargers	Oilers
First Downs	17	13
Rushing Yards	119	76
Passing Yards	206	90
Punts-Average	6-36.0	6-40.6
Fumbles-Lost	1-0	2-2
Penalties-Yards	4-56	1-15

Chargers' Leaders

Rushing Post 17-65, Foster 8-20, Allison 3-34, Hadl 2-9, Lowe 1-(-1)
Passing Hadl 20-39-1-213, Whitehead 0-1-0-0
Receiving Alworth 10-121, Frazier 4-69, Post 3-17, Foster 2-2, Garrison 1-4
Interceptions None

Oilers' Leaders

Rushing Blanks 13-35, Granger 10-25, Campbell 5-15, Trull 2-2, Burrell 1-2
Passing Lee 8-20-0-77, Trull 4-10-0-38
Receiving Granger 4-22, Frazier 3-31, Elkins 2-25, Poole 1-18, Burrell 1-14
Interceptions Jancik 1-0

Week 4 Games

San Diego 13, Houston 3
Boston 23, Buffalo 0
New York 38, Denver 24
Kansas City 24, Miami 0
Oakland - Bye

Week 4 Standings

East	W	L	T	West	W	L	T
Miami	1	1	0	Oakland	2	0	0
New York	1	1	0	San Diego	2	0	0
Buffalo	1	2	0	Kansas City	2	0	0
Houston	1	2	0	Denver	1	3	0
Boston	1	3	0				

OCTOBER 1, 1967
War Memorial Stadium – Buffalo, New York
Attendance – 39,310

					Total
Chargers	7	14	13	3	37
Bills	3	0	7	7	17

Bills	Mercer kicks a 26-yard field goal.
Chargers	Hadl 21-yard pass to Frazier for the touchdown. Van Raaphorst kicks the extra point.
Chargers	Hadl 3-yard pass to MacKinnon for the touchdown. Van Raaphorst kicks the extra point.
Chargers	Van Raaphorst kicks a 32-yard field goal.
Chargers	Van Raaphorst kicks a 30-yard field goal.
Chargers	Appleton recovers fumble and returns 2 yards for the touchdown.
Bills	Kemp 60-yard pass to Lincoln for the touchdown. Mercer kicks the extra point.
Chargers	Van Raaphorst kicks a 25-yard field goal.
Bills	Lincoln 18-yard run for the touchdown on a lateral from Kemp. Mercer kicks the extra point.

	Chargers	Bills
First Downs	26	12
Rushing Yards	202	54
Passing Yards	282	193
Punts-Average	1-38.0	5-45.4
Fumbles-Lost	0-0	1-1
Penalties-Yards	5-67	6-64

Chargers' Leaders
Rushing	Post 20-121, Hubbert 17-57, R. Smith 3-14, Hadl 3-10
Passing	Hadl 18-31-0-282, Alworth 0-1-0-0
Receiving	Frazier 5-106, Alworth 4-99, Garrison 4-50, Post 3-20, Hubbert 1-4
Interceptions	Erickson 1-17, Graham 1-8

Bills' Leaders
Rushing	Lincoln 8-34, Spikes 3-8, Kemp 2-12
Passing	Kemp 7-18-1-198, Flores 3-12-1-26, Rutkowski 0-1-0-0
Receiving	Powell 4-68, Lincoln 3-90, Dubenion 1-42, Masters 1-15, Spikes 1-9
Interceptions	None

Week 5 Games
San Diego 37, Buffalo 17
New York 29, Miami 7
Oakland 23, Kansas City 21
Houston 10, Denver 6
Boston - Bye

Week 5 Standings
East	W	L	T	West	W	L	T
New York	2	1	0	Oakland	3	0	0
Houston	2	2	0	San Diego	3	0	0
Miami	1	2	0	Kansas City	2	1	0
Buffalo	1	3	0	Denver	1	4	0
Boston	1	3	0				

Game Program - October 1, 1967

Game Program - October 8, 1967

OCTOBER 8, 1967
San Diego Stadium – San Diego, California
Attendance – 23,620

					Total
Chargers	7	10	0	14	31
Patriots	7	14	10	0	31

Chargers	Hadl 20-yard pass to Hubbert for the touchdown. Van Raaphorst kicks the extra point.
Patriots	Parilli 64-yard pass to Garron for the touchdown. Cappalletti kicks the extra point.
Chargers	Hadl 1-yard run for the touchdown. Van Raaphorst kicks the extra point.
Patriots	Nance 1-yard run for the touchdown. Cappalletti kicks the extra point.
Chargers	Van Raaphorst kicks a 32-yard field goal.
Patriots	Nance 18-yard run for the touchdown. Cappalletti kicks the extra point.
Patriots	Parilli 8-yard pass to Graham for the touchdown. Cappalletti kicks the extra point.
Patriots	Cappalletti kicks a 41-yard field goal.
Chargers	Hadl 4-yard pass to Frazier for the touchdown. Van Raaphorst kicks the extra point.
Chargers	Hadl 24-yard pass to Alworth for the touchdown. Van Raaphorst kicks the extra point.

	Chargers	Patriots
First Downs	17	21
Rushing Yards	61	123
Passing Yards	224	264
Punts-Average	6-38.2	4-37.5
Fumbles-Lost	1-1	2-0
Penalties-Yards	7-86	5-63

Chargers' Leaders
Rushing	Post 12-(-5), Hubbert 9-39, Hadl 4-20, Stephenson 1-7
Passing	Hadl 17-29-0-249, Stephenson 0-2-0-0
Receiving	Post 6-58, Alworth 4-62, Frazier 4-42, Hubbert 2-69, Garrison 1-18
Interceptions	Beauchamp 1-13

Patriots' Leaders
Rushing	Nance 29-127, Garron 3-0, Parilli 1-(-4)
Passing	Parilli 17-34-1-264
Receiving	Garron 5-96, Whalen 4-72, Graham 4-41, Cappalletti 3-33, Nance 1-22
Interceptions	None

Week 6 Games
San Diego 31, Boston 31
Buffalo 17, Denver 16
New York 27, Oakland 14
Kansas City 41, Miami 0
Houston - Bye

Week 6 Standings
East	W	L	T	West	W	L	T
New York	3	1	0	San Diego	3	0	1
Houston	2	2	0	Oakland	3	1	0
Buffalo	2	3	0	Kansas City	3	1	0
Miami	1	3	0	Denver	1	5	0
Boston	1	3	1				

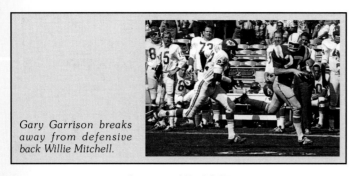

Gary Garrison breaks away from defensive back Willie Mitchell.

OCTOBER 15, 1967
San Diego Stadium – San Diego, California
Attendance – 45,355

					Total
Chargers	14	10	14	7	45
Chiefs	7	7	3	14	31

Chargers	Hadl 1-yard run for the touchdown. Van Raaphorst kicks the extra point.
Chargers	Duncan recovers fumble and returns 35 yards for the touchdown. Van Raaphorst kicks the extra point.
Chiefs	Taylor 24-yard run for the touchdown. Stenerud kicks the extra point.
Chargers	Van Raaphorst kicks a 15-yard field goal.
Chargers	Duncan intercepts Dawson pass, returns it 100 yards for the touchdown. Van Raaphorst kicks the extra point.
Chiefs	Garrett 1-yard run for the touchdown. Stenerud kicks the extra point.
Chargers	Post 67-yard run for the touchdown. Van Raaphorst kicks the extra point.
Chiefs	Stenerud kicks a 34-yard field goal.
Chargers	Hadl 60-yard pass to Alworth for the touchdown. Van Raaphorst kicks the extra point.
Chargers	Hadl 5-yard pass to Alworth for the touchdown. Van Raaphorst kicks the extra point.
Chiefs	Dawson 15-yard pass to Burford for the touchdown. Stenerud kicks the extra point.
Chiefs	Pitts 15-yard run for the touchdown. Stenerud kicks the extra point.

	Chargers	Chiefs
First Downs	24	20
Rushing Yards	145	121
Passing Yards	307	324
Punts-Average	2-39.0	4-47.0
Fumbles-Lost	3-1	1-1
Penalties-Yards	7-38	4-32

Chargers' Leaders
Rushing	Post 15-116, Hubbert 10-38, Foster 5-5, Hadl 3-(-7), Alworth 1-5
Passing	Hadl 17-32-1-307, Post 0-1-0-0
Receiving	Alworth 5-95, Garrison 4-108, Frazier 4-59, Post 4-45
Interceptions	Duncan 1-100, Beauchamp 1-28, Redman 1-23

Chiefs' Leaders
Rushing	Garrett 11-33, Dawson 4-16, McClinton 4-12, Coan 4-10, Pitts 2-25
Passing	Dawson 24-37-3-364
Receiving	Taylor 9-134, Garrett 4-15, Burford 3-58, Richardson 2-63, Coan 2-17
Interceptions	Hunt 1-39

Week 7 Games
San Diego 45, Kansas City 31
Oakland 24, Buffalo 20
Houston 28, New York 28
Boston 41, Miami 10
Denver - Bye

Week 7 Standings
East	W	L	T	West	W	L	T
New York	3	1	1	San Diego	4	0	1
Houston	2	2	1	Oakland	4	1	0
Boston	2	3	1	Kansas City	3	2	0
Buffalo	2	4	0	Denver	1	5	0
Miami	1	4	0				

OCTOBER 22, 1967
Bears Stadium – Denver, Colorado
Attendance – 34,465

					Total
Chargers	7	7	14	10	38
Broncos	7	0	7	7	21

Broncos	Wilson intercepts Hadl pass, returns it 40 yards for the touchdown. Humphreys kicks the extra point.
Chargers	Post 8-yard run for the touchdown. Van Raaphorst kicks the extra point.
Chargers	Post 2-yard run for the touchdown. Van Raaphorst kicks the extra point.
Broncos	Tensi 75-yard pass to Crabtree for the touchdown. Humphreys kicks the extra point.
Chargers	Hadl 66-yard pass to Post for the touchdown. Van Raaphorst kicks the extra point.
Chargers	Hadl 5-yard pass to Frazier for the touchdown. Van Raaphorst kicks the extra point.
Broncos	Tensi 10-yard pass to Denson for the touchdown. Humphreys kicks the extra point.
Chargers	Hadl 67-yard pass to Alworth for the touchdown. Van Raaphorst kicks the extra point.
Chargers	Van Raaphorst kicks a 30-yard field goal.

	Chargers	Broncos
First Downs	22	11
Rushing Yards	155	49
Passing Yards	335	206
Punts-Average	6-37.3	8-53.8
Fumbles-Lost	0-0	2-1
Penalties-Yards	3-33	2-20

Chargers' Leaders
Rushing	Post 15-70, Hubbert 9-36, Smith 5-35, Foster 3-29, Hadl 2-(-15)
Passing	Hadl 15-34-2-345, Post 0-1-0-0, Foster 0-1-0-0
Receiving	Alworth 5-142, Frazier 4-67, Garrison 3-66, Post 2-68, Hubbert 1-2
Interceptions	None

Broncos' Leaders
Rushing	Little 9-30, Mitchell 9-11, Tensi 3-6, Crabtree 2-2
Passing	Tensi 15-36-0-234
Receiving	Crabtree 6-123, Denson 3-55, Mitchell 2-28, White 2-23, Little 2-5
Interceptions	Wilson 1-40, Myrtle 1-1

Week 8 Games
San Diego 38, Denver 21
Oakland 48, Boston 14
Houston 24, Kansas City 19
New York 33, Miami 14
Buffalo - Bye

Week 8 Standings
East	W	L	T	West	W	L	T
New York	4	1	1	San Diego	5	0	1
Houston	3	2	1	Oakland	5	1	0
Buffalo	2	4	0	Kansas City	3	3	0
Boston	2	4	1	Denver	1	6	0
Miami	1	5	0				

Game Program - October 22, 1967

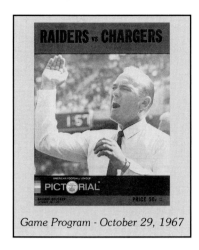

Game Program - October 29, 1967

OCTOBER 29, 1967

Oakland-Alameda County Coliseum – Oakland, California
Attendance – 53,474

					Total
Chargers	0	10	0	0	10
Raiders	9	7	14	20	51

Raiders	Post tackled in the end zone by Birdwell for a safety.
Raiders	Lamonica 40-yard pass to Daniels for the touchdown. Blanda kicks the extra point.
Chargers	Van Raaphorst kicks a 40-yard field goal.
Raiders	Lamonica 3-yard run for the touchdown. Blanda kicks the extra point.
Chargers	Hadl 71-yard pass to Alworth for the touchdown. Van Raaphorst kicks the extra point.
Raiders	Daniels 1-yard run for the touchdown. Blanda kicks the extra point.
Raiders	Lamonica 1-yard run for the touchdown. Blanda kicks the extra point.
Raiders	Lamonica 70-yard pass to Biletnikoff for the touchdown. Blanda kicks the extra point.
Raiders	Blanda 14-yard pass to Wells for the touchdown. Blanda kicks the extra point.
Raiders	Dixon 7-yard run for the touchdown. Blanda kicks the extra point.

	Chargers	Raiders
First Downs	16	18
Rushing Yards	54	127
Passing Yards	287	310
Punts-Average	8-42.1	6-51.0
Fumbles-Lost	1-0	0-0
Penalties-Yards	10-106	6-64

Chargers' Leaders

Rushing	Post 7-16, Lowe 6-29, Foster 5-(-1), 4-10
Passing	Hadl 19-39-3-318, Stephenson 0-6-1-0
Receiving	Alworth 10-213, Frazier 3-65, Post 3-5
Interceptions	Beauchamp 1-3, Tolbert 1-9

Raiders' Leaders

Rushing	Daniels 16-94, Dixon 12-24, Lamonica 3-4, Banks 1-3, Hagberg 1-2
Passing	Lamonica 13-30-1-316, Blanda 1-5-1-14
Receiving	Daniels 4-101, Dixon 4-65, Biletnikoff 2-81, Miller 2-48, Hagberg 1-21
Interceptions	Grayson 3-41, McCloughan 1-7

Week 9 Games

San Diego 10
Kansas City 52, Denver 9
New York 30, Boston 23
Houston 10, Buffalo 3
Miami - Bye

Week 9 Standings

East	W	L	T	West	W	L	T
New York	5	1	1	Oakland	6	1	0
Houston	4	2	1	San Diego	5	1	1
Buffalo	2	5	0	Kansas City	4	3	0
Boston	2	5	1	Denver	1	7	0
Miami	1	5	0				

Week 10 Games

San Diego – Bye
Buffalo 35, Miami 13
Boston 18, Houston 3
Kansas City 42, New York 18
Oakland 21, Denver 17

Week 10 Standings

East	W	L	T	West	W	L	T
New York	5	2	1	Oakland	7	1	0
Houston	4	3	1	San Diego	5	1	1
Buffalo	3	5	0	Kansas City	5	3	0
Boston	3	5	1	Denver	1	8	0
Miami	1	6	0				

Jacque MacKinnon (left) and Emil Karas (second from left) give a tour of San Diego Stadium during construction.

November 12, 1967
San Diego Stadium – San Diego, California
Attendance – 25,819

					Total
Chargers	7	0	0	17	**24**
Dolphins	0	0	0	0	**0**

Chargers	Hadl 9-yard pass to Frazier for the touchdown. Van Raaphorst kicks the extra point.
Chargers	Hadl 10-yard pass to Garrison for the touchdown. Van Raaphorst kicks the extra point.
Chargers	Van Raaphorst kicks a 42-yard field goal.
Chargers	Stephenson 13-yard pass to Alworth for the touchdown. Van Raaphorst kicks the extra point.

	Chargers	Dolphins
First Downs	17	13
Rushing Yards	103	121
Passing Yards	224	122
Punts-Average	4-37.5	8-45.1
Fumbles-Lost	0-0	4-1
Penalties-Yards	2-10	3-35

Chargers' Leaders

Rushing	Post 14-48, Lowe 5-13, Hubbert 4-19, Foster 4-1, Hadl 3-22
Passing	Hadl 14-27-4-211, Stephenson 1-1-0-13, Post 0-1-0-0
Receiving	Alworth 4-125, Garrison 3-31, Frazier 3-31, Post 3-17, Hubbert 2-20
Interceptions	None

Dolphins' Leaders

Rushing	Griese 6-36, Mitchell 6-16, Haynes 6-12, Harper 4-12, Price 3-11
Passing	Griese 13-39-0-186
Receiving	Clancy 5-71, Moreau 3-36, Noonan 2-16, Harper 1-34, Haynes 1-19
Interceptions	Neff 1-17, Erlandson 1-37, Warren 1-0, Bramlett 1-(-1)

Week 11 Games
San Diego 24, Miami 0
New York 20, Buffalo 10
Houston 20, Denver 18
Kansas City 33, Boston 10
Oakland - Bye

Week 11 Standings

East	W	L	T	West	W	L	T
New York	6	2	1	Oakland	7	1	0
Houston	5	3	1	San Diego	6	1	1
Buffalo	3	6	0	Kansas City	6	3	0
Boston	3	6	1	Denver	1	9	0
Miami	1	7	0				

Lance Alworth makes a reception against the Dolphins.

Jim Tolbert

November 19, 1967
Municipal Stadium – Kansas City, Missouri
Attendance – 46,738

					Total
Chargers	7	3	0	7	**17**
Chiefs	6	3	7	0	**16**

Chiefs	Stenerud kicks a 12-yard field goal.
Chiefs	Stenerud kicks a 48-yard field goal.
Chargers	Post 4-yard run for the touchdown. Van Raaphorst kicks the extra point.
Chargers	Van Raaphorst kicks a 12-yard field goal.
Chiefs	Stenerud kicks a 22-yard field goal.
Chiefs	Dawson 35-yard pass to Richardson for the touchdown. Stenerud kicks the extra point.
Chargers	Hadl 2-yard pass to Alworth for the touchdown. Van Raaphorst kicks the extra point.

	Chargers	Chiefs
First Downs	20	16
Rushing Yards	188	75
Passing Yards	139	222
Punts-Average	4-22.5	3-42.0
Fumbles-Lost	3-2	0-0
Penalties-Yards	6-70	4-32

Chargers' Leaders

Rushing	Post 18-108, Hubbert 8-84, Hadl 5-(-4)
Passing	Hadl 11-23-1-139
Receiving	Garrison 4-69, Frazier 4-44, Hubbert 2-24, Alworth 1-2
Interceptions	None

Chiefs' Leaders

Rushing	Garrett 26-83, McClinton 2-4, Dawson 2-(-12)
Passing	Dawson 18-31-0-232
Receiving	Richardson 4-79, Arbanas 4-69, Garrett 4-2, Taylor 3-50, Burford 2-27
Interceptions	E. Thomas 1-0

Week 12 Games
San Diego 17, Kansas City 16
Oakland 31, Miami 17
New York 29, Boston 24
Denver 21, Buffalo 20
Houston - Bye

Week 12 Standings

East	W	L	T	West	W	L	T
New York	7	2	1	Oakland	8	1	0
Houston	5	3	1	San Diego	7	1	1
Buffalo	3	7	0	Kansas City	6	4	0
Boston	3	7	1	Denver	2	9	0
Miami	1	8	0				

November 23, 1967
San Diego Stadium – San Diego, California
Attendance – 34,586

					Total
Chargers	0	7	3	14	24
Broncos	7	10	3	0	20

Broncos	Tensi 9-yard pass to Denon for the touchdown. Humphreys kicks the extra point.
Broncos	Tensi 5-yard pass to Crabtree for the touchdown. Humphreys kicks the extra point.
Chargers	Post 7-yard run for the touchdown. Van Raaphorst kicks the extra point.
Broncos	Humphreys kicks a 13-yard field goal.
Chargers	Van Raaphorst kicks a 24-yard field goal.
Broncos	Humphries kicks a 16-yard field goal.
Chargers	Humphreys kick blocked, recovered by Duncan and returned 72-yards for the touchdown. Van Raaphorst kicks the extra point.
Chargers	Post 8-yard run for the touchdown. Van Raaphorst kicks the extra point.

	Chargers	Broncos
First Downs	14	21
Rushing Yards	96	112
Passing Yards	204	246
Punts-Average	4-39.8	4-46.5
Fumbles-Lost	2-1	2-1
Penalties-Yards	5-70	4-40

Chargers' Leaders
Rushing	Post 21-72, Hubbert 6-14, Hadl 1-5
Passing	Hadl 13-26-1-202, Post 1-2-0-9
Receiving	Frazier 5-50, Garrison 4-119, Post 3-26, Hubbert 2-16
Interceptions	Allen 2-2

Broncos' Leaders
Rushing	Little 22-79, Hickey 8-24, Mitchell 4-13, Tensi 1-(-4)
Passing	Tensi 18-41-2-253
Receiving	Crabtree 8-107, Denson 7-97, Beer 2-46, Little 1-3
Interceptions	Lentz 1-0

Week 13 Games
San Diego 24, Denver 20
Miami 17, Buffalo 14
Oakland 44, Kansas City 22
Houston 27, Boston 6
New York - Bye

Week 13 Standings
East	W	L	T	West	W	L	T
New York	7	2	1	Oakland	9	1	0
Houston	6	3	1	San Diego	8	1	1
Buffalo	3	8	0	Kansas City	6	5	0
Boston	3	8	1	Denver	2	10	0
Miami	2	8	0				

Jeff Staggs unloads on Broncos' quarterback Steve Tensi.

George Gross (79) and Tom Day (88) bring down Daryle Lamonica.

December 3, 1967
San Diego Stadium – San Diego, California
Attendance – 52,661

					Total
Chargers	7	14	0	0	21
Raiders	17	14	7	3	41

Raiders	Lamonica 18-yard pass to Biletnikoff for the touchdown. Blanda kicks the extra point.
Chargers	Hadl 1-yard run for the touchdown. Van Raaphorst kicks the extra point.
Raiders	Lamonica 64-yard pass to Cannon for the touchdown. Blanda kicks the extra point.
Raiders	Blanda kicks a 24-yard field goal.
Chargers	Hadl 57-yard pass to Alworth for the touchdown. Van Raaphorst kicks the extra point.
Raiders	Lamonica 29-yard pass to Miller for the touchdown. Blanda kicks the extra point.
Raiders	Todd 2-yard run for the touchdown. Blanda kicks the extra point.
Chargers	Hadl 29-yard pass to Garrison for the touchdown. Van Raaphorst kicks the extra point.
Raiders	Lamonica 1-yard pass to Cannon for the touchdown. Blanda kicks the extra point.
Raiders	Blanda kicks a 21-yard field goal.

	Chargers	Raiders
First Downs	19	21
Rushing Yards	115	135
Passing Yards	303	325
Punts-Average	7-39.7	7-42.4
Fumbles-Lost	1-0	1-0
Penalties-Yards	5-75	7-100

Chargers' Leaders
Rushing	Hubbert 8-41, Post 7-15, Lowe 7-3, Hadl 5-40, Smith 1-16
Passing	Hadl 18-40-3-315
Receiving	Frazier 6-76, Alworth 4-86, Garrison 3-97, Hubbert 3-33, MacKinnon 1-14
Interceptions	None

Raiders' Leaders
Rushing	Todd 16-61, Dixon 8-41, Banaszak 8-26, Hagberg 2-7
Passing	Lamonica 21-34-0-349, Blanda 1-1-0-1
Receiving	Biletnikoff 6-69, Miller 5-96, Dixon 5-70, Cannon 3-92, Banaszak 3-22
Interceptions	Williams 2-55, Brown 1-0

Week 14 Games
Oakland 41, San Diego 21
Kansas City 23, Buffalo 13
Denver 33, New York 24
Houston 17, Miami 14
Boston - Bye

Week 14 Standings
East	W	L	T	West	W	L	T
New York	7	3	1	Oakland	10	1	0
Houston	7	3	1	San Diego	8	2	1
Boston	3	8	1	Kansas City	7	5	0
Buffalo	3	9	0	Denver	3	10	0
Miami	2	9	0				

Game Program - December 10, 1967

DECEMBER 10, 1967
The Orange Bowl – Miami, Florida
Attendance – 23,007

					Total
Chargers	3	7	14	0	24
Dolphins	0	13	14	14	41

Chargers	Van Raaphorst kicks a 23-yard field goal.
Dolphins	Harper kicks a 37-yard field goal.
Dolphins	Lusteg kicks a 14-yard field goal.
Chargers	Hadl 3-yard pass to Frazier for the touchdown. Van Raaphorst kicks the extra point.
Dolphins	Lusteg kicks a 19-yard field goal.
Chargers	Smith 14-yard run for the touchdown. Van Raaphorst kicks the extra point.
Dolphins	Griese 10-yard pass to Moreau for the touchdown. Lusteg kicks the extra point.
Dolphins	Griese 1-yard run for the touchdown. Lusteg kicks the extra point.
Chargers	Hadl 38-yard pass to Frazier for the touchdown. Van Raaphorst kicks the extra point.
Dolphins	Griese 10-yard pass to Twilley for the touchdown. Lusteg kicks the extra point.
Dolphins	Mitchell 1-yard run for the touchdown. Lusteg kicks the extra point.

	Chargers	Dolphins
First Downs	15	24
Rushing Yards	87	161
Passing Yards	182	164
Punts-Average	2-28.0	3-47.3
Fumbles-Lost	1-1	2-1
Penalties-Yards	5-60	6-50

Chargers' Leaders
Rushing Smith 13-50, Hubbert 12-47, Hadl 4-(-10)
Passing Hadl 9-21-4-166, Stephenson 1-2-1-16
Receiving Frazier 4-72, MacKinnon 3-80, Garrison 1-16, Hubbert 1-8, Smith 1-6
Interceptions None

Dolphins' Leaders
Rushing Mitchell 15-43, Harper 9-71, Griese 6-34, Auer 5-15, Moreau 1-(-2)
Passing Griese 15-28-0-145, Seiple 1-1-0-19, Lusteg 0-1-0-0
Receiving Clancy 8-96, Moreau 2-27, Mitchell 2-12, Beier 1-19, Twilley 1-10
Interceptions Bramlett 2-32, Bruggers 1-20, Westmoreland 1-14, Warren 1-0

Week 15 Games
Miami 41, San Diego 24
Buffalo 44, Boston 16
Oakland 19, Houston 7
Kansas City 21, New York 7
Denver - Bye

Week 15 Standings

East	W	L	T	West	W	L	T
New York	7	4	1	Oakland	11	1	0
Houston	7	4	1	San Diego	8	3	1
Buffalo	4	9	0	Kansas City	8	5	0
Boston	3	9	1	Denver	3	10	0
Miami	3	9	0				

DECEMBER 16, 1967
Rice Stadium – Houston, Texas
Attendance – 19,870

					Total
Chargers	0	7	0	10	17
Oilers	3	7	7	7	24

Oilers	Wittenborn kicks a 31-yard field goal.
Chargers	Hadl 3-yard pass to Hubbert for the touchdown. Van Raaphorst kicks the extra point.
Oilers	Granger 1-yard run for the touchdown. Wittenborn kicks the extra point.
Oilers	Beathard 8-yard pass to Campbell for the touchdown. Wittenborn kicks the extra point.
Chargers	Van Raaphorst kicks an 18-yard field goal.
Oilers	Beathard 15-yard pass to Reed for the touchdown. Wittenborn kicks the extra point.
Chargers	Hadl 16-yard pass to Frazier for the touchdown. Van Raaphorst kicks the extra point.

	Chargers	Oilers
First Downs	19	21
Rushing Yards	98	158
Passing Yards	198	176
Punts-Average	5-36.8	3-43.6
Fumbles-Lost	0-0	0-0
Penalties-Yards	6-53	3-56

Chargers' Leaders
Rushing Hubbert 13-65, Post 10-24, Hadl 1-9
Passing Hadl 23-40-0-198, Post 0-1-0-0
Receiving Newell 6-54, Frazier 5-64, Garrison 5-55, Post 4-13, Hubbert 3-12
Interceptions Duncan 1-0

Oilers' Leaders
Rushing Granger 27-107, Campbell 7-18, Beathard 5-22, Blank 3-11
Passing Beathard 14-24-1-188
Receiving Burrell 5-97, Campbell 4-38, Taylor 3-45, Reed 1-15, Granger 1-(-7)
Interceptions None

Week 16 Games
Houston 24, San Diego 17
Kansas City 38, Denver 24
Oakland 38, New York 29
Miami 41, Boston 32
Buffalo - Bye

Week 16 Standings

East	W	L	T	West	W	L	T
Houston	8	4	1	Oakland	12	1	0
New York	7	5	1	Kansas City	9	5	0
Buffalo	4	9	0	San Diego	8	4	1
Miami	4	9	0	Denver	3	11	0
Boston	3	10	1				

Willie Frazier streaks for the goal line.

San Diego Stadium – San Diego, California
Attendance – 34,580

					Total
Chargers	7	17	0	7	31
Jets	14	14	14	0	42

Chargers	Hadl 72-yard pass to Frazier for the touchdown. Van Raaphorst kicks the extra point.
Jets	Namath 13-yard pass to Maynard for the touchdown. J. Turner kicks the extra point.
Jets	Mathis 1-yard run for the touchdown. J. Turner kicks the extra point.
Chargers	Hubbert 46-yard run for the touchdown. Van Raaphorst kicks the extra point.
Jets	Namath 36-yard pass to Sauer for the touchdown. J. Turner kicks the extra point.
Chargers	Van Raaphorst kicks a 13-yard field goal.
Jets	Namath 36-yard pass to Maynard for the touchdown. J. Turner kicks the extra point.
Jets	Mathis 1-yard run for the touchdown. J. Turner kicks the extra point.
Jets	Namath 37-yard pass to Maynard for the touchdown. J. Turner kicks the extra point.
Chargers	Stephenson 8-yard pass to MacKinnon for the touchdown. Van Raaphorst kicks the extra point.

	Chargers	Jets
First Downs	19	23
Rushing Yards	230	113
Passing Yards	246	316
Punts-Average	3-48.5	5-46.6
Fumbles-Lost	2-2	0-0
Penalties-Yards	4-48	7-60

Chargers' Leaders

Rushing	Hubbert 15-189, Foster 6-21, Post 5-16, Stephenson 1-4
Passing	Hadl 8-17-1-173, Stephenson 9-15-0-88
Receiving	Garrison 8-115, Foster 3-15, Alworth 2-29, Frazier 1-72, Newell 1-14
Interceptions	None

Jets' Leaders

Rushing	Mathis 10-29, Joe 9-19, Haynes 8-34, Smolinski 7-17, Snell 5-9
Passing	Namath 18-26-0-343
Receiving	Maynard 8-141, Sauer 6-118, Mathis 1-33, Snell 1-21, Joe 1-17
Interceptions	Baird 1-3

Week 17 Games
New York 42, San Diego 31
Houston 41, Miami 10
Oakland 28, Buffalo 21
Kansas City, Denver and Boston - Bye

Week 17 Standings

East	W	L	T	West	W	L	T
Houston	9	4	1	Oakland	13	1	0
New York	8	5	1	Kansas City	9	5	0
Buffalo	4	10	0	San Diego	8	5	1
Miami	4	10	0	Denver	3	11	0
Boston	3	10	1				

Paul Lowe and Lance Alworth ask for an AFL championship for Christmas. But Santa didn't deliver.

1968 CHARGERS TEAM STATISTICS
(9-5 OVERALL) THIRD PLACE IN THE AFL WEST

Team Statistics	Chargers	Opponent
TOTAL FIRST DOWNS	270	225
Rushing	93	90
Passing	164	118
Penalty	13	17
TOTAL NET YARDS	5,388	4,333
Avg. Per Game	384.9	309.5
Avg. Per Play	5.9	4.9
NET YARDS RUSHING	1,765	1,641
Avg. Per Game	126.1	117.2
NET YARDS PASSING	3,623	2,692
Avg. Per Game	258.8	192.3
Gross Yards	3,813	2,896
Completions/Attempts	225/472	217/430
Completion Pct.	.477	.505
Had Intercepted	33	20
PUNTS/AVERAGE	56/40.7	74/42.3
PENALTIES/YARDS	72/654	63/692
FUMBLES/BALL LOST	20/12	26/15
TOUCHDOWNS	45	36
Rushing	12	13
Passing	29	20
Returns	4	3
QUARTERBACK SACKS	24.0	18.0

Rushing	No.	Yds.	Avg.	TD
Post	151	758	5.0	3
Smith	88	426	4.8	4
Foster	109	394	3.6	1
Hubbert	28	119	4.3	2
Allison	23	31	1.3	0
Alworth	3	18	6.0	0
Hadl	23	14	0.6	2
Lowe	1	9	9.0	0
Brittenum	2	-4	-2.0	0
Totals	**428**	**1,765**	**4.1**	**12**

Receiving	No.	Yds.	Avg.	TD
Alworth	68	1,312	19.3	10
Garrison	52	1,103	21.2	10
MacKinnon	33	646	19.6	6
Foster	23	224	9.7	0
Post	18	165	9.2	0
Frazier	16	237	14.8	3
Smith	7	71	10.1	0
Hubbert	5	11	2.2	0
Allison	2	22	11.0	0
Dyer	1	22	22.0	0
Totals	**225**	**3,813**	**16.9**	**29**

Passing	Att.	Comp.	Yds.	Comp. %	TD	Int.
Hadl	440	208	3,473	.473	27	32
Brittenum	17	9	125	.529	1	1
Foster	7	6	169	.857	0	0
Post	4	1	23	.250	0	0
Smith	3	0	0	.000	0	0
Allison	1	1	23	100.0	1	0
Totals	**472**	**225**	**3,813**	**.477**	**29**	**33**

Interceptions	No.	Yds.	TD
Beauchamp	5	114	2
Graham	5	87	0
Tolbert	2	42	0
Erlandson	2	22	0
Staggs	2	2	0
Allen	1	4	0
Duncan	1	4	0
Fetherston	1	0	0
Howard	1	0	0
Totals	**20**	**275**	**2**

Kicking	FG	Att.	PAT	Att.	Pts.
Partee	22	32	40	43	106

Punting	No.	Avg.
Partee	56	40.7

Punt Returns	No.	FC	Yds.	Avg.	TD
Duncan	18	5	206	11.4	1
Graham	13	10	61	4.7	0
Smith	8	3	25	3.1	0
Allison	0	1	0	0.0	0

Kickoff Returns	No.	Yds.	Avg.	TD
Duncan	25	586	23.4	0
Post	10	199	19.9	0
Allison	7	121	17.3	0
Baccaglio	2	0	0.0	0
Lincoln	2	37	18.5	0
Whitehead	2	81	40.5	0
Latzke	1	0	0.0	0
Smith	1	20	20.0	0
Speights	1	21	21.0	0

Above: *Halftime at San Diego Stadium.*

Left: *Walt Sweeney (78), Joe Madro and Ron Mix (74)*

SEPTEMBER 6, 1968
San Diego Stadium – San Diego, California
Attendance – 33,687

					Total
Chargers	10	0	13	6	29
Bengals	7	3	3	0	13

Bengals	Robinson 2-yard run for the touchdown. Livingston kicks the extra point.
Chargers	Partee kicks a 42-yard field goal.
Chargers	Post 48-yard run for the touchdown. Partee kicks the extra point.
Bengals	Livingston kicks a 22-yard field goal.
Chargers	Hubbert 1-yard run for the touchdown. Partee kicks the extra point.
Bengals	Livingston kicks a 35-yard field goal.
Chargers	Hadl 48-yard pass to Frazier for the touchdown.
Chargers	Hadl 6-yard pass to Frazier for the touchdown.

	Chargers	Bengals
First Downs	27	13
Rushing Yards	229	122
Passing Yards	325	104
Punts-Average	2-58.5	7-44.3
Fumbles-Lost	2-2	1-1
Penalties-Yards	9-100	6-56

Chargers' Leaders
Rushing	Post 16-140, Hubbert 11-54, Smith 2-20, Alworth 1-10, Lowe 1-9
Passing	Hadl 20-37-0-325
Receiving	Garrison 5-101, MacKinnon 4-87, Alworth 4-58, Frazier 3-66, Hubbert 3-17
Interceptions	Erlandson 1-6

Bengals' Leaders
Rushing	Robinson 16-33, Smiley 9-26, Johnson 2-16, McVea 1-28, Warren 1-12
Passing	Warren 14-26-1-125
Receiving	Smiley 6-51, McVea 4-32, Saffold 2-24, White 2-18
Interceptions	None

Week 1 Games
San Diego 29, Cincinnati 13
Kansas City 26, Houston 21
Boston 16, Buffalo 7
Miami and Oakland – Bye
New York and Denver - Bye

Week 1 Standings
East	W	L	T	West	W	L	T
Boston	1	0	0	San Diego	1	0	0
Buffalo	0	1	0	Kansas City	1	0	0
Houston	0	1	0	Cincinnati	0	1	0
New York	0	0	0	Oakland	0	0	0
Miami	0	0	0	Denver	0	0	0

Game Program - September 6, 1968

Clowning around with mascot, Charlie Charger.

Week 2 Games
San Diego and Boston - Bye
Cincinnati 24, Denver 10
Oakland 48, Buffalo 6
Houston 24, Miami 10
New York 20, Kansas City 19

Week 2 Standings
East	W	L	T	West	W	L	T
Boston	1	0	0	Oakland	1	0	0
New York	1	0	0	San Diego	1	0	0
Houston	1	1	0	Kansas City	1	1	0
Miami	0	1	0	Cincinnati	1	1	0
Buffalo	0	2	0	Denver	0	1	0

The new scoreboard at San Diego Stadium.

SEPTEMBER 21, 1968
San Diego Stadium – San Diego, California
Attendance – 46,217

					Total
Chargers	3	6	0	21	30
Oilers	0	7	7	0	14

Chargers	Partee kicks a 35-yard field goal.
Chargers	Partee kicks a 23-yard field goal.
Houston	Campbell 9-yard run for the touchdown. Wittenborn kicks the extra point.
Chargers	Partee kicks a 48-yard field goal.
Oilers	Granger 1-yard run for the touchdown. Wittenborn kicks the extra point.
Chargers	Hubbert 3-yard run for the touchdown. Partee kicks the extra point.
Chargers	Hadl 80-yard pass to Hadl for the touchdown. Partee kicks the extra point.
Chargers	Beauchamp intercepts Beathard pass, returns it 24 yards for the touchdown. Partee kicks the extra point.

	Chargers	Oilers
First Downs	20	19
Rushing Yards	97	124
Passing Yards	250	161
Punts-Average	2-53.5	5-40.5
Fumbles-Lost	2-1	0-0
Penalties-Yards	2-9	6-81

Chargers' Leaders
Rushing Hubbert 17-65, Post 5-7, Hadl 3-1, Smith 2-16, Foster 1-5
Passing Hadl 17-28-2-265, Post 0-1-0-0
Receiving Alworth 8-183, MacKinnon 3-32, Smith 2-30, Garrison 2-26, Hubbert 2-(-6)
Interceptions Duncan 1-4, Beauchamp 1-24, Tolbert 1-0

Oilers' Leaders
Rushing Blanks 12-39, Granger 12-31, Campbell 5-16, Beathard 3-25, Hopkins 1-13
Passing Beathard 17-28-2-170, Davis 1-2-1-6
Receiving Haik 7-80, Blanks 3-25, Granger 3-19, Frazier 2-32, Taylor 1-16
Interceptions Boyette 1-0, Houston 1-16

Week 3 Games
San Diego 30, Houston 14
Kansas City 34, Denver 2
Oakland 47, Miami 21
New York 47, Boston 31
Cincinnati 34, Buffalo 23

Week 3 Standings

East	W	L	T	West	W	L	T
New York	2	0	0	Oakland	2	0	0
Boston	1	1	0	San Diego	2	0	0
Houston	1	2	0	Kansas City	2	1	0
Miami	0	2	0	Cincinnati	2	1	0
Buffalo	0	3	0	Denver	0	2	0

SEPTEMBER 29, 1968
Nippert Stadium – Cincinnati, Ohio
Attendance – 28,642

					Total
Chargers	0	17	0	14	31
Bengals	3	0	7	0	10

Bengals	Livingston kicks a 21-yard field goal.
Chargers	Hadl 10-yard pass to Garrison for the touchdown. Partee kicks the extra point.
Chargers	Partee kicks a 21-yard field goal.
Chargers	Hadl 19-yard pass to Garrison for the touchdown. Partee kicks the extra point.
Bengals	Johnson 6-yard run for the touchdown. Livingston kicks the extra point.
Chargers	Hadl 2-yard run for the touchdown. Partee kicks the extra point.
Chargers	Hadl 2-yard run for the touchdown. Partee kicks the extra point.

	Chargers	Bengals
First Downs	18	14
Rushing Yards	101	66
Passing Yards	201	129
Punts-Average	3-51.0	5-40.0
Fumbles-Lost	0-0	2-0
Penalties-Yards	6-51	8-90

Chargers' Leaders
Rushing Foster 16-31, Post 14-61, Smith 4-16, Hadl 3-(-7)
Passing Hadl 9-22-1-132, Foster 2-2-0-83
Receiving Garrison 5-121, Foster 3-34, Frazier 1-33, Post 1-16, Alworth 1-11
Interceptions Graham 1-10, Howard 1-0

Bengals' Leaders
Rushing Robinson 12-26, Smiley 6-4, Banks 5-24, Johnson 1-6, Warren 1-6
Passing Stofa 12-21-1-100, Warren 5-8-1-53
Receiving Sherman 8-86, Herock 2-29, Trumpy 2-24, Robinson 2-(-7), Peterson 1-10
Interceptions Headrick 1-0

Week 4 Games
San Diego 31, Cincinnati 10
Buffalo 37, New York 35
Kansas City 48, Miami 3
Oakland 24, Houston 15
Boston 20, Denver 17

Week 4 Standings

East	W	L	T	West	W	L	T
New York	2	1	0	Oakland	3	0	0
Boston	2	1	0	San Diego	3	0	0
Houston	1	3	0	Kansas City	3	1	0
Buffalo	1	3	0	Cincinnati	2	2	0
Miami	0	3	0	Denver	0	3	0

John Hadl (21) and Lance Alworth (19)

Game Program - October 5, 1968

OCTOBER 5, 1968
Shea Stadium – New York City, New York
Attendance – 63,786

					Total
Chargers	0	7	6	7	20
Jets	3	6	7	7	23

Jets	J. Turner kicks a 26-yard field goal.
Chargers	Hadl 7-yard pass to Alworth for the touchdown. Partee kicks the extra point.
Jets	J. Turner kicks a 45-yard field goal.
Jets	J. Turner kicks an 11-yard field goal.
Jets	Snell 1-yard run for the touchdown. J. Turner kicks the extra point.
Chargers	Hadl 84-yard pass to Garrison for the touchdown.
Chargers	Hadl 5-yard pass to Garrison for the touchdown. Partee kicks the extra point.
Jets	Boozer 1-yard run for the touchdown. J. Turner kicks the extra point.

	Chargers	Jets
First Downs	15	19
Rushing Yards	28	82
Passing Yards	319	220
Punts-Average	6-37.5	6-47.8
Fumbles-Lost	3-1	2-0
Penalties-Yards	10-92	7-100

Chargers' Leaders
Rushing	Post 8-7, Foster 7-25, Smith 2-2, Hadl 2-(-11), Alworth 1-5
Passing	Hadl 17-37-3-326
Receiving	Alworth 8-137, Garrison 6-163, Foster 2-4, Dyer 1-22
Interceptions	None

Jets' Leaders
Rushing	Boozer 24-35, Snell 16-47
Passing	Namath 16-34-0-220
Receiving	Maynard 4-59, Sauer 4-58, Johnson 3-47, Smolinski 3-44, Boozer 1-7
Interceptions	Beverly 1-22, Gondon 1-0, Sample 1-39

Week 5 Games
New York 23, San Diego 20
Kansas City 18, Buffalo 7
Miami 24, Houston 7
Denver 10, Cincinnati 7
Oakland 41, Boston 10

Week 5 Standings
East	W	L	T	West	W	L	T
New York	3	1	0	Oakland	4	0	0
Boston	2	2	0	Kansas City	4	1	0
Miami	1	3	0	San Diego	3	1	0
Buffalo	1	4	0	Cincinnati	2	3	0
Houston	1	4	0	Denver	1	3	0

OCTOBER 13, 1968
Oakland-Alameda County Coliseum – Oakland, California
Attendance – 53,257

					Total
Chargers	10	7	3	3	23
Raiders	0	14	0	0	14

Chargers	Partee kicks a 24-yard field goal.
Chargers	Foster 1-yard run for the touchdown. Partee kicks the extra point.
Raiders	Partee punts to Atkinson, returned 82 yards for the touchdown. Balnda kicks the extra point.
Chargers	Hadl 38-yard pass to Alworth for the touchdown. Partee kicks the extra point.
Raiders	Lamonica 7-yard pass to Wells for the touchdown. Blanda kicks the extra point.
Chargers	Partee kicks a 27-yard field goal.
Chargers	Partee kicks a 27-yard field goal.

	Chargers	Raiders
First Downs	20	11
Rushing Yards	170	45
Passing Yards	214	215
Punts-Average	6-38.8	8-45.0
Fumbles-Lost	0-0	3-0
Penalties-Yards	4-40	2-20

Chargers' Leaders
Rushing	Foster 27-104, Smith 14-53, Post 8-13
Passing	Hadl 14-32-1-220, Foster 1-1-0-17, Smith 0-1-0-0
Receiving	Alworth 9-182, MacKinnon 3-16, Garrison 2-22, Foster 1-(-3)
Interceptions	Beauchamp 1-22, Graham 1-42

Raiders' Leaders
Rushing	Dixon 10-21, Banaszak 7-19, Lamonica 2-5
Passing	Lamonica 13-32-2-229
Receiving	Dixon 5-44, Miller 2-49, Wells 2-22, Biletnikoff 1-58, Kocourek 1-18
Interceptions	Bird 1-17

Week 6 Games
San Diego 23, Oakland 14
Denver 21, New York 13
Houston 16, Boston 0
Kansas City 13, Cincinnati 3
Miami 14, Buffalo 14

Week 6 Standings
East	W	L	T	West	W	L	T
New York	3	2	0	Kansas City	5	1	0
Boston	2	3	0	Oakland	4	1	0
Houston	2	4	0	San Diego	4	1	0
Miami	1	3	1	Denver	2	3	0
Buffalo	1	4	1	Cincinnati	2	4	0

Rick Redman

OCTOBER 20, 1968
San Diego Stadium – San Diego, California
Attendance – 42,953

					Total
Chargers	3	28	10	14	55
Broncos	3	7	7	7	24

Chargers	Partee kicks an 18-yard field goal.
Broncos	Howfield kicks a 15-yard field goal.
Chargers	Hadl 74-yard pass to Alworth for the touchdown. Partee kicks the extra point.
Chargers	Hadl 21-yard pass to Garrison for the touchdown. Partee kicks the extra point.
Chargers	Beauchamp intercepts Tensi pass, returns it 35 yards for the touchdown. Partee kicks the extra point.
Chargers	Hadl 50-yard pass to MacKinnon for the touchdown. Partee kicks the extra point.
Broncos	Briscoe 60-yard pass to Jones for the touchdown. Howfield kicks the extra point.
Chargers	Hadl 55-yard pass to Garrison for the touchdown. Partee kicks the extra point.
Broncos	Briscoe 28-yard pass to Van Heusen for the touchdown. Howfield kicks the extra point.
Chargers	Partee kicks a 27-yard field goal.
Chargers	Post 62-yard run for the touchdown. Partee kicks the extra point.
Chargers	Brittenum 17-yard pass to MacKinnon for the touchdown. Partee kicks the extra point.
Broncos	Briscoe 6-yard pass to Jones for the touchdown. Howfield kicks the extra point.

	Chargers	**Broncos**
First Downs	20	26
Rushing Yards	211	181
Passing Yards	370	295
Punts-Average	3-49.7	5-39.8
Fumbles-Lost	1-0	3-2
Penalties-Yards	4-50	5-34

Chargers' Leaders
Rushing	Post 11-121, Foster 8-52, Smith 7-30, Hadl 1-5
Passing	Hadl 9-18-1-321, Brittenum 3-5-0-38, Foster 1-1-0-28
Receiving	MacKinnon 6-172, Alworth 4-131, Garrison 2-77, Post 1-7
Interceptions	Beauchamp 1-35, Staggs 1-2, Graham 1-10

Broncos' Leaders
Rushing	Ford 8-30, Lynch 6-13, Briscoe 5-68, Erwin 5-32, Lindsey 4-17
Passing	Tensi 6-14-1-84, Briscoe 17-30-2-237
Receiving	Jones 8-128, Beer 3-36, Ford 3-22, Crabtree 2-45, Van Heusen 2-40
Interceptions	Jacquess 1-5

Week 7 Games
San Diego 55, Denver 24
New York 20, Houston 14
Miami 24, Cincinnati 22
Kansas City 24, Oakland 10
Boston 23, Buffalo 6

Week 7 Standings
East	W	L	T	West	W	L	T
New York	4	2	0	Kansas City	6	1	0
Boston	3	3	0	San Diego	5	1	0
Miami	2	3	1	Oakland	4	2	0
Houston	2	5	0	Denver	2	4	0
Buffalo	1	5	1	Cincinnati	2	5	0

Terry Owens

Larry Little

OCTOBER 27, 1968
Municipal Stadium – Kansas City, Missouri
Attendance – 50,344

					Total
Chargers	0	10	3	7	20
Chiefs	7	10	0	10	27

Chiefs	Holmes 6-yard run for the touchdown. Stenerud kicks the extra point.
Chargers	Partee kicks a 19-yard field goal.
Chargers	Hadl 9-yard pass to Garrison for the touchdown. Partee kicks the extra point.
Chiefs	Dawson 55-yard pass to Pitts for the touchdown. Stenerud kicks the extra point.
Chiefs	Stenerud kicks a 29-yard field goal.
Chargers	Partee kicks a 36-yard field goal.
Chargers	Hadl 5-yard pass to Frazier for the touchdown. Partee kicks the extra point.
Chiefs	Garrett 13-yard run for the touchdown. Stenerud kicks the extra point.
Chiefs	Stenerud kicks a 37-yard field goal.

	Chargers	**Chiefs**
First Downs	22	15
Rushing Yards	98	194
Passing Yards	297	180
Punts-Average	2-36.0	1-39.0
Fumbles-Lost	1-0	3-1
Penalties-Yards	4-43	2-20

Chargers' Leaders
Rushing	Foster 13-29, Post 12-61, Smith 1-8, Allison 1-0
Passing	Hadl 19-36-4-297
Receiving	Alworth 6-169, Garrison 4-60, Post 4-26, Frazier 3-22, MacKinnon 1-11
Interceptions	None

Chiefs' Leaders
Rushing	Holmes 20-69, Garrett 15-89, Hayes 3-16, Dawson 1-11, Pitts 1-9
Passing	Dawson 8-13-0-180
Receiving	Garrett 7-73, Pitts 2-94, Taylor 1-13
Interceptions	Robinson 2-0, Lynch 1-49, Kearney 1-0

Week 8 Games
Kansas City 27, San Diego 20
Oakland 31, Cincinnati 10
New York 48, Boston 14
Denver 21, Miami 14
Houston 30, Buffalo 7

Week 8 Standings
East	W	L	T	West	W	L	T
New York	5	2	0	Kansas City	7	1	0
Boston	3	4	0	San Diego	5	2	0
Houston	3	5	0	Oakland	5	2	0
Miami	2	4	1	Denver	3	4	0
Buffalo	1	6	1	Cincinnati	2	6	0

NOVEMBER 3, 1968
San Diego Stadium – San Diego, California
Attendance – 37,284

					Total
Chargers	7	10	7	10	34
Dolphins	7	7	7	7	28

Dolphins	Griese 10-yard pass to Twilley for the touchdown. Keyes kicks the extra point.
Chargers	Smith 26-yard run for the touchdown. Partee kicks the extra point.
Chargers	Hadl 14-yard pass to Garrison for the touchdown. Partee kicks the extra point.
Dolphins	Griese 15-yard pass to Moreau for the touchdown. Keyes kicks the extra point.
Dolphins	Partee kicks a 33-yard field goal.
Dolphins	Kiick 4-yard run for the touchdown. Keyes kicks the extra point.
Chargers	Allison 23-yard pass to Alworth for the touchdown. Partee kicks the extra point.
Chargers	Hadl 2-yard pass to Alworth for the touchdown. Partee kicks the extra point.
Chargers	Partee kicks a 23-yard field goal.
Dolphins	Griese 19-yard pass to Noonan for the touchdown. Keyes kicks the extra point.

	Chargers	Dolphins
First Downs	28	19
Rushing Yards	239	114
Passing Yards	240	238
Punts-Average	1-40.0	5-44.4
Fumbles-Lost	0-0	0-0
Penalties-Yards	2-20	2-30

Chargers' Leaders

Rushing Post 21-151, Smith 10-62, Allison 6-16, Hadl 3-10
Passing Hadl 17-28-2-228, Post 0-1-0-0, Allison 1-1-0-23
Receiving Alworth 5-60, Garrison 4-62, Post 3-49, Frazier 3-34, Smith 2-36
Interceptions Beauchamp 1-31

Dolphins' Leaders

Rushing Csonka 9-61, Kiick 8-9, Mitchell 4-5, Griese 3-39
Passing Griese 20-27-1-260
Receiving Twilley 7-124, Noonan 6-72, Kiick 3-28, Moreau 2-25, Cox 1-8
Interceptions West 2-59

Week 9 Games

San Diego 34, Miami 28
Oakland 38, Kansas City 21
Denver 35, Boston 14
Houston 27, Cincinnati 17
New York 25, Buffalo 21

Week 9 Standings

East	W	L	T	West	W	L	T
New York	6	2	0	Kansas City	7	2	0
Houston	4	5	0	San Diego	6	2	0
Boston	3	5	0	Oakland	6	2	0
Miami	2	5	1	Denver	4	4	0
Buffalo	1	7	1	Cincinnati	2	7	0

Dickie Post

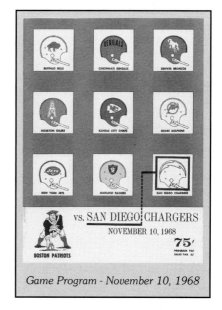

Game Program - November 10, 1968

NOVEMBER 10, 1968
Fenway Park – Boston, Massachusetts
Attendance – 19,278

					Total
Chargers	7	10	10	0	27
Patriots	3	0	7	7	17

Chargers	Smith 37-yard run for the touchdown. Partee kicks the extra point.
Patriots	Cappalletti kicks a 35-yard field goal.
Chargers	Partee kicks a 32-yard field goal.
Chargers	Hadl 67-yard pass to Garrison for the touchdown. Partee kicks the extra point.
Chargers	Smith 16-yard run for the touchdown. Partee kicks the extra point.
Chargers	Partee kicks a 33-yard field goal.
Patriots	Nance 1-yard run for the touchdown. Cappalletti kicks the extra point.
Patriots	Sherman 19-yard pass to Cappalletti for the touchdown. Cappalletti kicks the extra point.

	Chargers	Patriots
First Downs	11	11
Rushing Yards	144	121
Passing Yards	175	107
Punts-Average	7-31.0	5-33.4
Fumbles-Lost	4-2	2-1
Penalties-Yards	8-67	4-61

Chargers' Leaders

Rushing Post 16-41, Smith 13-93, Allison 7-12, Hadl 2-(-2)
Passing Hadl 5-23-2-152, Post 1-1-0-28
Receiving Garrison 3-89, MacKinnon 2-57, Alworth 1-29
Interceptions Tolbert 1-22, Erlandson 1-16, Fetherston 1-0

Patriots' Leaders

Rushing Nance 23-96, Thomas 4-13, Gamble 4-3, Sherman 3-10
Passing Sherman 12-36-3-107
Receiving Thomas 5-89, Murphy 2-36, Nance 2-13, Cappalletti 1-19, Gamble 1-0
Interceptions Satcher 1-1, B. Johnson 1-14

Week 10 Games

San Diego 27, Boston 17
Kansas City 16, Cincinnati 9
New York 26, Houston 7
Oakland 45, Denver 7
Miami 21, Buffalo 17

Week 10 Standings

East	W	L	T	West	W	L	T
New York	7	2	0	Kansas City	8	2	0
Houston	4	6	0	San Diego	7	2	0
Miami	3	5	1	Oakland	7	2	0
Boston	3	6	0	Denver	4	5	0
Buffalo	1	8	1	Cincinnati	2	8	0

Bills/Chargers

OFFICIAL PROGRAM MAGAZINE 50c

NOVEMBER 17, 1968

DICK CUNNINGHAM:
"Cuts It" As Versatile Bill — Page 9

AMERICAN FOOTBALL LEAGUE

PICTORIAL

Game Program - November 17, 1968

NOVEMBER 17, 1968
War Memorial Stadium – Buffalo, New York
Attendance – 27,993

					Total
Chargers	7	14	0	0	21
Bills	3	0	3	0	6

Chargers	Hadl 18-yard pass to MacKinnon for the touchdown. Partee kicks the extra point.
Bills	Alfred kicks a 25-yard field goal.
Chargers	Hadl 62-yard pass to MacKinnon for the touchdown. Partee kicks the extra point.
Chargers	Post 12-yard run for the touchdown. Partee kicks the extra point.
Bills	Alfred kicks a 16-yard field goal.

	Chargers	Bills
First Downs	15	7
Rushing Yards	76	90
Passing Yards	206	61
Punts-Average	10-34.3	5-35.6
Fumbles-Lost	2-2	0-0
Penalties-Yards	2-10	2-28

Chargers' Leaders
Rushing	Post 15-67, Smith 12-9, Hadl 1-0
Passing	Hadl 11-22-3-223, Smith 0-1-0-0
Receiving	MacKinnon 3-103, Garrison 3-74, Alworth 2-29, Post 2-13, Smith 1-4
Interceptions	Graham 1-25

Bills' Leaders
Rushing	Anderson 12-40, Cappadona 6-21, Rutkowski 4-24, Masters 1-4, McDermott 1-1
Passing	Darragh 8-21-0-38, Rutkowski 7-15-1-35, Russell 1-2-0-3
Receiving	Anderson 5-13, Cappadona 4-12, Moses 3-18, McDermott 2-9, Crockett 1-20
Interceptions	Guidry 1-21, Pitts 1-17, McDole 1-5

Week 11 Games
San Diego 21, Buffalo 6
Kansas City 31, Boston 17
Houston 38, Denver 17
Cincinnati 38, Miami 21
Oakland 43, New York 32

Week 11 Standings
East	W	L	T	West	W	L	T
New York	7	3	0	Kansas City	9	2	0
Houston	5	6	0	San Diego	8	2	0
Miami	3	6	1	Oakland	8	2	0
Boston	3	7	0	Denver	4	6	0
Buffalo	1	9	1	Cincinnati	3	8	0

NOVEMBER 24, 1968
San Diego Stadium – San Diego, California
Attendance – 51,175

					Total
Chargers	0	7	0	8	15
Jets	10	17	3	7	37

Jets	J. Turner kicks a 13-yard field goal.
Jets	Namath 87-yard pass to Maynard for the touchdown. J. Turner kicks the extra point.
Jets	Snell 3-yard run for the touchdown. J. Turner kicks the extra point.
Jets	J. Turner kicks a 20-yard field goal.
Chargers	Johnson punts to Duncan, returned 95 yards for the touchdown. Partee kicks the extra point.
Jets	Namath 19-yard pass to Maynard for the touchdown. J. Turner kicks the extra point.
Jets	J. Turner kicks a 23-yard field goal.
Jets	Mathis 1-yard run for the touchdown. J. Turner kicks the extra point.
Chargers	Hadl 3-yard pass to MacKinnon for the touchdown. Hadl 2-yard pass to MacKinnon for the 2-point conversion.

	Chargers	Jets
First Downs	12	22
Rushing Yards	45	142
Passing Yards	190	368
Punts-Average	8-43.4	4-54.5
Fumbles-Lost	0-0	0-0
Penalties-Yards	7-55	6-35

Chargers' Leaders
Rushing	Post 8-30, Foster 2-14, Hadl 1-2, Smith 1-(-1)
Passing	Hadl 19-46-4-190
Receiving	Foster 8-100, Garrison 3-38, Alworth 3-33, MacKinnon 2-10, Post 2-4
Interceptions	Graham 1-0

Jets' Leaders
Rushing	Snell 18-91, Snell 16-38, Mathis 4-12, Smolinski 2-1
Passing	Namath 17-31-1-137, Parilli 1-1-0-31
Receiving	Maynard 6-166, Sauer 5-124, Snell 3-13, Mathis 2-50, Lammons 1-11
Interceptions	Baird 1-22, Beverly 1-9, Baker 1-8, Gordon 1-0

Week 12 Games
New York 37, San Diego 15
Miami 34, Boston 10
Oakland 34, Cincinnati 0
Denver 34, Buffalo 32
Kansas City and Houston - Bye

Week 12 Standings
East	W	L	T	West	W	L	T
New York	8	3	0	Kansas City	9	2	0
Houston	5	6	0	Oakland	9	2	0
Miami	4	6	1	San Diego	8	3	0
Boston	3	8	0	Denver	5	6	0
Buffalo	1	10	1	Cincinnati	3	9	0

Steve DeLong (82) and Pete Barnes (59)

Jacque MacKinnon with one of his four receptions for the day.

December 1, 1968
Bears Stadium – Denver, Colorado
Attendance – 35,312

					Total
Chargers	**21**	**10**	**0**	**16**	**47**
Broncos	**3**	**14**	**6**	**0**	**23**

Chargers	Hadl 2-yard pass to Alworth for the touchdown. Partee kicks the extra point.
Chargers	Smith 35-yard run for the touchdown. Partee kicks the extra point.
Broncos	Howfield kicks a 30-yard field goal.
Chargers	Hadl 79-yard pass to Alworth for the touchdown. Partee kicks the extra point.
Chargers	Hadl 1-yard pass to Alworth for the touchdown. Partee kicks the extra point.
Chargers	Partee kicks a 19-yard field goal.
Broncos	Briscoe 14-yard pass to Crabtree for the touchdown. Howfield kicks the extra point.
Broncos	Briscoe 11-yard pass to McCarthy for the touchdown. Howfield kicks the extra point.
Broncos	Briscoe 24-yard pass to Crabtree for the touchdown. Howfield kicks the extra point.
Chargers	Hadl 9-yard pass to Garrison for the touchdown. Partee kicks the extra point.
Chargers	Briscoe tackled in the end zone on the kickoff for a safety.
Chargers	Hadl 4-yard pass to Alworth for the touchdown. Partee kicks the extra point.

	Chargers	Broncos
First Downs	27	15
Rushing Yards	161	110
Passing Yards	335	177
Punts-Average	3-33.7	5-49.4
Fumbles-Lost	1-0	3-2
Penalties-Yards	2-6	6-64

Chargers' Leaders
Rushing	Smith 18-106, Foster 12-48, Allison 3-3, Hadl 2-4
Passing	Hadl 21-35-1-325, Foster 1-2-0-18, Smith 0-1-0-0
Receiving	Alworth 9-171, Garrison 5-96, MacKinnon 4-39, Foster 3-34, Smith 1-3
Interceptions	None

Broncos' Leaders
Rushing	Little 12-43, Briscoe 6-56, McCarthy 5-11
Passing	Briscoe 15-33-0-218
Receiving	Crabtree 4-98, McCarthy 4-15, Denson 3-34, Beer 2-42, Haffner 1-19
Interceptions	Jaquess 1-8

Week 13 Games
San Diego 47, Denver 23
Boston 33, Cincinnati 14
Kansas City 26, Houston 10
New York 35, Miami 17
Oakland 13, Buffalo 10

Week 13 Standings
East	W	L	T	West	W	L	T
New York	9	3	0	Kansas City	10	2	0
Houston	5	7	0	Oakland	10	2	0
Miami	4	7	1	San Diego	9	3	0
Boston	4	8	0	Denver	5	7	0
Buffalo	1	11	1	Cincinnati	3	10	0

December 8, 1968
San Diego Stadium – San Diego, California
Attendance – 51,174

					Total
Chargers	**3**	**0**	**0**	**0**	**3**
Chiefs	**7**	**14**	**14**	**5**	**40**

Chargers	Partee kicks a 28-yard field goal.
Chiefs	Dawson 5-yard pass to Richardson for the touchdown. Stenerud kicks the extra point.
Chiefs	Dawson 7-yard pass to Garrett for the touchdown. Stenerud kicks the extra point.
Chiefs	Dawson 68-yard pass to Pitts for the touchdown. Stenerud kicks the extra point.
Chiefs	Garrett 1-yard run for the touchdown. Stenerud kicks the extra point.
Chiefs	Lanier intercepts Hadl pass, returns it 75 yards for the touchdown. Stenerud kicks the extra point.
Chiefs	Brittenum tackled in the end zone by Buchanan for a safety.
Chiefs	Stenerud kicks a 33-yard field goal.

	Chargers	Chiefs
First Downs	17	20
Rushing Yards	75	183
Passing Yards	136	188
Punts-Average	3-42.7	1-35.0
Fumbles-Lost	0-0	4-3
Penalties-Yards	5-30	5-53

Chargers' Leaders
Rushing	Post 10-47, Foster 5-20, Smith 1-12, Brittenum 1-0, Hadl 1-(-1)
Passing	Hadl 9-24-6-110, Brittenum 6-12-1-87, Post 0-1-0-0
Receiving	Garrison 4-46, Alworth 3-39, MacKinnon 2-31, Post 2-25, Foster 2-22
Interceptions	Beauchamp 1-2

Chiefs' Leaders
Rushing	Garrett 21-69, Holmes 11-56, Hayes 8-47, Coan 4-15, Taylor 2-(-2)
Passing	Dawson 7-12-1-153, Lee 2-5-0-35
Receiving	Garrett 3-33, Pitts 2-95, Holmes 1-20, Carolan 1-19, Taylor 1-16
Interceptions	Sellers 2-19, Bell 2-35, Kearney 1-23, Robinson 1-16, Lanier 1-75

Week 14 Games
Kansas City 40, San Diego 3
New York 27, Cincinnati 14
Miami 38, Boston 7
Oakland 33, Denver 27
Houston 35, Buffalo 6

Week 14 Standings
East	W	L	T	West	W	L	T
New York	10	3	0	Kansas City	11	2	0
Houston	6	7	0	Oakland	11	2	0
Miami	5	7	1	San Diego	9	4	0
Boston	4	9	0	Denver	5	8	0
Buffalo	1	12	1	Cincinnati	3	11	0

Ernie Ladd (99) and Dickie Post (22)

DECEMBER 15, 1968
San Diego Stadium – San Diego, California
Attendance – 40,698

					Total
Chargers	3	10	6	8	27
Raiders	3	7	14	10	34

Chargers	Partee kicks a 13-yard field goal.
Raiders	Blanda kicks a 28-yard field goal.
Chargers	Hadl 62-yard pass to MacKinnon for the touchdown. Partee kicks the extra point.
Raiders	Lamonica 13-yard pass to Biletnikoff for the touchdown. Blanda kicks the extra point.
Chargers	Partee kicks a 34-yard field goal.
Raiders	Bird intercepts Hadl pass, returns it 22 yards for the touchdown. Blanda kicks the extra point.
Raiders	Lamonica 55-yard pass to Wells for the touchdown. Blanda kicks the extra point.
Chargers	Partee kicks a 40-yard field goal.
Chargers	Partee kicks a 42-yard field goal.
Raiders	Lamonica 40-yard pass to Smith for the touchdown. Blanda kicks the extra point.
Raiders	Blanda kicks an 18-yard field goal.
Chargers	Partee punts to Wilson who fumbles. Ball recovered by Dyer in the end zone for the touchdown. Hadl 2-yard pass to Alworth for the 2-point conversion.

	Chargers	Raiders
First Downs	18	14
Rushing Yards	91	67
Passing Yards	365	249
Punts-Average	5-42.8	7-43.0
Fumbles-Lost	4-4	3-2
Penalties-Yards	7-81	1-5

Chargers' Leaders

Rushing	Foster 18-66, Post 7-12, Hadl 3-3, Smith 1-0
Passing	Hadl 21-52-2-359, Post 0-1-0-0, Foster 1-1-0-23
Receiving	Alworth 5-80, Garrison 4-128, Frazier 4-55, MacKinnon 3-68, Foster 3-24
Interceptions	Staggs 1-0, Allen 1-4

Raiders' Leaders

Rushing	Smith 13-10, Dixon 9-16, Lamonica 5-41
Passing	Lamonica 18-39-2-275
Receiving	Smith 5-79, Biletnikoff 5-61, Wells 4-113, Dixon 4-22
Interceptions	Bird 1-22, Grayson 1-32

Week 15 Games
Oakland 34, San Diego 27
Kansas City 30, Denver 7
New York 31, Miami 7
Houston 45, Boston 17
Buffalo and Cincinnati - Bye

Week 15 Standings

East	W	L	T	West	W	L	T
New York	11	3	0	Kansas City	12	2	0
Houston	7	7	0	Oakland	12	2	0
Miami	5	8	1	San Diego	9	5	0
Boston	4	10	0	Denver	5	9	0
Buffalo	1	12	1	Cincinnati	3	11	0

* On December 22, Oakland beat Kansas City 41-6 in the Western Division Playoff and went on to represent the West in the AFL Championship against the New York Jets on December 29, 1968.

Jacque MacKinnon heads down the sideline.

1969 Chargers Team Statistics
(8-6 Overall) Third Place in the AFL West

Team Statistics	Chargers	Opponent
TOTAL FIRST DOWNS	275	232
Rushing	119	71
Passing	131	148
Penalty	25	13
TOTAL NET YARDS	4,611	4,237
Avg. Per Game	329.4	302.6
Avg. Per Play	4.9	5.1
NET YARDS RUSHING	1,985	1,442
Avg. Per Game	141.8	103.0
NET YARDS PASSING	2,626	2,795
Avg. Per Game	187.6	199.6
Gross Yards	2,927	3,075
Completions/Attempts	444/208	423/241
Completion Pct.	.468	.570
Had Intercepted	21	31
PUNTS/AVERAGE	71/44.6	76/40.3
PENALTIES/YARDS	63/731	71/791
FUMBLES/BALL LOST	27/13	13/6
TOUCHDOWNS	35	34
Rushing	18	11
Passing	13	22
Returns	4	1
QUARTERBACK SACKS	35.0	33.0

Rushing	No.	Yds.	Avg.	TD
Post	182	873	4.8	6
Hubbert	94	333	3.5	4
Foster	64	236	3.7	0
Smith	51	211	4.1	2
Domres	19	145	7.6	4
Hadl	26	109	4.2	2
Sayers	14	53	3.8	0
Alworth	5	25	5.0	0
Totals	**455**	**1,985**	**4.4**	**18**

Receiving	No.	Yds.	Avg.	TD
Alworth	64	1,003	15.7	4
Garrison	40	804	20.1	7
Post	24	235	9.8	0
Frazier	17	205	12.1	0
Foster	14	83	5.9	1
Hubbert	11	43	3.9	0
Queen	10	148	14.8	0
Smith	10	144	14.4	0
Eber	9	141	15.7	1
MacKinnon	7	82	11.7	0
Trapp	2	39	19.5	0
Totals	**208**	**2,927**	**14.1**	**13**

Passing	Att.	Comp.	Yds.	Comp. %	TD	Int.
Hadl	324	158	2,253	.488	10	11
Domres	112	47	631	.420	2	10
Foster	5	2	39	.400	1	0
Post	2	1	4	.500	0	0
Hubbert	1	0	0	.000	0	0
Mikolajewski	0	0	0	-	0	0
Totals	**444**	**208**	**2,927**	**.468**	**13**	**21**

Interceptions	No.	Yds.	TD
Hill	7	92	0
Duncan	6	118	1
Howard	6	50	0
Barnes	5	64	0
Graham	4	112	2
Bruggers	1	5	0
Redman	1	3	0
Campbell	1	0	0
Totals	**31**	**444**	**3**

Kicking	FG	Att.	PAT	Att.	Pts.
Partee	15	28	33	33	78

Punting	No.	Avg.
Partee	71	44.6

Punt Returns	No.	FC	Yds.	Avg.	TD
Duncan	27	7	280	10.4	0
Graham	3	24	15	5.0	0
Smith	1	0	5	5.0	0
Trapp	0	1	0	-	0

Kickoff Returns	No.	Yds.	Avg.	TD
Duncan	21	587	28.0	0
Smith	6	138	23.0	0
Post	4	74	18.5	0
Fetherston	3	0	0.0	0
Sayers	2	42	21.0	0
Briggs	1	0	0.0	0
Foster	1	1	1.0	0
Huey	1	0	0.0	0

Rick Redman (66) and Jeff Staggs (81)

Charlie Waller replaced Sid Gillman as head coach on November 14.

Ron Mix

SEPTEMBER 14, 1969
San Diego Stadium – San Diego, California
Attendance – 47,988

					Total
Chargers	3	0	6	0	9
Chiefs	3	10	7	7	27

Chiefs	Stenerud kicks a 35-yard field goal.
Chargers	Partee kicks a 50-yard field goal.
Chiefs	Hayes 1-yard run for the touchdown. Stenerud kicks the extra point.
Chiefs	Stenerud kicks a 17-yard field goal.
Chargers	Hadl 9-yard run for the touchdown.
Chiefs	Dawson 55-yard pass to Taylor for the touchdown. Stenerud kicks the extra point.
Chiefs	Dawson 9-yard pass to Taylor for the touchdown. Stenerud kicks the extra point.

	Chargers	Chiefs
First Downs	14	16
Rushing Yards	45	67
Passing Yards	250	206
Punts-Average	7-47.6	7-42.6
Fumbles-Lost	5-1	2-1
Penalties-Yards	1-41	1-15

Chargers' Leaders
Rushing Hubbert 8-9, Smith 5-9, Post 5-6, Hadl 3-9, Domres 1-12
Passing Hadl 16-29-4-220, Domres 6-14-0-50
Receiving Alworth 4-94, Garrison 4-63, Post 4-45, Hubbert 4-8, Smith 3-24
Interceptions Duncan 1-20, Hill 1-0

Chiefs' Leaders
Rushing Holmes 14-58, Hayes 5-8, Garrett 1-1
Passing Dawson 19-34-2-224
Receiving Garrett 7-40, Taylor 5-111, Richardson 2-39, Pitts 2-20, Holmes 2-3
Interceptions Robinson 2-30, Thomas 1-43, Lanier 1-2

Week 1 Games
Kansas City 27, San Diego 9
Denver 35, Boston 7
Oakland 21, Houston 17
Cincinnati 27, Miami 21
New York 33, Buffalo 19

Week 1 Standings

East	W	L	T	West	W	L	T
New York	1	0	0	Kansas City	1	0	0
Boston	0	1	0	Oakland	1	0	0
Houston	0	1	0	Denver	1	0	0
Miami	0	1	0	Cincinnati	1	0	0
Buffalo	0	1	0	San Diego	0	1	0

SEPTEMBER 21, 1969
Nippert Stadium – Cincinnati, Ohio
Attendance – 26,243

					Total
Chargers	3	10	7	0	20
Bengals	7	10	14	3	34

Bengals	Cook 9-yard run for the touchdown. Muhlmann kicks the extra point.
Chargers	Partee kicks a 29-yard field goal.
Chargers	Partee kicks a 14-yard field goal.
Bengals	Muhlmann kicks a 17-yard field goal.
Chargers	Hubbert 2-yard run for the touchdown. Partee kicks the extra point.
Bengals	Cook 9-yard pass to Thomas for the touchdown. Muhlmann kicks the extra point.
Bengals	Cook 78-yard pass to Trumpy for the touchdown. Muhlmann kicks the extra point.
Chargers	Briggs recovers Cook fumble in the end zone for the touchdown. Partee kicks the extra point.
Bengals	Cook 39-yard pass to Coslet for the touchdown. Muhlmann kicks the extra point.
Bengals	Muhlmann kicks a 23-yard field goal.

	Chargers	Bengals
First Downs	17	19
Rushing Yards	180	180
Passing Yards	215	292
Punts-Average	5-47.0	3-45.0
Fumbles-Lost	0-0	2-1
Penalties-Yards	8-103	5-35

Chargers' Leaders
Rushing Post 15-147, Hubbert 6-21, Hadl 2-4, Alworth 1-5, Smith 1-3
Passing Hadl 12-30-1-229, Domres 1-3-0-2
Receiving Garrison 3-109, Post 3-6, MacKinnon 2-25, Hubbert 2-23, Alworth 2-18
Interceptions Hill 1-0

Bengals' Leaders
Rushing Phillips 12-59, Robinson 12-55, Cook 3-33, Turner 3-10, Lamb 2-5
Passing Cook 14-22-1-327
Receiving Crabtree 4-86, Trumpy 3-118, Thomas 2-27, Robinson 2-10, Myers 1-44
Interceptions Hunt 1-0

Week 2 Games
Cincinnati 34, San Diego 20
Kansas City 31, Boston 0
Oakland 20, Miami 17
Denver 21, New York 19
Houston 17, Buffalo 3

Week 2 Standings

East	W	L	T	West	W	L	T
New York	1	1	0	Kansas City	2	0	0
Houston	1	1	0	Oakland	2	0	0
Boston	0	2	0	Denver	2	0	0
Miami	0	2	0	Cincinnati	2	0	0
Buffalo	0	2	0	San Diego	0	2	0

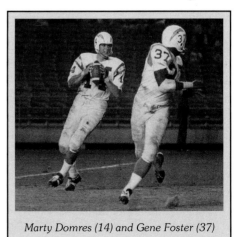

Marty Domres (14) and Gene Foster (37)

Dickie Post (22) and
Brad Hubbert (26)

SEPTEMBER 28, 1969
San Diego Stadium – San Diego, California
Attendance – 54,042

					Total
Chargers	7	17	3	7	34
Jets	0	10	3	14	27

Chargers	Hadl 9-yard pass to Alworth for the touchdown. Partee kicks the extra point.
Chargers	Partee 42-yard field goal.
Jets	Namath 21-yard pass to Sauer for the touchdown. J. Turner kicks the extra point.
Chargers	Smith 5-yard run for the touchdown. Partee kicks the extra point.
Chargers	Hadl 13-yard pass to Garrison for the touchdown. Partee kicks the extra point.
Jets	J. Turner kicks a 47-yard field goal.
Jets	J. Turner kicks a 37-yard field goal.
Chargers	Partee kicks a 27-yard field goal.
Jets	Boozer 1-yard run for the touchdown. J. Turner kicks the extra point.
Chargers	Hadl 29-yard pass to Garrison for the touchdown. Partee kicks the extra point.
Jets	Namath 14-yard pass to Sauer for the touchdown. J. Turner kicks the extra point.

	Chargers	Jets
First Downs	22	24
Rushing Yards	150	81
Passing Yards	268	333
Punts-Average	5-45.0	4-38.7
Fumbles-Lost	2-1	0-0
Penalties-Yards	8-106	3-45

Chargers' Leaders
Rushing	Post 12-58, Hubbert 10-39, Smith 10-28, Hadl 4-14, Foster 1-6
Passing	Hadl 19-31-0-281
Receiving	Garrison 10-188, Post 4-44, Alworth 4-33, MacKinnon 1-16
Interceptions	Barnes 1-25, Hill 1-2

Jets' Leaders
Rushing	Boozer 7-45, Snell 5-11, Mathis 4-10, White 3-15
Passing	Namath 29-51-2-344
Receiving	Sauer 9-118, Lammons 7-80, Mathis 6-71, Maynard 5-76, Snell 2-(-1)
Interceptions	None

Week 3 Games
San Diego 34, New York 27
Houston 22, Miami 10
Oakland 38, Boston 23
Cincinnati 24, Kansas City 19
Buffalo 41, Denver 28

Week 3 Standings
East	W	L	T	West	W	L	T
Houston	2	1	0	Cincinnati	3	0	0
New York	1	2	0	Oakland	3	0	0
Buffalo	1	2	0	Denver	2	1	0
Miami	0	3	0	Kansas City	2	1	0
Boston	0	3	0	San Diego	1	2	0

OCTOBER 4, 1969
San Diego Stadium – San Diego, California
Attendance – 52,748

					Total
Chargers	7	7	0	7	21
Bengals	7	0	7	0	14

Bengals	Thomas 16-yard run for the touchdown. Muhlmann kicks the extra point.
Chargers	Hubbert 8-yard run for the touchdown. Partee kicks the extra point.
Chargers	Hubbert 2-yard run for the touchdown. Partee kicks the extra point.
Bengals	Wyche 62-yard pass to Trumpy for the touchdown. Muhlmann kicks the extra point.
Chargers	Hubbert 1-yard run for the touchdown. Partee kicks the extra point.

	Chargers	Bengals
First Downs	23	8
Rushing Yards	199	151
Passing Yards	214	70
Punts-Average	4-42.7	9-38.6
Fumbles-Lost	2-2	2-1
Penalties-Yards	2-10	2-20

Chargers' Leaders
Rushing	Post 19-123, Hubbert 17-72, Smith 1-4
Passing	Hadl 17-27-1-238, Hubbert 0-1-0-0
Receiving	Alworth 8-125, Garrison 4-85, Frazier 2-27, Post 2-7, Hubbert 1-(-6)
Interceptions	None

Bengals' Leaders
Rushing	Phillips 13-103, Robinson 9-31, Wyche 3-14, Thomas 2-3
Passing	Wyche 7-18-0-115
Receiving	Crabtree 3-31, Trumpy 2-74, Thomas 1-10, Phillips 1-0
Interceptions	Bergey 1-4

Week 4 Games
San Diego 21, Cincinnati 14
New York 23, Boston 14
Oakland 20, Miami 20
Kansas City 26, Denver 13
Houston 28, Buffalo 14

Week 4 Standings
East	W	L	T	West	W	L	T
Houston	3	1	0	Oakland	3	0	1
New York	2	2	0	Cincinnati	3	1	0
Buffalo	1	3	0	Kansas City	3	1	0
Miami	0	3	1	Denver	2	2	0
Boston	0	4	0	San Diego	2	2	0

Houston Ridge brings down Bengals' quarterback Sam Wyche.

OCTOBER 11, 1969
The Orange Bowl – Miami, Florida
Attendance – 34,585

					Total
Chargers	0	14	0	7	21
Dolphins	0	0	7	7	14

Chargers	Hadl 40-yard pass to Garrison for the touchdown. Partee kicks the extra point.
Chargers	Hadl 26-yard pass to Garrison for the touchdown. Partee kicks the extra point.
Dolphins	Griese 5-yard pass to Noonan for the touchdown. Kremser kicks the extra point.
Chargers	Graham intercepts Griese pass, returns it 65 yards for the touchdown. Partee kicks the extra point.
Dolphins	Kick 2-yard run for the touchdown. Kremser kicks the extra point.

	Chargers	Dolphins
First Downs	15	16
Rushing Yards	126	67
Passing Yards	155	138
Punts-Average	7-41.7	6-39.5
Fumbles-Lost	1-0	2-1
Penalties-Yards	2-20	5-96

Chargers' Leaders

Rushing Post 14-38, Foster 9-27, Hubbert 5-9, Hadl 2-23, Smith 2-22
Passing Hadl 13-28-1-195
Receiving Garrison 4-103, Frazier 4-34, Alworth 3-55, Foster 1-5, Hubbert 1-(-2)
Interceptions Graham 1-65, Duncan 1-0

Dolphins' Leaders

Rushing Kiick 11-29, Csonka 9-24, Griese 2-14
Passing Griese 18-31-2-171
Receiving Clancy 5-46, Kiick 5-36, Seiple 4-64, Csonka 2-16, Noonan 1-5
Interceptions Weisacosky 1-0

Week 5 Games
San Diego 21, Miami 14
Oakland 24, Denver 14
New York 21, Cincinnati 7
Kansas City 24, Houston 0
Buffalo 23, Boston 16

Week 5 Standings

East	W	L	T	West	W	L	T
Houston	3	2	0	Oakland	4	0	1
New York	3	2	0	Kansas City	4	1	0
Buffalo	2	3	0	San Diego	3	2	0
Miami	0	4	1	Cincinnati	3	2	0
Boston	0	5	0	Denver	2	3	0

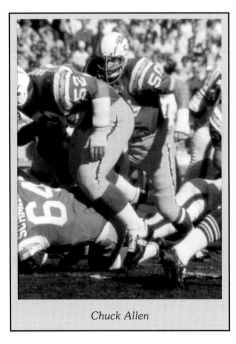

Chuck Allen

Sam Gruneisen (65) and Marty Domres (14)

OCTOBER 19, 1969
Boston College Stadium – Boston, Massachusetts
Attendance – 18,346

					Total
Chargers	0	3	3	7	13
Patriots	7	0	0	3	10

Patriots	Taliaferro 7-yard pass to Garrett for the touchdown. Cappalletti kicks the extra point.
Chargers	Partee kicks a 12-yard field goal.
Chargers	Partee kicks a 28-yard field goal.
Chargers	Hadl 6-yard run for the touchdown. Partee kicks the extra point.
Patriots	Cappalletti kicks a 32-yard field goal.

	Chargers	Patriots
First Downs	24	11
Rushing Yards	171	127
Passing Yards	163	90
Punts-Average	3-27.0	5-36.6
Fumbles-Lost	2-2	0-0
Penalties-Yards	0-0	3-31

Chargers' Leaders

Rushing Foster 13-62, Smith 9-46, Post 8-14, Hubbert 7-30, Hadl 7-19
Passing Hadl 15-26-0-163, Foster 0-1-0-0
Receiving Alworth 7-95, Garrison 4-40, Post 2-13, Foster 1-10, Smith 1-5
Interceptions Hill 1-21, Howard 1-10

Patriots' Leaders

Rushing Nance 13-69, Garrett 12-54, Blanks 1-4
Passing Taliaferro 11-25-2-90
Receiving Nance 4-1, Garrett 3-30, Whalen 2-43, Frazier 1-13, Blanks 1-3
Interceptions None

Week 6 Games
San Diego 13, Boston 10
New York 26, Houston 17
Denver 30, Cincinnati 23
Kansas City 17, Miami 10
Oakland 50, Buffalo 21

Week 6 Standings

East	W	L	T	West	W	L	T
New York	4	2	0	Oakland	5	0	1
Houston	3	3	0	Kansas City	5	1	0
Buffalo	2	4	0	San Diego	4	2	0
Miami	0	5	1	Cincinnati	3	3	0
Boston	0	6	0	Denver	3	3	0

OCTOBER 26, 1969
San Diego Stadium – San Diego, California
Attendance – 54,008

					Total
Chargers	3	3	0	6	12
Raiders	7	7	7	3	24

Chargers	Partee kicks a 25-yard field goal.
Raiders	Lamonica 48-yard pass to Todd for the touchdown. Blanda kicks the extra point.
Raiders	Lamonica 16-yard pass to Wells for the touchdown. Blanda kicks the extra point.
Chargers	Partee kicks a 46-yard field goal.
Raiders	Lamonica 15-yard pass to Hagberg for the touchdown. Blanda kicks the extra point.
Chargers	Hadl 3-yard pass to Alworth for the touchdown.
Raiders	Blanda kicks a 28-yard field goal.

	Chargers	Raiders
First Downs	20	19
Rushing Yards	71	171
Passing Yards	182	228
Punts-Average	7-47.6	6-41.1
Fumbles-Lost	0-0	0-0
Penalties-Yards	5-63	12-180

Chargers' Leaders

Rushing	Post 12-35, Foster 5-9, Smith 2-10, Hadl 1-14, Domres 1-3
Passing	Hadl 12-45-3-167, Domres 3-6-1-49, Post 0-1-0-0
Receiving	Alworth 6-96, Queen 2-32, Post 2-29, MacKinnon 2-29, Trapp 1-15
Interceptions	Barnes 2-18, Duncan 1-0

Raiders' Leaders

Rushing	Banaszak 25-123, C. Smith 10-25, Todd 6-23
Passing	Lamonica 19-26-3-237
Receiving	Wells 4-64, Banaszak 4-41, Todd 3-45, Biletnikoff 3-40, C. Smith 2-11
Interceptions	Grayson 1-13, Nilson 1-22

Week 7 Games
Oakland 24, San Diego 12
Houston 24, Denver 21
New York 23, Boston 17
Kansas City 42, Cincinnati 22
Miami 24, Buffalo 6

Week 7 Standings

East	W	L	T	West	W	L	T
New York	5	2	0	Oakland	6	0	1
Houston	4	3	0	Kansas City	6	1	0
Buffalo	2	5	0	San Diego	4	3	0
Miami	1	5	1	Cincinnati	3	4	0
Boston	0	7	0	Denver	3	4	0

Jacque MacKinnon hauls in a reception.

Walt Sweeney (78) and Dickie Post (22)

NOVEMBER 2, 1969
Denver Mile High Stadium – Denver, Colorado
Attendance – 45,511

					Total
Chargers	0	0	0	0	0
Broncos	0	0	13	0	13

Broncos	Tensi 2-yard pass to Danson for the touchdown.
Broncos	Little 2-yard run for the touchdown. Howfield kicks the extra point.

	Chargers	Broncos
First Downs	10	19
Rushing Yards	50	114
Passing Yards	20	199
Punts-Average	10-48.6	6-39.0
Fumbles-Lost	0-0	0-0
Penalties-Yards	2-20	7-72

Chargers' Leaders

Rushing	Post 9-11, Foster 5-9, Hadl 4-23, Domres 1-7, Hubbert 1-0
Passing	Hadl 8-20-0-51, Domres 2-9-0-8, Foster 1-1-0-9
Receiving	Frazier 3-19, Foster 3-1, Smith 2-30, Alworth 2-13, Eber 1-5
Interceptions	Howard 2-19

Broncos' Leaders

Rushing	Lynch 13-34, Little 10-42, Quayle 9-30, Tensi 1-8
Passing	Tensi 15-32-2-219
Receiving	Denson 6-93, Haffner 4-56, Little 4-56, Pivec 1-14
Interceptions	None

Week 8 Games
Denver 13, San Diego 0
New York 33, Miami 31
Boston 24, Houston 0
Cincinnati 31, Oakland 17
Kansas City 29, Buffalo 7

Week 8 Standings

East	W	L	T	West	W	L	T
New York	6	2	0	Kansas City	7	1	0
Houston	4	4	0	Oakland	6	1	1
Buffalo	2	6	0	San Diego	4	4	0
Miami	1	6	1	Cincinnati	4	4	0
Boston	1	7	0	Denver	4	4	0

Brad Hubbert

NOVEMBER 9, 1969
Municipal Stadium – Kansas City, Missouri
Attendance – 51,104

					Total
Chargers	3	0	0	0	3
Chiefs	0	10	10	7	27

Chargers	Partee kicks a 25-yard field goal.
Chiefs	Garrett 5-yard run for the touchdown. Stenerud kicks the extra point.
Chiefs	Stenerud kicks a 30-yard field goal.
Chiefs	Stenerud kicks a 47-yard field goal.
Chiefs	McVea 50-yard pass to Pitts for the touchdown. Stenerud kicks the extra point.
Chiefs	McVea 2-yard run for the touchdown. Stenerud kicks the extra point.

	Chargers	Chiefs
First Downs	10	17
Rushing Yards	70	99
Passing Yards	104	209
Punts-Average	6-46.1	5-43.0
Fumbles-Lost	1-0	1-0
Penalties-Yards	4-40	5-35

Chargers' Leaders

Rushing	Smith 8-30, Hubbert 3-21, Domres 2-6, Post 2-(-3), Alworth 1-16
Passing	Domres 10-31-5-132
Receiving	Eber 3-66, Alworth 3-43, Queen 2-27, Post 1-1, Hubbert 1-(-5)
Interceptions	Duncan 1-26, Barnes 1-13, Howard 1-0

Chiefs' Leaders

Rushing	Garrett 9-46, Holmes 9-22, McVea 6-14, Hayes 4-11, Livingston 1-16
Passing	Dawson 17-24-3-169, Livingston 2-4-0-26, McVea 1-1-0-50
Receiving	Garrett 7-43, Pitts 4-99, Holmes 3-30, Richardson 2-35, Hayes 2-15
Interceptions	Thomas 2-0, Marsalis 1-4, Lanier 1-16, Kearney 1-34

Week 9 Games
Kansas City 27, San Diego 3
Cincinnati 31, Houston 31
Miami 17, Boston 16
Oakland 41, Denver 10
Buffalo 28, Miami 3

Week 9 Standings

East	W	L	T	West	W	L	T
New York	6	2	0	Kansas City	8	1	0
Houston	4	4	1	Oakland	7	1	1
Buffalo	3	6	0	Cincinnati	4	4	1
Miami	2	6	1	San Diego	4	5	0
Boston	1	8	0	Denver	4	5	0

NOVEMBER 16, 1969
Oakland-Alameda County Stadium – Oakland, California
Attendance – 54,372

					Total
Chargers	0	7	3	6	16
Raiders	0	14	0	7	21

Chargers	Duncan intercepts Lamonica pass, returns it 72 yards for the touchdown. Partee kicks the extra point.
Raiders	Lamonica 19-yard pass to Biletnikoff for the touchdown. Blanda kicks the extra point.
Raiders	Conners recovers fumble and returns 25 yards for the touchdown. Blanda kicks the extra point.
Chargers	Partee kicks an 18-yard field goal.
Chargers	Partee kicks a 31-yard field goal.
Chargers	Partee kicks a 14-yard field goal.
Raiders	Lamonica 80-yard pass to Wells for the touchdown. Blanda kicks the extra point.

	Chargers	Raiders
First Downs	17	13
Rushing Yards	117	74
Passing Yards	107	235
Punts-Average	6-42.7	4-41.0
Fumbles-Lost	5-3	2-1
Penalties-Yards	4-46	8-67

Chargers' Leaders

Rushing	Post 20-113, Hubbert 13-13, Foster 2-4, Hadl 1-(-5), Alworth 1-(-8)
Passing	Hadl 12-32-0-127
Receiving	Eber 3-28, Alworth 3-25, Queen 2-59, Frazier 2-27, Foster 1-(-6)
Interceptions	Duncan 2-72, Hill 1-42

Raiders' Leaders

Rushing	Dixon 14-64, Smith 10-11, Todd 3-7, Wells 1-(-8)
Passing	Lamonica 15-29-3-235
Receiving	Dixon 8-49, Biletnikoff 3-47, Wells 2-105, Hagberg 2-34
Interceptions	None

Week 10 Games
Oakland 21, San Diego 16
Houston 20, Denver 20
Boston 25, Cincinnati 14
Kansas City 34, New York 16
Buffalo 28, Miami 3

Week 10 Standings

East	W	L	T	West	W	L	T
New York	7	3	0	Kansas City	9	1	0
Houston	4	4	2	Oakland	8	1	1
Buffalo	3	7	0	Cincinnati	4	5	1
Miami	2	7	1	Denver	4	5	1
Boston	2	8	0	San Diego	4	6	0

Dennis Partee

Dickie Post (22) runs behind the blocks of Sam Gruneisen (65), Terry Owens (76) and Bill Lenkaitis (51).

NOVEMBER 23, 1969
San Diego Stadium – San Diego, California
Attendance – 34,664

					Total
Chargers	14	3	21	7	45
Broncos	7	10	7	0	24

Broncos	Tensi 6-yard pass to Denson for the touchdown. Howfield kicks the extra point.
Chargers	Post 7-yard run for the touchdown. Partee kicks the extra point.
Chargers	Post 1-yard run for the touchdown. Partee kicks the extra point.
Broncos	Tensi 38-yard pass to Denson for the touchdown. Howfield kicks the extra point.
Chargers	Partee kicks a 33-yard field goal.
Broncos	Howfield kicks a 22-yard field goal.
Chargers	Domres 10-yard run for the touchdown. Partee kicks the extra point.
Chargers	Post 10-yard run for the touchdown. Partee kicks the extra point.
Broncos	Tensi 10-yard pass to Embree for the touchdown. Howfield kicks the extra point.
Chargers	Domres 8-yard run for the touchdown. Partee kicks the extra point.
Chargers	Domres 14-yard pass to Foster for the touchdown. Partee kicks the extra point.

	Chargers	Broncos
First Downs	27	23
Rushing Yards	235	34
Passing Yards	227	329
Punts-Average	1-38.0	4-37.8
Fumbles-Lost	2-0	0-0
Penalties-Yards	8-87	7-87

Chargers' Leaders

Rushing	Post 17-128, Foster 11-23, Domres 6-58, Smith 4-17, Sayers 2-9
Passing	Domres 11-20-2-235, Foster 0-2-0-0
Receiving	Garrison 3-55, Foster 3-48, Smith 2-69, Alworth 2-52, Queen 1-11
Interceptions	Graham 2-36, Bruggers 1-5

Broncos' Leaders

Rushing	Quayle 5-22, Lynch 5-8, Williams 1-4
Passing	Tensi 19-26-1-301, Liske 7-10-2-62
Receiving	Embree 9-122, Denson 6-140, Quayle 4-35, Pivec 3-34, Lynch 3-23
Interceptions	Cavness 1-29, Thompson 1-0

Week 11 Games
San Diego 45, Denver 24
New York 40, Cincinnati 7
Houston 32, Miami 7
Oakland 27, Kansas City 24
Boston 35, Buffalo 21

Week 11 Standings

East	W	L	T	West	W	L	T
New York	8	3	0	Oakland	9	1	1
Houston	5	4	2	Kansas City	9	2	0
Buffalo	3	8	0	San Diego	5	6	0
Boston	3	8	0	Cincinnati	4	6	1
Miami	2	8	1	Denver	4	6	1

NOVEMBER 27, 1969
The Astrodome – Houston, Texas
Attendance – 40,065

					Total
Chargers	0	7	7	7	21
Oilers	7	10	0	0	17

Oilers	Beathard 2-yard run for the touchdown. Gerela kicks the extra point.
Chargers	Domres 23-yard pass to Garrison for the touchdown. Partee kicks the extra point.
Oilers	Trull 3-yard pass to Granger for the touchdown. Gerela kicks the extra point.
Oilers	Gerela kicks a 42-yard field goal.
Chargers	Smith 2-yard run for the touchdown. Partee kicks the extra point.
Chargers	Graham intercepts Trull pass, returns it 11 yards for the touchdown. Partee kicks the extra point.

	Chargers	Oilers
First Downs	20	18
Rushing Yards	139	109
Passing Yards	186	103
Punts-Average	4-42.8	6-36.0
Fumbles-Lost	3-1	1-1
Penalties-Yards	4-38	5-53

Chargers' Leaders

Rushing	Post 10-26, Smith 8-32, Foster 6-15, Domres 5-34, Hubbert 5-26
Passing	Hadl 12-17-0-144, Domres 4-11-2-52
Receiving	Alworth 7-85, Garrison 4-63, Frazier 2-22, Foster 1-12, Post 1-7
Interceptions	Redman 1-3, Graham 1-11

Oilers' Leaders

Rushing	Hopkins 13-25, Campbell 12-37, Granger 5-25, Beathard 4-11, Trull 2-11
Passing	Beathard 10-14-1-91, Trull 5-12-1-30
Receiving	Hopkins 5-36, Beirne 4-41, Granger 2-14, Campbell 2-13, Levias 1-13
Interceptions	Farr 1-35, Hicks 1-7

Week 12 Games
San Diego 21, Houston 17
Oakland 27, New York 14
Kansas City 31, Denver 17
Boston 38, Miami 23
Buffalo 16, Cincinnati 13

Week 12 Standings

East	W	L	T	West	W	L	T
New York	8	4	0	Oakland	10	1	1
Houston	5	5	2	Kansas City	10	2	0
Buffalo	4	8	0	San Diego	6	6	0
Boston	4	8	0	Cincinnati	4	7	1
Miami	2	9	1	Denver	4	7	1

Sam Gruneisen

DECEMBER 7, 1969
San Diego Stadium – San Diego, California
Attendance – 33,146

					Total
Chargers	7	7	14	0	28
Patriots	0	3	0	15	18

Chargers	Post 4-yard run for the touchdown. Partee kicks the extra point.
Patriots	Cappalletti kicks a 34-yard field goal.
Chargers	Domres 1-yard run for the touchdown. Partee kicks the extra point.
Chargers	Hadl 17-yard pass to Garrison for the touchdown. Partee kicks the extra point.
Chargers	Hadl 76-yard pass to Alworth for the touchdown. Partee kicks the extra point.
Patriots	Nance 9-yard run for the touchdown. Cappalletti kicks the extra point.
Patriots	Nance 3-yard run for the touchdown. Hammond 2-yard run for the 2-point conversion.

	Chargers	Patriots
First Downs	24	16
Rushing Yards	190	110
Passing Yards	240	183
Punts-Average	4-40.5	3-38.3
Fumbles-Lost	3-2	0-0
Penalties-Yards	5-60	6-76

Chargers' Leaders

Rushing	Post 20-71, Foster 7-47, Hubbert 6-32, Sayers 5-19, Domres 2-16
Passing	Domres 9-17-0-78, Hadl 6-10-1-176
Receiving	Alworth 6-147, Garrison 3-57, Foster 2-1, Hubbert 1-18, Post 1-12
Interceptions	Hill 2-27, Howard 1-0, Barnes 1-8

Patriots' Leaders

Rushing	Nance 11-58, Garrett 10-49, Taliaferro 1-3
Passing	Taliaferro 13-23-4-169
Receiving	Brown 5-54, Nance 4-15, Sellers 3-102, Garrett 2-8, Cappalletti 1-21
Interceptions	Bramlett 1-26

Week 13 Games
San Diego 28, Boston 18
Miami 27, Denver 24
New York 34, Houston 26
Oakland 37, Cincinnati 17
Kansas City 22, Buffalo 19

Week 13 Standings

East	W	L	T	West	W	L	T
New York	9	4	0	Oakland	11	1	1
Houston	5	6	2	Kansas City	11	2	0
Buffalo	4	9	0	San Diego	7	6	0
Boston	4	9	0	Cincinnati	4	8	1
Miami	3	9	1	Denver	4	8	1

Jim Schmedding looks for someone to block.

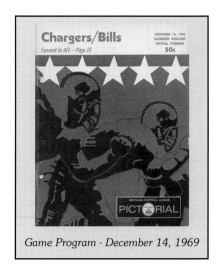

Game Program - December 14, 1969

DECEMBER 14, 1969
San Diego Stadium – San Diego, California
Attendance – 47,582

					Total
Chargers	10	14	7	14	45
Bills	0	0	0	6	6

Chargers	Hadl 41-yard pass to garrison for the touchdown. Partee kicks the extra point.
Chargers	Partee kicks a 33-yard field goal.
Chargers	Foster 30-yard pass to Eber for the touchdown. Partee kicks the extra point.
Chargers	Hadl 1-yard pass to Alworth for the touchdown. Partee kicks the extra point.
Chargers	Post 34-yard run for the touchdown. Partee kicks the extra point.
Chargers	Post 2-yard run for the touchdown. Partee kicks the extra point.
Chargers	Domres 9-yard run for the touchdown. Partee kicks the extra point.
Bills	Sherman 19-yard pass to grate for the touchdown.

	Chargers	Bills
First Downs	30	15
Rushing Yards	242	58
Passing Yards	305	180
Punts-Average	2-54.0	8-45.2
Fumbles-Lost	2-1	1-0
Penalties-Yards	3-21	5-55

Chargers' Leaders

Rushing	Post 19-106, Hubbert 13-61, Sayers 6-22, Foster 5-34, Smith 1-10
Passing	Hadl 16-29-0-262, Foster 1-1-0-30, Post 1-1-0-4, Domres 1-1-0-25
Receiving	Alworth 7-122, Post 3-77, Queen 3-19, Eber 2-42, Frazier 2-14
Interceptions	Howard 1-5, Campbell 1-0

Bills' Leaders

Rushing	Simpson 7-27, Patrick 4-9, Sherman 2-14, Enyart 2-6, Anderson 1-16
Passing	Kemp 16-33-2-164, Sherman 1-1-0-20
Receiving	Briscoe 6-94, Enyart 3-36, Simpson 3-(-8) Grate 1-19, Masters 1-16
Interceptions	None

Week 14 Games
San Diego 45, Buffalo 6
Denver 27, Cincinnati 16
Houston 27, Boston 23
Oakland 10, Kansas City 6
New York 27, Miami 9

Week 14 Standings

East	W	L	T	West	W	L	T
New York	10	4	0	Oakland	12	1	1
Houston	6	6	2	Kansas City	11	3	1
Buffalo	4	10	0	San Diego	8	6	0
Boston	4	10	0	Denver	5	8	1
Miami	3	10	1	Cincinnati	4	9	1

MEMBERS OF THE LOS ANGELES AND SAN DIEGO CHARGERS, 1960-1969

HEAD COACHES

NAME	COLLEGE	YEARS WITH CHARGERS (AFL)
Sid Gillman	Ohio State	1960-1969
Charlie Waller	Georgia	1969

ASSISTANT COACHES

NAME	COLLEGE	YEARS WITH CHARGERS (AFL)
Tom Bass	San Jose State	1964-1967
Al Davis	Syracuse	1960-1962
Jack Faulkner	Miami of Ohio	1960-1961
Walt Hackett	Whittier	1962-1966
Harry Johnston	Nebraska	1966-1967
Joe Madro	Ohio State	1960-1969
Chuck Noll	Dayton	1960-1965
Bum Phillips	Stephen F. Austin	1967-1969
Jim Phillips	Auburn	1968-1969
Jackie Simpson	Mississippi	1967-1969
Bones Taylor	Oklahoma City	1963
Chuck Weber	Westchester, PA	1968-1969

PLAYERS

NAME	POSITION	COLLEGE	YEARS WITH CHARGERS (AFL)
Ben Agajanian	Kicker	New Mexico	1960-1961, 1964
Harold Akin	Tackle	Oklahoma State	1967-1968
Chuck Allen	Linebacker	Washington	1961-1969
Jim Allison	Running Back	San Diego State	1965-1968
Lance Alworth	Flanker	Arkansas	1962-1969
Scott Appleton	Defensive Tackle	Texas	1967-1968
Martin Baccaglio	Defensive End	San Jose State	1968
John Baker	Linebacker	Mississippi State	1967
Al Bansavage	Guard	Southern California	1960
Ernie Barnes	Guard	North Carolina College	1960-1962
Al Barry	Guard	Southern California	1960
Joe Beauchamp	Cornerback	Wisconsin	1966-1969
George Belotti	Guard	Southern California	1961
Bob Bethune	Safety	Mississippi State	1962
Ron Billingsley	Defensive Tackle	Wyoming	1967-1969
George Blair	Kicker/Cornerback	Mississippi	1961-1964
Hubert Bobo	Linebacker	Ohio State	1960
Ron Botchan	Linebacker	Occidental	1960
Hezekiah Braxton	Running Back	Virginia Union	1962
Don Breaux	Quarterback	McNeese State	1964-1965
Bob Briggs	Defensive End	Heidelberg, Ohio	1968-1969
Jon Brittenum	Quarterback	Arkansas	1968
Charlie Brueckman	Linebacker	Pittsburgh	1960
Bob Bruggers	Linebacker	Minnesota	1968-1969

Ron Mix, Lance Alworth, Walt Sweeney and John Hadl

Frank Buncom	Linebacker	Southern California	1962-1967
Jim Campbell	Linebacker	West Texas State	1969
Reg Carolan	Tight End	Idaho	1962-1963
Ron Carpenter	Linebacker	Texas A&M	1964-1965
Levert Carr	Tackle	North Central Illinois	1969
Kern Carson	Half Back	San Diego State	1965
Dick Chorovich	Defensive Tackle	Miami of Ohio	1960
Howard Clark	Tight End	Tennessee-Chattanooga	1960-1961
Bobby Clatterbuck	Quarterback	Houston	1960
Doug Cline	Linebacker	Clemson	1966
Bert Coan	Running Back	Kansas	1962
Fred Cole	Guard	Maryland	1960
Ollie Cordill	Wide Receiver	Memphis State	1967
Tom Day	Defensive End	North Carolina A&T	1967
Dick Degan	Linebacker	Long Beach State	1965-1966
Steve DeLong	Defensive End	Tennessee	1965-1969
Sam DeLuca	Guard	South Carolina	1960-1961, 1963
Marty Domres	Quarterback	Columbia	1969
Ben Donnell	Defensive End	Vanderbilt	1960
Leslie Duncan	Cornerback	Jackson State	1964-1969
Ken Dyer	Wide Receiver	Arizona State	1968
Rick Eber	Wide Receiver	Tulsa	1969
Hunter Enis	Quarterback	Texas Christian	1961
Bernard Erickson	Linebacker	Abilene Christian	1967-1968
Tom Erlandson	Linebacker	Washington State	1968
Don Estes	Guard	Louisiana State	1966
Earl Faison	Defensive End	Indiana	1961-1966
Dick Farley	Safety	Boston University	1968-1969
Miller Farr	Cornerback	Wichita State	1965-1966
John Farris	Guard	San Diego State	1965-1966
Lane Fenner	Wide Receiver	Florida State	1968
Eugene Ferguson	Tackle	Norfolk State	1969
Howard Ferguson	Running Back	No College	1960
Orlando Ferrante	Guard	Southern California	1960-1961
Jim Fetherston	Linebacker	California	1968-1969
Gary Finneran	Defensive Tackle	Southern California	1960
Charlie Flowers	Running Back	Mississippi State	1960-1961
Fred Ford	Running Back	Cal Poly San Luis Obispo	1960
Gene Foster	Running Back	Arizona State	1965-1969
Wayne Frazier	Center	Auburn	1962
Willie Frazier	Tight End	Arkansas M&N	1966-1969
Bob Garner	Cornerback	Fresno State	1960
Gary Garrison	Split End	San Diego State	1966-1969
Claude Gibson	Cornerback	North Carolina State	1961-1962
Fred Gillett	Linebacker	Los Angeles State	1962
Gary Glick	Safety	Colorado State	1963
Art Gob	Linebacker	Pittsburgh	1960
Tom Good	Linebacker	Marshall, West Virginia	1966
Kenny Graham	Safety	Washington State	1964-1969
Tom Greene	Quarterback	Holy Cross	1961

From San Diego State to the Chargers, Gary Garrison (27), Houston Ridge (80), Jeff Staggs (81), Jim Allison (32) and Bob Howard (24).

Miss San Diego with Gerry McDougall (20), Ron Mix (74), Keith Kinderman (24) and Ernie Park (61).

Give to the United Way.

Jim Griffin	Defensive Tackle	Grambling	1966-1967
George Gross	Defensive Tackle	Auburn	1963-1967
Sam Gruneisen	Center	Villanova	1962-1969
John Hadl	Quarterback	Kansas	1962-1969
Dick Harris	Cornerback	McNeese State	1960-1965
Luther Hayes	Split End	Southern California	1961
Dan Henning	Quarterback	William & Mary	1966
Jim Hill	Safety	Texas A&I	1969
Bob Horton	Linebacker	Boston University	1964-1965
Bob Howard	Cornerback	San Diego State	1967-1969
Brad Hubbert	Running Back	Arizona	1967-1969
Bill Hudson	Defensive Tackle	Clemson	1961-1962
Richard Hudson	Tackle	Memphis State	1962
Gene Huey	Wide Receiver	Wyoming	1969
Bob Jackson	Wide Receiver	New Mexico State	1962-1963
Curtis Jones	Guard	Missouri	1968
Emil Karas	Linebacker	Dayton	1960-1964, 1966
Val Keckin	Quarterback	Southern Mississippi	1962
Jack Kemp	Quarterback	Occidental	1960-1962
Charles Kempinska	Guard	Mississippi	1960
Keith Kinderman	Running Back	Florida State	1963-1964
Howard Kindig	Defensive End	Los Angeles State	1965-1967
Gary Kirner	Tackle	Southern California	1964-1969
Jack Klotz	Defensive Tackle	Penn Military	1962
Dave Kocourek	Tight End	Wisconsin	1960-1965
John Kompara	Defensive Tackle	South Carolina	1960
Ernie Ladd	Defensive Tackle	Grambling	1961-1965
Bob Lane	Linebacker	Baylor	1963-1964
Bob Laraba	Quarterback/ Linebacker	Texas Western	1960-1961
Paul Latzke	Center	Pacific	1966-1968
Bill Lenkaitis	Guard	Penn State	1968-1969
Keith Lincoln	Running Back	Washington State	1961-1966, 1968
Larry Little	Guard	Bethune-Cookman	1967-1968
Mike London	Linebacker	Wisconsin	1966
Rommie Loudd	Linebacker	UCLA	1960
Paul Lowe	Running Back	Oregon State	1960-1968
Jacque MacKinnon	Tight End	Colgate	1961-1969
Paul Maguire	Linebacker/ Punter	The Citadel	1960-1963
Frank Marsh	Cornerback	Oregon State	1967
Blanche Martin	Running Back	Michigan State	1960
Larry Martin	Defensive Tackle	San Diego State	1966
Archie Matsos	Linebacker	Michigan State	1966
Ron McCall	Linebacker	Weber State	1967-1968
Lloyd McCoy	Guard	San Diego State	1966
Gerry McDougall	Running Back	UCLA	1962-1964, 1968
Charlie McNeil	Safety	Compton Junior College	1960-1964
Mario Mendez	Wide Receiver	San Diego State	1964
Pete Mikolajewski	Quarterback	Kent State	1969
Jack Milks	Linebacker	San Diego State	1966
Paul Miller	Defensive Tackle	Louisiana State	1962
Ed Mitchell	Guard	Southern Louisiana	1965-1966
Bob Mitinger	Linebacker	Penn State	1963-1966, 1968
Ron Mix	Tackle	Southern California	1960-1969
Fred Moore	Defensive Tackle	Memphis State	1964-1966
Ron Nery	Defensive End	Kansas State	1960-1962

Steve Newell	Wide Receiver	Long Beach State	1967
Doyle Nix	Cornerback	Southern Methodist	1960
Trusse Norris	Wide Receiver	UCLA	1960
Don Norton	Wide Receiver	Iowa	1960-1966
Terry Owens	Tackle	Jacksonville State, AL	1966-1969
Ernest Park	Guard	McMurray, Texas	1963-1965
Dennis Partee	Kicker/Punter	Southern Methodist	1968-1969
Volney Peters	Defensive Tackle	Southern California	1960
Bob Petrich	Defensive End	West Texas State	1963-1966
Dave Plump	Wide Receiver	Fresno State	1966
Sherman Plunkett	Tackle	Maryland State	1961-1962
Dick Post	Running Back	Houston	1967-1969
Bob Print	Linebacker	Dayton	1967-1968
Jeff Queen	Running Back	Morgan State	1969
Rick Redman	Linebacker	Washington	1965-1969
Larry Rentz	Cornerback	Florida	1969
Houston Ridge	Defensive Tackle	San Diego State	1966-1969
Bo Roberson	Wide Receiver	Cornell	1961
Jerry Robinson	Wide Receiver	Grambling	1962-1964
Don Rogers	Center	South Carolina	1960-1964
Tobin Rote	Quarterback	Rice	1963-1964
Dan Sartin	Center	Mississippi	1969
Ron Sayers	Running Back	Nebraska – Omaha	1969
Bob Scarpitto	Defensive Back	Notre Dame	1961
Maury Schleicher	Defensive End	Penn State	1960-1962
Jim Schmedding	Guard	Weber State	1968-1969
Henry Schmidt	Defensive Tackle	Southern California	1961-1964
Jim Sears	Safety	Southern California	1960
Gene Selawski	Tackle	Purdue	1961
Pat Shea	Guard	Southern California	1962-1965
Russ Smith	Running Back	Miami, FL	1967-1969
Dick Speights	Wide Receiver	Wyoming	1968
Jeff Staggs	Linebacker	San Diego State	1966-1969
Kay Stephenson	Quarterback	Florida	1967
Walt Sweeney	Guard	Syracuse	1963-1969
Sammie Taylor	Wide Receiver	Grambling	1964
Steve Tensi	Quarterback	Florida State	1965-1966
Jesse Thomas	Safety	Michigan State	1960
Jim Tolbert	Safety	Lincoln, MO	1966-1969
Richard Trapp	Wide Receiver	Florida	1969
Herb Travenio	Kicker	Texas College	1965
Phil Tuckett	Wide Receiver	Weber State	1968
Dick Van Raaphorst	Kicker	Ohio State	1966-1967
Henry Wallace	Cornerback	Pacific	1960
Ron Waller	Running Back	Maryland	1960
Jim Warren	Defensive Back	Illinois	1964-1965
Russ Washington	Tackle	Missouri	1968-1969
Robert Wells	Tackle	J.C. Smith	1968-1969
Dick Westmoreland	Cornerback	North Carolina A&T	1963-1965
Andre White	Tight End	Florida A&M	1968
Bud Whitehead	Safety	Florida State	1961-1968
Nat Whitmyer	Cornerback	Washington	1966-1967
Royce Womble	Flanker	North Texas State	1960
Dick Wood	Quarterback	Auburn	1962
Ernie Wright	Tackle	Ohio State	1960-1967
Bob Zeman	Safety	Wisconsin	1960-1961, 1965-1966

Chargers Basketball Team. Back; Walt Sweeney, Earl Faison, Sam Gruneisen, Speedy Duncan, Jacque MacKinnon. Front; Steve Tensi, Ernie Wright, ball boy, Bob Mitinger.

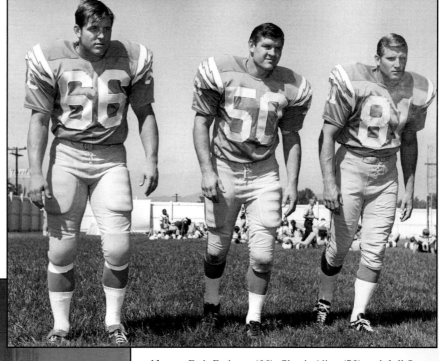

Above: *Rick Redman (66), Chuck Allen (50) and Jeff Staggs (81).*

Left: *Don Norton and Ron Mix*

INDEX